COMMENTARY ON
THE DELHI EXCISE ACT, 2009
AND
THE DELHI EXCISE RULES, 2010

The daring publisher, Universal Law Publishing Company, among the foremost in the law publishing field and progressive in venturing to bring out rare legal literature of avant garde *character has rightly enriched the* corpus juris *of India*

Justice V R Krishna Iyer
Random Reflections, page 14

COMMENTARY ON

THE DELHI EXCISE ACT, 2009 AND THE DELHI EXCISE RULES, 2010

M.U. SIDDIQUI

M.Com., LL.B., Diploma in IPR
Retired Deputy Secretary, Home
Consultant Excise Deptt.

&

MRS. RANA PARWEEN SIDDIQUI

M.A., LL.B.,
Advocate, Supreme Court of India

Universal
Law Publishing Co. Pvt. Ltd.
NEW DELHI - INDIA

2011 Edition

ISBN: 978-93-5035-073-7

Published by
UNIVERSAL LAW PUBLISHING CO. PVT. LTD.
C-FF-1A, Dilkhush Industrial Estate,
(Near Azadpur Metro Station) G.T. Karnal Road,
Delhi-110 033
Tel.: 011-27438103, 27215334, 42381334
Fax : 011-27458529
E-mail *(For sales inquiries)* : sales@unilawbooks.com
E-mail *(For editorial inquiries)* : edit@unilawbooks.com
Website : www.unilawbooks.com

Recommended citation: M.U. Siddiqui & Mrs. Rana Parween Siddiqui, *Commentary on The Delhi Excise Act, 2009 and The Delhi Excise Rules, 2010* (New Delhi: Universal Law Publishing Co. Pvt. Ltd., 2011) .

Computer Typeset at Aesthetic and *Printed* at Vishal Binding House, NOIDA

JAMIA MILLIA ISLAMIA

(A Central University by an Act of Parliament)

FACULTY OF LAW

Maulana Mohammad Ali Jauhar Marg, New Delhi-110025

Tel.: 91-11-26983946, 26981208/26985603/6167/1717 Extn. 3100/3101/3102

Fax: 91-11-26983946

جامعہ ملیہ اسلامیہ

FOREWORD

This book, the Delhi Excise Act authored by Mr. M.U. Siddiqui and Mrs. Rana Parween Siddiqui ventures to explain the provisions of the Delhi Excise Act, 2009 (Act 10 of 2010) with precision and clarity. It is pertinent to note that the Delhi Excise Act, 2009 replaces the Punjab Excise Act, 1914, which was previously applicable to Delhi. In XIV Chapters the authors have succinctly enumerated the law relating to licensing, possession, import, export, transport, purchase and sale of intoxicants, the levy of special duty thereon and punishment for the violation of law in the National Capital Territory of Delhi. The book provides a comparative analysis of the provisions of the Delhi Excise Act, 2009 and the Punjab Excise Act, 1914 as extended to the National Capital Territory of Delhi. Further, the book highlights the salient features of the present Act. It also brings out numerous judgments of the Supreme Court and High Courts on various provisions of the Act. There has not been any commentary on the Punjab Excise Act, 1914, as extended to the National Capital Territory of Delhi and therefore this is a pioneer work in this field.

It may be noted that Mr. M.U. Siddiqui was instrumental and in fact involved in the drafting of the present Act and the Rules thereunder. Having comprehended the subject, he has presented it to the legal fraternity in a lucid manner. This is a commendable work which would be useful to the Bench and the Bar and to everyone interested in this field of law.

March 3, 2011

Prof. Rose Varghese
Dean, Faculty of Law
Jamia Millia Islamia

PREFACE

In the year 1905 an Excise Committee was appointed by the Government of India to investigate various systems of excise administration obtaining in each province of the then British India, and to report how far they calculated to give the fullest practical effect to the general policy of the Government of India in excise matters, as declared in resolution dated September 7,1905. Before this, the Excise Act, 1895 (XII of 1896) was applicable in the then British India, which the Committee recommended to repeal and frame new Act, stating that the Act of 1895 was unsuited to the modern conditions. Government of India accepted the recommendations of the Excise Committee, which formulated a draft bill but left to each province to legislate the Excise Acts, making modifications in the draft bill to suit their needs.

The Punjab Excise Act, 1914 was enacted broadly on the model draft, prepared by the Excise Committee with suitable modifications. Similarly other provinces also passed their own Acts with certain modifications to suit their requirements. The said Act was extended to the then Union territory of Delhi. With the creation of Haryana and Himachal States, it was also extended to those States.

In the National Capital Territory of Delhi, the Punjab Excise Act, 1914 was applicable, which was originally extended to Delhi *vide* Government of India notification No. 3246-39 dated the 2nd May, 1914. The amendments in the original Act by the State of Punjab were extended to Delhi from time to time. The Punjab Excise Act, 1914, as in force in the National Capital Territory of Delhi was last amended by the Parliament, since there was no Legislative Assembly in Delhi at the relevant time, by the Punjab Excise (Delhi Amendment) Act, 1979 (No. 12 of 1979) w.e.f. 29-03-1979, with retrospective effect under Entry 97 (Any other matter not enumerated in List II or List III including any tax not mentioned either in those Lists) of list I of the Seventh Schedule to the Constitution as a result of the judgment of the Delhi High Court where it was held that since no liquor was produced in Delhi, it was not authorized to levy excise duty or the countervailing duty, hence special duty was levied in Delhi by the said amending Act, which is a tax on the import of any excisable article being an article on which countervailing duty as is mentioned in entry 51 of List II in the Seventh Schedule to the Constitution is not imposable on the ground that such article is not being manufactured or produced in the territory to which this Act extends. Delhi is the only State/Union territory where, instead of excise duty, special duty is levied on the excisable articles. After the creation of Haryana and Himachal Pradesh, the Punjab Excise Act, 1914 was also extended to those States.

With the passage of time, it was felt that the Excise Acts framed about a century back needed thorough review. The Government of India constituted a Joint Working Group of the Union Ministries concerned and the State Excise Commissioners to frame model Excise Act and the Rules for possible adoption by the States and the Union territories. The Joint Working Group had held a number of meetings and as a result of consensus reached, draft Model Excise Bill, 2005 was framed which had the broad approval of the Committee of Secretaries. It was desired that efforts should be made to make the existing excise regime in various States uniform and rationale and also to harmonize all excise regimes with WTO commitment. The draft Model Excise Bill was also discussed in the Planning Commission.

The Government of National Capital Territory of Delhi had started the process to draft its own Act. It was on an advance stage when the draft Model Excise Bill, 2005 was forwarded, *inter alia* to the National Capital Territory of Delhi for consideration. The draft Bill was examined and it was noticed that it lacked in certain aspects, so suitable modifications were made in various chapters, which has improved its utility and its implementation has been made more effective. In the Delhi Excise Act, 2009 (Act 10 of 2010), the provision for the levy of special duty has been made by virtue of the powers conferred by Entry 52 List II of the Seventh Schedule to the Constitution, under the head "Taxes on the entry of goods into a local area for consumption, use or sale therein"

The Delhi Excise Rules, 2010 have also been framed under the Delhi Excise Act, 2009. The comparison of the Punjab Excise Act, 1914 as extended to the National capital Territory of Delhi with the Delhi Excise Act, 2009 (Delhi Act 10 of 2010), salient features of the Act of 2009 and the Rules framed thereunder have been given separately in this book for easy comprehension, hence they are not being repeated here.

No commentary on the Punjab Excise Act, 1914 as extended to the National Capital Territory of Delhi has been written. The said Act and the Rules made thereunder are also not available in the market. In this book important judgments delivered by various courts in India have been given under the relevant sections and the Rules. It shall be helpful in understanding not only the Excise Act but other criminal matters also. We are in a better position to write this book as one of the authors (M.U. Siddiqui) was assigned the job to draft Delhi Excise Act, 2009 and the Delhi Excise Rules, 2010 by the Government of National Capital territory of Delhi.

To err is human and we are not an exception. Any suggestion would be welcome with gratitude.

July 2011

M.U. Siddiqui
Mrs. Rana Parween Siddiqui

CONTENTS

THE DELHI EXCISE ACT, 2009

CHAPTER II
ESTABLISHMENT AND CONTROL

CHAPTER III
LICENCE AND PERMIT FOR MANUFACTURE, POSSESSION, SALE, ETC., OF INTOXICANTS

CHAPTER IV

EXCISE REVENUE

CHAPTER V

OFFENCES AND PENALTIES

CHAPTER VI

DETECTION, INVESTIGATION AND TRIAL OF OFFENCES

CHAPTER VII

REVIEW, APPEAL AND REVISION

CHAPTER VIII

MISCELLANEOUS PROVISIONS

THE DELHI EXCISE RULES, 2010

CHAPTER I

PRELIMINARY AND DEFINITIONS

CHAPTER II

IMPORT, EXPORT, TRANSPORT, POSSESSION, PERMITS AND PASSES OF INTOXICANTS

CHAPTER III

SALE AND LICENCE OF INTOXICANTS

CHAPTER IV

LICENSING OF LIQUOR

CHAPTER V

LICENCE AND PERMIT FOR SALE OF DENATURED, SPECIAL DENATURED AND RECTIFIED SPIRIT

CHAPTER VI

ESTABLISHMENT OF WAREHOUSES FOR LIQUOR

CHAPTER VII

SUPPLY AND SALE OF HEMP DRUGS (BHANG)

CHAPTER VIII

IMPORT, EXPORT, TRANSPORT, POSSESSION AND SALE OF INTOXICATING SPIRITUOUS PREPARATIONS

CHAPTER IX

MISCELLANEOUS

CHAPTER X

FISCAL MEASURES

FORMS

TABLE OF CASES

A

D

E

F

G

L

M

Q

R

S

W

Y

SALIENT FEATURES OF THE DELHI EXCISE ACT, 2009

(Delhi Act 10 of 2010)

1. Some new definitions have been added and some have been modified.

2. The provision of review has been added.

3. Powers of compounding of offences have been enlarged.

4. Provision for the disposal of confiscated goods has been made by the Deputy Commissioner, either by destruction or by sale, irrespective of the pendency of the case in the court.

5. Apart from prosecution of offenders, the powers to confiscate the intoxicants and other goods have been conferred on the Deputy Commissioner. This will enable the Excise department to confiscate carrier vehicles, receptacles, liquor, etc., and sell the goods and the liquor, if it is found fit for human consumption, after analysis.

6. Quantum of punishment has been enhanced in all cases, imprisonment has been made rigorous and minimum punishment has been prescribed in many cases, which was earlier in the case of possession of working still for manufacture of intoxicants only. Amount of fine has been enhanced substantially.

7. Rectification of denatured spirit for sale, which is a serious offence, was being dealt with leniently in the repealed Act as the maximum punishment prescribed, was one year. It has now been the enhanced to five years with fine up to Rs. 2 lakh.

8. Powers to close liquor shops in case of riots have been transferred from Collector/SDM to the Excise Commissioner.

9. Provision for punishment for the commission of offence by the Companies has been made.

10. Enabling provision has been made to grant reward to the officers responsible for seizure of intoxicants and vehicles, carrying the intoxicants and to the informers out of the amount realized from the disposal of potable liquor, and vehicles used for carrying such intoxicants, without burdening the Government revenue. It shall encourage the enforcement wing of excise department and the police to apprehend the offenders more zealously and discourage the smuggling of liquor. Effective enforcement on this front shall enhance the Government revenue through authorized sales of liquor.

11. Some of the offences in the Act have been made triable summarily, to have speedy disposal of cases.

12. In order to facilitate quick recovery of excise revenue, powers have been conferred on the Excise Commissioner, with the approval of the Government to remit/reduce interest.

13. Provision to levy interest @12% per annum on arrears of excise revenue has been made in the Act, which was not there in the repealed Act.

14. The words "Lieutenant Governor", have been substituted by the word "Government".

15. The word 'Collector' has been substituted by the words 'Deputy Commissioner'.

16. The words 'Union territory of Delhi' have been substituted by the word 'Delhi' and the word 'Delhi' has been defined.

17. Order of sections has been changed to have a better look of the Act, *viz.* Appeals, Revisions, Rule making powers and Repeal and Savings have been shifted at the end of the Act.

18. Filing of challan, within one year of the commission of an offence has been dispensed with, so as to bring it at par with other offences under section 468 of the Code of Criminal Procedure, 1973, to avoid confusion.

19. Jurisdiction of courts in certain cases has been barred.

20. Restriction of the employment of women, where liquor is served has been removed. Age of employment where liquor is served has been reduced from 25 years to 21 years.

21. Government has been authorized to make Rules with retrospective effect and a provision has been made to place the Rules before the Legislative Assembly to confer them more authenticity.

22. Provision for disposing of appeals within one year has been made.

23. The appellant has to pay excise revenue, or in the discretion of the appellate authority, file security. In the case stay is granted, appeal is to be decided preferably within a month.

24. Malkhanas, in police stations are full of liquor, which is consumed or bottles are broken, during long trial and its non-production of case property before the court affects trial. A provision has been made for its disposal and its non-production will not be a bar in the conviction of the accused. It will improve conviction rate.

25. Provision of affixing seal by the SHO, apart from the seal of the Investigation officer, has been dispensed with.

26. Manufacturers of liquor may now be arrayed as accused along-with other offenders, if the court is satisfied of their involvement.

27. Power of Metropolitan Magistrates, to award higher punishment than permitted under section 29 of the Cr. P.C, has been enhanced to enable them to try offences with enhanced punishment under the Act.

28. Earlier the offence of possession of working still for manufacture of any intoxicant was a non-bailable offence. Now offences, entailing punishments for two years or more, have been made non-bailable.

29. Provision for stringent penalties have been made and minimum penalties have been prescribed.

30. Government has been empowered to vary duty.

COMPARISON OF THE DELHI EXCISE ACT, 2009

(Delhi Act 10 of 2010)

with

THE PUNJAB EXCISE ACT 1914

As Extended to the National Capital Territory of Delhi

Sections	The Delhi Excise Act, 2009.	Section of The Punjab Excise Act, 1914 exten-ded to the National Capital Territory of Delhi	Modifications.
(1)	(2)	(3)	(4)
1.	Short title, extent, commencement and application	1	1. Title of the Act has been made as Delhi Excise Act, 2009. (Delhi Act 10 of 2010)
2.	Definitions	3	Some new definitions have been added and some definitions have been modified to suit the changing needs. With the enactment of the Narcotic Drugs and Psychotropic Substance Act, 1985 (Act 61 of 1985), the definition of Intoxicating Drugs has been modified to retain only the 'bhang' in its definition.
3.	Appointment of Excise Commissioner	9	Minor changes in the appointment of Excise Commissioner have been made.
4.	Powers and functions of Excise Commissioner.		
5.	Appointment of certain officers and staff	9	(i) Language has slightly been changed but the contents are the same. (ii) Earlier such appoint-ments were prescribed in the rules. They have now been defined in the Act to provide more respectability to the officers.

1	2	3	4
6.	Excise Intelligence Bureau.	—	New section of Excise Intelligence Bureau has been added.
7.	Excise administration.	—	Excise Administration has been expressly defined.
8.	Delegation and withdrawal of powers	10	(i) Excise officers have been mentioned by designations with some modifications (ii) Delegation of powers has been made more precisely.
9.	Investing persons with special powers	11	Minor modifications have been made.
10.	Reward for seizure of intoxicants and vehicles, etc.	—	Sustentative provision has been made enabling the grant of reward to excise officers and informers.
11.	Prohibition of import, export, transport, manufacture, possession, sale etc. of liquor.	16	Language has been amended but the contents are similar.
12.	Grant of letter of intent, licence or permit	17	Instead of negative, positive language has been used.
13.	Qualifications for grant of licence		New sections have been added. Earlier, the subject was part of the Rules.
14.	Power to take security and counterpart agreement		
15.	Technical defects in licence and permit	24	No major change
16.	Power to withdraw licence and permit	41	No major change, except provision of payment of compensation in the case of withdrawal of licence has been deleted.
17.	Power to suspend or cancel licence and permit	36, 37, 38	Minor modifications have been made.
18.	Bar to the right of renewal and to compensation	43	No major change has been made.
19.	Surrender of licence	44	No major change

(1)	(2)	(3)	(4)
20.	Transfer of licence or permit	—	New provision has been made.
21.	Grant of exclusive privilege of manufacture, etc.	27	Minor changes have been made.
22.	Removal of liquor from manufactory, warehouse, etc., on payment of duty.	31	Language of the section has been modified. Proviso barring levy of duty on customs duty paid liquor has been deleted.
23.	Prohibition of sale to certain persons	29	The age has been retained as 25 years.
24.	Prohibition of employment of certain persons	30	The age of employment has been reduced to 21 years and bar on employment of women has been removed.
25.	Closing of shops for preservation of public peace	54	Powers to close shops have been conferred on the Excise Commissioner instead of District Magistrate and Sub-divisional Magistrates with minor modifications.
26.	Nature and components of excise revenue	3(a)	Earlier "excise revenue" was defined in section 3 which contains definitions. Now it has been defined in separate sections with minor modifications.
27.	Excise duty, countervailing duty and special duty	31	Substantive provision for the levy of fee and collection of equalisation amount as duty has been made, in fixing the retail price of liquor by the Excise Commissioner.
28.	Power of Government to vary duty	—	Special provision has been made to increase duty by the Government, in exceptional circumstances, instead of approaching the Legislative Assembly for the purpose.
29.	Recovery of duty and other levies and lien on the property of defaulter	—	Special provision has been made to recover excise levies.

(1)	(2)	(3)	(4)
30.	Interest payable for failure to pay excise revenue	—	Substantive provision for levy of interest has been made which did not exist in the Act.
31.	Power to reduce or waive interest in certain cases	—	Special provision has been made to reduce or waive interest, with the approval of the Government, to have effective realisation of excise revenue, in special circumstances.
32.	Accounts and returns	—	Provision to maintain accounts and submission of returns has been made in the Act.
33.	Penalty for unlawful import, export, transport, manufacture, possession, sale etc.	61	Punishment has been made dependent on the quantity of intoxicants. Scope of minimum imprisonment has been widened and fine has been enhanced from Rs. 5,000.00 to one lakh.
34.	Penalty for rendering denatured spirit fit for human consumption	63	Imprisonment from one year and fine upto Rs.1,000.00 has been enhanced to 5 years with minimum of 2 years and fine upto Rs. 2 lakh respectively.
35.	Penalty for mixing noxious substance with liquor	—	Special stringent provision has been made for mixing noxious substance causing grievous hurt of the penalty of death and the imprisonment for life, and fine up to Rs. 10 lakh, depending upon the gravity of the offence.
36.	Order to pay compensation	—	Provisions for payment of compensation, depending upon the gravity of injury to the victim by the accused, has been made.
37.	Penalty for selling spurious liquor	—	New section has been added to punish the persons selling spurious liquor.

(1)	(2)	(3)	(4)
38.	Penalty for possession of liquor unlawfully imported, non-duty paid, etc.		Possession of non-duty paid liquor has been made an offence.
39.	Penalty for consumption of liquor in chemist's shop	66	Punishment has been enhanced from imprisonment for three months and fine of one thousand rupees to six months imprisonment and fine up to Rs.5,000.00.
40.	Penalty for consumption of liquor in public place	68	Fine has been enhanced from Rs. 200.00, from 5000 to 50,000 rupees and imprisonment from 3 months to six months has been provided for causing nuisance, after drinking at public place.
41.	Penalty for unlawful advertisement	—	New provision has been made to award punishment up to six months and fine up to Rs. 10 lakh. Earlier it was part of the Rules, entailing a fine of Rs. 200.
42.	Penalty for employing minors or selling liquor to minors	62	Fine has been enhanced from Rs. 500 to Rs. 10,000
43.	Penalty for assault and obstruction	—	New provision has been made for assault and obstruction to excise officer in the discharge of his official duties, providing imprisonment for one year and fine up to Rs. 1 lakh.
44.	Liability of employer for offence committed by his employee or agent.	65	For an offence committed by the employee, the employer has been made equally liable unless he proves that he exercised due precaution. Minor modifications have been made.
45.	Penalty for manufacture, sale or possession by one person on account of another	67	No change

(1)	(2)	(3)	(4)
46.	Penalty for non-payment of duty or fee	—	New section has been added, providing imprisonment for one year and fine up to Rs. one lakh for non-payment of duty by the licensee, apart from liability to pay the duty with interest.
47.	Penalty for allowing premises, etc., to be used for commission of an offence	—	New section has been added to punish for allowing the premises in the commission of excise offence.
48.	Penalty for attempt to commit an offence	69	Penalty for attempt has been reduced to half of the punishment, provided in the case of accomplished offence.
49.	Penalty on excise officer for making vexatious search, seizure, detention or arrest.	70(a)(b)(c)	Fine has been enhanced from Rs. 500 to Rs. 10,000.
50.	Penalty on excise officer refusing to do duty	70(d)	Fine has been enhanced from Rs. 500 to Rs. 10,000.
51.	Penalty for offences not provided for.	68	Imprisonment for six months has been added and fine has been enhanced from Rs. 200 to Rs. 10,000.
52.	Presumption as to commission of offence in certain cases	76	Minor modifications have been made.
53.	Enhanced punishment after previous conviction	68 A	Minor amendments have been made.
54.	Power of court to implead manufacturer, etc.	—	New provision has been made to implead manufacturer as provided in the Prevention of Food Adulteration Act, as without the connivance of manufacturer, liquor on large scale cannot be dumped in the Delhi market.

(1)	(2)	(3)	(4)
55.	Magistrate's power to impose enhanced penalties	69	Since the powers of a Magistrate are limited to 3 years imprisonment and fine upto Rs. 7,000.00 under section 29 Cr. P.C. and penalties provided in the Act are much higher, the Metropolitan Magistrates have been empowered to award higher punishment provided for in the Delhi Excise Act.
56.	Commission of offence by companies.	—	This section has been added to prosecute the companies.
57.	Compounding of certain offences.	80	Provisions of compounding have been modified and minor offences have been included.
58.	Certain things liable to Confiscation	78(1)	No major changes.
59.	Confiscation by Deputy Commissioner in certain cases.	78(2)	Powers of confiscation have been conferred on the Deputy Commissioner, instead of the courts. Also powers of disposal of confiscated property have been conferred on the Deputy Commissioner, independent of the pendency of the case in the court.
60.	Order of confiscation and destruction not to interfere with other punishment	—	Special provision has been made so that non-production of case property may not be a bar in prosecution.
61.	Bar of jurisdiction in confiscation	—	Jurisdiction of courts has been barred in confiscation of property connected with excise offence.

(1)	(2)	(3)	(4)
62.	Relevancy of statements under certain circumstances.	—	Statements made before the gazetted excise Officers have been made admissible in courts, as is provided in the Customs Act, 1962 to get better conviction rate.
63.	Power to obtain information	49 A	Minor modifications have been made.
64.	Landholders, officers and others to give information	52	Minor modifications have been made.
65.	Power of search and seizure	49	Minor modifications have been made.
66.	Duty of police to accept seized articles	53	The last sentence "All samples so taken shall also be sealed with the seal of the officer, in-charge of the police stations" has been deleted
67.	Offences under this Act to be cognizable	53	More precise provision has been made.
68.	Certain offences to be non-bailable	72	In the existing Act offence of possession of working still was non-bailable. In the new Bill offences punishable with imprisonment of 2 years and more shall be non-bailable.
69.	Power of court to try cases summarily	—	This provision has been made as per the provision of the Prevention of Food Adulteration Act, so as the cases are decided speedily.
70.	Security for good conduct and abstaining from committing offence	69 A	Minor changes have been made.
71.	Review.	—	New provision of review has been made to remove omissions, irregularity or illegality apparent on record.

(1)	(2)	(3)	(4)
72.	Appeal	14	eDeta Details, which were part of the Rules have been incorporated in the Act. A provision has been added that the appeal shall be decided within one year from its institution.
73.	Order of appellate authority	—	New provision has been made that the copy of the order shall be sent to the officer who passed the order as well as to the appellant.
74.	Revision of orders by Excise Commissioner	15	Minor changes have been made.
75.	Deposit of excise revenue pending appeal	—	New provision has been made to deposit Excise Revenue or get stay subject to furnishing surety and in case stay is granted the appeal is to be decided preferably within 30 days.
76.	Power of Government to declare what shall be deemed to be liquor	4	Minor modifications have been made.
77.	Power of Government to regulate drinking and to enforce prohibition	—	New provision has been made to regulate and enforce prohibition.
78.	Power of Government to regulate molasses, black jaggery, mahua flower, etc. to prevent misuse	—	New provision has been made.
79.	Power to regulate advertisement	Rule 15 of the Delhi Intoxicants Licence and Sale Rules	Comprehensive provision, which earlier existed in the Rules, has been made in the Act.
80.	Bar and limitation of certain suits	7	No material change has been made.
81.	Power of Government to make rules	58	(i) In the earlier Act all the important powers to make rules, were vested with the Excise Commissioner, whereas the rules were framed by the

(1)	(2)	(3)	(4)
			Government. In the present Act this anomaly has been removed. (ii) Provision for making rules with retrospective effect has been made, as sometimes it is felt necessary. (iii) Provision of previous publication of the rules has been dispensed with as it is rarely done and power to dispense with this provision is exercised. (iv) Placement of rules before the Assembly has been provided to confer more credibility to the Rules.
82.	Power to remove difficulties		New provision has been made to remove any difficulty within three years of the enactment
83.	Repeal and savings	2	Provision of repeal has been made broad based,

NEW AND OLD NUMBERS OF LICENCES AND PERMITS

New licences No.	Old licences No.	Description
(1)	(2)	(3)
L-1	L-1	Wholesale vend for Indian liquor
L-1F	L-1F	Wholesale vend of Foreign Liquor
L-1B	L-2	Wholesale vend of Draught Beer
L-9	L-3	Wholesale vend of Country liquor
L-16	L-4	Wholesale vend of Rectified spirit
L-12	L-5	Wholesale vend of Denatured spirit
L-2	L-6	Retail vend of Indian Liquor in public sector
L-2F	L-6FG	Retail vend of Foreign Liquor in public sector to the holder of licence in form L-6
L-2FE	L-6FE	Retail Vend of Foreign Liquor in public sector
L-52	L-7	Retail vend of Indian Liquor in private sector
L-52F	L-7FG	Retail vend of Foreign Liquor in private sector to the holder of licence in form L-7
L-52FE	L-7FE	Retail vend of Foreign Liquor in private sector
L-10	L-8	Retail vend of Country Liquor in public sector
L-52D	L-9	Retail vend of Indian liquor to holders of licence in Form L-1.
L-56	L-10	Retail vend of Indian Liquor and Foreign Liquor in Shopping Malls
L-55	L-11	Retail vend of Beer, manufactured by Microbrewery.
L-53	L-12	Retail vend of Beer and Wine in Departmental Store
L-53F	L-12F	Retail vend of Foreign Beer and Wine in Departmental Store to the holder of licence in form L-12
L-54	L-13	Retail vend of Indian Liquor for home delivery
L-54F	L-13F	Retail vend of Foreign Liquor for home delivery to the holder of licence in form L-13

(1)	(2)	(3)
L-2A	L-14	Retail vend of economy Indian Liquor and Beer to the holders of licence in Form L-8
L-3	L-15	Service of Indian Liquor in a hotel to residents in their rooms
L-3F	L-15F	Service of Foreign Liquor in a hotel to residents in their rooms to the holder of licence in form L-15
L-5	L-16	Service of Indian Liquor in a bar/restaurant attached to a hotel
L-5F	L-16F	Service of Foreign Liquor in a bar/restaurant attached to a hotel to the holder of licence in form L-16
L-4	L-17	Service of Indian Liquor in independent restaurant
L-4F	L-17F	Service of Foreign Liquor in independent restaurant to the holder of licence in form L-17
L-4D	L-18	Service of Wine, Beer and alcopop in independent restaurant
L-4B	L-19	Round the clock service of Indian Liquor in independent restaurant located either in arrival or departure area of International Airport.
L-4BF	L-19F	Round the clock service of Foreign Liquor in independent restaurant located either in arrival or departure area of International Airport to the holder of licence in form L-19
L-5A	L-20	Service of Indian Liquor in a bar/dining car in a luxury train
L-5AF	L-20F	Service of Foreign Liquor in a bar/dining car in a luxury train to the holder of licence in form L-20
L-5B	L-21	Round the clock service/sale of Indian Liquor in a bar attached to a hotel located either in arrival or departure area of International Airport
L-5BF	L-21F	Round the clock service/sale of Foreign Liquor in a bar attached to a hotel located either in arrival or departure area of International Airport to the holder of licence in form L-21
L-6	L-22	Retail vend of Indian liquor in duty free shop for consumption "off" the premises, located at departure lounge of International Airport

(1)	(2)	(3)
L-7	L-23	Retail vend of Indian Liquor in military canteen.
L-7A	L-23F	Retail vend of Indian Foreign Liquor in military canteen to the holder of licence in form L-23
L-8	L-24	Retail vend of Medicated Wine
L-11	L-25	Retail vend of Denatured Spirit
L-15	L-26	Retail vend of Rectified Spirit
H-1	L-27	Retail vend of Bhang
L-19	L-28	Service of Indian Liquor in a club
L-19F	L-28F	Service of Foreign Liquor in a club to the holder of licence in form L-28
L-19A	L-29	Service of Indian Liquor at a club/mess whose membership is exclusively for Government servants, retired Government servants and the club/mess is not run on commercial lines.
L-19AF	L-29F	Service of Foreign Liquor at a club/mess whose membership is exclusively for Government servants, retired Government servants and the club/mess is not run on commercial lines to the holder of licence in form L-29
L-49	L-30	Licence for possession of liquor at home in excess of individual possession limit
	L-31	Licence for Warehouse for storage of Indian Liquor,
	L-32	Licence for Warehouse for storage of Foreign Liquor
CLW-1	L-33	Licence for Warehouse for storage of Country Liquor
	L-34	Licence for Warehouse for storage of denatured spirit
	L-35	Licence for Warehouse for storage of rectified spirit
I.S.P-1	L-36	Licence to a registered medical practitioner, a chemist, a druggist for sale of intoxicating spirituous preparations
	L-37	Licence for Hotel Management Institute for keeping liquor for the purpose of training
L-34	P-1	Permit to import rectified spirit, denatured spirit, special denatured spirit and absolute alcohol

(1)	(2)	(3)
L-35/F-34	P-2	Permit for possession of denatured spirit, exceeding five litres up to ten litres.
L-39/L-42A/F-21	P-3	Permit for possession of denatured spirit, exceeding ten litres (in bulk quantity)
L-42C/F-23	P-4	Permit for possession of special denatured spirit in bulk quantity.
L-42 B& J. D/F-22	P-5	Permit for possession of rectified spirit, in bulk quantity to educational institutions, etc.
L-42D	P-6	Permit for possession of denatured spirit by industrial manufacturers.
I.S.P2A	P-7	Permit for possession of Intoxicating Spirituous Preparations
I.S.P.3	P-8	Permit for import or transport of Intoxicating Spirituous Preparations.
L-39	P-9	Permit for import of Indian Liquor and Country Liquor for troops.
L-49A	P-10	Permit for service of Indian Liquor and Foreign Liquor at a place other than the licensed premises.
L-49C	P-11	Permit for Liquor Exhibitors
H-2	P-12	Permit for import export or transport of bhang.
L-20	P-13	Service of Indian Liquor and Foreign Liquor at a temporary place at hotel, club and restaurant.
	P-14	Permit for the import of liquor for the holder of licence in form L-1, L-1F, L-3
	P-15	Transport permit for the transport of liquor

THE DELHI EXCISE ACT, 2009[1]

(Delhi Act 10 of 2010)

An Act to consolidate, amend and update the Excise Laws, relating to manufacture, import, export, transport, possession, purchase, sale, etc., of liquor and other intoxicants, in the National Capital Territory of Delhi and for matters connected therewith or incidental thereto.

WHEREAS it is expedient to provide for a uniform law relating to licensing, possession, import, export, transport, purchase and sale of intoxicants, the levy of special duty thereon and punishment for the violation of law in the National Capital Territory of Delhi, the Delhi Excise Act, 2000 is hereby enacted.

BE it enacted by the Legislative Assembly of the National Capital Territory of Delhi in the Sixtieth Year of the Republic of India as follows:—

SYNOPSIS

1. **Preamble is the Introduction of Statute**
2. **No Resort to Preamble when Words used in the Act are Clear and Unambiguous**
3. **Preamble can be Looked into when the Words of the Act are Ambiguous**
4. **Proceedings in Legislature not an Aid of Construction**
5. **Statement cannot be used as an Aid to Construction of Enactment**
6. **Statement of Objects and Reasons can be used for the Purpose of Appreciating the Background**
7. **Statement of Objects and Reasons can be used as Aid to Find out the Legislative Intent when the Language is Obscure or Ambiguous**
8. **Interpretation by the Court**
9. **Taxing Act**
10. **Special Act, Later Act**
11. **Fiscal Statutes to be Interpreted Strictly**
12. **Taxing Statute – Rule of Construction**
13. **Ordinarily Statutes are Considered to be Prospective**
14. **Subsequent Act Affords no Useful Guide**
15. **Heading cannot Control the Plain Words**
16. **Interpretation of Words in Different Acts may be Different**
17. **Whether Particular Provision is Mandatory or Directory**
18. **Literal Construction**
19. **Precedent**
20. **Entry in Fiscal Statute should be given Popular Meaning**
21. ***Obiter dicta* of Supreme Court is Binding on All Courts**
22. **Fiscal Statutes should be Construed Strictly**
23. **Provision in Special Act *vis-a-vis* General Act**
24. **Rule of Harmonious Construction**

---

1. *Vide* Notification No. F. 14(2)/LA-2008/L.J./10/IClaw/288, dated 28th July, 2010, published in the Delhi Gazette, Extra., Pt. IV, come into force w.e.f. 4th October, 2010 *vide* Notifications No. 10(5)/Fin(T&E) 2009-10.

Comments

1. Preamble is the Introduction of Statute

Preamble is the introduction of a statute giving its reason and purpose. It is thus the introductory part of a statute of Parliament or State legislature. It is said that the face is the index of mind. It can also be said that a Preamble is the index of a statute. The Preamble of a statute has been said to be a good means of finding out its meanings and as if it were a key to the understanding of it.[1]

2. No Resort to Preamble when Words used in the Act are Clear and Unambiguous

No resort to the Preamble would be justified in interpreting the provision in the Act when the words used in it are clear and unambiguous. A Preamble is a key to the interpretation of a statute but is not ordinarily an independent enactment conferring rights or taking them away and cannot restrict or widen the enacting part, which is clear and unambiguous. The motive for legislation is often recited in the Preamble but the remedy may extend beyond the cure of the evil, intended to be removed.[2]

3. Preamble can be Looked into when the Words of the Act are Ambiguous

The ambiguity can be resolved by taking into consideration the Preamble and the statement of objects and reasons. The Preamble suggests what the act was intended to deal with. If the language used by Parliament is ambiguous the court is permitted to look into the Preamble for construing the provisions of an Act.[3]

A Preamble of a statute has been said to be a good means of finding out its meaning and, as it were, the key of understanding of it, said this Court.[1]

The Preamble is a key to unlock the legislative intent. If the words employed in an enactment may spell a doubt as to their meaning it would be useful to so interpret the enactment as to harmonise it with the object, which the Legislature had in its view.[5]

4. Proceedings in Legislature not an Aid of Construction

The proceedings of the Legislature cannot be called in aid for constructing a section. The statement of objects and reasons is not admissible in evidence for construing a statute.

The history of a legislation would be admissible for ascertaining the legislative intent when the question is one of severability. But the statement of objects and reasons is not a part of the history of the legislation. It is merely an expression of what according to the mover of the Bill are the scope and purpose of the legislation.

1. *A. Thangal Kunju Musaliar* v. *M. Venkatachalam Potti,* AIR 1956 SC 246: (1955) 2 SCR 1196.
2. *R.V. Naidu* v. *Narain Das,* (1966) 1 SCR 110: AIR 1966 SC 361.
3. *Burrakur Coal Co. Ltd. & East Indian Coal Co. Ltd.* v. *Union of India,* AIR 1961 SC 954: 1961 (2) SCA 523: (1962) 1 SCR 44: 1962 (2) SCJ 216.
4. *A. Thangal Kunju Musaliar* v. *M. Venkatachalam Potti,* AIR 1956 SC 246: (1955) 2 SCR 1196.
5. *Arnit Das* v *State of Bihar,* 2000 (2) Crimes 334 SC: AIR 2000 SC 2264: 2000 Cr LJ 2971: 2000 AIR SCW 2037: 2000 (3) All Cri LR 289: 2000 Cal Cr LR 336: JT 2000 (6) SC 320: (2000) 5 SCC 488: 2000 (6) SRJ 378: (2000) 4 SCALE 515: 2000 SCC (Cri) 962: 2000 (4) Supreme 186: 2000 (2) UJ (SC) 1062.

But the question of severability has to be judged on the intention of the legislature as expressed in the bill as passed, and to ascertain it the statement of the mover of the bill is no more admissible than a speech made on the floor of the House.

The statement of objects and reasons might be admissible not for construing the Act but for ascertaining the conditions which prevailed when the legislation was enacted.[1]

5. Statement cannot be used as an Aid to Construction of Enactment

Statement of objects and reasons accompanying a Bill when introduced in Parliament cannot be used to determine the true meaning and effect of the substantive provisions of the statute, they cannot be used except for a limited purpose of understanding the background and the antecedent state of affairs leading up to the legislation. But the courts cannot use this statement as an aid to the construction of the enactment.[2]

6. Statement of Objects and Reasons can be used for the Purpose of Appreciating the Background

For determining the purpose or object of the legislation, it is permissible to look into the circumstances, which prevailed at the time when the law was passed and which necessitated the passing of that law. For the limited purpose of appreciating the background and the antecedent factual matrix leading to the legislation, it is permissible to look into the Statement of Objects and Reasons of the Bill which actuated the step to provide a remedy for the then existing malady.[3]

7. Statement of Objects and Reasons can be used as Aid to find out the Legislative intent when the Language is Obscure or Ambiguous

It is a cardinal rule of interpretation that objects and reasons of a statute is to be taken into as an extrinsic aid to find out legislative intent only when the meaning of the statute by its ordinary language is obscure or ambiguous. But if the words used in the statute are clear and unambiguous, then the statute itself declares the intention of the legislature, and in such a case it will not be permissible for a court to interpret the statute by examining the Objects and Reasons for the statute in question.[4]

8. Interpretation by the Court

It is not legitimate for the Courts to re-write the sub-sections, particularly when on the alternative construction it is found that there is no repugnance between the two sub-sections. That clearly is the function of the Legislature which enacts laws and not of the court which interprets them.[5]

---

1. *Jia Lal* v. *Delhi Administration,* AIR 1962 SC 1781: 1963 1 Cr LJ 1: 1962 All Cri R 431: (1963) 2 SCR 864: 1962 All WR (HC) 765.
2. *State of West Bengal* v. *Union of India, Defendant,* AIR 1963 SC 1241: 1963 (2) SCA 448: (1964) 1 SCR 371.
3. *Shashikant Laxman Kale* v. *Union of India,* AIR 1990 SC 2114: 1990 Tax LR 877: JT 1990 (3) SC 267
4. *S.S. Bhola* v. *B.D. Sardana,* AIR 1997 SC 3127: 1997 AIR SCW 3172: (1997) 8 SCC 522: 1997 (5) SCJ 278: (1997) 5 SCALE 90: 1997 (7) Supreme 427.
5. *Madan Lal Fakirchand Dudhediya* v. *Shree Changdeo Sugar Mills Ltd.,* AIR 1962 SC 1543: 1962 (32) Com Cas 604: 65 Bom LR 162.

9. Taxing Act

In a taxing statute one has to look merely at what is clearly said. There is no room for any intendment. There is no equity about a tax. There is no presumption as to a tax. Nothing is to be read in, nothing is to be implied. One can only look fairly at the language used.[1]

10. Special Act, Later Act

Special Act overrides the general Act and later Act will prevail over the earlier Act.[2]

11. Fiscal Statutes to be Interpreted Strictly

In interpreting a fiscal statute the Court cannot proceed to make good the deficiencies, if there be any in the statutes; it shall interpret the statute as it stands and in case of doubt, it shall interpret it in a manner favourable to the tax payer. In considering a taxing Act, the Court is not justified in straining the language in order to hold a subject liable to tax.[3]

12. Taxing Statute – Rule of Construction

In a Taxing Act one has to look merely at what is clearly said. There is no room for any intendment. There is no equity about a tax. Nothing is to be read in, nothing is to be implied. One can only look fairly at the language used. In a case of reasonable doubt, the construction most beneficial to the subject is to be adopted. But even so, the fundamental rule of construction is the same for all statutes, whether fiscal or otherwise. The underlying principle is that the meaning and intention of a statute must be collected from the plain and unambiguous expression used therein rather than from any notions which may be entertained by the court as to what is just or expedient. The expressed intention must guide the court. The maxim *"generalia specialibus non derogant"* means that when there is a conflict between a general and a special provision, the latter shall prevail.[4]

13. Ordinarily Statutes are Considered to be Prospective

The general rule is that all statutes, other than those which are merely declaratory, or which relate only to matters of procedure or of evidence, are *prima facie* prospective; and retrospective effect is not to be given to them unless, by express words or necessary implication, it appears that this was the intention of the legislature. In fact, the court must look to the general scope and purview of the statute, and at the remedy sought to be applied, and consider what was the former state of the law, and what it was that the Legislature contemplated.[5]

---

1. *Cape Brandy Syndicate* v. *IRC*, (1921) 1 KB 64 (71), as *per* Rowallt J: (1921) 12 Tax Cas 358 (366): 90 LJ KB 118.
2. *Jasbir Singh* v. *Vipin Kumar Jaggi*, 2001 VI AD (SC) 245: 2001 Cr LJ 3993: JT 2001 (6) SC 419: 2001 (3) Ker LT 346: (2001) 8 SCC 289: 2001 (4) SCJ 465: (2001) 5 SCALE 258: 2001 (6) Supreme 135: 2001 (2) UC 506: 2001 (2) UJ (SC) 1421.
3. *State of Punjab* v. *Jullundur Vegetables Syndicate*, AIR 1966 SC 1295: 1966 (17) STC 326: 1966 (1) SCJ 665: 68 Pun LR 434: (1966) 2 SCR 457.
4. *Commissicner of Income Tax* v. *M/s Shahzada Nand*, AIR 1966 SC 1342: 1966 Cur LJ 488: 1966 (1) SCJ 715.
5. *Income Tax Officer* v. *T.S.D. Nadar*, AIR 1968 SC 623: 1968 (1) SCA 444: 1968 (1) SCJ 733: (1968) 2 SCR 33..

14. Subsequent Act Affords no Useful Guide

Generally speaking a subsequent Act of Parliament affords no useful guide to the meaning of another Act, which came into existence before the later one was ever framed. Under special circumstances, the law does, however, admit of a subsequent Act to be resorted to for this purpose but the conditions under which the latter Act may be resorted to for the interpretation of the earlier Act are strict; both must be laws on the same subject and the part of the earlier Act which it is sought to construe must be ambiguous and capable of different meanings.[1]

15. Heading cannot Control the Plain Words

The headings prefixed to sections or sets of sections in some modern statutes are regarded as preambles to those sections. They cannot control the plain words of the statute but they may explain ambiguous words.[2]

16. Interpretation of Words in Different Acts may be Different

Interpretation given to words in one Act cannot be given to the words occurring in another Act, which is not kindered in nature.[3]

17. Whether Particular Provision is Mandatory or Directory

There are no ready tests or invariable formulae to determine whether a particular provision in a statute is mandatory or directory. The broad purpose of the statute is important. The object of the particular provision must be considered. The link between the two is most important. The weighing of the consequence of holding a provision to be mandatory or directory is vital and, more often than not, determinative of the very question whether the provision is mandatory or directory. Where the design of the statute is the avoidance or prevention of public mischief, but the enforcement of a particular provision literally to its letter will tend to defeat that design, the provision must be held to be directory, so that proof of prejudice in addition to non-compliance of the provision is necessary to invalidate the act complained of.[4]

18. Literal Construction

The dominant purpose in construing a statute is to ascertain the intention of the Parliament. One of the well recognized canons of construction is that the legislature speaks its mind by use of correct expression and unless there is any ambiguity in the language of the provision the court should adopt literal construction if it does not lead to an absurdity. The first question to be posed is whether there is any ambiguity in the language used in the provision. If there is none, it would mean the language used, speaks the mind of Parliament and there is no need to look somewhere else to discover the intention or meaning. If the literal construction leads to an absurdity, external aids to construction can be resorted to. To ascertain the literal meaning it is equally necessary first to ascertain the

1. *Income Tax Officer* v. *Mani Ram*, AIR 1969 SC 543: (1969) 1 SCR 724.
2. *Ajit Singh* v. *State*, 1970 Cr LJ 1075 (FB): AIR 1970 Punj 351: 72 Pun LR 396: ILR (1970) 2 Punj 69.
3. *S. Mohan Lal* v. *R. Kondaiah*, AIR 1979 SC 1132: (1979) 3 SCR 12.
4. *Dalchand* v. *Municipal Corporation*, 1983 Cr LJ 448: AIR 1983 SC 303.

juxtaposition in which the rule is placed, the purpose for which it is enacted and the object which it is required to subserve and the authority by which the rule is framed.[1]

19. Precedent

A decision is available as a precedent only if it decides a question of law. Thus, the temporary lecturers in a writ petition before High Court, would not be entitled to rely upon an order of Supreme Court which directs a temporary employee to be regularised in his service without assigning reasons. It has to be presumed that for special grounds, which must have been available to the temporary employees in those cases, they were entitled to the relief granted. Merely because grounds are not mentioned in a judgment of the Supreme Court, it cannot be understood to have been passed without an adequate legal basis therefore. On the question of the requirement to assessing reasons for an order, a distinction has to be kept in mind between a court whose judgment is not subject to further appeal and other courts. One of the main reasons for disclosing and discussing the grounds in support of a judgment is to enable a higher court to examine the same in case of a challenge. It is, of course, desirable to assign reasons for every order or judgment, but the requirement is not imperative in the case of Supreme Court. It is, therefore not proper to suggest that if the Supreme Court has issued an order in the circumstances the similar order can also be issued by the High Court. There is still another reason why the High Court cannot be equated with the Supreme Court. The Constitution has, by article 142, empowered the Supreme Court to make such orders as may be necessary "for doing complete justice in any case or matter pending before it", which authority the High Court does not enjoy.[2]

20. Entry in Fiscal Statute should be given Popular Meaning

In construing the relevant item or entry in fiscal statutes, if it is one of every day use, the concerned authority must normally, construe it as to how it is understood in common parlance or in the commercial world or trade circles. It must be given its popular meaning. The meaning given in the dictionary must not prevail. Nor should the entry be understood in any technical or botanical or scientific sense. In case of technical words, it may call for a different approach.[3]

21. *Obiter dicta* of Supreme Court is Binding on All Courts

The doctrine of judicial precedents applicable is that a judgment of the Supreme Court is binding on all the courts in India. The judgment of the Supreme Court means not only the ratio of a particular judgment but even *obiter dicta* in particular judgment rendered by the Supreme Court is binding on all the courts in India. As against this, the *obiter dicta* of a High Court, may it be contained in the judgment of the Full Bench or a Division Bench is not binding on the Single Judge of that court nor such *obiter dicta* of the Full Bench, Division Bench or Single

---

1. *Prithi Pal Singh* v. *Union of India*, 1983 Cr LJ 647 SC: AIR 1982 SC 1413: (1982) 3 SCC 140: 1983 (1) SCJ 10: (1983) 1 SCR 393: 1982 SCC (Cri) 642: 1982 UJ (SC) 695.
2. *State of Punjab* v. *Surinder Kumar*, AIR 1992 SC 1593· 1992 AIR SCW 1728: JT 1991 (6) SC 540: (1992) 1 SCC 489: 1992 (1) Serv LR 335: 1992 (2) UPTC 814.
3. *Indian Cable Company Ltd.* v. *Collector of Central Excise*, AIR 1995 SC 64: 1995 (1) SCT 56: 1994 (5) Serv LR 605: 1994 AIR SCW 4071: JT 1994 (6) SC 243: (1994) 6 SCC 610.

Judge is binding on all courts subordinate to a particular High Court. It is only the ratio of a particular case decided by the High Court, which is binding on all the courts subordinate to it.[1]

22. Fiscal Statutes should be Construed Strictly

Lord Cairns said many years ago in (1869) 4 HL 100 (2) at p. 122: "As I understand the principle of all fiscal legislation it is this. If the person sought to be taxed comes within the letter of the law he must be taxed, however great the hardship may appear to the judicial mind to be. On the other hand if the Crown, seeking to recover the tax, cannot bring the subject within the letter of the law, the subject is free, however, apparently within the spirit of the law the case might otherwise appear to be.[2]

23. Provision in Special Act *vis-a-vis* General Act

There can be a situation in law where the same statute is treated as a special statute *vis-à-vis* one legislation and again as a general statute *vis-à-vis* yet another legislation. Such situations do arise as held in *LIC of India* v. *D.J. Bahadur*, AIR 1980 SC 2181: (1981) 1 SCC 315. It was there observed:

> "....for certain cases, an Act may be general and for certain other purposes, it may be special and the court cannot blur a distinction when dealing with the finer points of law."

For example, a Rent Control Act may be a special statute as compared to the Code of Civil Procedure. But *vis-à-vis* an Act permitting eviction from public premises or some special class of buildings, the Rent Control Act may be a general statute. In fact in *Damji Valji Shah* v. *LIC of India*, AIR 1965 SC 135: (1965) 3 SCR 665, this Court has observed that *vis-à-vis* the LIC Act, 1956, the Companies Act, 1956 can be treated as a general statute. This is clear from para 19 of that judgment. It was observed.

> "Further, the provisions of the special Act, *i.e.*, the LIC Act, will override the provisions of the general Act, *viz.*, the Companies Act which is an Act relating to companies in general."

Thus, some High Courts rightly treated the Companies Act as a general statute, and the RDB Act as a special statue overriding the general statute.

Alternatively, the Companies Act, 1956 and the RDB Act can both be treated as special laws, and the principle that when there are two special laws, the latter will normally prevail over the former if there is a provision in the latter special Act giving it overriding effect, can also be applied. Such a provision is there in the RDB Act, namely, section 34. A similar situation arose in *Maharashtra Tubes Ltd.* v. *State Industrial and Investment Corpn. of Maharashtra Ltd.*, (1993) 2 SCC 144: (1993) 1 SCR 340 where there was inconsistency between two special laws, the Finance Corporation Act, 1951 and the Sick Industries Companies (Special Provisions) Act, 1985. The latter contained section 32, which gave overriding effect to its provisions

1. *Food Corporation of India* v. *Viramgam Nagar Palika*, AIR 2000 Guj 91.
2. *Mathuram Aggrawal* v. *State of Madha Pradesh*, AIR 2000 SC 109: 1999 AIR SCW 4069: (1999) 8 SCC 667: 2000 (1) SCJ 239: (1999) 6 SCALE 667: 1999 (9) Supreme 503: 2000 (1) UJ (SC) 345.

and was held to prevail over the former. It was pointed out by Ahmadi, J. that both special statutes contained *non-obstante* clauses but that the "1985 Act being a subsequent enactment, the *non-obsante* clause therein would ordinarily prevail over the *non-obstante* clause in section 46B of the 1951 Act unless it is found that the 1985 Act is general statue and the 1951 Act is special one".

Therefore, in view of section 34 of the RDB Act, the said Act overrides the Companies Act; to the extent there is anything inconsistent between the Acts.[1]

24. Rule of Harmonious Construction

The expression "any other law" employed in sub-section (3) of section 32 of Drugs and Cosmetics Act, 1940 is of wide amplitude and it embraces within its fold the Excise Act also. It is well-settled that a particular act or omission to do a thing may constitute an offence under two or more statutes. In such an event the competent authorities are not prevented from taking any action under various statutes. Section 26 of the General Clauses Act provides that where an act or omission constitutes an offence under two or more enactments, then the offender shall be liable to be punished under either or any of those enactments; but he shall not be liable to be punished twice for the same offence. The only restriction is indicated in article 20(2) of the Constitution, which directs that no person shall be prosecuted and punished for the same offence more than once. As noticed earlier, the Act of 1940 does not provide for prevention of misuse of medicinal preparations and drugs containing alcohol as alcoholic beverages. The incidental provisions about manufacture, transport, possession and licence. etc., in the rules framed under the Act of 1940 will have the effect of repealing only *pro tanto* similar provision in the Excise Act, *i.e.*, only insofar as they have bearing with regard to levy and collection of duties and control of quality of medicinal preparations and drugs. They will not have the effect of repealing provisions of the Excise Act insofar as they relate to the prevention of misuse of medicinal preparations and drugs containing alcohol as alcoholic beverages. As a necessary corollary, provisions regulating misuse of medicinal preparations and drugs containing alcohol can be made by the State Government as also by the Competent Authority in the exercise of the powers conferred on them by the Excise Act. Such an interpretation would be in conformity with the rule of interpretation about "harmonious construction"' making an endeavour "to solve the conflict" and attempting a reconciliation as laid down by the Supreme Court.[2] Thus the Excise Authorities or the police can proceed under section 61 of the Excise Act or any other provision of the Excise Act against a dealer under the Act of 1940, if he commits any offence under the Excise Act, although he might also be liable under the Act of 1940. That being so, the plea of the petitioner that he cannot be proceeded against by the police under the Excise Act even if he contravenes the provisions of the Excise Act is not tenable.[3]

---

1. *Allahabad Bank* v. *Canara Bank,* (2000) 4 SCC 406: 2000 AIR SCW 1347: AIR 2000 SC 1535: 2000 CLC 913.
2. *Harak Chand* v. *Union of India,* AIR 1970 SC 1453.
3. *Anoop Khanna* v. *State,* 83 (2000) DLT 516 (DHC).

CHAPTER 1

PRELIMINARY

1. Short title, extent and commencement.—(1) This Act may be called the Delhi Excise Act, 2009 (Delhi Act 10 of 2010).

(2) It extends to the whole of the National Capital Territory of Delhi.

(3) It shall come into force on such date* as the Government may, by notification in the Official Gazette, appoint.

SYNOPSIS

Notification

Comments

Notification

1.'We hold that a Central Excise Notification can be said to have been published, except when it is provided other wise, when it is so issued as to make it known to the public. It would be a proper publication if it is published in such a manner that persons can, if they were so interested, acquaint themselves with its contents. If publication is through a Gazette then mere printing of it in the Gazette would not be enough. Unless Gazette containing the notification is made available to the public, the notification cannot be said to have been duly published.[1]

2. Unless and until there is clear intention expressed in notification that it would also apply retrospectively, the same cannot be given retrospective effect and would always apply prospectively.[2]

2. Definitions.—In this Act, unless the context otherwise requires,—

(1) "alcohol" means ethyl alcohol of any strength and purity having the chemical composition C_2H_5OH;

(2) "alcoholic beverage or potable liquor" means any beverage containing alcohol in conformity with the BIS standards which may be intoxicating and is fit for human consumption;

(3) "alcoholic strength by volume (% vol.) of a mixture of water and alcohol" means the ratio of volume of alcohol, measured at 20°C, contained in the mixture to the total volume of the mixture;

---

* Came into force on 4-10-2010. *Vide* Notification No. F-10(5)/Fin(T&E)/2009-10/SSF/103, dated 4th October, 2010.

1. *Collector Central Excise* v. *New Tobacco Company*, 1998 (97) ELT 388 (SC).
2. *Union of India* v. *Kartick Chandra Mondol*, I (2010) SLT 475.

(4) "appellate authority" means the Deputy Commissioner, the Excise Commissioner, or the Financial Commissioner, as the case may be, for the purposes of this Act;

(5) "authorized officer" means an officer authorized to exercise any power or to perform any duties and functions conferred on or imposed under this Act;

(6) "Assistant Commissioner" means an officer appointed by the Government as Assistant Commissioner of Excise under section 5 of this Act;

(7) "beer" means alcoholic beverage prepared from malt or grain with or without addition of sugar and hops and includes black beer, ale, stout, porter and such other substance as may be notified by the Government;

(8) "BIS standards" means standard prescribed by Bureau of Indian Standards or the standards prescribed by any other Central Government authority, constituted under the relevant Act;

(9) "black jaggery" means coarse brown sugar made from palm tree or cane juice ordinarily unfit for human consumption but contains sufficient quantity of fermentable sugar for manufacture of ethyl alcohol;

(10) "blending" means mixing of two or more spirits which may be of different strengths and different qualities;

(11) "bonded warehouse" means a licensed private bonded warehouse or part of a public bonded warehouse, established under this Act for storing liquor on which duty has not been paid;

(12) "bottling" means transfer of liquor from a cask or other vessel to a bottle or other approved receptacle for the purpose of sale whether any process of rectification be employed or not and includes rebottling;

(13) "bottling plant" means premises where bottling of liquor is done and includes every place therein where it is stored or wherefrom it is issued;

(14) "brewery" means premises where beer is manufactured and includes every place therein where beer is stored or wherefrom it is issued;

(15) "compounding" means the manufacture of alcoholic beverage by addition to spirit of a flavouring or colouring matter or both;

(16) "counterfeit liquor" means a liquor in respect of which—

(a) there is any violation of any right under the Trade Marks Act, 1999 (47 of 1999) or the Copyright Act, 1957 (14 of 1957) or any other similar Act in force, or

(b) in respect of which an offence under section 481 or section 483 or section 486 of the Indian Penal Code, 1860 (XLV of 1860) has been committed;

(17) "country or traditional liquor" means plain or spiced spirit which has been manufactured in India from material recognized as base for country or traditional spirit namely mahua, rice, gur, molasses, etc., and notified as such liquor by the Government;

(18) "Delhi" means the National Capital Territory of Delhi;

(19) "denaturant" means any substance completely miscible in spirit and of such a character that its addition renders the material, or any aqueous dilution of it, non-potable;

(20) "denatured spirit" means spirit with added denaturant to render it effectively and permanently unfit for human consumption;

(21) "Deputy Commissioner" means the officer appointed by the Government as Deputy Commissioner of Excise under section 5 of this Act;

(22) "distillery" means premises where spirit is manufactured and includes every place therein where it is stored or wherefrom it is issued;

(23) "duty" means the excise duty or the countervailing duty as mentioned in Entry 51 of List II of Seventh Schedule of the Constitution, or as the case may be special duty;

(24) "excisable article" means any alcoholic liquor for human consumption or any other similar article which the Government may declare to be an excisable article;

(25) "Excise Commissioner" means the officer appointed by the Government as Excise Commissioner under section 3 of this Act;

(26) "excise officer" means any officer or person appointed or invested with powers under this Act;

(27) "excise revenue" means revenue derived or derivable from any payment, duty, fee, tax, confiscation or fine, imposed or ordered under the provisions of this Act, or of any other law

for the time being in force relating to intoxicants but does not include fine imposed by a court of law;

(28) "excise tree" includes the gul, mahua, coconut, palm, palmyra, date, begani or doddasal tree or any other tree, the fermented or unfermented juice of which contains alcohol and from which toddy or any other liquor can be prepared;

(29) "export" means to take out of Delhi to any other State within the country;

(30) "export out of India" with its grammatical variations and cognate expressions means taking out of Delhi to any place outside India;

(31) "extra neutral alcohol or silent spirit" means spirit as may be specified by the relevant Central Government Authority;

(32) "fermented liquor" means liquor obtained by the process of fermentation and includes beer, ale, stout, porter, wine, pachwai, fermented tari and any other similar liquor;

(33) "Financial Commissioner" means the Financial Commissioner of the National Capital Territory of Delhi;

(34) "foreign liquor" means any liquor imported by land, sea or air into India;

(35) "Government" means the Lieutenant Governor of the National Capital Territory of Delhi appointed by the President under article 239 and designated as such under article 239AA of the Constitution;

(36) "illicit liquor" means any liquor manufactured or stored or distributed or sold, in contravention of the provisions of this Act or the rules framed thereunder or liquor on which appropriate duty or fee leviable under this Act or the rules framed there under, has not been paid and includes foreign liquor on which appropriate duty of customs has not been paid;

(37) "import" means to bring into Delhi from any other State of the country;

(38) "import into India" with its grammatical variations and cognate expressions, means bringing into Delhi from any place out side India;

(39) "Indian liquor" means liquor manufactured in India by process of distillation or using alcohol obtained by distillation such as whisky, brandy, rum, gin, vodka, liqueurs, but does not include country liquor or fermented liquor;

(40) "intoxicant" means and includes,—

(a) any liquor,

(b) any spirit,

(c) any intoxicating drug,

(d) any other article, which the Government may from time-to-time declare to be intoxicant, except the substances covered under the Narcotic Drugs and Psychotropic Substances Act, 1985, for the purpose of this Act;

(41) "intoxicating drug" means,—

(a) the dried leaves of the Indian hemp plant known as bhang, siddhi or patti or cannabis sativa;

(b) any mixture with or without natural materials of bhang, siddhi or patti or cannabis sativa or any drink prepared therefrom;

(42) "Legislative Assembly" means the Legislative Assembly of the National Capital Territory of Delhi;

(43) "licence" means a licence granted under this Act and the rules framed thereunder;

(44) "licensing authority" means an officer who is authorized to grant, suspend and cancel licence, permit and pass under this Act;

(45) "Lieutenant Governor" means the Lieutenant Governor of Delhi appointed by the President under article 239 of the Constitution;

(46) "liquor" means any alcoholic beverage and includes whisky, brandy, beer, wine, toddy, tari, pachwai, vodka, gin, tequila, country liquor, arrack and intoxicating liquid consisting of or containing alcohol as may be specified under BIS standard besides any similar substance which the Government may by notification declare to be liquor for the purpose of this Act;

(47) "major and minor offences"

(a) major offences mean—

(i) adulteration;

(ii) sale of non-duty paid liquor, (NDPL);

(iii) illicit manufacture, possession, transport, transit and sale of liquor;

(iv) rendering denatured spirit fit for human consumption;

(v) mixing noxious substance with liquor;

(vi) tampering with sealed bottles;

(vii) sale to minor;

(b) the remaining offences under this Act shall be minor offences;

(48) "manufactory" means any distillery, brewery, winery or any establishment distilling, brewing, manufacturing, blending or bottling liquor;

(49) "manufacture" includes any process—

(a) incidental or ancillary to the completion of manufactured intoxicants,

(b) whether natural or artificial, by which any intoxicant is produced or prepared and also re-distillation and every process for the rectification, reduction, flavouring, blending or colouring of liquor, or

(c) which in relation to intoxicant involves packing or repacking of such article in bottle or unit package or labelling or re-labelling of bottles or unit package, including the declaration or alteration of maximum retail price (MRP) on it or adoption of any other treatment on the intoxicant for sale to the consumers;

Explanation.—For the removal of doubt, it is hereby clarified that labelling of bottles or unit packages, imported into India or into Delhi, to comply with statutory requirements shall not be construed as manufacture;

(50) "manufacturer" means any person who manufactures intoxicants and includes a manufacturer of alcohol subject to excise duty under the Central Excise Act, 1944 (1 of 1944);

(51) "molasses" means heavy viscous liquid produced, in the final stage of manufacture of gur or sugar including khandsari, sugar from sugar cane or gur, when liquid as such or in any form or ad-mixture containing sugar which can be fermented;

(52) "MRP" means the maximum price at which the liquor may be sold to the ultimate consumer and shall include all taxes, freight, transport charges, commission or trade margin payable to dealers, and all charges towards marketing, delivery, packing, forwarding and the like as the case may be;

(53) "notification" means a notification issued under the Act and the rules framed thereunder and published in the Official Gazette;

(54) "officer-in-charge" means the excise officer authorized to supervise and control manufactory or warehouse;

(55) "pachwai" means fermented rice, millet or other grain, and includes liquid obtained therefrom, whether diluted or undiluted, but does not include beer;

(56) "permit" means an authorization granted under this Act and/or the rules framed thereunder;

(57) "place" includes a house, building, shop, booth, tent enclosure, vessel, boat, raft and vehicle;

(58) "police station" means a police station having jurisdiction over the place and any other place, which the Government may, by notification, declare to be a police station for the purpose of this Act;

(59) "prescribed" means prescribed by rules made under this Act;

(60) "rectification" includes every process whereby spirit is purified or is coloured or flavoured by mixing any material therewith;

(61) "rectified spirit" means un-denatured alcohol, including absolute alcohol, extra neutral alcohol and alcohol derived from malt as may be specified by the BIS standard;

(62) "relevant laws" means the Indian Power Alcohol Act, 1948 (22 of 1948), the Motor Spirit Taxation Act the Medicinal and Toilet Preparations (Excise Duties) Act, 1955 (16 of 1955), the Narcotic Drugs and Psychotropic Substances Act, 1985 (61 of 1985) and such other Acts relevant to excise revenue;

(63) "retail price" means the price fixed by the Excise Commissioner for the sale of intoxicant at which the licensee is bound to sell the intoxicants;

(64) "retail sale" means sale in quantities not exceeding the limits of sale by retail for any consideration or not;

(65) "special duty" means a tax on the import of any excisable article being an article on which countervailing duty as is mentioned in Entry 51 of List II in the Seventh Schedule to the Constitution is not imposable on the ground merely that such article is not being manufactured or produced in the territory to which this Act extends;

(66) "spirit" means any liquid containing alcohol obtained by distillation, whether denatured or not;

(67) "spirituous preparation" means—

(a) any medicinal or toilet preparation containing alcohol,

(b) any antiseptic preparation or solution containing alcohol,

(c) any flavouring extract, essence or syrup containing alcohol;

(68) "still" includes any apparatus or part thereof, for distillation or manufacture of spirit;

(69) "sub-standard liquor" means liquor, which does not meet the BIS standards and includes liquor whose nature, substance or quality is so affected—

(a) by liquor itself, or the package thereof which is composed, whether wholly or in part of poisonous or deleterious substances;

(b) by virtue of unhygienic processing or presence in that article of any harmful substance;

(c) by substitution of any inferior or cheaper substance whether wholly or in part;

(d) by addition of substance directly or as an ingredient which is not permitted;

(e) by the presence of any colouring matter preservative other than specified in respect thereof;

(f) by the presence of worm, weevil or insect;

(g) by virtue of its being prepared, packed or kept under insanitary conditions, or

(h) by dilution;

(70) "toddy and tari" means fermented or unfermented juice drawn from a coconut, palmyra, date or any other kind of palm tree;

(71) "transit" means to move from one State to another through Delhi;

(72) "transport" means to move from one place to another within Delhi;

(73) "VAT" means tax on sale or purchase of goods referred to in Entry 54 of the State List (List-II) of the Seventh Schedule to the Constitution;

(74) "warehouse" means a place where storage of liquor is permitted and includes the relevant part of manufactory;

(75) "wholesale sale" means sale in quantities exceeding the limit of sale by retail;

(76) "wine" means a fermented juice of grapes or other fruits with or without the addition of sugar or jaggery containing self-generated alcohol and includes fortified wine;

(77) "winery" means – premises where wine is manufactured and includes every place therein where wine is stored or wherefrom it is issued.

SYNOPSIS

Comments

1. Means

When in a definition clause, given in any statute the word 'means' is used, what follows is intended to speak exhaustively. When a phrase "means" is used in a definition, it is 'hard and fast' definition and no meaning other than that which is put in the definition can be assigned to the same. On the other hand, when the word 'includes' is used in a definition, the legislature does not intend to restrict the definition, makes the definition enumerative but not exhaustive. That is to say, the term defined will retain its ordinary meaning but its scope would be extended to bring within its matters, which in its ordinary meaning may or may not comprise'.[1]

Beer means:

(i) fermented alcoholic beverage brewed from malt and hops.

Source: Word Net (R) 1.6, (c) 1997 Princeton University.

(ii) fermented extract of the roots and other parts of various plants, as spruce, ginger, sassafras, etc.

Source: Webster's Revised Unabridged Dictionary, (c) 1996, 1998 MICRA, Inc.

(iii) The definition of liquor is wide enough to include beer. The mere fact that beer is defined separately does not mean or show that it is separate from liquor. The beer having been specifically declared as foreign liquor, the licensee in forms L-4 and L-5 cannot be restrained from selling it under the said licences.[2]

(iv) 'Beer' would mean fermented liquor from malt when it is potable and in consumable condition as beverage.[3]

2. (a) 'Ale' means:

(i) fermented alcoholic beverage similar to but heavier than beer.

Source: Word Net (R) 1.6, (c) 1997 Princeton University.

(ii) The word 'ale', in England and the United States, usually designates a heavier kind of fermented liquor, and the word beer a lighter kind. The word beer is also in common use as the generic name for all malt liquors.

Source: Webster's Revised Unabridged Dictionary, (c) 1996, 1998 MICRA, Inc.

(b) 'Ale' means a beverage made from an infusion of malt by fermentation flavoured with hops (The Readers Digest Great Encyclopaedia Dictionary).

Providing of ethyl alcohol content: Provision that alcoholic contents of toddy kept for sale drawn from coconut trees should not exceed 8.1% v/v is liable to be struck down, being unworkable and unreasonable. Contents of ethyl alcohol in toddy would depend on various factors including weather, season or pot in which it is kept, the statute must be definite. Where it is vague, the same is liable to be struck down. Unless the statutory intention otherwise provides, existence of *mens rea* must be read in penal statute.[4]

3.(a) 'Porter' a malt liquor, of a dark colour and moderately bitter taste, possessing tonic and intoxicating qualities.

1. *Bharat Co-op. Bank Ltd.* v. *Cooperative Bank Employees' Union*, AIR 2007 SC 2320: 2007 Lab IC 2823: 2007 AIR SCW 4020: (2007) 4 SCC 685: 2007 (2) SCT 505: (2007) 5 SCALE 57: 2007 (2) UPLBEC 1804: 2007 (4) AIR Bom R 649: 2007 (3) Bom CR 673.
2. *Milkha Singh Hardial Singh & Co.* v. *State of Punjab*, 1967 PLR 890.
3. *Mohan Meakin Ltd.* v. *Excise and Taxation Commissioner, Himachal Pradesh*, (1997) 2 SCC 193.
4. *State of Kerala* v. *Unni*, AIR 2007 SC 819: (2007) 2 SCC 365: (2006) 13 SCALE 208: 2007 (1) Supreme 179: 2007 AIR SCW 531: 2007 (1) Ker LJ 97.

Note.—Porter is said to be so called as having been first used chiefly by the London porters, and this application of the word is supposed to be not older than 1750.

Source: Webster's Revised Unabridged Dictionary, (c) 1996, 1998 MICRA, Inc.

(b) "Porter" is dark brown bitter beer, like stout but weaken, brewed from charred or browned malt (The Reader's Digest C.E. Dictionary).

No excise duty on un-drawn liquor: 1. Licence fee stipulated to be paid by the licensee was the price or consideration or rental which the government charged them for parting its privilege and that it was a normal incident of trading or business transaction. It is true no excise duty could be collected on undrawn liquor.[1]

4.(a) 'Stout' a dark brown beer, brewed from black malt in the grist and strongly flavoured with hops.

Source: New Webster's comprehensive Dictionary of English Language, 1990 Edition.

(b)"Stout" is stronger and better quality of porter. Extra strong porter (Chambers Dictionary).

2. Duty on Left over Stock

A fair reading of the rule giving full effect to the words used in rule XXVI of the Excise Rules and the *Explanation* added to rule IV (of the Foreign Liquor Rules) leave no doubt that the balance of stock envisioned by the rules and subjected to enhancement or reduction of duty is such surplus stock as is held immediately before the expiry of the previous licence. So construed, in this case the quantity held over in March, 1964 becomes liable to enhancement of licence fee on April 1, 1964, for, otherwise, some persons who by accident have huge stocks left over will not have to pay the enhanced rate of licence fee while others with 'virgin' licences for that year and who begin with no stock-on-hand have to pay at a higher rate. The respondent, therefore, must pay higher fee on the balance of stock as on April 1, 1964.[2]

3. Countervailing Duty

The expression 'countervailing duties' has not been defined in the Constitution or the Bihar and Orissa Act 2 of 1915. To be seen in etymological sense and the context in which it has been used in Entry 51. In its etymological sense, it means to counter-balance; to avail against with equal force or virtue; to compensate for something or serve as an equivalent of or substitute for see *Black's Law Dictionary*, 4th Edn., p. 421. This would suggest that a countervailing duty is imposed for the purpose of counter-balancing or to avail against something with equal force or to compensate for something as an equivalent. Entry 51 in List II of the Seventh Schedule of the Constitution gives power to the State Legislature to impose duties of excise on alcoholic liquors for human consumption where the

1. *Panna Lal* v. *State of Rajasthan*, AIR 1975 SC 2008: (1975) 2 SCC 633: (1976) 1 SCR 219: 1975 Tax LR 2005.
2. *State of Madhya Pradesh* v. *Tikamdas*, AIR 1975 SC 1429: 1975 Tax LR 1751: (1975) 2 SCC 100: 1975 SCC (Tax) 310: 1975 Jab LJ 704: 1975 Supp SCR 234.

goods are manufactured or produced in the State. It also gives power to levy countervailing duties at the same or lower rates on similar goods manufactured or produced elsewhere in India. The fact that countervailing duties may be imposed at the same or lower rates suggests that they are meant to counter-balance the duties of excise imposed on goods manufactured in the State. They may be imposed at the same rate as excise duties or at a lower rate, presumably to equalise the burden after taking into account the cost of transport from the place of manufacture to the taxing State. It seems, therefore, that countervailing duties are meant to equalise the burden on alcoholic liquors manufactured or produced in the State. If no alcoholic liquors similar to those imported into the State are produced or manufactured, the right to impose counter-balancing duties of excise levied on the goods manufactured in the State will not arise. It may, therefore, be accepted that countervailing duties can only be levied if similar goods are actually produced or manufactured in the State on which excise duties are being levied.[1]

4. Duty on Alcohol not for Human Consumption only by the Centre

It is clear that the State legislature had no authority to levy duty or tax on alcohol, which is not for human consumption as that would only be levied by the centre.[2]

5. Countervailing Duty is Imposed on the Import of Excisable Article

"Excise duty" and "countertvailing duty" are well-known concepts and are attracted in different situations. "Excise duty" is essentially a duty on manufacture of goods, and the taxable event is the manufacture of the excisable goods. "Countervailing duty", on the other hand, is imposed when excisable articles are imported into the State, in order to counter balance the excise duty, which is leviable on similar goods if manufactured within the State. So far as countervailing duty is concerned, the incidence of the impost is on the import of the excisable articles, *i.e.*, at the time of entry into the State.[3]

6. Excisable Article

Excisable article would mean any alcoholic liquor for human consumption or any intoxicating drug. The levy or impost of excise duty would be only on alcoholic liquor for human consumption or for being produced in the brewery. Beer would mean fermented liquor from malt, when it is potable or in consumable condition as beverage. The levy is in terms of Entry 51 of List II of the Seventh Schedule which envisages that duties of excise on the goods manufactured or produced in the State and countervailing duties at the same or lower rates on similar goods manufactured or produced elsewhere in India. The range of potable alcohol varies between country spirit to whisky and the ethyl alcohol. The alcohol strength of each excisable article and its percentage varies as per the ISI

---

1. *Mohan Meakin Breweries Ltd.* v. *Excise and Taxation Commissioner, Chandigarh,* (1976) 3 SCC 421: AIR 1976 SC 2020: 1976 SCC (Tax) 318: 1976 Supp SCR 510.
2. *Synthetics & Chemicals Ltd.* v. *State of Uttar Pradesh,* AIR 1990 SC 1927: JT 1989 (4) SC 267.
3. *S.K. Pattanaik* v. *State of Orissa,* AIR 2000 SC 612: 2000 AIR SCW 41: (2000) 1 SCC 413: 2000 (1) SCJ 232: (1999) 7 SCALE 557: 1999 (10) Supreme 259: 2000 (89) Cut LT 706: JT 1999 (10) SC 48: 2000 (1) SRJ 438: 2000 SC Cr R 306.

specifications but intoxicating liquor necessarily means only that liquor which was consumable by human beings as it was. The stage of levying excise duty upon alcoholic liquor arises when excisable article is brought to the stage of human consumption with the requisite alcoholic strength thereof. It is only the final product which is relevant.[1]

7. Fee on Non-potable Liquor:

State of Himachal Pradesh levied permit fee on the import of malt spirit of over proof strength and denatured spirit. *Held*: State government is not competent to levy fee on non-potable liquor.[2]

8. Excise Revenue

It is the revenue derived or derivable from any payment, duty, fee, tax, confiscation or fine, imposed or ordered under the provisions of the Act or any other law for the time being in force relating to liquor or intoxicating drugs but does not include a fine imposed by court of law. The term excise revenue covers all excise fees or other dues including arrears thereof, recoverable under section 60 of the Act.[3]

Includes: Where the definition is inclusive definition, the use of the word, "includes" indicates an intention to enlarge the meaning of the word, used in the statute. Consequently, the word must be construed comprehending not only such things, which they signify according to their natural import, but also those things, which the interpretation clause declares that they shall include. Thus where a definition uses the word "includes" as constructed from "means" the word defined not only bears its ordinary, popular and natural meaning, but in addition also bears the extended statutory meaning.

9. Import is Complete when it Crosses the Border

An article under transport across the frontier of a State implies import with all the cognate variations in its definition. The offence is complete as soon as the contraband reaches the other side of the border.[4]

10. Bhang/Ganja

1. Section 2(iii)(b) of the NDPS Act, 1985 defines Ganja which means the flowering or fruiting tops of cannabis plant excluding the seeds and when not accompanied by the tops, by whatever name they may be known for designated. Bhang, Siddhi, Patti or Cannabis Sativa consists of dead leaves and fruiting shoots whereas Ganja has a rusty green colour and a characteristic odour and counts of flowering or fruiting tops. IV (1995) CCR 636 Raj.

2. As the leaves of Bhang as such are not within the definition of cannabis (hemp) contained in section 2(iii) of the NDPS Act, the provision of section 20 of the Act would not apply to the recovery made. However, this recovery would be

---

1. *Mohan Meakin Ltd.* v. *Excise and Taxation Commissioner, Himachal Pradesh,* (1997) 2 SCC 193: (1997) 2 Supreme 33.
2. *Mohan Meakin Breweries Ltd.* v. *State of Himachal Pradesh,* 1 (2009) DLT 635.
3. *Ravinder Nath Giani Chand* v. *State of Punjab,* 1969 CLJ 786.
4. *Emperor* v. *Mubarak Mian,* 1934 Sind 147.

in violation of section 3(13) of the Punjab Excise Act, 1914 punishable under section 61 of the Excise Act.[1]

11. Licence for Liquor

Licence fee/rental is the consideration for the privilege granted by the Government for manufacturing of vending liquor. Licence fee imposed on undrawn liquor, in advance, neither violates article 14 or section 25 of the M.P. Excise Act, 1915.[2]

12. Definition of Liquor is Constitutional

The definition of liquor as given in the Act is not violative of article 13 of the Constitution.[3]

13. Lahan

Lahan means a mixture of any substance together with a fermenting agent. A mixture of gur and water will become lahan only if some fermenting agent is added.[4]

14. Maha Shakti Sudha is Liquor

The possession of Maha Shakti Sudha being not exempt from the operation of notification No.10(27/61-Fin(E)(I), dated 7th Dec., 1961 issued under section 3(14) of the Act, is violative of the Excise Rules.[5]

15. Spirituous Preparations

For spirituous preparations or medicinal and toilet preparations containing alcohol, the requirement of obtaining licence is not inconsistent with the provisions of the Act and the rules framed by the State Government.[6]

16. Excise Act – M&TP

Medicinal preparation containing alcohol in excess of the contents given in the notification are subject to the prosecution under the Punjab Excise Act (section 61).[7]

17. Ayurvedic Preparations Containing Alchocol

State is competent to regulate Ayurvedic preparations containing alcohol under State Excise Law – State is entitled to call upon the manufacturer to take licence on payment of fee, such fee is regulatory and no *quid pro quo* is required. It will be immune from challenge under article 301.[8]

---

1. *Gurdial Singh* v. *State of Punjab,* 2002 (3) RCR (Criminal) 334 (P&H).
2. *State of Madhya Pradesh* v. *Lalit Jaggi,* (2008) 10 SCC 607.
3. *Dr. Bishamber Nath* v. *State of Punjab,* AIR 1953 Punj 77.
4. *State* v. *Teja Singh,* ILR 1957 Punj 238.
5. *Chaman Lal* v. *The Excise Commr. of Delhi,* 1996 PLR (Del) 181.
6. *K.D.S and A.V. Sangam* v. *Government of Tamil Nadu,* AIR 1996 SC 1314.
7. *Anoop Khanna* v. *State,* 83 (2000) DLT 516.
8. *State of Bihar* v. *Shree Baidyanath Ayurvedic Bhawan,* AIR 2005 SC 932: 2005 AIR SCW 515: 2005 (1) JCR SC 190: JT 2005 (1) SC 314: (2005) 2 SCC 762: 2005 (1) SCJ 529: (2005) 1 SCALE 320: 2005 (1) Supreme 297.

18. Excise Act

Issuing licence on payment of fee to regulate activities like use/misuse of medicines containing alcohol is within the competence of Bihar Excise Act and not in conflict with M & TP or Drugs Act.[1]

"Manufacture" has been defined in its true sense in this Act but every artificial or natural process by which any intoxicant can be produced, its re-distillation and every process for the rectification, reduction, flavouring, blending or colouring of liquor are included in view of the definition under this section. Mere dilution of the denatured spirit with water cannot be termed as manufacture. (Under the Bengal Excise Act of 1910).[2]

The definition of the word "place" under the Act includes vehicles, which could include a car.[3]

19. Special Duty

"It was incidentally urged that Entry 52 in the State List which enables the levying of taxes on entry of goods in local area for consumption, use or sale therein was also within the contemplation of the founding fathers and that power under Entry 52 having been exercised by the Delhi Municipal Administration in the form of terminal tax the same cannot be arrogated by Parliament to itself. Terminal tax is entirely different from the special duty sought to be imposed by the impugned Ordinance. The impost is on entry of country liquor into Delhi to be recovered by the Delhi Administration for its own use. Delhi Administration and Delhi Municipal Administration are entirely different and, therefore, it cannot be said that Entry 52 excludes the power of the Parliament to levy duty on import of country liquor in Delhi."

"Incidentally, the argument is that the taxing event being the import of liquor in Delhi, is exposed to double taxation, namely, the special duty levied by Parliament and the terminal tax imposed by the Municipal Administration and that is impermissible. This has merely to be mentioned to be rejected in view of the decision of this Court in *Arvinder Singh* v. *State of Punjab*,[4] wherein it was observed that if on the same subject the legislature chooses to levy tax twice over there is no inherent invalidity in the fiscal adventure save where ever prohibitions exist."[5]

20. Industrial Alcohol

Industrial alcohol as it is, incapable of being consumed by a normal human being, the expression "consumption" must also be understood in the sense of direct physical intake by human beings in this context. It is true that utilisation

---

1. *State of Bihar* v. *Shree Baidyanath Ayurvedic Bhawan,* AIR 2005 SC 932: 2005 AIR SCW 515: 2005 (1) JCR SC 190: JT 2005 (1) SC 314: (2005) 2 SCC 762: 2005 (1) SCJ 529: (2005) 1 SCALE 320: 2005 (1) Supreme 297.
2. *U.N. Vishwash* v. *Emperor,* AIR 1914 Cal 603.
3. *K.L. Subbayya* v. *State of Karnataka,* AIR 1979 SC 711: 1979 Cr LJ 651: (1979) 2 SCC 115: 1979 SCC (Cri) 367: 1979 (2) SCJ 29: (1979) 2 SCR 1131: 1979 Cri App R (SC) 125: 1979 (1) Kant LJ 410: ILR (1979) 1 Kant 457: 1979 Chand LR (Cri) 145: 1979 Cr LJ (SC) 419.
4. (1979) 1 SCC 137: AIR 1979 SC 321.
5. *Sat Pal and Co.* v. *Lt. Governor of Delhi,* AIR 1979 SC 1550: (1979) 3 SCR 651: 1979 Tax LR 2486: 1979 UJ (SC) 631: (1979) 4 SCC 232: 1979 SCC (Tax) 322

in some form or the other is consumption for the benefit of human being if industrial alcohol is utilised for production of rubber, tyres used , the utilisation of those tyres in the vehicle of man cannot in the context in which the expression has been used in the Constitution, be understood to mean that the alcohol has been for human consumption. The expression 'alcohol for human consumption' means that liquor which as it is consumable in the sense capable of being taken by human being as such as beverage or drink.[1]

21. Ethyl Alcohol (95%)

Ethyl Alcohol is not alcoholic liquor for human consumption but can be used as raw material input after processing and substantial dilution in the production of whisky, gin, country liquor, etc.[1]

22. Ethanol AR

"The product Ethanol AR (analytical reagent) is a product consisting of alcohol of very high purity, *i.e.*, 99.9 per cent. cannot be termed as rectified spirit. The same cannot be said to have been prepared by any process where liquor is purified or refined. It is not liquor as it is not spirit, denatured spirit, wine, beer tody or a liquid consisting or containing alcohol. It is not intoxicant as it is not liquor and we are constrained to hold that the provisions of the Bombay Prohibition Act are not attracted and hence the prosecution sought to be launched against the petitioner is misconceived.[2]

23. Transporting in a Car

Four accused were caught transporting a large quantity (65 Gallons) of illicit liquor in light motor tubes by a motor car at 1.00 a.m. The accused put forward a false plea and did not account for their possession of the liquor. They were found seated in the car at that time the car was stopped and searched. The accused were held to be guilty under section 31 in view of presumption under section 38 of the Hyderabad Abkari Act.[3]

24. Movement inside the State is 'transport'

Liquor moved from Pondy to Madras without permit and the lorry was intercepted several kilometer inside Tamil Nadu. The movement inside Tamil Nadu was held to be 'transport' and transport includes element of 'possession'.[4]

---

1. *Synthetics and Chemicals Ltd.* v. *State of Uttar Pradesh*, AIR 1990 SC 1927: JT 1989 (4) SC 267.
2. *M/s. Raj and Co.* v. *State of Maharashtra*, 1994 Cr LJ 2022 Bom (DB).
3. *In re Rajiab*, 1958 Cr LJ 1294 (AP).
4. *Ganesh* v. *State*, 1997 Cr LJ 126 Mad.

CHAPTER II

ESTABLISHMENT AND CONTROL

3. Appointment of Excise Commissioner.—The Government may, by notification, appoint an officer as Excise Commissioner who, subject to the control and orders of the Government in this behalf, shall be the chief controlling authority in all matters connected with the administration of this Act.

SYNOPSIS

Conferment of Power by Name

Comments

Conferment of Power by Name

Conferment of powers on an Excise Commissioner by name will not confer those powers on his successor.[1]

4. Powers and functions of Excise Commissioner.—The powers and functions of the Excise Commissioner shall be—

(a) to regulate, control and monitor manufacture, possession, import, export, transport, sale and consumption of liquor and other intoxicants;

(b) to curb illegal trade in liquor and illicit distillation;

(c) to protect excise revenue and ensure prompt recovery;

(d) to submit returns and information as required by this Act or the rules framed thereunder, to the Government upon all matters concerning excise;

(e) to ensure social well-being through education for responsible drinking;

(g) to submit to the Government an annual report on the administration of this Act in the format prescribed;

(h) to perform such other functions and to exercise such other powers as may, from time to time, be entrusted or delegated to him.

5. Appointment of certain officers and staff.—The Government may appoint such numbers of Additional Commissioners, Joint Commissioners, Deputy Commissioners, Assistant Commissioners,

---

1. *Mohammad Aslam* v. *The Crown,* AIR 1949 Lah 210: 50 Cr LJ 984.

Excise Inspectors and such other officers and staff as it may deem fit for the purpose of performing the functions under this Act.

6. Excise Intelligence Bureau.—(1) There shall be an Excise Intelligence Bureau, headed by the Excise Commissioner, consisting of such number of excise officers and staff as may be appointed by the Government and such other officers and staff as may be appointed by the Excise Commissioner with the prior approval of the Government.

(2) The Excise Intelligence Bureau shall—

(a) collect intelligence, keep surveillance and maintain information of excise offences;

(b) collect and disseminate information regarding prominent excise offenders and history-sheeters;

(c) detect, monitor detection, investigation and trial of offences under this Act.

7. Excise administration.—(1) The Deputy Commissioner shall be the licensing authority who shall exercise all powers and functions under this Act, subject to the control and supervision of the Excise Commissioner.

(2) The Deputy Commissioner shall, within the limits of his jurisdiction, exercise such powers and perform such duties and functions as are assigned by or under the provisions of this Act subject to such control as the Government may from time-to-time direct.

(3) The Assistant Commissioner and other subordinate officers shall assist the Deputy Commissioner in exercising his functions.

SYNOPSIS

Licensing Authority

Comments

Licensing Authority

It is the Collector who has to grant country liquor vend licence subject to rules made by the Financial Commissioner. However, such rules cannot derogate in any manner from the statutory power vested in the matter of grant of licences. The rules can only regulate the manner in which and the circumstances under which that power can be exercised.

Where the District Excise and Taxation Officer who was vested with the authority to grant allotment of country liquor vends, acted on the directions of higher authorities in making allotments and not independently, it was held that the allotments were not in accordance with law.[1]

8. Delegation and withdrawal of powers.—(1) The Government may delegate its powers to the Excise Commissioner subject to such

1. *Kans Raj Nathu Ram* v. *Deputy Excise and Taxation Commr.*, AIR 1965 Punj 284.

limitations and conditions as may be specified in the order of delegation.

(2) The Excise Commissioner and the Deputy Commissioner may, by order, delegate their powers under this Act to any subordinate officer subject to such limitations and conditions as may be specified in the order of delegation.

(3) The Excise Commissioner or the Deputy Commissioner, as the case may be, may by an order also withdraw from any officer or person any or all the powers so delegated.

9. Investing persons with special powers.—The Government may, by notification, invest in any Government functionary not being an excise officer, with powers to perform all or any of the functions of any excise officer under this Act, and such person shall, in the exercise of these functions, be deemed to be an excise officer.

10. Reward for seizure of intoxicants and vehicles, etc.—The Excise Commissioner may grant reward to excise officers out of the sum collected from the sale of intoxicants, apparatus and vehicles carrying such intoxicants, or otherwise and also to such informers for such work subject to such terms and conditions as may be prescribed.

Comments

The expression, etc., used is significant and the said entry includes all the employees who are described as artisans by whatever name they might have been known, like polishers, carpenters, tailors, upholsters, cameras and all other artisans doing similar jobs in the Farash Khana and that they are all included in the category of class IV employees.[1]

---

1. *Kamruddin* v. *State of Rajasthan*, AIR 1995 SC 223: (1994) 6 SCC 605: 1994 AIR SCW 4290: JT 1994 (6) SC 356: 1995 (1) SCT 125: 1994 (3) SCC (Supp) 511.

CHAPTER III

LICENCE AND PERMIT FOR MANUFACTURE, POSSESSION, SALE, ETC., OF INTOXICANTS

11. Prohibition of import, export, transport, manufacture, possession, sale, etc., of intoxicant.—(1) No person shall construct or establish any manufactory or warehouse, bottle, import, export, transport, transit, manufacture, collect, possess, sell or purchase any intoxicant or use, keep or have in his possession any material whatsoever, still, utensil, implement, apparatus, label, cork, capsule or seal for manufacture of any intoxicant except under the authority and in accordance with the terms and conditions of a licence or letter of intent or permit granted under this Act and the rules framed thereunder.

(2) The possession of labels, corks or capsules by its printer or manufacturer, as the case may be, will not amount to illegal possession and offence under this section if printed or manufactured under the authority from the holder of licence to manufacture intoxicant, issued under this Act.

12. Grant of letter of intent, licence or permit.—Every letter of intent, licence or permit under this Act shall be granted on payment of such fees, for such period and subject to such restrictions, conditions and in such form and contain such particulars, as may be prescribed.

SYNOPSIS

1. **Licence Fee**
2. **Excise Duty**
3. **No Fundamental Right to Trade in Liquor**
4. **Charges for Parting with Privileges**
5. **Consideration to Part with Privilege**
6. **Jurisdiction of State/Central Government over Manufacture**
7. **Demarcation of Control between States and Union for the Manufacture of Spirit**

Comments

1. Licence Fee

Discrimination: Although it is the discretion of the Excise Commissioner to either grant or withhold licence, but the discretion has to be exercised judiciously and not arbitrarily or capriciously. Thus where the Excise Commissioner allowed the sale of liquor to the members of one Civilian Club but refused such permission to another Civilian Club, having similar rules, it was held that there being no warrant for this unjust discrimination, the order refusing grant of licence to the other Club was *ultra virus* of article 14 of the Constitution.[1]

2. Excise Duty

Excise duty is primarily a duty on the production or manufacture of goods produced or manufactured within the country. The amounts charged to the licensees in the instant case are, evidently, neither in the nature of a tax nor of excise duty. But then, the 'licence fee' which the State Government charged to the licensees through the medium of auctions or the 'fixed fee' which it charged to the vendors of foreign liquor holding licences need bear no *quid pro quo* to the services rendered to the licensees. The word 'fee' is not used in the Act or the Rules in the technical sense of the expression. By 'licence fee' or 'fixed fee' is meant the price or consideration which the Government charges to the licensees for parting with its privileges and granting them to the licensees. As the State can carry on a trade or business, such a charge is the normal incident of a trading or business transaction.

The 'licence fee' or 'fixed fee' in the instant case does not have to conform to the requirement that it must bear a reasonable relationship with the services rendered to the licensees. The amount charged to the licensees is not a fee properly so-called nor indeed a tax but is in the nature of the price of a privilege, which the purchaser has to pay in any trading or business transactions.[2]

3. No Fundamental Right to Trade in Liquor

After consideration all the decisions of five Constitution Benches Chandrachud J., as he then was summed up the position as follows:

> "These unanimous decisions of five Constitution Benches uniformly emphasized after a careful consideration of the problem involved that the State has the power to prohibit trades which are injurious to the health and welfare of the public is inherent in the nature of liquor business that no person has an absolute right to deal in liquor and that all forms of dealings in liquor have, from their inherent nature, been treated as a class by themselves by all civilized communities."

There is no fundamental right to do trade or business in intoxicants. The State under its regulatory powers, has the right to prohibit absolutely every form of activity in relation to intoxicants, its manufacture, storage, export, import, sale and possession.[2]

Where the State overlooked the claim of the petitioner who had offered tender for supply of liquor in the district where he had a distillery and granted the privilege to a person who had no distillery in that district, the action of the Excise Commissioner was held to be not in accordance with law.[3]

---

1. *Lumsden Club* v. *State of Punjab*, AIR 1957 Punj 20: 58 PLR 426.
2. *Har Shankar* v. *Deputy Excise and Taxation Commissioner*, AIR 1975 SC 1121: (1975) 1 SCC 737: (1975) 3 SCR 254: 1975 Tax LR 1569.
3. *Sir Shadi Lal Distillery & Chemical Works* v. *State of Uttar Pradesh*, AIR 1977 All 349.

4. Charges for Parting with Privileges

The amounts, which are charged to the licensees who offer their bids in auction sales of vends are neither tax, nor fee properly so called which would require the existence of a *quid pro quo*, nor in the nature of excise duty, which by reason of the Constitutional constraints has to be primarily a duty on the production or manufacture of goods produced or manufactured within the country. The true nature of the charge which the government levies in such cases is that it is a price which the State charges as a consideration for parting with its privileges in favour of the licensee. Such a charge is a normal incident of a trading or business transaction. Since rights in regard to the manufacture and sale of intoxicants are vested in the State, it is open to it to part with those rights for consideration.[1]

The classification which can be sustained must have a reasonable nexus with objective sought to be achieved by the impugned action. If the licences issued in 1993-94 to licensees operating from before and to the appellants were issued afresh as the rules do not make discrimination between renewal and fresh grant then all licences were on same footing and the attempt to pick and choose the appellants, in our opinion, was contrary to rules without any valid justification.[2]

The State can adopt any mode of selling the licences for trade or business with a view to maximize its revenue so long as the method adopted is not discriminatory".[3]

5. Consideration to Part with Privilege

Since the State in exercise of its regulatory power can even absolutely prohibit all activities relating to intoxicants, it is competent to part with its rights for consideration – Fee charged under the Rules is the price or consideration and not 'fee' in technical sense which requires *quid pro quo* – Enhancement or imposition of fee of Rs. 25,000 constitutes only a small percentage of the total turnover of various products to which the labels are affixed and hence cannot be considered exorbitant.[4]

6. Jurisdiction of State/Central Government over Manufacture

Prohibition is referable to Entry 8, of List II, of Schedule 7 to the Constitution and is within the competence of State legislature. The industries producing and manufacturing intoxicating liquors fall within the purview of Entry 24 of List II which is a general entry relating to industries whereas Entry 8 is a specific and special entry relating, *inter alia*, to industries engaged in production and manufacture of intoxicating liquor. As per rule of interpretation (special excludes general), the industries engaged in production of intoxicating liquor, do not fall within Entry 24 but do fall within Entry 8. As such the Parliament cannot take over the control of industries engaging in the manufacture of intoxicating liquors by

1. *State Bank of Haryana* v. *Jage Ram,* (1980) 3 SCC 599: 1980 Tax LR 2362.
2. *R. Vijay Kumar* v. *The Commissioner of Excise,* 1 (1994) CCR 70 SC.
3. *Khoday Distilleries Ltd.* v. *State of Karnataka,* (1995) 1 SCC 574: 1995 AIR SCW 313.
4. *Khoday Distilleries Ltd.* v. *State of Karnataka,* (1996) 10 SCC 304.

making declaration under Entry 52 of List I since the said entry governs only Entry 24 in List II and not Entry 8 in List II.

The prohibition of manufacture of intoxicating liquor squarely falls within the four corners of Entry 8 read with Entry 6 in List II. Item 26 of the 1st Schedule to the Industrial Regulation Act must be read subject to Entry 8 and for that matter Entry 6 in List II. The ambit and scope of Constitutional entry cannot be determined with reference to a Parliamentary enactment.

A law made by legislature can be struck down by courts on two grounds and two grounds alone; *viz.*, (1) Lack of legislative competence, and (2) Violation of any of the fundamental rights guaranteed in Part III of the Constitution or any other Constitutional provision.

Trade and business in intoxicating liquors can be restricted, severely curtailed or even prohibited. Imposition of prohibition has to be treated as reasonable restriction in view of directive principles to bring about prohibition.[1]

7. Demarcation of control between States and Union for the Manufacture of Spirit

So far as demarcation of control between States and Union of India in all respect such as setting up of distillery, manufacture, transport, distribution, etc., over rectified spirit is concerned, following position emerges:—

So far as industries engaged in manufacturing rectified spirit meant exclusively for supply to industries, whether after denaturing it or without denaturing it, are concerned, they shall be under the total and exclusive control of the Union. The power of State is only to ensure that the rectified spirit is not diverted or misused for potable purposes and for that purpose post staff on the distillery and levy regulatory fee to defray the cost of such staff. So far as industries engaged in the manufacture of rectified spirit meant exclusively for the purpose of obtaining or manufacturing potable liquor are concerned, they shall be under the total and exclusive control of the State in all stages, including the establishment of distillery and levy of duty.

Where the industries manufacture for both the purposes, the establishment of the distillery shall be in the exclusive domain of the Union, the duty on rectified spirit cleared for industries, other than the industries engaged in obtaining or manufacturing potable liquor, shall be levied by the Union and the duty on rectified spirit cleared/removed for the purpose of obtaining or manufacturing potable liquor shall be levied by the concerned State. The disposal, *i.e.*, clearance or removal of rectified spirit shall be under the joint control of the Union and the State concerned.

'Ethyl alcohol' and 'industrial alcohol' which is of 95 per cent. and above purity cannot be treated as potable liquor.

---

1. *State of Andhra Pradesh* v. *Mc Dowell & Co.*, AIR 1996 SC 1627: 1996 AIR SCW 1679: JT 1996 (3) SC 679: (1996) 3 SCC 709: (1996) 3 SCR 721: 1997 (1) Mad LJ 82.

The potability of liquor is determined by the standards specified by I.S.I (now Bureau of Indian Standards) *i.e.,* alcohol *i.e.,* contents not exceeding 43 per cent. v/v.[1]

13. Qualifications for grant of licence.—(1) While considering an application for grant of licence or permit, the licensing authority shall have regard that the applicant—

(a) is a citizen of India;

(b) is not a defaulter, or black-listed or debarred from holding an excise licence;

(c) possesses good moral character and has no criminal background or has not been convicted of any offence punishable under this or other relevant Acts:

Provided that in case he is selected as licensee, he shall furnish within thirty days of the grant of licence a certificate issued by the Superintendent of Police of the district or the Commissioner of Police, as the case may be, of which place he is the resident, showing that he possesses good moral character and has no criminal background or criminal record;

(d) is not in arrears of any Government or public dues; and

(e) is solvent and has the necessary funds or has made arrangements for it, for conducting the business:

Provided that the details of such funds shall be made available to the licensing authority, if required;

(f) possesses or has an arrangement for taking on rent suitable premises for the licence and such premises have not been constructed in violation of any law;

(g) shall not employ any salesman or representative who has criminal background or suffers from any infectious and contagious disease or is below twenty one years of age.

(2) The licence shall be liable for cancellation, if any document produced with the application is found to be false or forged.

14. Power to take security and counterpart agreement.—Subject to such rules as may be prescribed, any authority granting a licence under this Act may require the licensee—

(a) to give security for the observance of the terms of his licence; and

1. *Bihar Distillery* v. *Union of India,* AIR 1997 SC 1208: 1997 AIR SCW 1240: (1997) 2 SCC 727: (1997) 1 SCR 680: (1997) 1 SCALE 573.

(b) to execute a counterpart agreement in conformity with the tenor of his licence.

15. Technical defects in licence and permit.—(1) No licence or permit granted under this Act shall be deemed to be invalid by reason merely of any technical defect, irregularity or omission in the licence or permit, or in any proceedings conducted prior to grant thereof.

(2) The decision of the licensing authority, as to what is a technical defect, irregularity or omission shall be final and binding.

16. Power to withdraw licence and permit.—(1) Whenever the authority which granted a licence or permit under this Act, considers that such licence or permit should be withdrawn for any reason, it may do so on expiry of fifteen days' notice of its intention to do so or forthwith for reasons to be recorded.

(2) If any licence or permit is withdrawn, the licensee or the permit holder shall be refunded any fee paid in advance or deposit made by the licensee or the permit holder in respect thereof after deducting the amount recoverable by the Government.

17. Power to suspend or cancel licence and permit.—(1) Subject to such restrictions as the Government may prescribe, the authority granting any licence or permit under this Act may suspend or cancel it in the following circumstances after giving reasonable opportunity of being heard—

(a) if the licence or permit is transferred or sublet by the holder thereof without the permission of the licensing authority;

(b) if any excise revenue payable by the holder thereof is not duly paid;

(c) in the event of any breach by the holder of such licence or permit or by his servant, or by any one acting on his behalf, with his express or implied permission, of any of the terms and conditions of such licence or permit;

(d) if the holder of licence or permit or his agent or employee is convicted of an offence punishable under this Act or any other law for the time being in force, relevant and connected with excise matters relating to excise revenue or of any cognizable and non-bailable offence under any other relevant law;

(e) if the purpose for which the licence or permit was granted ceases to exist;

(f) if the licence or permit has been obtained through misrepresentation or fraud.

(2) When a licence or permit is cancelled under sub-section (1), the aforesaid authority may cancel any other licence or permit granted to such person under this Act or under any other law relating to excise revenue.

(3) In the case of cancellation or suspension of licence under sub-section (1), the fee payable for the balance of the period for which any licence would have been current but for such cancellation or suspension, may be recovered from the ex-licensee as excise revenue.

(4) The holder of a licence or permit shall neither be entitled to any compensation for the cancellation or suspension thereof nor to refund of any fee paid or deposit made in respect thereof.

SYNOPSIS

1. **Cancellation of Licence**
2. **Revival Notice**
3. **Default in Payment of Penalty No Ground for Cancellation**
4. **Sections not *ultra vires* the Constitution**
5. **Principles of Natural Justice to be Followed**
6. **Rules of Natural Justice to be followed before Ordering Penalty**
7. **Single Order Setting Aside Different Auctions, Bad in Law**
8. **Principles of Natural Justice**

Comments

1. Cancellation of Licence

Transfer or sub-letting in violation of the provisions of the Statute would be illegal.[1]

2. Revival Notice

A notice terminating a licence when kept in abeyance, cannot be revived by a notice of revival.[2]

3. Default in Payment of Penalty no Ground for Cancellation

"In our opinion section 80(2) does not authorise the Commissioner to make a conditional order in the form in which he purported to do by his order of June 5, 1963. There was no cancellation of licence by that order. The Commissioner merely intimated the appellant that its licence had become liable to cancellation or suspension but instead of cancelling the licence he was imposing a penalty of Rs. 500 to be paid within a fortnight failing which action for cancellation would be taken under section 36(c). The Commissioner's show-cause notice, dated October 16, 1964 proceeds on the basis that as the penalty had not been paid within the period fixed, the licence had to be cancelled in terms of the order of June 5, 1963. Section 36 does not permit the taking of such a course. The grounds for cancellation or suspension of the licence are specified in sub-clauses (a) to (g) of the section and default in payment of penalty levied under the Act does not find

1. *Hari Bandu* v. *Gopal,* AIR 1943 Pat 374.
2. *Karnal Distillery* v. *State,* AIR 1965 Punj 217.

a place therein. The imposition of a penalty by way of threat of cancellation of licence was also not permissible under the Act.[1]

The right to impose lesser penalty is included in the right to impose higher penalty.[2]

4. Sections not *ultra vires* of the Constitution

Section 36(c) read with sections 40 and 80 are not *ultra vires* articles 14 and 19(i)(f) and (g) of the Constitution.[3]

5. Principles of Natural Justice to be Followed

Action under section 36(c) and section 40 is taken on the proof of violation of any condition of the licence, permit or pass. The order is made as a result of *quasi-*judicial proceeding after compliance with the principles of natural justice.[3]

6. Rules of Natural Justice to be followed before Ordering Penalty

Rules of natural justice should be followed while passing order of penalty.[4]

7. Single Order Setting Aside Different Auctions, Bad in Law

Single order setting aside different auctions (of licence for foreign liquor, country liquor and bhang vend) without applying mind separately to question of maintainability of each auction, held, bad and must be set aside.[5]

8. Principles of Natural Justice

Natural justice is an inseparable ingredient of fairness and reasonableness. It is even said that the principles of natural justice must be read into unoccupied interstices of the Statute, unless there is clear mandate to the contrary. Natural justice is the essence of the adjudication, deeply rooted in tradition and conscience, to be ranked as fundamental. The purpose of following principles of natural justice is the prevention of miscarriage of justice.[6]

"Even God did not pass a sentence upon Adam, before he was called upon to make his defence. Adam says God "where art thou has those not eaten of the tree where of I commanded thee that 'thou should not eat'.[7]

18. Bar to the right of renewal and to compensation.—No person to whom a licence or permit has been granted, shall be entitled to claim any renewal thereof, and no claim shall lie for damages or otherwise in consequence of any refusal to renew a licence or permit on the expiry of the period for which the same remains in force.

---

1. *Karnal Distillery Co. Ltd.* v. *State of Haryana*, (1970) 1 SCC 116.
2. *Samand Singh Sohan Singh and Co.* v. *State of Punjab*, 1974 PLR 561.
3. *Bhagat Singh* v. *State of Punjab*, 1975 PLR 506.
4. *Satya Paul Joginder Nath* v. *Excise & Taxation Commr., Himachal Pradesh Govt.*, ILR 1977 HP 258.
5. *Excise Commissioner* v. *Chander Shekhar*, AIR 1983 SC 1050.
6. In the celebrated case of *Cooper* v. *Wandsworth Board of Works*, 1963 (143) ER 414, the principle was thus stated.
7. *Suresh Chandra Nanhorya* v. *Rajendra Rajak*, VI (2006) SLT 568.

19. Surrender of licence.—No holder of a licence granted under this Act shall surrender his licence except on the expiration of one month's notice in writing given by him to the licensing authority of his intention to surrender the same on payment of the fee payable for the licence for the whole period for which it would have been current but for the surrender:

Provided that if the licensing authority is satisfied that there are sufficient reasons for surrendering the licence, he may remit to the holder thereof the sum so payable, or any portion thereof, on surrender.

SYNOPSIS

Proviso

Comments

Proviso

The effect of an excepting or qualifying proviso, according to the ordinary rules of construction, is to except out of the preceding portion of the enactment, or to qualify some thing enacted therein, which but for the proviso would be within it.[1]

It is a cardinal rule of interpretation that a proviso to a particular provision of a statute only embraces the field, which is covered by the main provision. It carves out an exception to the main provision to which it has been enacted by the proviso and to no other. The proper function of a proviso is to except and deal with a case, which would otherwise fall within the general language of the main enactment, and its effect is to confine to that case. Where the language of the main enactment is explicit and unambiguous, the proviso can have no repercussion on the interpretation of the main enactment, so as to exclude from it, by implication what clearly falls within its express terms. The scope of the proviso, therefore, is to carve out an exception to the main enactment and it excludes something which otherwise would have been within the rule. It has to operate in the same field and if the language of the main enactment is clear, the proviso cannot be torn apart from the main enactment nor can it be used to nullify by implication what the enactment clearly says nor set at naught the real object of the main enactment, unless the words of the proviso are such that it is its necessary effect.[2]

The normal function of a proviso is to except some thing out of an enactment or to qualify something created therein, which but for the proviso would be within the purview of the enactment. As a general rule a proviso is added to an enactment to qualify or to create an exception to what is in the enactment and ordinarily, a proviso is not interpreted as stating a general rule.[3]

---

1. *Kedarnath Jute Manufacturing Co. Ltd.* v. *Commercial Tax Officer*, AIR 1966 SC 17.
2. *A.N. Sehgal* v. *Raje Ram Sheoran*, AIR 1991 SC 1406: 1991 Lab IC 1227: JT 1991 (2) SC 123: 1991 (2) Lab LJ 50: (1991) 2 SCR 198: 1991 AIR SCW 1246: 1992 (1) SCC (Supp) 304.
3. *Nagar Palika Nigam* v. *Krishi Upaj Mandi Samiti*, AIR 2009 SC 187: 2008 AIR SCW 7114: (2008) 12 SCC 364: (2008) 13 SCALE 228.

20. Transfer of licence or permit.—The licence or permit granted under this Act is not transferable except with the prior approval of the licensing authority subject to such terms and conditions as may be prescribed.

21. Grant of exclusive privilege of manufacture, etc.—Subject to the provisions of this Act and the terms and conditions as may be prescribed, the Government may grant to any person a licence either jointly or severally, for the exclusive privilege of manufacturing, supplying by wholesale and sale by retail within any local area.

22. Removal of liquor from manufactory, warehouse, etc., on payment of duty.—No liquor shall be removed from any manufactory, warehouse or other place of storage established under this Act without a relevant pass and unless duty and fee payable has been paid or a bond as may be prescribed, has been executed for the payment thereof.

23. Prohibition of sale to certain persons.—No person or licensed vendor or his employee or agent shall sell or deliver any liquor to any person apparently under the age of twenty five years, whether for consumption by self or others.

24. Prohibition of employment of certain persons.—No licensee shall employ or permit to be employed in his premises any person under the age of twenty-one years, or suffering from contagious disease.

25. Closing of shops for preservation of public peace.—The Deputy Commissioner or any other officer authorized by him may, by notice in writing to the licensee, require that any shop in which any liquor is sold shall be closed at such time or for such period as he may think necessary for preservation of public peace:

Provided that the total closure days in the licensing year shall not exceed fifteen days in all or more than three days continuously at any one time:

Provided further that if the Excise Commissioner is of the opinion that any particular shop or all shops in any particular area shall be closed for a period exceeding fifteen days in a year or more than three days continuously at any one time, he may do so for reasons to be recorded.

CHAPTER IV

EXCISE REVENUE

26. Nature and components of excise revenue.—Excise revenue shall be levied and recovered under the following heads, namely:—

(a) duty;

(b) licence fee;

(c) label registration fee; and

(d) import or export fee.

SYNOPSIS

Vend Fee

Comments

Vend Fee

Levy of vend fee on denatured spirit is not without legislative competence.[1]

27. Excise duty, countervailing duty and special duty.—(1) There shall be levied and collected duty on all intoxicants which are produced, manufactured, transported or imported into Delhi at such rates as may be prescribed, not exceeding the rates set forth in the Schedule.

(2) There shall be levied and collected fee for terms, conditions and form of, and duration of, licence, permit and pass.

(3) In computing the retail price, notwithstanding anything contained in sub-section (1) of section 27, the duty shall be so increased and computed that the retail price is rounded off up to the next higher multiple of ten rupees, as notified by the Government and such increased duty shall be collected by the Government in the manner prescribed.

SYNOPSIS

1. **Levy of Excise Duty on Wastage Beyond Permissible Limit**
2. **Levy of Excise Duty on Undrawn Liquor**
3. **Duty on Non-lifted Liquor**
4. **Duty on Wastage**
5. **Incidence of Duty**

---

1. *State of Uttar Pradesh* v. *Synthetics & Chemicals Ltd.*, AIR 1980 SC 614: 1980 All LJ 258: 1980 Tax LR 2294: (1980) 2 SCC 441: (1980) 2 SCR 531.

6. **Excise Duty Paid by Monopoly Corporation shall form Part of Turnover of Manufacture**
7. **Duty on Liquor Unfit for Human Consumption**
8. **Payment of Duty on Sedimented Stock**

Comments

1. Levy of Excise Duty on Wastage Beyond Permissible Limit

In the present case, the liquor for which permits were obtained by the appellant was admittedly in existence and was meant for human consumption and did leave the appellant's distilleries in Uttar Pradesh for being transported to its warehouse in Chandigarh at its own risk and responsibility. It is also not denied on behalf of the appellant that a portion of the liquor which exceeded the permissible limit of wastage did not reach the appellant's warehouse and was not found therein and the shortage remained unaccounted for. It is thus evident that duty is not sought to be charged on an excisable article which was not in existence, as contended on behalf of the appellant. It is sought to be charged on liquor which was actually manufactured and left Uttar Pradesh but was found short beyond the permissible limit and no reasonable explanation was tendered by the appellant in respect thereof. There is accordingly no merit or substance in the second contention advanced on behalf of the appellant as well.[1]

2. Levy of Excise Duty on Undrawn Liquor

Levy of excise duty on undrawn liquor was beyond the power of the State Government and that, therefore, the rule imposing the condition to that effect was invalid.[2]

3. Duty on Non-lifted Liquor

Merely because the quota for which they gave their bid is required to be multiplied by a certain figure per proof litre and further because they were given the facility of paying the amount in instalments while lifting the quota from time-to-time, it cannot be said that the payment made by them represented excise duty. What they agreed to pay was the price of a privilege which the state parted on the ground that the payment which they were called upon to make, is truly in the nature of excise duty and that no such duty can be imposed on liquor not lifted or purchased by them.[3]

4. Duty on Wastage

Levy of excise duty on wastage during transportation in containers of high strength spirit of 80 to 85 per cent. from distillery to warehouse by State of Uttar Pradesh, held beyond its competence.[4]

---

1. *Mohan Meakin Breweries Ltd.* v. *Excise and Taxation Commissioner, Chandigarh,* (1976) 3 SCC 421: 1976 SCC (Tax) 318: AIR 1976 SC 2020: 1976 Supp SCR 510.
2. *State of Madhya Pradesh* v. *Firm Gappu Lal,* AIR 1976 SC 633: 1976 UJ (SC) 182: (1976) 1 SCC 791: 1976 Jab LJ 597: 1976 SCC (Tax) 71: 1976 Tax LR 1465: 1976 (2) Serv SCR 1041.
3. *State Bank of Haryana* v. *Jage Ram,* (1980) 3 SCC 599: 1980 Tax LR 2362: AIR 1980 SC 2018.
4. *State of Uttar Pradesh* v. *Modi Distillery,* (1995) 5 SCC 753: 1995 AIR SCW 3791.

5. Incidence of Duty

It is an indirect duty which the manufacturer or producer passes on to the ultimate consumer, that is ultimate incidence will always be on the consumer.[1]

6. Excise Duty Paid by Monopoly Corporation shall form Part of Turnover of Manufacture

The assessee manufactured IMFL. A monopoly of supply was created in favour of State Marketing Corporation. The excise duty was to be paid by the Corporation as per rules. The assessee contended that the excise duty so paid would not form part of assessee's turnover.

Held: Primary obligation to pay excise duty on IMFL is that of manufacturer thereof. Rule 22 provides convenient method for its collection. This does not absolve the manufacturer of his liability to pay excise duty. Excise duty paid by the Corporation would form part of assessee's turnover. Fact that excise duty does not physically enter assessee's till notwithstanding.[2]

7. Duty on Liquor Unfit for Human Consumption

The fact that the liquor was rendered unfit for human consumption and destroyed, after its import, which itself attracted the levy of duty could not wipe of the liability of the appellant, for payment of duty on the excisable goods, after their (sic) import, in the bonded warehouse.[3]

8. Payment of Duty on Sedimented Stock

Excise duty is leviable on sedimented stock.—The appellant imported into the State of Orissa; Indian made foreign liquor and stored it in a licensed bonded warehouse from where the liquor was to be released for sale. While liquor was so stored in the warehouse, a portion of the imported stock became sedimented and was rendered unfit for human consumption. That stock was, therefore, destroyed. A notice was issued to the appellant for payment of countervailing duty on the stock to the tune of Rs. 10,02,182.

In this view of the matter, the demand of countervailing duty from the appellant in the established facts and circumstances of the case was perfectly justified. The fact that the liquor was rendered unfit for human consumption and destroyed, after its import, which by itself attracted the levy of duty could not wipe of the liability of the appellant, for payment of duty on excisable goods, after their import, in the bonded warehouse.[3]

It is now well-settled principle of law that the regulatory powers are generally to be widely construed. However, empowering the State Government to impose taxes, fees or duties and such demands must be authorised by the Statute and must contain sufficient guidelines.[4]

---

1. *McDowell & Co.'s* case, AIR 1997 SC 1459.
2. *Mohan Breweries and Distilleries Ltd.* v. *Commercial Tax Officer, Madras,* AIR 1997 SC 3497: 1997 AIR SCW 3589: JT 1997 (8) SC 36: (1997) 7 SCC 542: 1997 (3) SCJ 441: 1998 (5) Supreme 422: 1997 (2) UPTC 1181: 1998 BRLJ 26: 1997 (107) STC 212.
3. *S.K. Pattanaik (Dead) Thru LRs.* v. *State of Orissa,* (1999) 7 SCALE 557: AIR 2000 SC 612: 2000 AIR SCW 41: (2000) 1 SCC 413: 2000 (1) SCJ 232: 2000 (1) SRJ 438: 1999 (10) Supreme 259: JT 1999 (10) SC 48: 2000 (1) LRI 387.
4. *Gupta Modern Breweries* v. *State of Jammu & Kashmir,* (2007) 5 SCALE 842.

28. Power of Government to vary duty.—(1) Where, in respect of any intoxicant, the Government is satisfied that the duty leviable thereon under section 27 of this Act should be increased or decreased and that circumstances exist which render it necessary to take immediate action, the Government may, by notification in the Official Gazette, direct an amendment of the Schedule to be made so as to substitute for the rate of duty specified in the Schedule in respect of such intoxicant.

(2) Every notification under sub-section (1) shall be laid before the Legislative Assembly, if it is sitting, as soon as may be after the issue of the notification, and, if it is not sitting, within seven days of its re-assembly, and the Government shall seek the approval of the Legislative Assembly to the notification by a resolution moved within a period of fifteen days beginning with the day on which the notification is so laid before the Legislative Assembly. If the Legislative Assembly makes any modification in the notification or directs that the notification should cease to have effect, the notification shall thereafter have effect only in such modified form or be of no effect, as the case may be, but without prejudice to the validity of anything previously done thereunder.

29. Recovery of duty and other levies and lien on the property of defaulter.—(1) All excise revenue, payable to the Government under this Act, may be recovered from the person liable to pay the same or his legal successors or from his surety or his agent as if they were the arrears of land revenue.

(2) In the event of default in payment of excise revenue or otherwise, by any person licensed under this Act, his manufactory, warehouse, shop or premises and all fittings, apparatus, stocks of liquor or material for the manufacture of the same, held therein shall be liable to be attached towards any claim for excise revenue or in respect of any loss incurred by the Government through such default and be sold to satisfy such claim which shall be the first charge upon the proceeds of such sale.

(3) Where duty due is not levied or not paid or short-levied or short paid or erroneously refunded;—

(a) the Assistant Commissioner may, within four years from the relevant date, serve notice on the person chargeable with the duty or fee which has not been levied or paid or which has been short-levied or short-paid or to whom the refund has erroneously been made, requiring him to show cause why he should not pay the amount specified in the notice;

Explanation I.—Where the service of the notice is stayed by an order of the court , the period of such stay shall be excluded in computing the aforesaid period of four years;

Explanation II.—For the purposes of this clause "relevant date" means—

(i) in the case of intoxicants on which duty has not been levied or paid or has been short-levied or short-paid, the date on which the duty is to be paid under this Act or the rules made thereunder;

(ii) in the case where duty is provisionally assessed under this Act or the rules made thereunder, the date of adjustment of duty after the final assessment thereof;

(iii) in the case of intoxicants on which duty has been erroneously refunded, the date of such refund;

(b) the Assistant Commissioner shall, after considering the representation, if any, made by the person on whom notice is served under clause (a), determine the amount of duty due from such person (not being in excess of the amount specified in the notice) and thereupon such person shall pay the amount so determined.

SYNOPSIS

1. **Civil Prison in Default of Payment of Dues**
2. **Refund of Tax Collected**

Comments

The explanation must be read so as to harmonise with and clear up any ambiguity in the main section. It should not be so construed as to widen the ambit of the section.[1]

The scope of an explanation to the main provisions of law is very limited and at any rate the explanation does not take place of the substantive law.[2]

1. Civil Prison in Default of Payment of Dues

Civil prison shall not be construed in any manner as discharge of debt in terms of section 58 (2) of Code of the Civil Procedure.[3]

2. Refund of Tax Collected

Refund claim shall be allowed/decreed only when he establishes that he has not passed on the burden of the duty or to the extent he has not passed on, as the case may be. The real loss or prejudice is suffered in such a case by the person who has ultimately borne the burden and it is only the person who can legitimately claim its refund. But where such person does not come forward or where it is not

1. *Development and Cane Marketing Union Ltd.* v. *Bank of Bihar,* AIR 1967 SC 389.
2. *Jiwan Nath Razdan* v. *State of Maharashtra,* AIR 1991 Bom 196.
3. *Samiran Sen* v. *Arpita Sen,* AIR 2009 Cal 229.

possible to refund the amount to him for one or the other reason, it is just and appropriate that the amount is retained by the State, *i.e.*, by the people.

The doctrine of unjust enrichment is inapplicable to the State. State represents the people of the country.

30. Interest payable for failure to pay excise revenue.—If the excise revenue payable by a person under this Act or the rules made thereunder is not paid within time, he shall be liable to pay on the sum due, a simple interest at the rate of twelve per cent per annum from the date next following the day on which such payment became due.

Explanation.—Where the duty determined to be payable is reduced or increased by the appellate authority or court, the interest shall be payable on such reduced or increased amount of excise revenue, as the case may be.

SYNOPSIS

Comments

Interest

Interest is not a penalty or punishment at all, but it is the normal accretion on capital.[1]

Interest is compensation for forbearance or detention of money.[2]

31. Power to reduce or waive interest in certain cases.—Notwithstanding anything contained in this Act, the Excise Commissioner may, on the application made in this behalf by a person, with the approval of the Government and after recording his reason for so doing, reduce or waive the amount of any interest payable by him under this Act if he is satisfied that—

(a) to do otherwise would cause genuine hardship to the person having regard to the circumstances of the case; and

(b) the person has co-operated in any proceeding for the recovery of any amount due from him.

32. Accounts and returns.—Every licensee shall maintain such accounts and submit to the authorized officers such returns in such forms containing such particulars relating to stock, apparatus, duty, fee payable and paid to the Government and such other information at such intervals as may be prescribed.

---

1. *Alok Shankar Pandey* v. *Union of India,* III (2007) SLT 27: AIR 2007 SC 1198: 2007 AIR SCW 1233: (2007) 3 SCC 545: (2007) 3 SCALE 190: 2007 (2) JCR SC 358: 2007 (2) Supreme 249.
2. *Dharampal* v. *State Road Transport Corporation,* (2008) 12 SCC 208: AIR 2008 SC 2312: 2008 AIR SCW 3947: 2008 (2) Ker LT 691: 2008 (3) Punj LR 759: (2008) 7 SCALE 360.

CHAPTER V

OFFENCES AND PENALTIES

33. Penalty for unlawful import, export, transport, manufacture, possession, sale, etc.—Whoever, in contravention of provision of this Act or of any rule or order made or notification issued or of any licence, permit or pass, granted under this Act—

(a) manufactures, imports, exports, transports or removes any intoxicant;

(b) constructs or works any manufactory or warehouse;

(c) bottles any liquor for purposes of sale;

(d) uses, keeps or has in his possession any material, still, utensil, implement or apparatus, whatsoever, for the purpose of manufacturing any intoxicant other than toddy or tari;

(e) possesses any material or film either with or without the Government logo or logo of any State or wrapper or any other thing in which liquor can be packed or any apparatus or implement or machine for the purpose of packing any liquor;

(f) sells any intoxicant, collects, possesses or buys any intoxicant beyond the prescribed quantity,

shall be punishable with imprisonment for a term which shall not be less than six months but which may extend to three years and with fine, which shall not be less than fifty thousand rupees which may extend to one lakh rupees.

SYNOPSIS

Minimum Sentence

Comments

Minimum Sentence

(a) *Court cannot award less than the minimum prescribe punishment*: The proviso clearly restricts the discretion to the passing of a minimum sentence of three months imprisonment and a fine of Rs. 100 in regard to the first offence. It is hence, clear that no court can, while imposing sentence for a first offence under section 34 of the Act award a sentence less than the prescribed minimum of three months' imprisonment and a fine of Rs. 100.[1]

---

1. *State of Mysore* v. *Paimlee,* 1971 Cr LJ 1462.

(b) The statute prescribed a minimum sentence. It does not provide for any exception and does not vest the court with any discretion to award a sentence below the prescribed minimum under any special circumstances. The learned judge has himself noticed that the statute prescribes a minimum sentence for the offence, the High Court has understandably reduced the sentence of imprisonment to less than the minimum permissible. The High Court was clearly in error in doing so. We think we have said enough to correct the error. It is unnecessary to pursue the matter further by granting special leave.[1]

(c) Sentence lesser than prescribed minimum can be imposed only by reasoned order which should be adequate and special, not fanciful.[2]

34. Penalty for rendering denatured spirit fit for human consumption.—Whoever renders or attempts to render fit for human consumption any spirit, which has been denatured or has in his possession any spirit in respect of which he knows or has reason to believe that such attempt has been made, shall be punishable with imprisonment for a term which shall not be less than two years, which may extend to five years, and with fine which may extend to two lakh rupees.

35. Penalty for mixing noxious substance with liquor.—Whoever mixes or permits to be mixed with any liquor sold or manufactured or possessed by him any noxious drug or any foreign ingredient likely to cause disability or grievous hurt or death to human beings, shall be punishable—

(a) if as a result of such an act, death is caused, with death or imprisonment for life and shall also be liable to fine, which may extend to ten lakh rupees;

(b) if as a result of such an act, disability or grievous hurt is caused to any person, with imprisonment for a term which shall not be less than six years but which may extend to imprisonment for life, and with fine which may extend to five lakh rupees;

(c) if as a result of such an act, any other consequential injury is caused to any person, with imprisonment for a term which may extend to one year and fine which may extend to two lakh fifty thousand rupees;

(d) if as a result of such an act, no injury is caused, with imprisonment which may extend to six months and fine which may extend to one lakh rupees.

---

1. *State of Andhra Pradesh* v. *S.R. Rangadamappa,* AIR 1982 SC 1492: 1982 Cr LJ 2364: (1982) 3 SCC 223: 1982 All WC 798.
2. *State of Madhya Pradesh* v. *Munna Choubey,* AIR 2005 SC 682: 2005 Cr LJ 913: 2005 AIR SCW 443: JT 2005 (2) SC 122: (2005) 2 SCC 710: 2005 (1) SCJ 621: 2005 (1) Supreme 559.

Explanation.—For the purpose of this section the expression "grievous hurt" shall have the same meaning as in section 320 of the Indian Penal Code, 1860 (XLV of 1860).

36. Order to pay compensation.—Notwithstanding anything contained in the Code of Criminal Procedure, 1973 (2 of 1974) the court, when passing an order under this Act may, if it is satisfied that death or injury has been caused to any person due to consumption of liquor sold in any place, order the manufacturer and seller, whether or not he is convicted of an offence, to pay, by way of compensation, an amount not less than three lakh rupees to the legal representatives of each deceased or two lakh rupees to the person to whom grievous hurt has been caused, or twenty thousand rupees to the person for any other consequential injury:

Provided that where the liquor is sold in a licensed shop, the liability to pay the compensation under this section shall be on the licensee.

(2) Any person agrieved by an order under sub-section (1) may, within thirty days from the date of the order, prefer an appeal to the High Court:

Provided that no appeal can be filed by the accused unless the amount ordered to be paid under sub-section (1) is deposited by him in the court:

Provided further that the High Court may entertain an appeal after expiry of the said period of ninety days if it is satisfied that the appellant was prevented by sufficient cause from preferring the appeal in time.

37. Penalty for selling spurious liquor.—Whoever sells or keeps or exposes for sale as foreign liquor which he knows or has reason to believe to be Indian liquor shall be punishable with imprisonment which may extend to six months and fine which may extend to one lakh rupees.

38. Penalty for possession of liquor unlawfully imported, non-duty paid, etc.—Whoever has in his possession any liquor knowing the same to have been unlawfully imported, transported or manufactured or knowing the prescribed duty not to have been paid thereon, shall be punishable with imprisonment for a term which may extend to six months and fine which may extend to one lakh rupees.

39. Penalty for consumption of liquor in chemist's shop.—(1) If a chemist, druggist, apothecary or keeper of a dispensary, allows any liquor which has not been *bonafidely* medicated for medicinal purposes to be consumed on his business premises by any person, he shall be punishable with fine which may extend to five thousand rupees.

(2) If a person consumes any such liquor on such premises, he shall be punishable with fine which may extend to two thousand rupees.

40. Penalty for consumption of liquor in public place.—Whoever, in contravention of this Act or the rules, notification or order made thereunder—

(a) consumes liquor in a public place;

(b) consumes liquor in public place and creates nuisance;

(c) permits drunkenness or allows assembly of unsocial elements on the premises of liquor establishment;

shall be punishable,

(1) in case of an offence falling under clause (a), with fine which may extend to five thousand rupees.

(2) in case of an offence falling under clause (b), with imprisonment for a term which may extend to three months and fine which may extend to ten thousand rupees.

(3) in case of an offence falling under clause (c), with imprisonment for a term which may extend to six months and fine up to fifty thousand rupees.

41. Penalty for unlawful advertisement.—Whoever prints, publishes or gives an advertisement directly or indirectly in any media soliciting the use of any liquor, shall be punishable with imprisonment for a term which may extend to six months or with fine which may extend to ten lakh rupees, or with both:

Provided that this section shall not apply to catalogue and price list and advertisement generally or specially approved by the Excise Commissioner for display at the points of sale for consumer information and education.

42. Penalty for employing minors or selling liquor to minors.—(1) If any licence holder or any person acting on his behalf, sells or delivers any liquor to any person apparently under the age of twenty-five years, he shall be punishable with fine which may extend to ten thousand rupees.

(2) If a licence holder employs any person under the age of twenty-one years, he shall be punishable with imprisonment for a term which may extend to three months, or with fine which may extend to fifty thousand rupees, or with both.

43. Penalty for assault and obstruction.—Notwithstanding anything contained in the Indian Penal Code, 1860 (XLV of 1860) any person who assaults or threatens to assault or obstructs or attempts to obstruct any excise officer in the discharge of his official duties shall be punishable with imprisonment for a term which may extend to one year and with fine which may extend to one lakh rupees.

44. Liability of employer for offence committed by his employee or agent.—The holder of a licence or permit granted under this Act, as well as the actual offender, shall be liable for an offence committed by his employee or his agent, unless he proves that due and reasonable precautions were exercised by him to prevent commission of such offence.

45. Penalty for manufacture, sale or possession by one person on account of another.—(1) Where any intoxicant has been manufactured or sold or is possessed by any person on account of any other person and such other person knows or has reason to believe that such manufacture or sale was or that such possession is, on his account, the intoxicant shall, for the purposes of this Act, be deemed to have been manufactured or sold by or to be in the possession of such other person.

(2) Nothing in sub-section (1) shall absolve any person who manufactures, sells or has in possession any intoxicant on account of another person, from liability to any punishment under this Act for unlawful manufacture, sale or possession of such intoxicant.

46. Penalty for non-payment of duty or fee.—If any person fails to pay any duty or fee, which under this Act he is liable to pay, he shall be punishable with imprisonment for a term which may extend to one year and also with fine which may extend to one lakh rupees.

47. Penalty for allowing premises, etc., to be used for commission of an offence.—Whoever, being a licensee under this Act and having the control or use of any house, room, enclosure, space, animal, or conveyance, knowingly permits it to be used for commission by any other person of an offence punishable under any provision of this Act, shall be punishable in the same manner as if he had himself committed the said offence.

48. Penalty for attempt to commit an offence.—Whoever attempts to commit an offence punishable under this Act, shall be liable for half the punishment provided for the offence under this Act.

49. Penalty on excise officer for making vexatious search, seizure, detention or arrest.—Any excise officer or other person who vexatiously and without reasonable ground for suspicion—

(a) enters or searches or causes to be entered or searched any closed place under colour of exercising any power conferred by this Act;

(b) seizes the moveable property of any person on the pretext of seizing or searching for any article liable to confiscation under this Act;

(c) searches, detains or arrests any person;

(d) in any other way exceeds his lawful powers under this Act,

shall be liable to imprisonment for a term which may extend to three months, or with fine which may extend to ten thousand rupees or with both.

50. Penalty on excise officer refusing to do duty.—Any excise officer who, without lawful excuse, refuses to perform or withdraws himself from the duties of his office, unless expressly allowed to do so in writing by the Excise Commissioner, or unless he shall have given to his official superior officer two months' notice in writing of his intention to do so, or who shall be guilty of cowardice shall be punishable with imprisonment which may extend to three months, or with fine which may extend to ten thousand rupees, or with both.

51. Penalty for offences not otherwise provided for.—Whoever does any act in contravention of any of the provisions of this Act or any rule or order made thereunder and punishment for which has not been otherwise provided for such contravention, shall be punishable with imprisonment for a term which may extend to six months or with fine which may extend to ten thousand rupees, or with both.

52. Presumption as to commission of offence in certain cases.—(1) In prosecution under section 33, it shall be presumed, until the contrary is proved, that the accused person has committed the offence punishable under that section in respect of any intoxicant, still, utensil, implement or apparatus, for the possession of which he is unable to account satisfactorily.

(2) Where any animal, vessel, cart or other vehicle is used in the commission of an offence under this Act, and is liable to confiscation, the owner thereof shall be deemed to be guilty of such offence and such owner shall be liable to be proceeded against and punished accordingly, unless he satisfies the court that he had exercised due care in the prevention of the commission of such an offence.

SYNOPSIS

Comments

1. Accused to Account for Possession

When once possession of the intoxicant is proved, the presumption under section 40 comes into operation and it is for the accused to account satisfactorily for its possession.[1]

2. Possession should be with Knowledge

Mere possession of an unlawfully manufactured intoxicant is not made punishable under section 34. It is possession with knowledge that it is unlawfully manufactured that is made punishable.

Once it is established that the accused was in possession of an intoxicant and that the intoxicant was unlawfully manufactured, then a presumption that the accused had the requisite knowledge can be raised under section 40. But the presumption under section 40 does not extend to the extent of presuming that an intoxicant is unlawfully manufactured.[2]

53. Enhanced punishment after previous conviction.—If any person, after having been previously convicted of an offence punishable under this Act, subsequently commits and is convicted of an offence under this Act, he shall be liable to twice the punishment, provided for the first conviction.

SYNOPSIS

1. **Second Offence, not Necessary of the same Kind**

Comments

1. Second Offence, not Necessary of the same Kind

Second offence contemplated is not only "offence of the same kind as another" for which accused was convicted and punished on the earlier occasion but it also included any contravention of the Act committed on the second occasion.[3]

54. Power of court to implead manufacturer, etc.—Where at any time during the trial of an offence under this Act, alleged to have been committed by any person, not being the manufacturer, distributor or dealer of any intoxicant, the court is satisfied, on the evidence adduced before it, that such manufacturer, distributor or dealer is also concerned with that offence then the court may, notwithstanding anything contained in sub-section (3) of section 319 of the Code of Criminal Procedure, 1973 (2 of 1974), proceed against him under any section of this Chapter.

SYNOPSIS

1. ***Non-obstante* Clause**

---

1. *Yamanappa* v. *State of Karnataka*, 1972 (2) Kar LJ 132.
2. *State of Karnataka* v. *Hosbu Kush Gowda*, 1973 (1) Kar LJ 92.
3. *Jagdish Prasad* v. *State of Uttar Pradesh*, AIR 1966 SC 290: 1965 Cur LJ 793: 1965 All LJ 933: (1965) 2 SCWR 692: 1966 Cr LJ 194: 1966 (1) SCJ 15: 1966 (1) SCA 134: 1966 SCD 114: (1965) 3 SCR 806: ILR (1966) 1All 1.

Comments

1. *Non-obstante* Clause

Non-obstante clause is of wide amplitude; it not only overrides the provisions of the said Act but also overrides the provisions of any other Act for the time being in force. Such a *non-obstante* clause must be given its full effect.[1]

There is no doubt that by *non-obstante* clause the Legislature devices means which are usually applied to give overriding effect to certain provisions over some contrary provisions that may be found either in the same enactment or some other statue. In other words such a clause is used to avoid the operation and effect of all contrary provisions. The phrase is equivalent to showing that the Act shall be no impediment to measure intended. To attract the applicability of the phrase, the whole of the section, the scheme of the Act and the objects and reasons for which such an enactment is made has to be kept in mind.[2]

Non-obstante clause is generally incorporated to give overriding effect to a particular section or the statute as a whole. While interpreting the *non-obstante* clause, the court is required to find out the extent to which the legislature intended to do so and extent in which the *non-obstante* clause is used.

55. Magistrate's power to impose enhanced penalties.—Notwithstanding anything contained in section 29 of the Code of Criminal Procedure, 1973 (2 of 1974), it shall be lawful for any Metropolitan Magistrate to pass any sentence, authorized by this Act, except a sentence of imprisonment for life or for a term exceeding six years, in excess of his powers under the said section.

56. Commission of offence by companies.—(1) If the person committing an offence under this Act is a company, the company as well as every person in charge of and responsible to, the company for the conduct of its business at the time of the commission of the offence, shall be deemed to be guilty of offence, and shall be liable to be proceeded against and punished accordingly:

Provided that where a company has different establishments or branches or different units in any establishment or branch, the concerned Chief Executive and the person in charge of such establishment, branch, unit nominated by the company as responsible for the conduct of the business shall be liable for contravention in respect of such establishment, branch or unit:

---

1. *M. Venugopal* v. *Divisional Manager*, AIR 1994 SC 1343: 1994 AIR SCW 778: JT 1994 (1) SC 281: (1994) 2 SCC 323: 1994 (2) SCJ 62: (1994) 1 SCR 433: 1994 (1) SCT 858: 1994 (2) UJ (SC) 73: 1994 (1) UPLBEC 413.
2. *Vishin N. Khanchandani* v. *Vidya Lachmandas Khanchandani*, AIR 2000 SC 2747: 2000 AIR SCW 2932: JT 2000 (9) SC 321: (2000) 6 SCC 724: 2000 (3) SCJ 120: (2000) 5 SCALE 592: 2000 (5) Supreme 574: 2000 (2) UJ (SC) 1309.

Provided further that nothing in this sub-section shall render any such person liable to any punishment if he proves that the offence was committed without his knowledge or that he exercised all due diligence to prevent the commission of such offence.

(2) Notwithstanding anything contained in sub-section (1), where an offence under this Act has been committed by a company and it is proved that the offence has been committed with the consent or connivance of, or that the commission of the offence is attributable to any neglect on the part of any director, manager, secretary, or other officer of the company, such director, manager, secretary or other officer shall be liable to be proceeded against and punished accordingly.

Explanation.—For the purpose of this section—

"company" means any body corporate and includes a firm or other association of individuals; and "director", in relation to firm, means a partner in the firm.

SYNOPSIS

11. Evidentiary Value of Medical Evidence
12. Conviction Solely on Evidence of Handwriting Expert not Permissible
13. Ascendance by itself is of no Consequence
14. Expert Opinion
15. Non-bringing on Record and Non-proving Affidavits Extra-link Fatal
16. In Case of Large Number of Accused Conviction can be Sustained if two or more Witnesses give Consistent Account of Incident
17. I.O. has a Right to Refer to the Record before Giving Evidence

XII. FIR
1. FIR is Admissible to Prove Admission against the Person who Lodged the Report
2. Evidentiary Value
3. Object and Use of FIR
4. Evidentiary Value
5. FIR to be Sent to Magistrate Forthwith
6. Not Necessary to contain all the Facts in FIR
7. Only Officer-in-Charge of Police Station is Empowered to Record FIR
8. Telephonic Message may be Treated as an FIR if certain Conditions are Fulfilled
9. Statement of Complainant Recorded by Superior Officer than the Officer-in-Charge Police Station FIR
10. Officer-in-Charge Police Station has no Option but to Register FIR in a Cognizable Offence
11. FIR cannot be Used as Substantive Evidence
12. Unsigned FIR is an Irregularity not an Illegality
13. Delay in Sending FIR to the Magistrate
14. Investigation before FIR

XIII. Final Report
Accepting of Final Report of Police no Bar to take Cognizance

XIV. Jurisdiction
1. Jurisdiction of High Court under Artice 227 of the Constitution
2. Places through which Contraband was Transported have Jurisdiction

XV. Leading Question

XVI. Limitation for Filing Charge Sheet
1. Benefit of Time Spent by one Party in Obtaining Certified Copy cannot be Availed by other
2. Limitation Starts from Knowledge of the Order and not the Date of Order
3. Section 468 Condonation of Delay under Section 473 should be Liberally Construed
4. Limitation to be in Relation to Offence in which the Accused was Convicted
5. Limitation shall not be Counted with Reference to Maximum Sentence
6. Limitation to be Counted from the Next Date of Arrest
7. Period of Limitation Starts from the Date of Receipt of Report of Public Analyst
8. Charge-sheet not Filed in Time

XVII. Liquor Adulterated
1. Prosecution to Prove Illicit Origin of Liquor

2. Food Inspector Found the Contents of Liquor Less by 9% Case of Adulteration made out
3. Mentioning Wrong Section

XVIII. Penalty Measure

XIX. Plea Bargaining

XX. Police Custody

1. Police Custody while Interrogated
2. Police Custody, when Information given
3. Police Custody can be Ordered During the First Period of 15 days

XXI. Possession

1. Mere Joint Owner of House and Field not Enough
2. Possession Relative only to Husband, where the House was in his Name but Occupied Jointly with his Wife
3. Conviction under Section 61 Proper if Liquor in Excess of Prescribed is Found Outside the Licensed Premises
4. If Three Brothers Living Together, the Eldest Brother shall be Regarded as House Master
5. Individual Possession of Liquor
6. Handing Over Keys of House
7. Awareness of Existence of Article in the House
8. Possession in Transit
9. Possession of Key *Prima Facie* Evidence
10. Home to be in Occupation and Control
11. Recovery of Whisky from the Drawer of the Table Amounts to Conscious Possession
12. Conscious Possession
13. Bottles of Foreign Liquor Found in Luggage of Appellant; Luggage in Full Control of Appellant's Servant
14. Conscious and Intelligent Possession
15. Exclusive Possession
16. Recovery made from the House of the Accused
17. Conscious Possession
18. Constructive Possession
19. Conscious Possession to be Distinguished with Custody
20. Recovery from Dickey of the Car
21. Recovery in the Absence of the Accused
22. When Contraband in the Custody, *Onus* Shifts to the Accused
23. Recovery of Liquor from Car Belonging to other
24. Contraband Found in "Bada" not Exclusive Possession
25. Recovery from the Driver's Seat Amounts to Conscious Possession
26. Brief Case Underneath the Feet of the Accused
27. Ownership and Possession not Proved
28. Not mere Knowledge but Positive Possession to be Proved
29. Possession

XXII. Precedent

1. Binding Nature of Decision
2. Supreme Court may Overrule Earlier Decisions
3. Principle of *Stare-decisis* not on a Constitutional Point

13. **Investigation Officer is not at all a Material Witnesses**
14. **Witness – Relatives**
15. **Recalling of Witnesses**
16. **Official Witness**
17. **Solitary Witness**
18. **Relative Witness**
19. **Relative Witness**
20. **Interested Witness**

Comments

1. Prosecution of Company

No immunity to companies from prosecution merely because it is in respect of offences for which punishment of imprisonment is mandatory. In such cases in lieu of imprisonment fine can be imposed.[1]

Company did not enjoy any immunity from prosecution in respect of offences for which mandatory punishment of imprisonment has been prescribed. Only sentence of fine can be imposed on company or incorporated body.[2]

I. Accused

1. Accused of an Offence

In order to claim the benefit of the guarantee against testimonial compulsion embodied in clause (3) of article 20 it must be shown, firstly, that the person who made the statement was "accused of any offence"; secondly, that he made this statement under compulsion. The phrase "accused of any offence" includes within its ambit only a person against whom a formal accusation relating to the commission of an offence has been levelled which in the normal course may result in his prosecution. Here when the statement of the appellant was recorded by the customs officer under section 108, the appellant was not a person "accused of any offence" under the Customs Act, 1962. An accusation which would stamp him with the character of such a person was levelled only when the complaint was filed against him, by the Assistant Collector of Customs complaining of the commission of offences under section 135(a) and section 135(b) of the Customs Act. So the statement was not hit by article 20(3).[3]

2. Presence of Accused in the Court is not Necessary on All Dates

Scheme of the provisions under sections 205, 273 and 317 is that a Magistrate has to dispense with the personal appearance of the accused and allow him to appear by his pleader except when the personal attendance of the accused before court is necessary in the interest of justice. If, for example, a witness has to identify the accused then the Magistrate has to direct the accused to be present in court.

1. *Standard Chartered Bank* v. *Directorate of Enforcement*, AIR 2005 SC 2622 (Const. Bench): 2005 Cr LJ 4917: 2005 AIR SCW 2829: 2005 (2) Crimes 258: 2005 (119) DLT 687: JT 2005 (5) SC 267: (2005) 4 SCC 530: 2005 (4) SCJ 645: (2005) 5 SCALE 97: 2005 (4) Supreme 290.
2. *Standard Chartered Bank* v. *Directorate of Enforcement*, II (2006) SLT (3J): AIR 2005 SC 2622: 2005 Cr LJ 4917.
3. *Veera Ibrahim* v. *State of Maharashtra*, 1976 SCC (Cri) 278: (1976) 2 SCC 302.

But it cannot be said that the personal attendance of the accused in court is necessary on a day when the case is adjourned on the request of the complainant. In that case if the accused applies for permission to appear by his pleader, a Magistrate has no power under the Code to reject that application. Rejection of the application will only result in injustice. The discretion the Magistrate has in these matters is a judicial discretion.[1]

II. Affidavit

1. Affidavit should be Verified as Required by Order XIX, Rule 3 of CPC.

We wish, however, to observe that the verification of the affidavit produced here is defective. The body of the affidavit discloses that certain matters were known to the Secretary, who made the affidavit personally. The verification, however, states that everything was true to the best of his information and belief. We point this out as slipshod verifications of this type might well in a given case lead to a rejection of the affidavit. Verifications should invariably be modelled on the lines of Order XIX, rule 3 of the Civil Procedure Code, whether the Code applies in terms or not. And when the matter deposed to is not based on personal knowledge the sources of information should be clearly disclosed.[2]

2. Consequence of False Affidavit

False affidavit sworn by witness in proceeding before Court. Offence would fall under sections 191 and 192 rather than under section 199 of the Penal Code. For purpose of starting prosecution procedure under section 479A, the Cr.P.C. must be followed. Section 476, the Cr.P.C. cannot be invoked because of sub-section (6) of section 479.[3]

3. In the Absence for Proper Verification Affidavit cannot be Admitted in Evidence

The reasons for verification of affidavit are to enable the court to find out which facts can be said to he proved on the evidence of rival parties. Allegations may be true to knowledge or allegations may be true on information received from persons or allegations may be based on record. The importance of verification is to test the genuineness and authenticity of allegations and also to make the deponent responsible for allegations. In evidence, verification is required to enable the court to find out as to whether it will be safe to act on such affidavit evidence. In the absence of proper verification, affidavit cannot be admitted in evidence.[4]

4. Knowledge, Belief and the Grounds of Belief should Clearly be Indicated

Every affidavit should clearly express how much is a statement of the deponent's knowledge and how much of the statement was in his belief and the grounds of the belief must be stated with sufficient particularity.[5]

---

1. *N. Dinesan* v. *K.V. Baby,* 1981 Cr LJ 1551 Ker.
2. *State of Bombay* v. *Purushottam Jog Naik,* AIR 1952 SC 317: 1952 Cr LJ 1269: 1952 SCJ 503: 1953 SCA 893.
3. *A. Baban Singh* v. *Jagdish Singh,* AIR 1967 SC 68.
4. *A.K.K. Nambiar* v. *Union of India,* AIR 1970 SC 652: 1970 Lab IC 566.
5. *Shivajirao, N. Patil* v. *Mukesh Madhav Gosai,* AIR 1987 SC 294: JT 1986 SC 1071: (1987) 1 SCC 227: 1987 (2) SCJ 1: 1987 (2) Supreme 97.

5. Improper Verification Would Entitle the Accused to Acquittal

Where prosecution led evidence by way of affidavits and those affidavits were found to be not properly verified, the accused was held entitled to acquittal.[1]

6. Affidavit should be Verified Properly

In the Supreme Court evidence in support of the statements contained in writ petitions, special leave petitions, applications and other miscellaneous matters, is accepted in the form of affidavits filed by the parties concerned. It is, therefore, necessary that the party stating facts must disclose as to what facts are true to his personal knowledge, information or belief. If the statement of fact is based on information the source of information must be disclosed in the affidavit. An affidavit, which does not comply with the provisions of Order 11 of the Supreme Court Rules, has no probative value and it is liable to be rejected. In a matter where allegations of *mala fides* or disobedience of the court's order are made against a person or party it is all the more necessary that the person filing affidavit in this regard must take care to verify the facts stated in the affidavit strictly in accordance with the rules 5 and 13. The purpose underlying rules 5 and 13 is to enable the court to find out as to whether it would be safe to act on such evidence and to enable the court to know as to what facts are based in the affidavit on the basis of personal knowledge, information and belief as this is relevant for the purpose of appreciating the evidence placed before the court, in the form of affidavit. The importance of verification has to be judged by the purpose for which it is required. Only on the basis of verification, it is possible to decide the genuineness and authenticity of the allegations and the deponent can be held responsible for the allegations made in the affidavit.

Where in a contempt petition, the affidavit of the complainant was defective as it did not indicate as to what facts were true to her personal knowledge, information and belief and clerk of the advocate for the accused filing counter-affidavit had verified the affidavit saying that the statements of the case of the accused were true and correct which were based on the records maintained in the office of the advocate and based on the instructions received from the clients, affidavit in support of contempt petition and affidavit in reply to contempt petition were liable to be rejected. The affidavits, being liable to be rejected, contempt petition was also liable to be dismissed.[2]

7. Proper Verification is Essential to Accept it in Evidence and no Amendment is Possible Subsequently

Affidavits are not meant for stating facts relating to the subject-matter in question. The affidavits are required to be verified as per para 5 of Chapter VII page 141 of *Criminal Manual,* 11th Edn., as revised by this court. Para 5 reads thus:—

> "5(1) Every affidavit should clearly specify what portion of the statement is made on the declarant's knowledge and what portion of the statement is made on his information or belief.

1. *Piara Singh* v. *State of Punjab,* 1988 CCC 72 (P&H): 1988 Cr LJ 164 (SC): AIR 1987 SC 2377: JT 1987 (5) SC 74: (1987) 4 SCC 550: 1987 (3) SCJ 643.
2. *Savitramma* v. *Cicil Naronha,* 1989 Cr LJ 85 SC: JT 1988 (3) SC 432.

(2) When a particular portion is not within the declarant's own knowledge but it is stated from information obtained from others, the declarant must use the expression 'I am informed' and, if it is made on belief, should add 'I verily believe it to be true'. He must also state the source or ground of the information or belief and give the name and address of, and sufficiently describe for the purpose of identification, the person or persons from whom he had received such information.

(3) When the statement rests on facts disclosed in documents or copies of documents procured from any court or other person, the declarant shall state the source from which they were procured and his information, or belief, as to the truth of the facts disclosed in such documents. The learned Counsel for the petitioner orally applies for amendment of the petition and thereby wants to correct the verification of the petition. I am unable to see how a party can be allowed to amend the affidavit, which has been already made by him.

(4) The affidavit once made cannot be allowed by amending the same. Consequently, the prayer of the learned counsel for the petitioner for permission to amend the petition cannot be granted.[1]

8. Affidavit not Stating the Basis of Knowledge and Belief Separately not Accepted in Evidence

Further the affidavits filed by police officials were not properly sworn. It was not specified as to which part of the statement in the affidavits was verified on the basis of knowledge and which on the basis of information received. Both the affidavits had been verified on the basis of knowledge and information and cannot be accepted as legal evidence.[2]

9. Affidavit with Improper Verification cannot be taken in Evidence

Affidavit was sworn by constable who took the sample to the office of chemical examiner and deposited it there. The affidavit's verification was to the effect that it was true and correct. The affidavit was not properly sworn, as it was not mentioned, as to which part of the statement was verified on knowledge and which on the basis of information received by the deponent. In the absence of proper verification, affidavit cannot be taken into consideration.[3]

10. Not Properly Verified Affidavit Snaps the Link Evidence

Moreover, affidavits constituting link evidence in the case are not duly verified and have to be excluded from the consideration and thus the link evidence is missing and the omission to produce link evidence is fatal to the case.[4]

11. Without Proper Verification Affidavit cannot be used as Evidence

Affidavit of two witnesses on point of sample taken and deposited with chemical examiner did not indicate as to which part was true to their knowledge and which part was true to their information. Record also did not indicate that

1. *Nandakumar* v. *Dayanand*, 1989 Cr LJ 715 Bom: 1989 (1) Bom CR 112.
2. *Gurvel Singh* v. *State of Punjab*, I (1992) CCR 231 (P&H).
3. I (1992) CCR 240 (P&H).
4. *Nanak* alias *Kaddul* v. *State of Punjab*, 1992 (III) Crimes 457 (P&H).

when affidavits were tendered, witnesses were present for cross-examination — Link evidence could not be said proved. Conviction was liable to be set aside.[1]

12. Defect in Verification of Affidavit can be Cured by Filing a Fresh Affidavit

Even otherwise substantial compliance of rules is enough. Rules are undoubtedly statutory and forms are adopted wherever they are applicable. Rules relating to verification of affidavit and verification cannot be ordinarily brushed aside, but then what is required to be seen is whether petition substantially complies with requirements and secondly even when there is some breach or omission, whether it can be fatal to the petition?[2]

III. Appeal

1. Appeal may be Dismissed in Absentia but cannot be Decided on Merit, without Hearing the Appellant

It is an admitted position that neither the appellants nor counsel for the appellants in support of the appeal challenging the order of conviction and sentence were heard. It is no doubt true that if counsel does not appear when criminal appeals are called out it would hamper the working of the court and create a serious problem for the court. And if this happens often the working of the court would become well-nigh impossible. We are fully conscious of this dimension of the matter but in criminal matters the convicts must be heard before their matters are decided on merit. The court can dismiss the appeal for non-prosecution and enforce discipline or refer the matter to the Bar Council with this end in view. But the matter can be disposed of on merits only after hearing the appellant or his counsel. The court might as well appoint a counsel at State cost to argue on behalf of the appellants. Since the order of conviction and sentence in the present matter has been confirmed without hearing either the appellants or counsel for the appellants, the order must be set aside and the matter must be sent back to the High Court for passing an appropriate order in accordance with law after hearing the appellants or their counsel and on their failure to engage counsel, after hearing counsel appointed by the Court to argue on their behalf.[3]

2. Dismissal of Appeal in Default

It is now well-settled that no criminal appeal can be dismissed on the ground of default in appearance. The court has to go through the record of the case even in the absence of the appellants or their counsel and decide the matter on merit. Inasmuch as the High Court dismissed the appeal without going into the merit of the matter, the impugned order is set aside and the matter is remanded to the High Court for decision on merit.[4]

3. Dismissal of Appeal in the Absence of Accused/Lawyer should be no Merit

It is the duty of the appellant and his lawyer to remain present on the appointed day, time and place when the appeal is posted for hearing. This is the

1. *Jagdish* v. *State of Haryana,* 2000 (4) Crimes 74 P&H.
2. *Associated Journals* v. *Mysore Paper Mills,* VI (2006) SLT 545: (2006) 6 SCC 197: (2006) 7 SCALE 51: 2006 (5) Supreme 452.
3. *Ram Naresh Yadav* v. *State of Bihar,* 1987 Cr LJ 1856 SC: AIR 1987 SC 1500.
4. *Parasuram Patel* v. *State of Orissa,* 1994 SCC (Cri) 1320: (1994) 4 SCC 664.

requirement of the Code on a plain reading of sections 385-386 of the Code. The law does not enjoin that the court shall adjourn the case if both the appellant and his lawyer are absent. The Code envisages disposal of appeal on merits after perusal and scrutiny of record. The plain language of sections 385-386 does not contemplate dismissal of the appeal for non-prosecution simplicitor.[1]

IV. C.F.S.L. Form

1. *Non-Deposit of CFSL form in Malkhana along with case Property and not Sending of CFSL form with Sample Seal would Vitiate Conviction*

But in the present case the evidence of the prosecution is lacking to the effect that CFSL form was neither deposited in the malkhana alongwith the case property nor sent to CFSL with the sample parcel. The very name given to this form as CFSL form suggests the object of its preparation at the time of seizure of a contraband article and separation of its representative sample. The specimen seal impressions used at that time are affixed on it, so that it can be deposited with case property in malkhana and forwarded to CFSL parcel so that seal impression affixed on the sample parcel may be tallied with the seal impression on the CFSL form. The idea behind taking such precautions is to complete a material link in the prosecution evidence by eliminating the possibility of the sample, being tampered with. It provides a material link, conviction set aside."[2]

2. *Absence of Filling CFSL form at the Time of Recovery and Deposit with Analyst with Seal Fatal to Conviction*

Absence of evidence that CFSL form was filled when the recovery of contraband was affected or that such CFSL form was deposited with analyst with sample is fatal to the prosecution.[3]

V. Chemical Analysis

1. *Quantity of Liquor for Analysis*

It was contended that only one out of the articles recovered at the raid was sent for analysis and it was not proved that the bottles and the drums were recovered from the godown contained rectified spirit. These might well have contained phenyl, the manufacture of which the company admittedly was carrying on in that godown. This argument cannot be seriously considered. *Held*, it was wholly unnecessary to send all the bottles recovered by the police in the presence of panchas and which contained the same stuff for purpose of analysis.[4]

2. *Expert Evidence: Scientific Analysis by Technical Person should be Preferred over Smelling Sense of Prohibition Officer*

Merely trusting to the smelling sense of the prohibition officers and basing a conviction on an opinion expressed by those officers, under the circumstances,

---

1. *Bani Singh* v. *State of Uttar Pradesh*, 1996 Cr LJ 3491 SC: AIR 1996 SC 2439: 1996 AIR SCW 2986: 1996 All LJ 1399: 1996 (2) Cr CJ 277: 1996 (3) Crimes 54: JT 1996 (6) SC 287: (1996) 4 SCC 720: 1996 SCC (Cri) 848.
2. *Mool Chand* v. *State*, (1993) 2 CCR 964 Del.
3. 1996 (1) Crimes 604 Del.
4. *Vijendrajit* v. *State of Bombay*, AIR 1953 SC 247: 1953 SCA 395: 1953 Cr LJ 1097: 1953 SCJ 328.

cannot justify the conviction of the respondent. In such a case better proof by a technical person who has considered the matter from a scientific point of view is not only desirable but even necessary to establish that the article seized is one coming within the definition of 'liquor'. The fact that the accused have not challenged effectively the answers given by the prosecution witness that the commodity is arrack will not absolve the prosecution for establishing the ingredients of the offence, for justifying the conviction.[1]

3. Ordinarily Examination of Chemical Examiner is not Necessary but in Case of Doubt, he should be Examined

As long as the expert's report shows that the opinion is based on observation which lead to a conclusion that the opinion can be accepted, there is no necessity of examining the person making the report but should there be any doubt, it can always be resolved by calling and examining the person making the report.[2]

It is not desirable to lay down an inflexible rule on questions of fact even though their determination requires the adoption of scientific methods and tests. It is really for the court of fact to decide whether, upon a consideration of the totality of the facts in a case, it has been satisfactorily established that the objects recovered from the possession of the accused included liquor of prohibited strength. The excise inspector having 21 years experience employing smelling and other tests could reasonably be treated as an expert under section 45 of the Evidence Act.[3]

4. When Application to Summon Expert is Filed, Court is Bound to Summon him

The report of the expert was used as evidence by the prosecution without examining him in Court and neither the Court thought it fit nor the prosecution/ the accused filed any application to summon and examine the report as to the subject-matter of his report and if such an application was filed for the examination of expert, the court was bound to summon the expert.[4]

5. Chemical Analysis not Allowed at a Later Stage

Accused found in possession of brandy bottles with seals intact. Bottles were not sent for chemical analysis. Accused was prosecuted and convicted under section 61(a) of the Tamil Nadu Excise Act, 1971. On appeal by accused prosecution on application under section 428 was allowed to send the bottles for chemical examination. Application by prosecution under section 428 for sending bottles for chemical analysis cannot be allowed.[5]

---

1. *State of Andhra Pradesh* v. *Madiga Boosenna,* AIR 1967 SC 1550: 1967 Cr LJ 1398: 1967 Mad LW (Cri) 103: 1968 (1) SCJ 160: 1967 SCD 565: (1967) 3 SCR 871.
2. *Himachal Pradesh Administration* v. *Om Prakash,* AIR 1972 SC 975: 1972 Cr LJ 606: 1972 (1) SCJ 691: 1972 Cur LJ 654: (1972) 2 SCR 765.
3. *Chand Batra* v. *State of Uttar Pradesh,* 1974 SCC (Cri) 409: AIR 1974 SC 639: 1974 Cr LJ 590.
4. *Phool Kumar* v. *Delhi Administration,* AIR 1975 SC 905: 1975 Cr LJ 778: (1975) 1 SCC 797: (1975) 3 SCR 917.
5. *In re Subramaniam Gounder,* 1976 Cr LJ 1200 Mad.

6. Examination of one Bottle out of Ten would be Bad to Presume that other Bottles would also Contain Intoxicant

Ten bottles having labels of brand, etc., were seized from the petitioner. The contents of one bottle were sent to the chemical examiner, and it contained 650 Mls.

Held.-In the absence of evidence to show that the other nine bottles also contained brandy or other intoxicant, petitioner could not be convicted under section 34 (Karnataka Excise Act) by merely relying on the labels on the bottles. 1966 (2) Kar LJ 91, followed. Even granting that the bottle sent to the chemical examiner contained brandy, the quantity was less than the quantity permitted under rule 21 of the rules.[1]

7. Accused has no Right to Require the Court to Send Additional Sample

The accused has no right to require the court to send an additional representative sample of the substance recovered to the chemical examiner.[2]

8. All the Persons in whose Custody Samples Remained need be Examined

Where the samples of opium changed several hands before reaching the public analyst and yet none of those in whose custody the samples remained were examined by the prosecution to prove that while in their custody the seals on the samples were not tampered with, the inevitable effect of the omission was that the prosecution failed to rule out the possibility of the samples being changed or tampered with during the period in question a fact which had to be proved affirmatively by the prosecution. Consequently, the accused could not be convicted. In such a case, the prosecution could not be allowed to fill up the gaps in the prosecution story at the appellate or revisional stage.[3]

9. Non-examination of a Person to whom the Sample was...........Fatal to the Case

Where the sample of liquor recovered from the accused was sent to the chemical examiner and was handed over to some functionary in the office of the chemical examiner but that functionary was not examined and no evidence was led that the sample remained intact till it was handed over to the chemical examiner for analysis it was held that the report of the chemical examiner could not be relied upon.[4]

10. Report of Chemical Analyzer

A charge-sheet without report of chemical analyzer is a report under section 173(2).

A charge-sheet submitted to the Court without report of the chemical analyzer is a report as contemplated by sub-section (2) of section 173 of the Code.[5]

11. Blue Litmus and Hydrometer Test Admissible in Evidence

Whether the seized liquor was identified correctly to be illicit distilled liquor, it was seen that both blue litmus test and hydrometer test were done, and the liquor

1. *Mahapursha Durga* v. *State of Karnataka*, 1977 (2) Kar LJ 463.
2. *Joginder Kaur* v. *State of Punjab*, 1978 PLR 617 Punj.
3. *State of Rajasthan* v. *Daulat Ram*, AIR 1980 SC 1314: 1980 Cr LR (SC) 84: 1980 UJ (SC) 140 (2): (1980) 3 SCC 303: 1980 SCC (Cri) 683.
4. *Buta Singh* v. *State of Punjab*, 1981 CCC 207 (P&H).
5. *Vihabhai Ramdas Patel* v. *Hemtuji Shivaji Dabhi*, 1984 (2) 25 Guj LR 883.

seized was found to be illicit distilled liquor. The officer conducting the test had long experience of about 22 years as an Excise Officer, and he had undergone training in the line. Therefore, there is no reason to discard the evidence of this witness so far as identity of the seized liquor is concerned.[1]

Statement of Station House Officer that he tasted and examined the seized stuff and found the same to be opium – Station House Officer was not cross-examined on this aspect – *Held,* in the circumstances of the case, the prosecution has proved that it was opium which was seized from the accused – Conviction upheld.[2]

Expert evidence is a weak type of evidence, which cannot be safely relied upon without independent and reliable corroboration. On facts, the testimony of the handwriting expert was not clinching enough.[3]

It is well-settled that the approver's evidence must pass the double test of reliability and corroboration in material particulars. It is said that the approver is a most unworthy friend and he having bargained for his immunity must prove his worthiness for credibility in court. Ordinarily, combined effect of sections 133 and 114 of the Evidence Act, 1872 is that conviction can be based on uncorroborated testimony of an approver but as a rule of prudence it is unsafe to place reliance on the uncorroborated testimony of an approver. Section 14 illustration (b) incorporates a rule of caution of which the courts should have regard.[4]

Testimony is not liable to be discarded merely because they are police officials. However, their evidence should be carefully scrutinised and independently appreciated. On facts, their evidence regarding search and seizure of weapons from the accused is straightforward, consistent and specific. Non-examination of two panchas who were joined at the time of search and seizure and despite diligent efforts whose whereabouts could not be traced is not fatal to the prosecution case.[5]

12. Chemical Examination Report can be Submitted after Filing the Charge-sheet

In view of the provisions of section 173(8) of the Cr. P.C, submitting of chemical examiner's report subsequent to filing of charge-sheet in the court is in accordance with law and there was no need for the investigation officer to have filed an application for that purpose.[6]

13. Charge-sheet Would not be Vitiated by Non-supply of Forensic Report

Non-supply of forensic report shall not vitiate the charge sheet itself.[7]

---

1. *Subodh Sethi* v. *State,* 1991 Cr LJ 3266 Ori: 1992 (73) Cut LT 28.
2. *Ridmal* v. *State of Rajasthan,* 1994 SCC (Cri) 1664.
3. *S. Gopal Reddy* v. *State of Andhra Pradesh,* 1996 SCC (Cri) 792: 1996 Cr LJ 3237: 1996 (3) Crimes 35: 1997 (2) DMC 100: JT 1996 (6) SC 268: (1996) 4 SCC 596: 1996 SCC (Cri) 792: 1996 UP Cri R 708.
4. *Niranjan Singh* v. *State of Punjab,* 1996 SCC (Cri) 939: 1996 Cr LJ 2506: 1996 AIR SCW 2220: JT 1996 (5) SC 582: (1996) 9 SCC 98.
5. *Anil Nandoskar* v. *State of Maharashtra,* 1996 SCC (Cri) 356: 1996 Cr LJ 1698: 1996 (1) Crimes 103: JT 1996 (3) SC 120: (1996) 2 SCC 589: (1996) 2 SCR 807.
6. *State* v. *Nagaraj,* 1996 Cr LJ 3361 Kant: 1996 (2) Cr CJ 32: 1996 (2) EFR 431: 1996 (2) Kant LJ 178.
7. *Suresh Mahato* v. *State of West Bengal,* 1997 Cr LJ 1790 Cal (DB): 1997 (1) All Cr LR 741: 1997 Cal Cr LR 122: 1997 (2) Cal HN 16: 1997 (2) Cr CJ 183.

14. Evidence of Expert is of Advisory Character

An expert is not a witness of fact. His evidence is really of an advisory character. The duty of an expert witness is to furnish the Judge with the necessary scientific criteria for testing the accuracy of the conclusion so as to enable the judge to form his independent judgment by the application of this criterion to the fact proved by the evidence of the case. The scientific opinion evidence, if intelligible, convincing and tested becomes a factor and often an important factor for consideration along with the other evidence of the case. The credibility of such a witness depends on the reasons stated in support of his conclusions and the data and materials furnished which form the basis of his conclusions.[1]

15. Expert Witness is not a Witness of Fact

His evidence is of advisory character. Credibility of such witness depends on reasons stated in support of his conclusions, data and material furnished which forms basis of his conclusions.[2]

16. Difference in Sample Numbers

Sample sent to public analyst was numbered as OSA/52-87 whereas the sample sent to Central Food Laboratory under section 13(2) of the Act was numbered as OSA/57-87. Results of both the samples were different. Conviction set aside.[3]

VI. Charge

1. Principles of Section 10, General Clauses Act are Applicable

90th day from the date of arrest fell on Sunday. Charge-sheet was filed on 91st day – section 10 of the General Clauses Act or principles thereunder would apply. There is due compliance with provisions of section 167(2) Proviso (a)(i).[4]

2. Order Framing Charge is not Interlocutory Order

An order framing charge is an order of moment. It deprives the liberty of a citizen and puts him to jeopardy of a trial. Such an order finally rejects the plea of the accused that he is entitled to discharge or that he is not liable to be tried. Such an order concludes the enquiry and the pre-trial proceedings against the accused. The order framing charge takes away a very valuable right of the accused. Hence, an order framing charge is not an interlocutory order within the meaning of section 397(2) and such an order is amenable to the supervisory jurisdiction of the court of sessions.[5]

---

1. *State of Himachal Pradesh* v. *Jai Lal*, (1999) 5 SCALE 445: AIR 1999 SC 3318: 1999 AIR SCW 3309: 1999 (4) Crimes 4: JT 1999 (6) SC 548: (1999) 7 SCC 280: 2000 (2) SCJ 344: 1999 (9) SRJ 357: 1999 SCC (Cri) 1184: 1999 (8) Supreme 401: 2000 (1) UJ (SC) 121.
2. *Ramesh Chandra Aggarwal* v. *Regency Hospital Ltd.*, AIR 2010 SC 806.
3. *Ramesh Gupta* v. *State*, 2001 VII AD (Del) 300.
4. *N. Sureya Reddy* v. *State of Orissa*, 1985 Cr LJ 939 Ori (DB): 1985 (1) Ori LR 105.
5. *Jarnail Singh* v. *State of Rajasthan*, 1992 Cr LJ 810 (FB): 1992 (1) Crimes 777: 1991 (1) Raj LR 1: 1991 (1) Raj LW 384..

VII. Computation of Days for the Purpose of Limitation

Section 9 of the General Clauses Act states that in any Central Act it shall be sufficient for the purpose of excluding the first in a series of days or any other period of time, to use word "from" and for the purpose of including the last in a series of days or: any other period of time, to use the word "to". This section has no application, in the present case, because the words "from" and "to" are not used in sub-section (2) of section 110. The principles underlying section 9 has been applied even in the case of judicial orders passed by courts, even though in terms of the section it is not applicable. The material words in sub-section (2) of section 110 (Customs Act, 1962) are "within six months of the seizure of the goods". In such provisions the word "of" has been held to be equivalent to "from".

Whether the day on which the goods were seized can be excluded in view of the fact that the period of six months referred to in sub-section (2) of section 110 (Customs Act, 1962) is to be reckoned not from a particular day but from the happening of an event, *viz.*, the seizure of the goods. The relevant words are "within six months of the seizure of the goods" and not "within six months of the day of the seizure of the goods". The law on this point has been stated by *Halsbury* to be as follows:

> "The general rule in case in which a period is fixed within which a person must act or take the consequences is that the day of the act or even from which the period runs should not be counted against him".
>
> "This general rule applies irrespective of whether the limitation of time is imposed by the act of a party or by statute, thus, where a period is fixed within which a criminal prosecution or a civil action may be commenced, the day on which the offence is committed or the cause-of-action arises is excluded in the computation."[1]

VIII. Confessional Statement

Administering oath is barred in the recording of confessional statement by the clear provision of sub-section (5) of section 164 of the Cr.P.C. Confession should be recorded in the manner provided for recording for statement of an accused/ suspect and not in the manner provided for recording evidence. If it is recorded in the manner provided for recording evidence by administering oath, then it loses its character in so far the maker is concerned. The fact of administering oath at the recording of confession virtually means that the maker is compelled to give evidence against him, placing him in the status of a witness at the stage of investigation in violation of article 20(3) of the Constitution of India read with sub-section (5) of section 164 of the Code of Criminal Procedure. Administering oath for recording confession will only mean the recording of evidence of the maker for use in subsequent stage against the maker and which is prohibited in law. Such confession is bad in law, and is inadmissible in evidence.[2]

---

1. *Williams* v. *Burgess and Walcot*, (1849) 12 Ad. & E.I. 635: 113 ER 955. P. 335 of Customs Act.
2. *Akanman Bora* v. *State of Assam*, 1988 Cr LJ 573 Gau (DB): 1987 (3) Crimes 168: 1987 (2) Gau LR 90.

1. Non-asking any Question to Ascertain whether Confession was Voluntary, Would Vitiate the Admission

The magistrate cautioned the accused that he was not bound to make a confession and that if he did, it might be used against him. The other requirement that obligates the magistrate to put questions to the accused satisfying himself that the confession was voluntary so as to enable him to give requisite certificate under sub-section (4) of section 164 has not been fulfilled for, the learned magistrate did not ask any question whatsoever to ascertain whether appellant was making the confession voluntarily.

Held: In view of the flagrant omission to comply with the mandatory requirement of section 164 (2), the Cr.P.C the confession cannot be admitted as a piece of evidence.[1]

IX. Consecutive/Concurrent Sentence

1. If the Transactions are Different, Consecutive Sentence can be Accorded

Section 427 relates to administration of criminal justice and provides procedure for sentencing. The sentencing court is, therefore, required to consider and make an appropriate order as to how the sentence passed in the subsequent case is to run. Whether it should be concurrent or consecutive? The basic rule of thumb over the years has been the so-called single transaction rule for concurrent sentences. If a given transaction constitutes two offences under two enactments generally, it is wrong to have consecutive sentences. It is proper and legitimate to have concurrent sentences. But this rule has no application if the transaction relating to offences is not the same or the facts constituting the two offences are quite different.

Where the accused was in the first instance prosecuted under the Gold (Control) Act for possession of primary gold prohibited under section 8 of that Act and in the second case prosecuted under the Customs Act for smuggling of gold, the two offences for which the accused was prosecuted were quite distinct and different though the case under the Customs Act may, to some extent, overlap the case under the Gold (Control) Act, the courts would not be unjustified in directing that the sentences should be consecutive and not concurrent.[2]

2. Discretion of the Court

It is true that it is left to the discretion of the court while ordering the sentence to run either consecutively or concurrently. However, such discretion has to be exercised judicially, having regard to the facts of the case. In the facts of the cases, when the two occurrences of rape are separated from each other, sufficiently within time and place and are separate and distinct from each other. The fact that offences, being rape in both the cases and are, therefore, some what akin to each other cannot be a ground to exercise the discretion in favour of concurrent running of sentences.[3]

1. *Preetam* v. *State of Madhya Pradesh,* AIR 1997 SC 445: 1996 Cr LJ 4458: 1996 AIR SCW 3829: (1996) 10 SCC 432: (1996) 3 SCR 939: 1996 SCC (Cri) 1343.
2. *Mohd. Akhtar Hussain* v. *Asstt. Collector, Customs (Prevention),* 1989 Cr LJ 283 SC: AIR 1988 SC 2143: 1988 (3) Crimes 291: JT 1988 (3) SC 586: (1988) 4 SCC 183: 1988 (3) SCJ 577.
3. *State of Gujarat* v. *Zaverabhai Kababhai,* 1996 Cr LJ 1298 Guj: 1996 (1) Guj LH 31: 1996 (1) Guj LR 423.

3. Consecutive Sentence

Cannot be more than 14 years in view of section 31 of the Cr.PC.[1]

X. Drunkenness

Drunkenness cannot be said to be conclusively proved unless urine or blood test is carried out. Mere smelling of alcohol, unsteady gait, dilation of pupils and incoherence in speech is not enough.[2]

XI. Evidence

1. Evidentiary Value of Opinion of Handwriting Expert

The writing may be proved to be in the hand writing of a particular individual by the evidence of a person familiar with the hand writing of that individual or by the testimony of an expert competent to the comparison of hand writings on scientific basis. A third method is comparison by the court with the writing made in the presence of the court or admitted or proved to by the writing or the person. Both under section 45 and section 47 the evidence is an opinion, in the former by a scientific comparison and in the latter on the basis of familiarity resulting from frequent observations and experience. In either case the court must satisfy itself by such means as are open that the opinion may be given, the court must see for itself and with the assistance of the expert to come to its own conclusion whether it can safely be held that the two writings are by the same person. This is not to say that the court must play the role of an expert but to say that the court may accept the fact proved only when it has satisfied itself on its observation that it is safe to accept the opinion whether of the expert or other witness. The Supreme Court in an appeal also is entitled to call for the writings for making a comparison thereof.[3]

2. Tape Recorded Evidence

If a statement is relevant an accurate tape record of the statement is also relevant and admissible. The time and place and accuracy of the recording must be proved by a competent witness and the voices must be properly identified. One of the features of magnetic tape recording is the ability to erase and re-use the recording medium. Because of this facility of erasure and reuse, the evidence must be received with caution. The court must be satisfied beyond reasonable doubt that the record has not been tampered with.[4]

3. Tape Recorded Evidence is Admissible in Evidence

The Apex Court has put six conditions, enumerated in the judgment for the admissibility of tape recorded statement.[5]

---

1. *Chatar Singh* v. *State of Madhya Pradesh,* AIR 2007 SC 319: 2007 Cr LJ 796: AIR 2006 SCW 6133: 2007 (1) Crimes 171: 2007 (2) Ker LJ 13: (2006) 12 SCALE 381: (2007) 2 SCC (Cri) 370.
2. *Bachubhai Hassanalli Karyani* v. *State of Maharashtra,* 1972 SCC (Cri) 178: (1971) 3 SCC 930.
3. *Fakhruddin* v. *State of Madhya Pradesh,* AIR 1967 SC 1326: 1967 All LJ 303: 1967 MPLJ 473: 1967 (2) Andh LT 571: 1967 Cr LJ 38: 1967 (2) SCA 135: 1967 (2) SCJ 885.
4. *Yusufalli Esmail Nagree* v. *State of Maharashtra,* AIR 1968 SC 147: 70 Bom LR 76.
5. *R.K. Anand* v. *Registrar, Delhi High Court,* 161 (2009) DLT 130 SC.

4. Evidence of Accomplice

The court will not accept the evidence of an accomplice unless it was corroborated in material particulars.[1]

5. Criminal Trial

Circumstantial evidence - nature of conviction of appellant under section 34(a) of the Madhya Pradesh Excise Act – Appellant, a resident of Varanasi sent his car and his driver to his brother in Sasaram for election work – Two days after appellant lodged report that his car was missing and suspected that his driver had run away with the car – Meanwhile police arrested appellant's driver and two other accused in Khandwa for taking Ganja in the appellant's car – Prosecution contended that appellant had visited Khandwa to meet his driver and the accused in jail and had deposited Rs. 50 for their expenses in jail. In order to sustain the conviction of an accused on circumstantial evidence, it is necessary that such circumstantial evidence should be of a conclusive character and should be consistent only with the hypothesis of the guilt of the accused. The same cannot be said of the evidence against the appellant. Appeal allowed.[2]

6. Evidence of Interested Witness

Non-examination of disinterested neighbours residing near the place of occurrence is no ground for disbelieving the eye-witnesses even though they are related to or interested in the complaint when there is no evidence to show that any person other than the eye-witnesses saw the occurrence.[3]

7. Enmity between a Police Constable and Accused of Little Consequence

Mere enmity between a police constable and an accused in a murder case does not by itself affect the value of the otherwise trustworthy evidence of the police constable when there is no possibility of the police constable developing enmity with the accused so as to implicate him in the murder case.[4]

8. Evidence Recorded in one Case cannot be used in another Case

Each case must be decided on the evidence recorded in it and evidence recorded in another case cannot be taken into account in arriving at a decision.[5]

9. Statement before Police Officer

Statements of witnesses recorded by Police under section 161 can be used only to contradict witnesses in court. They have only negative value.[6]

---

1. *Mohd. Husain Umar Kochhra* v. *Dalip Singhjee*, AIR 1970 SC 45: 1970 Cr LJ 9: 1970 (1) SCJ 149: 1970 SCD 58: 1970 SC Cri R 76: (1970) 1 SCR 130.
2. *Thakur Jainarain Singh* v. *State of Madhya Pradesh*, 1973 SCC (Cri) 909.
3. *Amar Singh* v. *State of Haryana*, 1973 Cr LJ 1409 SC: AIR 1973 SC 2221: 1973 SCC (Cri) 789.
4. *Prem Datta Gautam* v. *State of Uttar Pradesh*, 1973 Cr LJ 1767 SC: 1973 SCC (Cri) 912: 1973 Cr LJ 1767.
5. *Mitthulal* v. *State of Madhya Pradesh*, 1975 Cr LJ 236 SC: 1975 MPLJ 137: 1975 SCC (Cri) 93: (1975) 3 SCC 529: 1975 (2) SCJ 217: 1975 Mad LJ (Cri) 484: 1975 All Cr C 39.
6. *Ponnuswami* v. *State*, 1975 Cr LJ 509 Mad.

10. Evidentiary Value of Retracted Confession

A retracted confession can form the legal basis of conviction if the court is satisfied that it is true and has been voluntarily made. It is no doubt true that as a general rule or practice it is unsafe to reply on a confession much less on a retracted confession unless the court is satisfied that retracted confession is true and voluntarily made and has been corroborated in material particulars, but it is neither an inflexible rule of law nor practice, nor prudence that in no circumstances the conviction can be made on the basis of a retracted confession without corroboration for a court may in particular case, be convinced of the absolute truth of a confession and be prepared to act upon it without corroboration.[1]

11. Evidentiary Value of Medical Evidence

In a case where there is conflict between the medical evidence and the occular account of witness, the court can either believe the prosecution witnesses without reservation or rely upon the medical evidence and approach the oral testimony with caution testing it in the light of the medical evidence. Medical evidence cannot override cogent and convincing testimony of eyewitnesses.[2]

It is a settled rule of circumstantial evidence that where circumstances are susceptible of two equally possible inferences, the courts should accept that inference which favours the accused rather than an inference, which goes in favour of the prosecution.[3]

12. Conviction Solely on Evidence of Handwriting Expert not Permissible

It is now well-settled that expert opinion must always be received with great caution and perhaps none so with more caution than the opinion of a handwriting expert. It is unsafe to base a conviction solely on expert opinion without substantial corroboration. This type of evidence, being opinion evidence, is by its very nature, weak and infirm and cannot of itself form the basis for a conviction.[4]

13. Ascendance by itself is of no Consequence

Ascendance is a matter, which is equally consistent with innocence as with guilt and that by itself is a circumstance of no weight. Ascendance is a very small item of evidence. The fact that the accused were also absconding is a circumstance of no weight whatsoever, 1971 Cr LJ 913 (SC), followed.[5]

14. Expert Opinion

The report of an expert is not conclusive proof. It is after all opinion evidence. The opinion is to be supported by reasons. The court has to evaluate the same like any other evidence. The reasons in support of the opinion, if convincing, make the opinion acceptable. There is no place for *ipse dixit* of the expert. It is for the court

1. *Hukma* v. *State of Rajasthan,* 1976 Cr LJ 1480 Raj (DB).
2. *Vasudevan* v. *State,* 1977 Cr LJ 83 Kar (DB).
3. *Ram Das* v. *State of Maharashtra,* 1977 SCC (Cri) 254.
4. *Magan Bihari Lal* v. *State of Punjab,* 1977 Cr LJ 711 SC: AIR 1977 SC 1091: (1977) 2 SCC 210.
5. *Harasdhan Char* v. *State of West Bengal,* 1981 Cr LJ (NOC) 158 Cal (DB).

to judge whether the opinion has been correctly reached on the data available and for the reason stated, 1980 Cr LJ 396 (SC) followed.[1]

15. Non-bringing of Record and Non-proving Affidavits Extra-link Fatal

The affidavit of Moharrir Head Constable as also the constable who carried the sample of distilled liquor to the chemical examiner has not been brought on record and duly proved. Link evidence is, therefore, missing. It was held by this court in *Resham Singh* v. *The State of Punjab*,[2] *Gurvel Singh* v. *The State of Punjab*,[3] that omission to produce link evidence aforesaid is again fatal to the prosecution of the case.[4]

16. In Case of Large Number of Accused Conviction can be Sustained if two or more Witnesses give Consistent Account of Incident

Where large number of assailants and victims are involved, conviction can be sustained if it is supported by two or more witnesses who give a consistent account of the incident. Accused persons coming together in large number and assaulting the deceased and PWs belonging to the opposite group. Two or more persons specifically speaking about presence of the accused. Witnesses giving consistent account of the incident and role played by the individual accused. Injured eyewitnesses, since beginning, consistently assigning a specific role to a particular accused. In the circumstances, conviction under sections 148, 324, 341, 302 read with section 149, the IPC upheld. There is no question of giving benefit of doubt to some of the accused.[5]

17. I.O. has a Right to Refer to the Record before Giving Evidence

P.W.15 (Sub-Inspector) was asked during examination-in-chief about what happened on 30-1-1982, and he wanted to check up his record, as he could not remember without refreshing his memory. But then the defense counsel seriously objected and wanted the court to disallow him from looking into such records.

Trial court cannot overlook the reality that an Investigating Officer comes to the court for giving evidence after conducting investigation in many other cases also in the meanwhile. Evidence giving process should not bog down to memory tests of witnesses. An Investigating Officer must answer the questions in court, as far as possible, only with reference to what he had recorded during investigation. Such records are the contemporaneous entries made by him and hence for refreshing his memory it is always advisable that he looks into those records before answering any question.[6]

---

1. *State* v. *Kanhu Charan Barik*, 1983 Cr LJ 133 Ori (DB).
2. 1981 Cr LR 314.
3. 1992 (1) Recent Cr LR 114.
4. *Subeg Singh* v. *State of Haryana*, 1992 (III) Crimes 155 (P&H).
5. *Krishnegowda* v. *State of Karnataka*, (2000) 1 SCC 306: 2000 Cr LJ 501 (SC): AIR 2000 SC 373: 1999 AIR SCW 4510: (1999) 7 SCALE 199: 2000 SCC (Cri) 174.
6. *State of Karnataka* v. *K. Yarappa Reddy*, 2000 Cr LJ 400: 1999 AIR SCW 4276: (1999) 8 SCC 715: (1999) 6 SCALE 330: 2000 SCC (Cri) 61: 1999 (8) Supreme 496.

XII. FIR

1. FIR is Admissible to Prove Admission against the Person who Lodged the Report

Where the person who lodged the first information report regarding the occurrence of a murder is himself subsequently accused of the offence and tried and the report lodged by him is not a confessional first information report but is an admission by him of certain facts which have a bearing on the question to be determined by the court, *viz.*, how and by whom the murder was committed or whether the statement of the accused in the court denying the correctness of certain statements of the prosecution witnesses is correct or not, the first information report is admissible to prove against him, his admissions which are relevant under section 21.

The first information report being neither a confession nor a statement made to a police officer during the course of investigation its admissibility is not barred either by section 25 of the Evidence Act or by section 162.[1]

2. Evidentiary Value

The first information report recorded under section 154, the Criminal Procedure Code as such is not substantive evidence, but may be used to corroborate the informant under section 157 of the Evidence Act or to contradict him under section 145 of the Act, if the informant is called as a witness. Where the accused himself gives the first information the fact of his giving the information is admissible against him as evidence of his conduct under section 8 of the Evidence Act. If the information is non-confessional, it is admissible against the accused as an admission under section 21 of the Evidence Act and is relevant. But a confessional first information report by the accused to a police officer cannot be used against him in view of section 25 of the Evidence Act.[2]

3. Object and use of FIR

The object of first information report from the point of view of the informant is to set the Criminal Law in motion. From the point of view of the investigating authorities it is to obtain information about the alleged criminal activity so as to be able to take suitable steps for tracing and bringing to book the guilty party. The report does not constitute substantive evidence though it is important as conveying the earliest information about the occurrence. It can be used only as a previous statement for the purpose contemplated under section 157 or section 145 of the Evidence Act that is for corroborating or contradicting its maker and not of other witness.[3]

4. Evidentiary Value

No doubt, an FIR is a previous statement which can, strictly speaking, be only used to corroborate or contradict the maker of it. But omission of important facts,

---

1. *Faddi* v. *State of Madhya Pradesh*, AIR 1964 SC 1850: 1964 Jab LJ 252: (1964) 2 SCWR 140: 1964 MPLJ 609: 1964 Mah LJ 519: 1964 SCD 779: (1964) 2 Cr LJ 744: 1965 (1) SCJ 203: 1965 MLJ (Cri) 93: (1964) 6 SCR 312.
2. *Aghnoo Nagesia* v. *State of Bihar*, AIR 1966 SC 119: 1965 (2) SCA 367: (1965) 2 SCWR 750: 1966 Cr LJ 100: 1966 MPLJ 49: 1966 Mah LJ 113: 1966 (1) SCJ 193.
3. *Hasib* v. *State of Bihar*, 1972 Cr LJ 233 SC: (1972) 4 SCC 773.

affecting the probabilities of the case, are relevant under section 11 of the Evidence Act in judging the veracity of the prosecution case.[1]

5. FIR to be Sent to Magistrate Forthwith

FIR in respect of cognizable offence should be sent 'forthwith' to a magistrate competent to take cognizance of offence. Unexplained delay of two days in sending FIR to magistrate makes the case suspect.[2]

6. Not Necessary to contain all the Facts in FIR

FIR is not required to contain all the facts and circumstances that the informant might know. Even if the same incident is observed by a group of persons simultaneously, reports lodged by each of them separately would not be identical. The contents would vary from person to person depending upon the importance attached by the informant to each fact or circumstances, to the details and upon his estimate of relevancy. The FIR is lodged with a view to setting the investigative process in motion and not for the purpose of setting down on paper all known facts and circumstances about the incident. There should be a common sense approach to such matters while evaluating the criticism levelled against an FIR. In the circumstances non-mention of a fact was not of any consequence.[3]

7. Only Officer-in-Charge of Police Station is Empowered to Record FIR

Section 154, the Cr.P.C. in very explicit term lays down that every information relating to the commission of a cognizable offence shall be given to an officer in charge of the Police Station. Officers-in-charge of police out posts are not officers -in-charge of police station within the meaning of section 154, the Cr.P.C. and the Police Officers at such out posts are not, therefore, empowered to record First Information Reports.[4]

8. Telephonic Message may be Treated as an FIR if certain Conditions are Fulfilled

Whether a telephonic message can be treated as an FIR or not would depend upon the facts and circumstances of each case. No hard and fast rule can be laid down in this connection. If the telephonic message has been given to officer-in-charge of a police station, the person giving the message is an ascertained one or is capable of being ascertained, the information has been reduced into writing as required by section 154, the Cr.P.C and it is a faithful record of such information and the information discloses commission of a cognizable offence and is not cryptic one or incomplete in essential details, it should constitute an FIR. An anonymous information, or information which is vague or cryptic and lacks in essential details or uninformative, which has not been faithfully recorded, would not constitute an FIR.[5]

---

1. *Ram Kumar Pande* v. *State of Madhya Pradesh,* 1975 Cr LJ 870 SC: AIR 1975 SC 1026.
2. *Ishwar Singh* v. *State of Uttar Pradesh,* 1976 Cr LJ 1883 SC: 1976 All Cri C 307: (1976) 4 SCC 355: 1976 SCC (Cri) 629.
3. *State* v. *Kanhu Charan Barik,* 1983 Cr LJ 133 Ori (DB).
4. *Mangal Singh* v. *State of Rajasthan,* 1985 Cr LJ 602 Raj (DB): 1984 Raj LR 953: 1984 WLN (UC) 187.
5. *Tehal Singh* v. *State of Rajasthan,* 1989 Cr LJ 1350 Raj (DB).

9. *Statement of Complainant Recorded by Superior Officer than the Officer-in-Charge Police Station FIR*

Where the officer superior in rank to the officer-in-charge of police station on receiving message about commission of cognizable offence rushed to the spot and recorded the statement of the complainant and sent it to the police station, the statement became the FIR.[1]

10. *Officer-in-Charge Police Station has no Option but to Register FIR in a Cognizable Offence*

If any information disclosing a cognizable offence is laid before the officer-in-charge of a police station, satisfying the requirements of section 154(1) of the Code the said officer has no other option except to enter the substance thereof in the prescribed form, that is, to say, to register a case on the basis of such information.[2]

11. *FIR cannot be used as Substantive Evidence*

Contents of FIR can be used for purpose of corroborating or contradicting person lodging FIR if he has been examined but not as substantive piece of evidence, in the case of person who had lodged FIR, had died.

Further statement allegedly made during inquest proceedings cannot be treated as substantive evidence in view of embargo of section 162 of the Cr. P.C.[3]

12. *Unsigned FIR is an Irregularity not an Illegality*

If Exh. 7/B is considered as First Information Report, same has not been signed by the person who had lodged the same. However, this would be a mere irregularity and cannot be treated, as illegality, which would vitiate the whole trial and, therefore, the contention raised in this regard, cannot be accepted.[4]

13. *Delay in Sending FIR to the Magistrate*

FIR was registered on 15-8-1981 at 7.30 p.m. and reached the court of magistrate on 17-8-1981 which was not very far away. The delay is fatal.[5]

FIR is only a report about the information as to the commission of an offence; it is not substantive evidence as the police has yet to investigate the offence.[6]

---

1. *Sherappa* v. *State*, 1991 Cr LJ 2215 Kar (DB): 1991 (1) All Cr LR 880: 1991 (1) Cr LC 556: 1990 (3) Crimes 645.
2. *State of Haryana* v. *Ch. Bhajan Lal*, AIR 1992 SC 604: 1992 Cr LJ 527: JT 1990 (4) SC 650: (1992) 3 SCR 735.
3. *Harkirat Singh* v. *State of Punjab*, AIR 1997 SC 3231: 1997 Cr LJ 3954: 1997 AIR SCW 3288: 1997 (3) Crimes 160: JT 1997 (7) SC 92: (1997) 11 SCC 215: (1997) 5 SCALE 76: 1997 SCC (Cri) 1068: 1997 (7) Supreme 246..
4. *Ashok Kamlakar* v. *State of Maharashtra*, IV (1998) CCR 194 (Bom) (DB).
5. *State of Rajasthan* v. *Teja Singh*, 2001 (I) AD (Cr) SC 385: AIR 2001 SC 990: 2001 (1) Crimes 232: JT 2001 (2) SC 347: (2001) 3 SCC 147: 2001 (3) SRJ 286: (2001) 1 SCALE 670: 2001 SCC (Cri) 439: 2001 (1) Supreme 621: 2001 (2) UJ (SC) 841.
6. *Sohan Lal* v. *State of Punjab*, 2003 Cr LJ 4569 SC: 2003 (4) Crimes 342: 2003 (2) DMC 645: (2003) 11 SCC 534: (2003) 8 SCALE 568: 2004 SCC (Cri) 226: 2003 (7) Supreme 386.

Law has not fixed any time for lodging the FIR. Hence a delayed FIR is not illegal.[1]

There is no hard and fast rule that F!R must always contain names of all persons who were involved in commission of offence. Very often names of culprits are not even mentioned in FIR and they surface only at the stage of investigation.[2]

14. Investigation before FIR

Investigation in the case had already commenced and once investigation commences, the FIR is hit by section 162 of the Cr.P.C.[3]

Telephonic messages received by the police did not constitute FIR under section 154 of the Code.[4]

XIII. Final Report

Accepting of Final Report of Police no Bar to take Cognizance

The Magistrate is not legally debarred from taking cognizance of the offence on the basis of the complaint or protest petition on same or similar allegations of the fact which were subject-matter of the investigation by the police on the basis of the FIR registered by the police and even though the Magistrate had earlier accepted the final report of the police.[5]

XIV. Jurisdiction

1. Jurisdiction of High Court under Artice 227 of the Constitution

Judicial order passed by the criminal courts are amenable to the jurisdiction of the High Court under article 227 of the Constitution.

Where appeals or revision applications or applications under section 482 of the Cr.P.C. are maintainable before the High Court for setting aside such orders there is no question of exercise of power under article 227.

Where appeals or revision applications or applications under section 482 of the Code cannot be entertained by the High Court for setting aside such orders, power under article 227 can be exercised in exceptional cases.

Where petitioner has already invoked the provisional jurisdiction of the sessions Judge under section 397 of the Cr.P.C. and his second revision applicant to the High Court is barred under section 397(3) it would indeed require very exceptional circumstances to warrant interference under article 227 of the Constitution, since the power of the superintendence under article 227 is not meant to circumvent the statutory bar.[6]

---

1. *Ravinder Kumar* v. *State of Punjab,* 2001 VII AD (SC) 209: AIR 2001 SC 3570: JT 2001 (7) SC 377: (2001) 7 SCC 690: 2001 (4) SCJ 419: 2001 (9) SRJ 80: (2001) 6 SCALE 119: 2001 SCC (Cri) 1384: 2001 (6) Supreme 549: 2001 (2) UC 631.
2. *Vinod G. Asrani* v. *State of Maharashtra,* II (2007) SLT 686: 2007 (1) JCC 723: (2007) 3 SCC 633: (2007) 3 SCALE 241: (2007) 2 SCC (Cri) 129: 2007 (2) Supreme 607.
3. *Ganesh Gogoi* v. *State of Assam,* AIR 2009 SC 2955: 2009 AIR SCW 4720: (2009) 7 SCC 404: (2009) 9 SCALE 135.
4. *Sidharth Vashisht @ Manu Sharma* v. *State (NCT) of Delhi,* III (2010) SLT 258.
5. *M.P. Srivastava* v. *Sqn. Ldr. K.V. Vashist,* 1991 Cr LJ 12 Del.
6. *Surendra Singh* v. *State of Bihar,* 1991 Cr LJ 3040 Pat (FB): 1992 APLJ (Cri) 10: 1992 (1) All Cri LR 260.

2. Places through which Contraband was Transported have Jurisdiction

Gold was transported from Pakistan to the place near Bahadurgarh in Haryana. *Prima facie* it appears that gold bars passed through Ambala also. The Ambala court would have jurisdiction to try the offence as carrying of smuggled gold is also an offence.[1]

FIR was filed in Shillong. Large number of events had taken place in Bombay. FIR registered in a particular State is not the sole criterion to decide that no cause of action has arisen even partly within the territorial limits of jurisdiction of another State. Nor are we to understand that any person can create a fake cause of action or even concoct one by simply jutting into the territorial limits of another State or by making a *sojourn* or even a permanent residence therein. The place of residence of the person moving a High Court is not the criterion to determine the contours of the cause of action in that particular writ petition. The High Court before which the writ petition is filed must ascertain whether any part of the cause-of-action has arisen within the territorial limits of its jurisdiction. It depends upon the facts in each case.

Held: Bombay High Court has the territorial jurisdiction.[2]

In terms of section 18(4) of the Cr.P.C. the accused can be prosecuted in the court within whose jurisdiction (i) the offence was committed, or (ii) any part of the property was received or retained, or (iii) any property or part of the property was required to be returned or accounted for by the accused.

Misappropriation was made in Hyderabad. All records of the company are maintained at New Delhi at the Head Office where statements of Hyderabad were sent. Delhi courts have jurisdiction.[3]

XV. Leading Question

Public prosecutor cannot put to the witnesses during examination-in-chief leading questions on material part of the evidence so as to elicit the evidence desired by him. Right to fair trial under article 21 would be otherwise affected vitiating the trial. It is not a curable irregularity.[4]

XVI. Limitation for Filing Charge-Sheet

1. *Benefit of Time Spent by one Party in Obtaining Certified Copy cannot be Availed by other*

Where a Government files the memorandum of appeal under section 417 of the Cr. P.C. along with the copy of a judgment obtained by the opposite party and sent to Government for purpose other than filing appeal, the time spent by the opposite party for obtaining that copy cannot be excluded in favour of Government.[5]

---

1. *Harbans Lal* v. *State of Haryana*, AIR 1995 SC 326: 1999 Cr LJ 455: 1998 AIR SCW 3728: 1998 (4) Crimes 107: JT 1998 (8) SC 48: (1998) 8 SCC 319: 1999 (1) SCJ 263: (1998) 6 SCALE 181: 1999 SCC (Cri) 11: 1998 (8) Supreme 436: 1999 (1) UJ (SC) 122.
2. *Navinchandra N. Majithia* v. *State of Maharashtra*, 2000 III AD (Cr) SC 13: AIR 2000 SC 2966: 2000 AIR SCW 3157: (2000) 7 SCC 640.
3. *Naveen Kumar Aditya* v. *Escorts Finance Ltd.*, 2002 I AD (Del) 762.
4. *Varkey Joseph* v. *State of Kerala*, 1993 SCC (Cri) 1117: AIR 1993 SC 1892: JT 1993 (3) SC 163: 1993 (2) SCJ 600: (1993) 3 SCR 390: 1993 (3) SCC (Supp) 745.
5. *State* v. *Hari Shankar*, 1972 Cr LJ 60 All (FB).

2. Limitation Starts from Knowledge of the Order and not the Date of Order

Under the proviso to sub-section (6) of section 488, the Criminal Procedure Code, 1898, a husband, against whom an *ex parte* order has been made fixing maintenance allowance, is entitled to reckon the periods of limitation of three months from the date of knowledge of the order for an application made to set aside that order on the ground that he had neither wilfully avoided service nor wilfully neglected to attend the court and pleads want of the knowledge of the order. *Terminus a quo* for reckoning the period of limitation in such a case is not the date of the order.[1]

Section 473 has overriding effect on section 468. The basic difference between section 5 of the Limitation Act and section 473 of the Cr. P.C. is that for exercising the power under section 5, the onus is on the applicant/appellant to satisfy the court that there was sufficient cause for condonation of delay whereas section 473 enjoins a duty on the court to examine not only whether such delay has been explained but as to whether it is requirement of the justice to condone or ignore such delay.[2]

3. Section 468 Condonation of Delay under Section 473 should be Liberally Construed

Whenever a complaint or a challan is filed at the instance of any person or any police officer, the Court must first see that section 468 is attracted or not. If it does, it should not register the case but give an opportunity to the person or the police officer filing the complaint or challan to satisfy it on the point of limitation for purposes of condonation of delay. As regards the condonation of delay it should not be done as a matter of course. The delay has to be condoned with exercise of judicial discretion.

Section 473 should also be liberally construed like section 5 of the Limitation Act so as to advance substantial justice when no negligence or inaction or want of *bona fides* is imputable to the prosecutor or prosecution is upon police report. After the delay is condoned by the court on its being satisfied then alone it would register the case and proceed with the same in accordance with law.

Natural justice demands that the accused persons must be heard before passing an order in that regard as such an order is bound to affect a valuable right which accrues to the accused and which cannot be allowed to be taken away lightly. As such, they have to be heard when an application under section 473 is moved by the prosecution before cognizance is taken.[3]

4. Limitation to be in Relation to Offence in which the Accused was Convicted

The accused Sarwan Singh was tried for the offence under section 408, the Indian Penal Code, on the basis of a charge-sheet filed against him on 13-10-1976. Though the trial court acquitted him of the offence under section 408, the I.P.C, it convicted him of the lesser offence punishable under section 406, the I.P.C, and

---

1. *Joginder Singh* v. *Balkaran Kaur,* 1972 Cr LJ 93 P&H (FB).
2. *Vanka Radhamanohari* v. *Vanka Venkata Reddy,* 1993 SCC (Cri) 571: (1993) 3 SCC 4: 1993 AIR SCW 3595: JT 1993 (4) SC 17.
3. *Krishna Sanghi* v. *State of Madhya Pradesdh,* 1977 Cr LJ 90 MP.

sentenced him to rigorous imprisonment for one year and also to pay a fine of Rs. 1,000. On appeal preferred by him, the High Court of Punjab and Haryana allowed the appeal and acquitted him on the ground that the prosecution launched against him was clearly barred by limitation. The State of Punjab having preferred an appeal before the Apex Court, their Lordships affirmed the decision of the High Court.[1]

5. Limitation shall not be Counted with Reference to Maximum Sentence

The expression, "imprisonment for a term of not less than six months" occurring in section 34 of the A.P. Excise Act, cannot be construed as a term not exceeding one year especially when the penal provision says that the offender is punishable not only with imprisonment but also with fine. It cannot be construed as term of six months and six months only. Whenever the statute says that imprisonment shall not be less than a particular term, the intention of Legislature is that in a given case the court may impose imprisonment for a greater period. Therefore, the offence punishable under section 34 of the Act does not fall within the ambit of section 468(2), the Cr. P.C and charge-sheet filed beyond period of one year from the date of the detection of the alleged offence is not time-barred under section 468, the Cr. P.C.[2]

6. Limitation to be Counted from the Next Date of Arrest

For filing charge-sheet, the limitation of one year would begin to run and be counted from the next date of arrest.[3]

7. Period of Limitation Starts from the Date of Receipt of Report of Public Analyst

In filing of complaint under the Drugs and Cosmetics Act, 1940, the period of limitation starts only from the date of receipt of report of public analyst and not from the date of taking sample by the Drugs Inspector as only on the receipt of the report of Government analyst it came to light that an offence was committed.[4]

8. Charge-sheet not Filed in Time

The proviso to section 167(2) of the Cr. P.C. does not create indefeasible right on accused to exercise at any time. This right is applicable after the maximum time allowed by law till the charge-sheet is filed. This right is not available after the charge-sheet is filed. But on the other hand if he exercises the right within the time allowed by law and is released on bail under such circumstances, he cannot be re-arrested on the mere filing of the charge-sheet.[5]

---

1. *State of Punjab* v. *Sarwan Singh,* AIR 1981 SC 1054: 1981 Cr LJ 722: (1981) 3 SCC 34: 1981 Cr LR (SC) 289: 1981 (2) SCJ 50: (1981) 8 Cr LT 188.
2. *K. Kasappa Naidu* v. *State of Andhra Pradesh,* 1992 Cr LJ 1214 (AP): 1991 (2) All Cri LR 944: 1991 (2) Andh WR 201: 1991 (3) Crimes 670.
3. *CBI* v. *Nazir Ahmad Sheikh,* AIR 1996 SC 2980.
4. *State of Rajasthan* v. *Sanjay Kumar,* 1998 Cr LJ 2531 SC: 1998 (2) Crimes 321 also by Delhi High Court in *R.S Arora* v. *State,* 1987 Cr LJ 1215: 1986 (11) DRJ 314: 1987 (1) FAC 283.
5. *Dr. Bipin Shanti Lal Panchal* v. *State of Guajrat,* AIR 1996 SC 2897: 1996 Cr LJ 1652: 1996 AIR SCW 734: 1996 (1) Cr CJ 629: 1996 (1) Mah LR 700: (1996) 1 SCC 718: 1996 (2) SCJ 198: (1996) 1 SCR 193.

XVII. Liquor Adulterated

1. Prosecution to Prove Illicit Origin of Liquor

It is for the prosecution to prove that the liquor found to be in possession of the accused was of illicit origin.[1]

In order to establish that an offence under section 272, the IPC has been committed, the prosecution has to prove that the article involved was food or drink meant to be consumed by live persons, that the accused adulterated it, that such adulteration rendered it noxious as food or drink, and that the accused at the time of such adulteration intended to sell such article as food or drink, or knew it to be likely that such article would be sold as food or drink. Noxious rendering is making it poisonous or harmful or both. The offence is complete on introduction of the adulterant in the food or drink, provided it is meant for the purposes of sale, actual or likely. That A-1 was found to be in possession of adulterated arrack would lead to the conclusion that the offences under section 272, the IPC and section 55(a) and (i) of the Abkari Act stood committed on the date of recovery itself. In spite of adulteration, the liquor remained as liquor. Section 2(10) of the Abkari Act defines 'liquor' to include spirits, wine, methylated spirits, toddy, beer and all liquor consisting of or containing alcohol. Methyl alcohol answers at least the description of being a liquor consisting of or containing alcohol.[2]

2. *Food Inspector Found the Contents of Liquor Less by 9 per cent. Case of Adulteration made out*

Food Inspector purchased liquor 'Masala Sarab'. On examination of the sample the alcoholic content was found to be 26.86 per cent. against the declared alcoholic content of 36 per cent.

Held prima facie a case of adulteration is made out and the High Court refused to quash the proceedings at that stage.[3]

3. Mentioning Wrong Section

Mere recital of a wrong provision of law does not have the effect of invalidating an order, which is otherwise within the power of the authority making it. The sessions Judge's order making over the case to the additional sessions Judge was within his power; the only error was that he recited a wrong section of the Code *viz.*, section 409(1) instead of section 194. Therefore, this order must be read as an order made under section 194 so far as the direction making over the case to the additional sessions Judge is concerned.[4]

XVIII. Penalty Measure

When statute creates criminal liability with provision for punishment, *mens rea* of the offender has to be established for awarding the punishment – But when statute imposes only a civil obligation with provision for penalty in the nature of fine, *mens rea* of the offender need not be established for imposing the penalty in

1. *State* v. *Bikar Singh*, 1965 PLR 1044.
2. *Joseph Kurian Philip Jose* v. *State of Kerala*, 1995 SCC (Cri) 20: 1994 AIR SCW 3989: (1994) 6 SCC 535: AIR 1995 SC 4.
3. *State of Uttar Pradesh* v. *Carew & Co. Ltd.*, II (1995) CCR 475 All.
4. *State of Karnataka* v. *Muniyalla*, 1985 SCC (Cri) 50.

absence of any indication to the contrary in the statute. Statute creating offence generally intends the punishment provided for to serve as deterrent.[1]

XIX. Plea Bargaining

No enhancement in sentence in plea bargaining: Where by reason of plea bargaining the accused pleaded guilty and was convicted and sentenced by Magistrate acting upon his plea of guilt, the enhancement of sentence by the appellate or revisional court in appeal or revision by acting on plea of guilt would not be reasonable, fair and just. It would be clearly violative of article 21 of the Constitution to induce or lead an accused to plead guilty under a promise or assurance that he would be let off lightly and then in appeal or revision, to enhance the sentence. The court of appeal or revision should, in such a case, set aside the conviction and sentence of the accused and remand the case to the trial court so that the accused can, if he so wishes, defend himself against the charge and if he is found guilty, proper sentence can be passed against him.[2]

XX. Police Custody

1. Police Custody while Interrogated

When a person is called to the police station and is interrogated as an accused he must be deemed to be in the custody of the police while he is so interrogated.[3]

2. Police Custody, when Information given

Accused will be deemed to be in constructive custody of police at the time of giving information and hence section 27 applies.[4]

3. Police Custody can be Ordered during the first period of 15 days

Taking the plain language into consideration, particularly the words otherwise than in the custody of the police beyond the period fifteen days in the provision it has to be held that the custody after the expiry of fifteen days can only be judicial custody during the rest of the period of ninety days or sixty days and that of police custody if found necessary can be ordered only during the first period of fifteen days.[5]

XXI. Possession

1. Mere Joint Owner of House and Field not Enough

The mere fact of a person being joint owner of a house and field, in which illicit liquor and distillery apparatus are found without anything further to connect him with the illicit distillation, is not sufficient to warrant his conviction under section 61 of the Excise Act.[6]

---

1. *Gujarat Travancore Agency* v. *Commissioner of Income Tax,* 1989 SCC (Cri) 509: AIR 1989 SC 1677.
2. *State of Gujarat* v. *Uttam Bhikhu Prajapati,* 1992 Cr LJ 626 Guj: 1990 (2) Guj LR 1244.
3. *Onkar* v. *State of Madhya Pradesh,* 1974 Cr LJ 120 (MP).
4. *Kanahiya* v. *State of Rajasthan,* 1976 Cr LJ 1652 Raj.
5. *C.B.I. Special Investigation* v. *Anupam J. Kulkarni,* AIR 1992 SC 1768: 1992 Cr LJ 2768: 1992 AIR SCW 1976: 1992 (2) Crimes 310: JT 1992 (3) SC 366: (1992) 3 SCC 141: 1992 (3) SCJ 50: (1992) 3 SCR 158.
6. *Mihan Singh* v. *Emperor,* 22 Cr LJ 30 Lah.

2. *Possession Relative only to Husband, where the House was in his Name but Occupied Jointly with his Wife*

When liquor and apparatus for manufacturing it are found in a house which is in the joint occupation of a husband and wife, but which belongs to the husband, the latter alone must be regarded as being in possession of the articles. The wife in such a case is not guilty of an offence under section 61 of the Punjab Excise Act.[1]

3. *Conviction under Section 61 Proper if Liquor in Excess of Prescribed is Found Outside the Licensed Premises*

A licensee in possession of liquor in excess of the prescribed quantity and out side the place of licence is rightly punishable under section 61 of the Act for contravening the provisions of section 24(3) of the Act.[2]

4. *If Three Brothers Living Together, the Eldest Brother shall be Regarded as House Master*

Where a house is in possession of three brothers living together as members of a family and if illicit article is found therein, the presumption is that it is in possession of the eldest of them who is to be regarded as house master.[3]

5. *Individual Possession of Liquor*

Seven persons were found sitting in a hotel around a table on which some tumblers were found, with liquor and others empty. Held all the person could not be convicted without proving that each accused was in individual possession of liquor.[4]

6. *Handing over Keys of House*

The mere fact that the keys of room from where the article was recovered were handed over to the police by the head of family, does not establish that he was in possession of the room especially when the keys were taken from the custody of one of his daughters-in-law. This circumstance alone does not lead to the inference that he was consciously in possession.[5]

7. *Awareness of Existence of Article in the House*

Merely because an incriminating article is found in a house occupied by some persons, the *onus* cannot be thrown either under section 106 of the Evidence Act or any other provision of law upon these persons to establish their innocence, unless the occupiers of the house are shown to have been aware of the existence of the article in the house.[6]

8. *Possession in Transit*

Possession of intoxicant in transit by a person on behalf of another but for the purpose of transit was not illegal.[7]

1. *Bishna* v. *Emperor,* AIR 1920 Lah 210 (V7): 22 Cr LJ 141 Lah.
2. *Emperor* v. *Puran Singh,* 24 Cr LJ 667 Lah.
3. *Bara Singh* v. *Emperor,* 39 Cr LJ 232 Punj.
4. *Dhani Cahnd* v. *Emperor,* 40 Cr LJ 341 Lah.
5. *Bhekha Ali* v. *Emperor,* AIR 1947 Pat 236: 48 Cr LJ 53.
6. *Sahendra* v. *Emperor,* AIR 1948 Pat 222: 49 Cr LJ 445.
7. *State* v. *Shantt Dutt,* 1952 Cr LJ 1350.

9. Possession of Key Prima Facie *Evidence*

Brandy and whisky found in room which was locked. Possession of key of the room by the accused is *prima facie* evidence of his possession of room.[1]

10. Home to be in Occupation and Control

Where a prosecution was lodged on the basis of recovery of certain incriminating articles from a house, unless the house is shown to have been in the occupation and control of the accused the mere factum of recovery of incriminating article, therefore, cannot fasten criminal liability on him.[2]

11. Recovery of Whisky from the Drawer of the Table Amounts to Conscious Possession

Where the whisky is recovered from the table of the Manager in the hotel premises it cannot be said that he had no knowledge of the fact that it was kept in his drawer within the hotel premises. He can thus be rightly held to be in conscious possession of incriminating article.[3]

12. Conscious Possession

Utensils containing illicit liquor were recovered from house in occupation of father, son and two ladies. It was held that unless it is proved that both the father and son were conscious of that the tins and other containers contained illicit liquor and also they had physical control over these articles, they cannot be held to be in possession of the incriminating articles.[4]

13. Bottles of Foreign Liquor Found in Luggage of Appellant; Luggage in Full Control of Appellant's Servant

Circumstantial evidence, held, not of that kind from which the only inference that could reasonably be drawn was that the appellant had knowledge of the contents of his luggage – A possession without knowledge is not actionable. Conviction set aside.[5]

14. Conscious and Intelligent Possession

Possession implies dominion and consciousness in mind of the person having domination over an object that he has it and that he can exercise it. Possession must be conscious and intelligent possession and not merely the physical presence of the accused in proximity or even in close proximity to the object.[6]

15. Exclusive Possession

When the discovery was made from a place to which four persons had access as inhabitants of the house and one of the inhabitants was convicted under section 9 of the Act, it was held that under the circumstances on facts there could

---

1. *Ghudusab Ibrahim Mujawar* v. *State,* AIR 1956 Bom 225: 1956 Cr LJ 495.
2. *State of Himachal Pradesh* v. *Booti Nath,* 1956 Cr LJ 747 (HP).
3. *Balbir Singh* v. *State,* 1958 Cr LJ 1461 (Assam).
4. *Partap Singh* v. *State,* 1959 Cr LJ 1436 J&K.
5. *Maharaja Prithvi Singh Ji Bhim Singh Ji* v. *State,* AIR 1960 SC 483: 1960 Cr LJ 672.
6. *In re Wahab Bosha,* AIR 1961 Mad 162.

be no question of exclusive possession by any member of the household. Conviction set aside.[1]

16. Recovery made from the House of the Accused

Where huge quantity of contraband was recovered from a house belonging to an accused. The key to the locked room from where contraband was recovered, was given by the wife of the accused while he was temporarily absent. The accused absconded and was arrested after some time. The accused was held to be in possession and convicted.[2]

17. Conscious Possession

Where more than one person was in possession of the house and a large quantity of opium was recovered from the house. The question arose whether the accused persons were in conscious possession of the opium recovered from their house. The court said that in the facts and circumstances of the case all the three persons can be said to be in conscious possession and the conviction was upheld.[3]

18. Constructive Possession

Possession need not be only physical or actual. It may be constructive.[4]

19. Conscious Possession to be Distinguished with Custody

It cannot be gainsaid that even a person who participates in a drinking party can in conceivable cases be guilty of the offence of possession of liquor. Suppose a person is found at a drinking party and he has a glass with him with liquor in it at the time when the raid is carried out, it would be correct to say that he was at the relevant time in possession of liquor. The liquor in his glass would be liquor in his possession. But at the same time it would not be correct to say that merely because a participant in a drinking party can stretch his hand and take liquor for his use and consumption, he can be held to be in possession of liquor. Possession again must be distinguished from custody and it must be conscious possession. If, for example, a bottle of liquor is kept by someone in the car or house of a person without his knowledge, he cannot be said to be in possession of the bottle of liquor. It cannot, therefore, be laid down as an absolute proposition that whoever is present at a drinking party must necessarily be guilty of the offence of possession of liquor and must be charged for such offence. Whether an accused is in possession of liquor or not must depend on the facts and circumstances of each case.[5]

20. Recovery from Dickey of the Car

The accused was found travelling in a car driven by the driver of the accused. The bottles of beer were recovered from the dickey of the car which was locked and

---

1. *Sadhu Singh* v. *State,* AIR 1967 Punj 14: 1966 Cur LJ 37: ILR (1966) 1 Punj 765.
2. *State of Rajasthan* v. *Anandi Lal,* 1968 Cr LJ 275 Raj (DB)
3. *Ashiq Miyan* v. *State of Madhya Pradesh,* AIR 1969 SC 4: 1969 1 SCR 188.
4. *Gunwanti Lal* v. *State of Madhya Pradesh,* AIR 1972 SC 1756: 1972 SCD 676: 1972 Cr LJ 1187: (1973) 1 SCR 508.
5. *Patel Jethabhai Chatur* v. *State of Gujarat,* AIR 1977 SC 294: 1976 Cr LR (SC) 518: (1976) 4 SCC 522: 1977 Cr LJ 201: 1977 SCC (Cri) 1: 18 Guj LR 360: (1977) 1 SCR 872: 1976 Guj Cri R 311.

opened with the key supplied by the driver. There was no material on record that the accused had any knowledge about the existence of beer in the dickey. The accused was acquitted.[1]

21. Recovery in the Absence of the Accused

48.5 kg. of opium recovered from the house of the accused. The recovery was made in the absence of accused when according to evidence he had gone over to Vaishnodevi five or six days before the raid.

Held: That the conscious possession of the accused was not proved. The conviction was held to be illegal.[2]

The prosecution case itself was that the illicit liquor was kept in a bag, which was closed and it was put into the dickey of the rickshaw. The appellant was merely a rickshaw driver. He cannot be imputed with the knowledge of the possession of the articles merely because the passenger put those articles in the dickey of that rickshaw. *Held* there was no legal evidence to connect the accused with the crime. Accordingly, the accused was acquitted.[3]

22. When Contraband in the Custody, Onus Shifts to the Accused

What the prosecution has to prove is that the accused was in some manner connected with the opium or dealt with it. The necessary animus for offence under section 9 can be inferred from the facts of a particular case. Further, under section 10 when the prosecution has shown by evidence that the accused has dealt with opium or has physical custody of the same or is directly connected with it, the onus shifts on the accused to prove by preponderance of probability that he is not knowingly possessing the opium.[4]

23. Recovery of Liquor from Car Belonging to Other

Illicit liquor was recovered from the car in which the petitioner was sitting. The car was owned and driven by somebody else and there was no evidence to connect the petitioner with the offence. The petitioner was acquitted of the charge.[5]

Recovery of liquor bottles in the presence of the wife of the accused, in his absence would not be deemed to be in conscious possession of the accused: Where the accused was not in his house at the time of raid leading to recovery of liquor bottles in the presence of his wife and the prosecution does not show the accused to have got out of his village the same day or a day prior to the search, it cannot be safely assumed that the accused was in possession of everything found inside his house.

Section 27 of the Penal Code extending the meaning of "possession" applies only to offences under the Penal Code and does not cover cases under the Rajasthan Prohibition Act, 1969. Hence, the word "possess" in section 4(2) of the Rajasthan Prohibition Act cannot be interpreted to include possession by the wife

1. *J.S.S. Sidhu Surinder Singh* v. *State of Punjab*, 1973-77 Ch LR (Supp) 381.
2. *Ram Rattan* v. *State of Punjab*, 1979 Cur LJ (Cr) 94 (SC): AIR 1979 SC 1249: 1979 Cr LJ 791.
3. *Jawar Arjan* v. *State of Gujarat*, 1979 SCC (Cri) 633: AIR 1979 SC 1500: 1980 Cr LJ 828.
4. *Karam Singh* v. *State*, 1981 Cr LJ (NOC) 123 (Raj).
5. *Brij Lal* v. *State of Punjab*, 1983 CCC 575 (P&H).

of the accused. It is imperative upon the prosecution to prove beyond reasonable doubt the conscious possession of the recovered liquor bottles by the accused. The mere fact of the accused being the head of the family is not sufficient for a finding that he must have been in conscious possession of the liquor bottles. Thus conviction of such accused is wrong.[1]

Possession of opium from the shop of the licensee when only salesman was present would be sufficient to convict the owner of the shop: Where opium was recovered from licensed ganja shop of the accused, the accused would be liable to be convicted for possession of opium and the mere fact that he was absent at the time of the raid and the salesman alone was present would not absolve him from criminal liability. In this connection, it could not be said that the accused was merely a licensee of the shop and he could not be held responsible for anything recovered from his shop when his servant was present. The concept of conscious possession could not be extended too far so as to defeat the very object of section 10.[2]

24. Contraband Found in "Bada" not Exclusive Possession

Articles used in preparing liquor along with one pitcher full of wash found from one 'Bada' situated behind the house of the petitioner, where everybody had access as such, it was not in the exclusive possession of the accused. Relying on AIR 1980 SC 1314 accused was let off.[3]

25. Recovery from the Driver's Seat Amounts to Conscious Possession

Where three bags containing large quantity of opium, about 66 kgs. were recovered from the truck driver's seat and from goods in truck, an inference could be drawn that the driver knowingly possessed opium. What the prosecution has to prove is that the accused was in some manner connected with the opium or dealt with it. The necessary animus for offence under section 9 can be inferred from the facts of a particular case.[4]

26. Brief Case Underneath the Feet of the Accused

Briefcase containing opium found underneath the feet of the appellant in the taxi in which he was traveling. Driver-cum-owner of the taxi deposing that appellant was the first passenger in his taxi on the day. Keys for opening the briefcase containing the opium, provided by the appellant himself. Briefcase thus in physical possession and custody of appellant. In the circumstances held, prosecution not only proved possession but also actual and conscious possession of opium.[5]

---

1. *Chela Ram* v. *State of Rajasthan*, 1984 Cr LJ 1143 Raj: 1983 Raj Cri C 305: 1984 Raj LR 579: 1983 Raj LW 392.
2. *Kailash Chandra Sahu* v. *Republic of India*, 1985 Cr LJ 1860 SC: AIR 1985 SC 1672: 1985 (2) Crimes 530: (1985) 3 SCC 708: 1985 SCC (Cri) 457: 1985 UJ (SC) 892.
3. *Nain Singh* v. *State of Rajasthan*, I (1992) CCR 808.
4. *Amreek Singh* v. *State of Rajasthan*, 1992 Cr LJ 2914 (Raj).
5. *Avtar Singh* v. *State of Punjab*, 1993 SCC (Cri) 422: AIR 1992 SC 1524: (1993) 1 SCC (Supp) 581.

27. Ownership and Possession not Proved

Ownership and possession of premises by accused from which contraband articles were seized were not established. Accused is entitled to be acquitted. The premises were searched in the absence of the accused.[1]

28. Not mere Knowledge but Positive Possession to be Proved

According to PWD-2 the police officer was asking him whether any charas was hidden and the accused number 1 was to show the place where the charas was hidden, but this will not attribute to the guilt of the accused in possessing the charas. In order to fasten the liability under section 20(b)(ii) of the NDPS Act, possession of charas was to be positively proved and mere knowledge of the person or the place where charas could be found cannot be equated with the possession in order to come under the ambit of section 20(b)(ii) of the Act.[2]

29. Possession

Where possession of a forbidden article constitutes an offence, the prosecution is duty bound to prove the ingredients thereof. Existence of *mens rea*, however, would be a question which has to be determined having regard to the provisions of the statute.[3]

The expression "possession" is polymorphous term which assumes different colours in different contexts. It may carry different meanings in contextually different backgrounds. It is impossible to work out a completely logical and precise definition of "possession" universally applicable to all situations in the context of all statutes. The word 'conscious' means awareness about a particular fact. It is a state of mind which is deliberate or intended. The possession may be constructive. It means the legal right to possess.[4]

XXII. Precedent

1. Binding Nature of Decision

A wrong decision by a court having jurisdiction is as much binding between the parties as a right one and may be superseded only by appeals to higher tribunals or other procedure like review, which the law provides.[5]

2. Supreme Court may Overrule Earlier Decisions

There was nothing in the Constitution, which prevented the Supreme Court from departing from a previous decision of its own if it was satisfied of its error and or its baneful effect on the general interest of the public. If the aforesaid rule of construction accepted by this court is inconsistent with the legal philosophy of our Constitution, it is our duty to correct ourselves and lay down the right rule. In constitutional matters, which affect the evolution of our policy, we must more

1. *Mohd Aslam Khan* v. *NCB*, AIR 1996 SC 3033: 1996 (1) Cri CJ 572: JT 1996 (2) SC 636: (1996) 9 SCC 462: (1996) 2 SCR 842.
2. *Milan Sarkariski* v. *State*, 1997 Cr LJ 2028 Bom (DB).
3. *P.K. Arjunan* v. *State of Kerala*, AIR 2007 SC 2331: 2007 AIR SCW 4035: (2007) 5 SCALE 92.
4. *State of Punjab* v. *Ram Lal*, V (2009) SLT 261.
5. *State of West Bengal* v. *Hemant Kumar Bhattacharjee*, AIR 1966 SC 1061: 1963 (2) SCJ 680: 1963 Supp (2) SCR 542: 1966 Cr LJ 805.

readily do so than in other branches of law, as perpetuation of a mistake will be harmful to public interest. While continuity and consistency are conducive to the smooth evolutions of the rule of law, hesitancy to set right deviations will retard its growth.[1]

3. Principle of Stare-decisis *not on a Constitutional Point*

It is true that the principle of *stare decisis* may not strictly apply to a decision on a constitutional point. There is no restriction in the Constitution itself which prevents this court from reviewing its earlier decisions or even to depart from them in the interest of public good. It is true that the problem of construing Constitutional provisions cannot be adequately solved by merely adopting the literal construction of the words used in various Articles. The Constitution is an organic document and it is intended to serve as a guide to the solution of changing problems, which the court may have to face from time-to-time. It is manifest that in a progressive and dynamic society the character of these problems is bound to change with the inevitable consequence that the relevant words used in the Constitution may also change their meaning and significance.[2]

Even assuming that a provision can receive a different interpretation and that interpretation is more reasonable than that adopted by the Supreme Court in its previous decision, in that event also the Supreme Court would not be justified in overruling its previous decision which has the force of law in view of article 141 of the Constitution. The decisions of the Supreme Court should not be overruled excepting under compelling circumstances. It is only when Supreme Court is fully convinced that public interest of a substantial character would be jeopardized by a previous decision of the court, Supreme Court should overrule that decision. Every time Supreme Court overrules its previous decision, the confidence of the public in the soundness of the decision of the court is bound to be shaken. Reconsideration of the decisions of the Supreme Court should be confined to questions of great public importance. In law finality is of utmost importance. Legal problems should not be treated as mere subjects for mental exercise. The Supreme Court must overrule its previous decisions only when it comes to the conclusion that it is manifestly wrong, not upon a mere suggestion that some or all of the members of the later court might arrive at a different conclusion if the matter was *res integra*.[3]

4. The Essence of Decision is its Ratio

A decision is only an authority for what it actually decides. What is of the essence in a decision is its ratio and not every observation found therein nor what logically follows from the various observations made in it. It is not a profitable task to extract a sentence here and there from a judgment and to build upon it.[4]

1. *State of West Bengal* v. *Corporation of Calcutta*, AIR 1967 SC 997: (1967) 1 SCWR 745: 1967 Cr LJ 950: 1967 (1) SCA 508: (1967) 2 SCR 170.
2. *Golak Nath* v. *State of Punjab*, AIR 1967 SC 1643: 1967 All LJ 813: 1967 (2) SCJ 486: 1967 (2) SCA 642: (1967) 2 SCR 762: (1967) 2 SCWR 1006.
3. *Income Tax Officer* v. *T.S. Devinatha Nadar*, AIR 1968 SC 623: 1968 (1) SCA 444: 1968 (1) SCJ 733: (1968) 2 SCR 33.
4. *State of Orissa* v. *Sudhansu Sekhar Misra*, AIR 1968 SC 647: (1967) 2 SCWR 846: (1968) 2 SCR 154: 1968 SCD 1: 1968 (1) SCA 428: 1968 (2) SCJ 236: 1970 (1) Lab LJ 662.

5. Conclusion may be Arrived by Different Reasoning

One may doubt the wisdom of attempting to trace a common *ratio decidendi* from divergent views expressed by different judges in support of a conclusion but it seems equally illogical to altogether ignore a clear conclusion arrived at by the majority of judges only because they arrived at that conclusion by different processes of reasoning. One would rather have thought that a conclusion stands more fortified when it can be supported not on one but on several lines of reasoning. At least for an identical problem, the final answer should be the same.[1]

6. In Case of Difference of Opinion, Case to be Referred to Larger Bench

Pursuit of the law, however, glamorous it is, has its own limitation on the Bench. In a multi-judge court, precedents and procedure bind the judges. They could use their discretion only when there is no declared principle to be found, no rule and no authority. The judicial decorum and legal propriety demand that where a learned single Judge or a Division Bench does not agree with the decision of a Bench of co-ordinate jurisdiction, the matter shall be referred to a larger Bench. It is a subversion of judicial process not to follow this procedure.[2]

7. Same Principles of Law may Apply Differently in Different Facts

It is often said that precedents are principles of law and cannot be applied to facts of all cases except in extraordinary situations. It is well to remember that precedents are not immutable dogma. Courts may evolve principles which are applicable to the facts involved in each case. Those principles may apply with marginal or substantial variations to other facts and situations of a similar nature. That is why the same principle of law may apply differently in different cases involving different sets of facts.[3]

8. A Co-ordinate Bench of a Court cannot Pronounce Judgment Contrary to Declaration of Law by Another Bench

Precedents which enunciate rules of law form the foundation of administration of justice under our system. This is a fundamental principle, which every Presiding Officer of a Judicial Forum ought to know, for consistency in interpretation of law alone can lead to public confidence in our judicial system. This court has laid down time and again precedent law must be followed by all concerned; deviation from the same should be only on a procedure known to law. A subordinate court is bound by the enunciation of law made by the superior courts. A co-ordinate Bench of a court cannot pronounce judgment contrary of declaration of law made by another Bench. It can only refer it to a larger Bench if it disagrees with the earlier pronouncement.[4]

---

1. *Ramesh Birch* v. *Union of India,* AIR 1990 SC 560: JT 1989 (2) SC 483: 1989 2 Rent LR 164.
2. *Sundarjas Kanyalal Bhathija* v. *Collector, Thane,* AIR 1991 SC 1893.
3. *Rumana Begum* v. *Govt. of Andhra Pradesh,* 1992 Cr LJ 3512 AP (DB): (1993) 2 (Supp) SCC 341: 1993 SCC (Cri) 551.
4. *S.I. Rooplal* v. *Lt. Governor, Delhi,* AIR 2000 SC 594: 2000 Lab IC 370: 2000 AIR SCW 19: (2000) 1 SCC 644: (1999) 7 SCALE 466: 1999 (10) Supreme 300: 2000 (1) UJ (SC) 252.

XXIII. Production of Accused – Before Magistrate within 24 Hours

The accused was arrested by Rajasthan Police, while he was in judicial custody. He was put under arrest by M.P. Police but he was not produced before the magistrate within 24 hours after formal arrest. Held: After arrest police was bound to produce accused before court within 24 hours as mandated by article 22 of the Constitution, and section 57 of the Cr.P.C. Detention beyond 24 hours was illegal, MP State's excuse that the accused was under detention at Rajasthan and as such could not be produced before court within 24 hours cannot be accepted. Arrest becomes otiose. MP Govt. cannot validly pray for further detention.[1]

XXIV. Promissory Estoppel

Understanding arrived at between Government and accused that if accused surrenders his licence, Government would not proceed further with the case. Later on Government reversed its decision.

Held: Acquittal on ground of promissory estoppels could not be sustained. Doctrine of promissory estoppels does not apply to criminal cases.[2]

XXV. Reasonable Belief

1. There should be prima facie *Justification for Reasonable Belief*

When we are dealing with question as to whether the belief in the mind of the officer who effected the seizure was reasonable or not, we are not sitting in appeal over the decision of the said officer. All that we can consider is whether there is ground which *prima facie* justifies the said reasonable belief.[3]

2. There should be Some Rational Basis

The words 'reason to believe' convey that there must be some rational basis to form the belief.[4]

3. *Conviction shall be Vitiated if No Satisfaction of Reason to Believe to take Search was Recorded*

Where in a prosecution under section 353 on the allegation that the accused had threatened to kill the Excise Inspector who proceeded to search the car of the accused on the belief that offences stated in section 74 of the Orissa Excise Act were committed, no material was produced to show that any reason was recorded by the Excise Officer before taking the search of the car as required by section 74, the search and seizure would be without jurisdiction and prosecution and conviction under section 353 would be vitiated.[5]

4. Reason to Believe

The expression 'reason to believe' is not synonymous with subjective satisfaction of the officer. The belief must be held in goods faith; it cannot merely

1. *Manoj* v. *State of Madhya Pradesh,* 1999 (2) Crimes 329 (SC).
2. *State of Maharashtra* v. *Jethmal Himatmal Jain,* 1994 Cr LJ 2613 Bom: 1994 (4) Bom CR 103.
3. *Pukhraj* v. *D.R. Kohli,* 1963 MPLJ 460: 1963 Mah LJ 468: 65 Bom LR 281: AIR 1962 SC 1559.
4. *Commissioner of Sales Tax* v. *Bhagwan Industries P. Ltd.,* (1973) 3 SCC 265: AIR 1973 SC 370: 1973 Tax LR 1703.
5. *Krishna Chandra* v. *State,* 1984 Cr LJ 1409 Ori: 1982 (55) Cut LT 7.

be pretence. It is open to the court to examine the question whether the reasons for the belief have a rational connection or a relevant bearing to the formation of the belief and are not extraneous or irrelevant to the purpose of the section.

It is not obligatory for an officer to record in writing prior to issuing the warrant the grounds for entertaining a reasonable belief that the documents useful for investigation or proceeding under the Act are secret and also to specify in such writing, as far as possible, the thing for which search is to be made. The material on which the belief is grounded may be secret, may be obtained through Intelligence or occasionally may be conveyed orally by informants and as such the officer is not bound to disclose his materials on mere allegation of absence of the reasons.[1]

XXVI. Remission of Sentence

Remission is not Available for Bail Period

A convicted prisoner, undergoing sentence of imprisonment cannot claim that he is entitled to remission of the period during which he was on bail under orders of the court.

While section 432 of the Code deals with power of the Government to suspend the sentence, section 389 of the Code deals with power of the court to suspend execution of sentence pending appeal or revision. Whenever the sentence is suspended by the court, the convict is entitled to be released on bail. The expression used in section 432(1) of the Code for remission is "remit the punishment to which he has been sentenced". It is, therefore, clear that remission can be granted only with reference to an operative punishment. In other words, when there is no operative punishment there is no need to remit any part of such punishment. Parole relates to executive action taken after the door has been closed on a convict. During parole period there is no suspension of sentence but sentence is actually continuing to run during that period also. Remission cannot be granted in respect of the period during which accused was released on bail.[2]

XXVII. Sale of Liquor by Licensee

Sale of Liquor by Licensee at a Place other than Licensed Premises

Where a licence holder for sale of liquor, sells Government licensed liquor at a place other than one specified in his licence, he is guilty under section 47(a) of the Bihar and Orissa Excise Act, section 57 is not applicable and non compliance with the provisions of section 87(b) will not vitiate the proceedings.[3]

XXVIII. Reference to Third Judge

Third Judge should Appreciate Evidence to come to its Conclusion

Where there was difference of opinion between the two Judges of High Court and the matter was placed before the third learned Judge and he, instead of

1. *Dr. Partap Singh* v. *Director of Enforcement, Foreign Exchange Regulation Act,* 1985 SCC (Cri) 312: AIR 1985 SC 989: 1986 Cr LJ 824.
2. *State of Haryana* v. *Nauratta Singh,* AIR 2000 SC 1179: 2000 Cr LJ 1710: 2000 AIR SCW 817: JT 2000 (3) SC 85: (2000) 3 SCC 514: 2000 (3) SCJ 174: (2000) 2 SCALE 321: 2000 (2) Supreme 249: 2000 (1) UJ (SC) 792.
3. *Appauna* v. *State,* 52 Cr LJ 119 (Ori).

appreciating the evidence, as a court of appeal would do, merely stated the conclusion of the two judges, who originally heard the appeal and differed from each other and then he agreed with the conclusion of one of the two judges, it was held that he failed to discharge his duty and obligation as an appellate court, in appreciating the evidence and coming to its conclusion one way or the other.[1]

XXIX. Remand

Non-production of Accused before the Court on Justifiable Ground

It is always open to either the prosecuting agency or the jail authority to put forward a plea of impossibility of production of an accused person before the learned Magistrate and if the learned Magistrate is satisfied that the plea is well-founded, he may, for special reason to be recorded in writing, extend the remand of the accused person even without his production. There may be cases where it may not be possible for the police or jail authorities to spare escort personnel for production of the accused; grave law and order situations necessitating diversion of the entire police force for that purpose are not uncommon contemporary phenomena. Natural disasters may sometimes compel the Government or District Administration to divert the police force to render help to the victims or to engage in salvaging operations. Communal riots, group clashes and inter-caste feuds threatening the even tempo of the society are no longer rare occurrences. It is not possible to enumerate instances or causes resulting in non-availability of escort personnel for production of the accused before a magistrate under section 167. Therefore, non-availability of police escort is a valid ground for non-production of the accused before the magistrate for extending remand under section 167, the Cr. P.C., provided there are justifiable causes for such non-availability of escort.[2]

XXX. Seal

1. Non-handing over of Seal not Inappropriate

Where in a case there is no independent witness or where the circumstances of the case so warrant, handing over of the seal of one police official to another police official cannot be held to be inappropriate.[3]

2. Handing over Seal to Third Person not Mandatory

There is neither a statutory requirement nor a Constitutional mandate for handing over the seal used by a police official in the course of an investigation to a third person forthwith. Even where it had been so done, the non-production of such witness cannot by itself affect the merits of the trial.[4]

3. Non-handing over of Seal may bring Doubt

Failure on the part of I.O. to make over his seal used on the sample of incriminating articles to another person for two days' time till those samples had

1. *Padam Singh* v. *State of Uttar Pradesh,* AIR 2000 SC 361.
2. *Kurra Dasaratha Ramaiah* v. *State of Andhra Pradesh,* 1992 Cr LJ 3485 AP (DB): 1992 (1) APLJ 186: 1992 APLJ (Cri) 109: 1992 (3) All Cr LR 775: 1992 (1) Andh LT 269: 1992 (1) LS AP 133.
3. *Joginder Singh* v. *State of Punjab,* 1981 CCC 236 P&H.
4. *Piara Singh* v. *State of Punjab,* 1982 CCC 450 (P&H) (FB).

reached the chemical examiner brings in the possibility of those samples being tampered with by the I.O. during transit initially from the place of recovery to the Malkhana of police station and thereafter to the office of chemical examiner.[1]

XXXI. Service of Notice

Notice shall be Deemed to have been Served, if Endorsement Contains that the Addressee was Out of Station

Notice sent by registered post for offence under section 138 of the Negotiable Instruments Act, 1881. Returned with the endorsement that addressee was out of station. Address on notice was correctly given. Notice would be deemed to have been duly served under section 27 of the General Clauses Act, 1897.[2]

XXXII. Withdrawal of Cases

1. Withdrawal to be by Prosecutor Dealing with the Case

The reasonable interpretation to be placed upon section 494, is that it is only the Public Prosecutor, who is in charge of a particular case and is actually conducting the prosecution, that can file an application under that section, seeking permission to withdraw from the prosecution. If a public prosecutor is not in charge of a particular case and is not conducting the prosecution, he will not be entitled to ask for withdrawal from prosecution, under section 494 of the Code.[3]

2. In Withdrawal of Cases the matter is not to be Determined Judicially

Section 321 providing for withdrawal from prosecution gives no indication as to the grounds on which the public prosecutor may make the application, or the considerations on which the court is to grant its consent. The initiative is that of the public prosecutor and what the court has to do is only to give its consent and not to determine any matter judicially. The judicial function implicit in the exercise of the judicial discretion for granting the consent would normally mean that the court has to satisfy itself that the executive function of the public prosecutor has not been improperly exercised, or that it is not an attempt to interfere with the normal course of justice for illegitimate reasons or purposes. When an application under section 321 is made, it is not necessary for the court to assess the evidence to discover whether the case would end in conviction or acquittal. The court's function is to give consent. This section does not obligate the court to record reasons before consent is given. However, it does not mean that consent of the court is a matter of course. When the public prosecutor makes the application for withdrawal after taking into consideration all the materials before him, the court exercises its judicial discretion by considering such material and on such consideration; either gives consent or declines consent. The section should not be construed to mean that the court has to give a detailed reasoned order when it gives consent. All that is necessary to satisfy the section is to see that the public prosecutor acts in good faith and that the Magistrate is satisfied that the exercise

1. *Subeg Singh* v. *State of Haryana,* 1992 (III) Crimes 155 (P&H).
2. *Aparna Agencies, Hyderabad* v. *P. Sudhakar Rao,* 2000 Cr LJ 1005: 2000 (1) All Cr LR 179: 1999 (5) Andh LD 16: 2000 (4) Civ LJ 54: 2000 (1) Crimes 86.
3. *State of Punjab* v. *Surjit Singh,* AIR 1967 SC 1214: (1967) 1 SCWR 90: 1967 (1) SCA 563: 1967 Cr LJ 1084: 1967 SCD 618: (1967) 2 SCR 347.

of discretion by the public prosecutor is proper. This will be clear on perusal of some other provisions in the Code such as sections 203, 227, 245, 257 and 258 which relate to the manner in which courts have to exercise their jurisdiction in pending cases when applications are made for their withdrawal or when the court finds that there is no ground to proceed with the cases and section 320 which is a kindred section. While sections 203, 227, 245, 257 and 258 require the magistrate to record his reasons for the order he passes, section 320 contemplates consent by the court only in a supervisory manner and not in an adjudicatory manner.

Where the application for withdrawal of prosecution by the Public Prosecutor was made in good faith after careful consideration of the materials placed before him and the order of consent given by the magistrate was also after due consideration of various details, it would be improper for the Supreme Court, keeping in view the scheme of section 321, to embark upon a detailed enquiry into the facts and evidence of the case or to direct retrial for that would be destructive of the object and intent of section 321.[1]

A magistrate cannot reject an application filed under section 321 of the Cr. P.C. for withdrawal from prosecution on the ground that the offences are exclusively triable by a court of sessions and, therefore, he is not competent to decide the application. Though the offences are exclusively triable by a court of sessions, the magistrate can give consent to the public prosecutor to withdraw from prosecution when he is satisfied that on facts and circumstances stated in the application under section 321 of the Cr. P.C. the prayer for withdrawal is justified and proper.[2]

3. *Public Prosecutor and the Court should Apply its Mind before Withdrawal of Cases*

The power of the court under section 321, the Cr.P.C. is supervisory but that does not mean that while exercising that power, the consent has to be granted on mere asking. The court has to examine that all relevant aspect have been taken into consideration by the public prosecutor and/or by the Government in exercise of its executive function.

Even if the State Government orders to withdraw prosecution proceedings, it is for the public prosecutor to apply his mind to all the relevant material and, in good faith, to be satisfied thereon that the public interest will be served by his withdrawal from the prosecution. In turn, the court has to be satisfied, after considering all that material, that the public prosecutor has applied his mind independently thereto, that the public prosecutor, acting in good faith, is of the opinion that his withdrawal from the prosecution is in the public interest, and that such withdrawal will not stifle or thwart the process of law or cause manifest injustice.

---

1. *Sheo Nandan Paswan* v. *State of Bihar,* 1987 Cr LJ 793 SC: JT 1986 SC 1132: 1987 SCC (Cri) 82: 1986 (4) Supreme 393: (1987) 1 SCC 288: 1987 Cr LR (SC) 51: 1987 (1) SCJ 595.
2. *Niranjan Pradhan* v. *State,* 1991 Cr LJ 224 Ori: 1991 (71) Cut LT 419: 1990 (2) Ori LR 384.

Prosecutor has to apply his mind in withdrawal of cases and court has also to satisfy itself about that before permitting withdrawal.[1]

XXXIII. Witness: Official/Independent

1. Single Witness is Sufficient to Prove Guilt

Even a single witness can be sufficient to prove the guilt of the accused, if found entirely reliable. Evidence has to be weighed and not counted.[2]

2. Conviction not to be Based on Stock Witness of Police

The conviction should not be based on the evidence of a person who is proved to be a stock witness of the police and has been going about, giving evidence in various police cases from different localities and who does not appear to have care to speak the truth in the witness box.

In order to avoid criticism, the police while arranging a raid should always make an earnest effort to associate with the outsiders, having some status in life. No hard and fast rule can be laid down about the association in a raiding party of an upper division clerk serving the Government. It cannot be said that such a witness has no such status as to justify conviction being based on his corroboration.[3]

3. Non-production of a Witness is a Serious Defect

A witness, who has been named as an eye-witness in the First Information Report, if not produced, would seriously affect the truth of the prosecution case. The mere presentation of an application to the effect that a witness had been won over was not conclusive of the question that the witness has been won over. The High Court rightly acquitted the accused.[4]

4. Supreme Court can Appraise Evidence in a Special Case

On going through the record and examining the evidence we are clear that there is no legal evidence on the record on which we can sustain the conclusions of the courts below that it was the appellant's house which was searched.

Normally this court of course, does not examine for appraisal under article 136 of the Constitution the evidence on questions of fact decided by the courts below. But when there are reasons to think that the conclusions may be based on no evidence, then this court is not only entitled but it has an obligation in the larger interests of justice to examine the evidence to see if there is legal evidence on which those conclusions can be sustained.[5]

5. Evidentiary Value of Signed Statement

The mere fact that signature of the witness was obtained on the statement by the investigating officer made by him does not by itself justify the rejection of his

1. *Abdul Karim* v. *State of Karnataka*, 2000 (4) Crimes 203 (SC): 2000 AIR SCW 3980: 2001 Cr LJ 148: (2000) 8 SCC 710.
2. *Thevar* v. *State of Madras*, AIR 1957 SC 614: 1957 Cr LJ 1000: 1957 All LJ 898: 1957 SCA 798: 1957 SCJ 527.
3. *Ved Parkash* v. *State*, 1965 PLR (Del Bench) 318.
4. *State of Uttar Pradesh* v. *Jaggo* alias *Jagadish*, AIR 1971 SC 1581.
5. *Ghuran Yadav* v. *State of Bihar*, AIR 1971 SC 1641: 1972 Pat LJR 96: 37 Cut LT 338: 1971 UJ (SC) 245: 1971 SCD 289: 1971 Cr LJ 1197.

evidence. But where the witness had been put under influence that since he had given a signed statement he was bound to repeat the same in court. The evidence given by him cannot be safely relied on 1968 Cr LJ 493 (Mad).[1]

6. Evidence of Partisan Witness can be Acted Upon

There is no hard and fast rule that the testimony of a partisan witness cannot be acted upon without corroboration. If his presence at the place of occurrence cannot be doubted and his evidence is consistent with the surrounding circumstances and the probability of the case strike the court as true, it can be a good foundation for conviction, more so, if assistance is available from medical evidence.[2]

7. Evidence of Investigating Officer can be Believed

If the evidence of the Investigating Officer who recovered the material is convincing, there is no reason to say that if the seizure witnesses did not support the prosecution version, it must fail.[3]

8. Minor Variation would not be Material

Where an eye-witness to the scene of occurrence stated that he saw 'S' giving blows with a stick to the accused and later diluted it by saying that he had seen S "trying'" or attempting to hit the accused with a stick when the latter had just started running away after stabbing *S's* father.

Held that such a minor variation between what he said on the point in examination-in-chief and cross-examination did not affect his credibility, when the witness was consistent as to the point of substance namely, those stick-blows to the accused were given or attempted by *S* after the accused had stabbed the deceased (*S's* father) in the abdomen and not before.[4]

9. Minor Discrepancies are Immaterial

The mere fact that the witnesses had succeeded in escaping unhurt or that there are discrepancies in the statements of the two witnesses as to whether they had gone to Amarkot with the deceased on the very day of occurrence or a day earlier, is no ground for jumping to the conclusion that the witnesses were not in the company of the deceased or near about the scene of occurrence when the deceased persons were shot dead.

Where the witnesses were examined at the trial 17 months after the incident, such discrepancies in regard to collateral or subsidiary facts or matters of details occur even in the statements of truthful witnesses, particularly when they are examined to depose to events which happened long before their examination. Such discrepancies are hardly a ground to reject the evidence of the witnesses when

---

1. *Vyas Tewari* v. *State,* 1973 Cr LJ 1420 All.
2. *Tameshawar Sahi* v. *State of Uttar Pradesh,* AIR 1976 SC 59: 1975 Cr LR (SC) 617: 1976 Cr LJ 6: 1976 SCC (Cri) 19: (1976) 1 SCC 401: ILR 1976 Kant 410: 1976 (2) SCJ 69: 1975 UJ (SC) 891.
3. *Modan Singh* v. *State of Rajasthan,* AIR 1978 SC 1511: 1978 Cr LJ 1531.
4. *State of Maharashtra* v. *Krishnamurti Laxmipati Naidu,* AIR 1981 SC 617: 1981 Cr LJ 9: 1981 Cr LR (SC) 145: 1981 SCC (Cri) 364: 1980 Supp SCC 455.

there is general agreement and consistency in regard to the substratum of the prosecution case.[1]

10. Evidence of Sole Witness of Close Relation of the Deceased unless he is very Reliable would not be Sufficient for Conviction

It is not necessary in law that more than one witness should be examined to prove a fact but unless the witness is very reliable, the court would ordinarily look for corroboration. Hence, where in a murder trial the only prosecution witness who supported the case was a close relation of the deceased and though he claimed to know the accused, it transpired from his evidence that he was a stranger so far as the accused were concerned; the High Court was justified in acquitting the accused.[2]

11. Accused can be Convicted on the Basis of Interested Witness

There is no law, which says that in the absence of any independent witness, the evidence of interested witness should be thrown out at the behest of or should not be relied upon for convicting an accused. What the law requires is that where the witnesses are interested, the court should approach their evidence with care and caution in order to exclude the possibility of false implication. The evidence of interested witnesses is not like that of an approver, which is presumed to be tainted and requires corroboration but the said evidence is as good as any other evidence. In a faction ridden village, it will really be impossible to find independent persons to come forward and give evidence and in a large number of such cases only partisan witnesses would be natural and probable witnesses. Once it is found by the court, on an analysis of the evidence of an interested witness that there is no reason to disbelieve him then the mere fact that the witness is interested cannot persuade the court to reject the prosecution case on that ground alone.[3]

12. Evidence of Police Official is Reliable

The police officials do not suffer from any disability to give evidence and the mere fact that they are police officials does not by itself give rise to any doubt about their creditworthiness. The independent panch witness could not be located in spite of serious efforts and could not be examined at the trial. Their non-production has not created any dent in the prosecution.[4]

13. Investigation Officer is not at all a Material Witnesses

It is unfortunate that investigating officer has not stepped into the witness box without any justifiable grounds. But this conduct of the investigating officer or

---

1. *State of Punjab* v. *Wassan Singh*, AIR 1981 SC 697: 1981 Cr LJ 410: 1981 Cr LR (SC) 122: (1981) 2 SCC 1: 1981 SCC (Cri) 292: (1981) 2 SCR 615.
2. *State of Uttar Pradesh* v. *Satish Chandra*, 1985 Cr LJ 1921 SC: AIR 1986 SC 313: 1986 All LJ 162: 1986 All Cr LJ 14 SC: 1985 (2) Crimes 861: 1985 SCC (Cri) 508: 1985 SCC (Supp) 596: 1986 (1) Supreme 35.
3. *State of Uttar Pradesh* v. *Ballabh Das*, 1985 Cr LJ 2009 SC: AIR 1985 SC 1384: 1986 All LJ 175: 1986 All Cr LJ 16 SC: (1985) 3 SCC 703: (1986) 1 SCWR 97: 1985 SCC (Cri) 452: 1985 UJ (SC) 906.
4. *Anil Nandoskar* v. *State of Maharashtra*, AIR 1996 SC 2493: 1996 (1) Crimes 103: (1996) 2 SCC 589: (1996) 2 SCR 807: 1996 SCC (Cri) 356: JT 1996 (3) SC 120.

other hostile witnesses cannot be a ground for discarding the evidence of PW5 and PW7 whose presence on the spot is established beyond reasonable doubt. They have suffered injuries and their evidence is corroborated by medical evidence. It is also in conformity with what has been stated in the FIR. In any case, investigating officer is not at all material witness for the purpose of establishing whether accused or the complainant party was the aggressor. Not only that, accused have examined the defense witnesses for establishing their say. Hence, non-examination of the investigation officer cannot be a ground for holding that injured witnesses should not be believed.[1]

14. Witness – Relatives

Evidence of close relations cannot be rejected merely on ground that they happened to be relatives – However, evidence of such witness must be scrutinized carefully – Both the witnesses giving minute details of weapons used by each of the accused and manner of assaulting the deceased – Their evidence corroborated from the fact that bloodstained earth seized from the place of occurrence contained human blood – In the facts and circumstances of the case non-explanation of one of the two gunshot injuries by the two witnesses would neither dilute their evidence nor could their presence be doubted.

Prosecution examining two relatives of the deceased – Non-examination of other independent witness who came to the place of occurrence cannot be a ground to discredit the evidence of the said two eyewitnesses.[2]

15. Recalling of Witnesses

Defence counsel expired after cross-examination. New defence counsel has right to recall witnesses for fresh cross-examination.[3]

16. Official Witness

There is no prohibition on a conviction being recorded on the basis of testimony of official witnesses if they are found to be trustworthy.[4]

17. Solitary Witness

Testimony of a solitary witness can be made the basis of conviction. The credibility of the witness requires to be tested with reference to the quality of his evidence which must be free from blemish or suspicion and must impress the court as natural, wholly truthful and so convincing that the court has no hesitation in recording a conviction solely on his uncorroborated testimony.[5]

---

1. *Ambika Prasad* v. *State (Delhi Administration, Delhi)*, 83 (2000) DLT 476 (SC): AIR 2000 SC 718: 2000 Cr LJ 810: 2000 AIR SCW 253: (2000) 2 SCC 646: 2000 (2) SCJ 472: (2000) 1 SCALE 219: 2000 SCC (Cri) 522: 2000 (2) Supreme 633.
2. *Hardev Singh* v. *Harbhaj Singh*, 1997 Cr LJ 727: 1997 AIR SCW 203: 1996 (4) Crimes 216: JT 1997 (1) SC 29: (1997) 1 SCC 80: 1996 (4) SCJ 173: 1997 SCC (Cri) 5.
3. *Hoffman Andreas* v. *Inspector of Customs*, (2000) 11 AD Cr SC 781: 2000 (4) Crimes 228 (SC).
4. *Khalek Sheikh* v. *State of West Bengal*, VI (2006) SLT 565: (2006) 7 SCC 439.
5. *Bhimappa Chandappa* v. *State of Karnataka*, VI (2006) SLT 587.

18. Relative Witness

In regard to the interestedness of the witness for furthering the prosecution version, relationship is not a factor to affect the credibility of a witness. It is more often than not that a relation would not conceal the actual culprit and make allegations against an innocent person. Foundation has to be laid if plea of false implication is made. In such cases the court has to adopt a careful approach and analyze evidence to find out whether it is cogent and credible.[1]

19. Relative Witness

Merely because eyewitnesses are family members their evidence cannot *per se* be discarded. When there is allegation of interestedness, the same has to be established. Mere statement that being relatives of the deceased they are likely to falsely implicate the accused cannot be aground to discard the evidence, which is otherwise cogent and credible.[2]

Relationship is not a factor to affect credibility of a witness. It is more often than not that a relation would not conceal actual culprit and make allegations against innocent persons leaving away to the real culprit to escape.[3]

20. Interested Witness

"It was contended that the only eye-witness was the son of the deceased. He was, therefore, 'highly interested' witness and his deposition should, therefore, be discarded as it has not been corroborated in material particulars by other witnesses. We are unable to uphold the contention. In our judgment, a witness who is a relative of the deceased or victim of a crime cannot be characterized as 'interested'. The term 'interested' postulates that the witness has some direct or indirect 'interest' in having the accused somehow or the other convicted due to animous or for some other oblique motive.[4]

57. Compounding of certain offences.—(1) Minor offences shall be compoundable under this Act.

(2) Any person who is reasonably suspected of having committed a minor offence under this Act, may apply to the Assistant Commissioner for compounding of the offence, before he is convicted.

(3) On receipt of such application, the Assistant Commissioner, having regard to the circumstances of the case, may in his discretion order for compounding of the offence on payment of a sum of money by way of compounding fee or compensation for the offence on such terms and conditions as he deems fit.

---

1. *Kalegura Padma Rao* v. *State of Andhra Pradesh,* II (2007) SLT 665: 2007 AIR SCW 1447: 2007 (2) Crimes 217: (2007) 3 SCALE 209: 2007 (2) Supreme 551.
2. *Vinay Kumar Rai* v. *State of Bihar,* 1 (2009) SLT 134: AIR 2008 SC 3276: (2008) 12 SCC 202: (2008) 11 SCALE 353: 2009 (1) SCC (Cri) 406.
3. *M.C. Ali* v. *State of Kerala,* III (2010) SLT 213 (224).
4. *Namdeo* v. *State of Maharashtra,* III (2007) SLT 666: 2007 AIR SCW 1835: (2007) 4 SCALE 337: 2007 (3) Supreme 643.

(4) On payment by the person such sum of money such person, if in custody, shall be set at liberty and no proceeding shall be instituted or continued against such person in any criminal court:

Provided that the sum of money fixed as compounding fee or compensation by the Assistant Commissioner under this section shall not be less than five times and not be more than ten times the duty involved or value of intoxicant, apparatus, vehicle and other material, whichever is higher:

Provided further that where intoxicant, apparatus, vehicle or other material is seized, the same shall not be released but shall be disposed of in such manner as may be prescribed.

58. Certain things liable to confiscation.—Whenever an offence has been committed, which is punishable under this Act, following things shall be liable to confiscation, namely—

(a) any intoxicant, material, still, utensil, implement, apparatus in respect of or by means of which such offence has been committed;

(b) any intoxicant unlawfully imported, transported, manufactured, sold or brought along with or in addition to, any intoxicant, liable to confiscation under clause (a);

(c) any receptacle, package, or covering in which anything liable to confiscation under clause (a) or clause (b), is found, and the other contents, if any, of such receptacle, package, or covering;

(d) any animal, vehicle, vessel, or other conveyance used for carrying the same.

59. Confiscation by Deputy Commissioner in certain cases.—(1) Notwithstanding anything contained in this Act or any other law for the time being in force, where anything liable for confiscation under section 58 is seized or detained under the provisions of this Act, the officer seizing and detaining such property shall, without any unreasonable delay, produce the said seized property before the Deputy Commissioner.

(2) On production of the said seized property under sub-section (1), the Deputy Commissioner if satisfied that an offence under this Act has been committed may, whether or not prosecution is instituted for the commission of such an offence, order confiscation of such property, otherwise he may order its return to the rightful owner.

(3) While making an order of confiscation under sub-section (2), the Deputy Commissioner may also order that such of the properties to

which the order of confiscation relates, which in his opinion cannot be preserved or are not fit for human consumption, be destroyed. Whenever any confiscated article has to be destroyed in conformity with these provisions, it shall be destroyed in the presence of the excise officer not below the rank of an inspector.

(4) Where the Deputy Commissioner, after passing an order of confiscation under sub-section (2), is of the opinion that it is expedient in the public interest so to do, he may order the confiscated property or any part thereof to be sold by public auction or dispose it of otherwise.

(5) When an order for confiscation of any property has been passed under section 58 and such order has become final in respect of the whole or any portion of such property, such property or portion thereof, as the case may be, shall vest in the Government free from all encumbrances.

(6) The Deputy Commissioner shall submit a report of all particulars of confiscation to the Excise Commissioner within one month of such confiscation.

(7) Any intoxicant, mahua flowers or molasses and any other property if confiscated in a case compounded under section 57 of the Act or in respect of which an offence has been committed and the offender is not known or cannot be found, shall be disposed of in the manner as prescribed.

60. Order of confiscation and destruction not to interfere with other punishment.—(1) The order of confiscation under section 58 shall not prevent imposition of any other punishment to which a person is liable under this Act.

(2) Notwithstanding anything contained in any other law for the time being in force, the disposal of goods in the manner, thereby non-production of case property before the trial court, shall not affect the conviction for an offence under this Act:

Provided that the samples of the intoxicants and the photographs of the confiscated property may be preserved to meet the evidentiary requirements.

SYNOPSIS

1. **Release of the Property Seized**
2. **Non-production of Case Property by itself Would not Vitiate Conviction**
3. **Non-production of Pitcher of Lahan Would not Warrant Acquittal**
4. **Non-production of Case Property Would not Vitiate Conviction**
5. **Conviction Would not be Safe when Empty Tube, which Contained 60 Bottles of Illicit Liquor was Produced in the Court**
6. **Non-production of Case Property Would not Vitiate Conviction**

7. Without Case Property Accused can be Convicted on other Reliable Evidence
8. Material Exhibits should be Kept Intact Till they are Produced in the Court
9. Destroying Remaining Liquor after taking Sample is Merely an Irregularity
10. Production of Case Property is only Corroborative Piece of Evidence
11. Seizure/Confiscation
(i) High Court has Power to Release Vehicle under Article 226
(ii) Goods can be Confiscated without Ascertaining the Real Owner
(iii) Release of Seized property to be a Rule
(iv) Inherent Powers of High Court cannot be Invoked to Return Seized Property
(v) Filing of Complaint in the Court Would not Divest the Officers of the Custody of Property
(vi) Special Provision to Prevail over General Provision
(vii) Notice Necessary before Confiscation
(viii) At the Stage of Notice Writ can be Entertained only for Want of Jurisdiction
(ix) Confiscating Authority has Power to Order Confiscation Irrespective of Pendency of Criminal Case
(x) Driver Employed by Owner Confiscation held Valid
(xi) Where the Court holds that there was no Misdeclaration the Authority Would Return Money Released on Sale of Goods with Interest
(xii) Confiscation no Bar to Prosecution

Comments

1. Release of the Property Seized

Chapter 34, the Cr.P.C., deals with disposal of property. Section 451 deals with property produced before Court, section 452 deals with property after the trial is concluded and section 457 with property seized and not produced before court, as in the present case. But the question of releasing the property to the claimant has to be decided by the Court on the merits in each case and this discretion of the court has to be exercised after due consideration of the interests of justice including the prospective necessity of the production of the seized property at the time of the trial. If the release of the property will, in any manner, affect or prejudice the course of justice at the time of trial, it will be a wise exercise of discretion to reject the claim for return.[1]

2. Non-production of Case Property by itself would not Vitiate Conviction

Held: Its presence or absence cannot render the statements of witnesses in admissible if the same are otherwise worthy of credit. The conviction was maintained.[2]

3. Non-production of Pitcher of Lahan Would not Warrant Acquittal

The mere fact that pitcher of lahan was not produced in court was held to be not sufficient to warrant acquittal.[3]

---

1. *Ram Prakash Sharma* v. *State of Haryana*, 1978 SCC (Cri) 309: AIR 1978 SC 1282: 1978 Cr LJ 1120.
2. *Ghulla Singh* v. *State of Punjab*, 1981 Cr LT 309.
3. *Teja Singh* v. *State of Punjab*, 1982 Ch LR 144.

4. Non-production of Case Property Would not Vitiate Conviction

Non-production of a part or whole of the case property in a criminal trial would not by itself vitiate the conviction of the accused.[1]

5. Conviction Would not be Safe when Empty Tube, which Contained 60 Bottles of Illicit Liquor was Produced in the Court

Where the petitioner was alleged to have been found in possession of a tube containing 60 bottles of illicit liquor and during trial only empty tube was produced, it was held that it was not safe to maintain the conviction.[2]

6. Non-production of Case Property would not Vitiate Conviction

Mere non-production of case property would not by itself vitiate the conviction of the accused.[3]

7. Without Case Property Accused can be Convicted on other Reliable Evidence

Production of such liquor at trial tends assurance to the fact of possession. If I.D. liquor is not produced, it cannot be conclusively held that accused was not in possession of it. Without such production also, court can convict a person if otherwise it accepts the evidence that accused was in possession of I.D. liquor.[4]

8. Material Exhibits should be Kept Intact Till they are Produced in the Court

When the articles of still were produced in the court they did not bear identification marks. The boiler was not fit for use and in the plastic can there was no liquor. It was the duty of the prosecution to have kept the material exhibits of the case intact till they were produced in the court.[5]

9. Destroying Remaining Liquor after taking Sample is Merely an Irregularity

After seizure of liquor PW-3 took three samples of the liquor in three bottles and destroyed the remaining part of the liquor.

Held: It is true that the Act does not empower the seizing officer, to destroy any part of the illicit liquor seized and, on the other hand, it requires him to produce the seized articles before the court but, his action destroying the remaining part of liquor after taking samples is only an irregularity which does not vitiate either the seizure or the prosecution of the trial. Revision petitioner can take advantage of this irregularity only if he satisfies the court that such irregularity has prejudiced the defence.[6]

10. Production of Case Property is only Corroborative Piece of Evidence

Production of case property in the court is only corroborative piece of evidence. If the direct evidence is credible and unimpeachable and in the view of the court is sufficient to establish the charge and a consequent conviction, it cannot be said

1. *Balraj Singh* v. *State of Punjab,* 1982 CCC 204 (P&H).
2. *Shubeg Singh* v. *State of Punjab,* 1983 CCC 1 (P&H).
3. *Jasbir Singh* v. *State of Haryana,* 1989 CCC 517 (P&H).
4. *Tirtha Naik* v. *State of Orissa,* 1991 Cr LJ 2182 Ori: 1991 (4) OCR 209.
5. *Nanak* alias *Kaddul* v. *State of Punjab,* 1992 (III) Crimes 457 (P&H).
6. *Sukhlal* v. *State of Madhya Pradesh,* 1995 Cr LJ 1234 MP.

that the whole of it would lose its value by the mere non-production of the case property, which is merely corroborative. The trial of offences and their punishments is a matter of substance which turns on the weight and the credibility of the direct evidence and not merely on the technicalities of the procedure. This view finds affirmation in a Division Bench judgment of this court rendered in *Balraj Singh* case.[1]

11. Seizure/Confiscation

(i) High Court has Power to Release Vehicle under Article 226

It has never been disputed that this court has powers under article 226 to entertain application for release of vehicle, pending confiscation proceedings.[2]

(ii) Goods can be Confiscated without Ascertaining the Real Owner

Proceedings for confiscation of contraband or smuggled goods under section 167(8), Sea Customs Act are proceedings in rem and therefore such goods can be confiscated without proceeding against any person and without ascertaining who is their real owner or who was actually concerned in their illicit import.[3]

We find that a later division bench consisting of Kondaiah, C.J. and Punnayya, J. in *Mohd. Yaseen* v. *Forest Range Officer, Flying Squad, Rayachoti,* (1980) 1 Andh LT 8 approved of the view expressed by Jeewan Reddy, J. in *P.K. Mohammad* case, and held that the Act contemplates two procedures, one for confiscation of goods forming the subject-matter of the offence by the Authorized Officer under sub-section (2A) of section 44 of the Act, and the other for trial of the person accused of the offence so committed under section 20 or 29 of the Act. The learned Judges held that the Act provides for a special machinery for confiscation of illicitly felled timber or forest produce by the Authorized Officer under sub-section (2A) of section 44 enacted in the general public interest to suppress the mischief of ruthless exploitation of government forests by illicit felling and removal of teak and other valuable forest produce. They further held that merely because there was an acquittal of the accused in the trial before the Magistrate due to paucity of evidence or otherwise did not necessarily entail in nullifying the order of confiscation of the seized timber or forest produce by the Authorized Officer under sub-section (2A) of section 44 of the Act based on his satisfaction that a forest offence had been committed in respect thereof. We affirm the view expressed by Jeewan Reddy, J. in *P.K. Mohammad* case and by Kondaiah, C.J. and Punnayya, J. in *Mohd. Yaseen's* case.[4]

There is no reason why the ordinary grammatical meaning of the term "goods" should not be applied for the purpose of section 110 of the Customs Act, 1962.

1. *Balraj Singh* v. *State of Punjab,* 1982 Cr LJ 1374.
2. *J. Palnitkar* v. *State of Andhra Pradesh,* 1955 (3) Andh Leg Dec 80.
3. *Collector of Customs* v. *D. Bhoormull,* 1975 Cr LJ 545 SC: 1974 (2) SCJ 238: (1974) 2 SCC 544: 1974 SCC (Cri) 784: 1975 Cr LJ 545.
4. *Divisional Forest Officer* v. *G.V. Sudhakar Rao,* 1986 SCC (Cri) 34: AIR 1986 SC 328: 1986 (1) Crimes 313: (1985) 4 SCC 573.

There is only one limitation introduced by the section and that is that the goods seizable are only those that are confiscateable under section 115 of the Customs Act, 1962. The dictionary defines "goods" as movables. There is no other meaning attributed to goods in the general sense which would not include a vehicle. It is difficult to give any limited meaning to the term "goods" even if it is to be read with the Preamble to the Act and rule. The purpose of the Act will include effective prevention of the evasions of duty on goods which are manufactured in India and which are subject to duty under the Act. This will involve often confiscation or seizure of goods utilized for the purpose of evading duty on the goods which are chargeable under the Act.[1]

(iii) Release of Seized Property to be a Rule

The release of the seized property should be a rule and rejection may be an exception.[2]

(iv) Inherent Powers of High Court cannot be Invoked to Return Seized Property

Section 482, the Cr. P.C. cannot be invoked for return of goods, seized under the Essential Commodities Act.[3]

(v) Filing of Complaint in the Court Would not Divest the Officers of the Custody of Property

The fact remains that the trucks in question were seized by the customs authorities in exercise of the statutory powers conferred on them by the Act, and as such mere filing of the complaint in court would not divest them of the custody and control of the same so as to vest the same in the criminal court within the meaning of section 451 of the Code of Criminal Procedure, 1973; which will have no application unless the property is produced before the court during the inquiry of trial.[4]

(vi) Special Provision to Prevail over General Provision

It is settled principle of law that when there are two provisions in an Act, one of which is specific or of a special character and the other of a general character, the specific or special provision qualifies the general one and ought to be applied in preference to and unaffected by the general one. Thus where there is a specific provision in an Act which covers a particular case, it is not proper to apply another general provision, the application of which is not free from doubt.[5]

(vii) Notice Necessary before Confiscation

Even if there is no express provision for a notice of hearing such requirement has to be read into the provisions of law. The order of confiscation passed without notice stands vitiated owing to the lapse-committed in not affording opportunity of hearing or showing cause against such application being allowed.[6]

---

1. *P.S.N. Lorry Transport* v. *Collector of Customs and Central Excise,* ILR (1967) 2 Ker 660.
2. *B.K. Patil* v. *State of Mysore,* AIR 1977 SC 1749.
3. *P. Shevaputhiran* v. *The State,* 1982 Cr LJ 556 Mad.
4. *Randhir Singh* v. *Directorate of Revenue, Intelligence,* 1986 Cr LJ 1208 (1213) Del.
5. *Shyam Kishore* v. *MCD,* AIR 1991 Del 104 (FB).
6. *Ishwar Parasram Punjabi* v. *Union of India,* 1990 (48) DLT 224 Del.

(viii) At the Stage of Notice Writ can be Entertained only for Want of Jurisdiction

Writ petition cannot be made at the stage of show cause notice. It cannot be entertained except for want of jurisdiction.[1]

(ix) Confiscating Authority has Power to Order Confiscation Irrespective of Pendency of Criminal Case

It was contended that while the vehicle was ordered to be returned on executing a bond by the trial court, the confiscating officer had no powers to confiscate, by invoking section 14(4) of the Act. It was held by first appellate authority that the confiscating authority has got powers to order confiscation, irrespective of the pending of the criminal case.[2]

(x) Driver Employed by Owner Confiscation held Valid

The truck was confiscated by the authorised officer under the Forest Act as it was carrying unauthorised timber. Petitioner having failed to prove that the driver of offending vehicle was not employed by him, the confiscation of truck was held to be valid.[3]

Where the evidence on record showed that the authorities had failed to establish that the owner of the truck had any knowledge of likelihood of the truck being used for carrying forest produce in contravention of the provisions of the Act, order of confiscation of the truck rightly set aside by High Court under article 227.[4]

(xi) Where the Court holds that there was no Mis-declaration the Authority Would return Money Released on Sale of Goods with Interest

"As the order of confiscation was declared illegal by this Court on the ground that there was no mis-declaration of the goods and that the applicant was entitled to import those goods on the OGL, the confiscated goods, if they had not been disposed of, would have been required to be released in favour of the applicant and the applicant could have claimed damages for the damage to the goods and loss caused to it as a result of illegal retention of the goods by the respondent. The goods having been sold away, the respondent is now not in a position to return the goods to the applicant. The applicant has become entitled to the value of the goods as on the date or time when the goods ought to have been cleared by the respondent for home consumption. This court also cannot accept the contention of the learned counsel for the respondent that if the applicant has suffered any loss as a result of wrongful act of the respondent, then he should file an action in the tort and this court cannot order payment of any amount on these applications. Directed to return the amount with simple interest @ 12 per cent.[5]

---

1. *A. Abdul Samath* v. *Union of India,* 1996 Cr LJ 727 Mad (DB).
2. *Ganesh* v. *State,* 1997 Cr LJ 126 Mad.
3. *Ram Chandra Singh* v. *State of West Bengal,* 1997 Cr LJ 3576 Cal: 1998 (3) Cur Cri R 60.
4. *Asstt. Forest Conservator* v. *Sharad Ramchandra Kale,* 1998 SCC (Cri) 260: AIR 1998 SC 2927: 1998 AIR SCW 2318: (1998) 1 SCC 48.
5. *Northern Plastics Ltd.* v. *Collector of Customs & Central Excise,* (1999) 6 SCALE 9: 1999 AIR SCW 3664: (2000) 1 SCC 545.

(xii) Confiscation no Bar to Prosecution

"By the impugned judgment the High Court of Karnataka in exercise of power under section 482 of the Code of Criminal Procedure has quashed a criminal proceeding initiated for commission of offence under section 135(B)(2) of the Customs Act, 1962 read with section 85 of the Gold (Control) Act, 1968. The High Court was of the opinion that the gold in question having been confiscated in a proceeding under Chapter XIV of the Customs Act the accused need not be penalized again by being pursued for commission of offence under section 135. This view of the High Court on the face of it is erroneous inasmuch as a confiscation proceeding under Chapter XIV of the Act has got nothing to do with the criminal prosecution under Chapter XVI of the Act. We, therefore, find sufficient substance in the argument of Mr. Veerappa, the learned counsel appearing for the State that the High Court committed error in quashing the criminal proceedings on an erroneous view of the law. But at the same time, we do not think any fruitful purpose will be served by interfering with the said order of the High Court and directing the prosecution to go on after lapse of 18 years. We, therefore, decline to interfere with the impugned order of the High Court. The appeal is accordingly dismissed".[1]

61. Bar of jurisdiction in confiscation.—Whenever any intoxicant, material, still, utensil, implement, apparatus or any receptacle, package, vessel, animal, cart, or other conveyance used in committing any offence, is seized or detained under this Act, no court shall, notwithstanding anything to the contrary contained in any other law for the time being in force, have jurisdiction to make any order with regard to such property.

SYNOPSIS

1. **Special Law Provision will Prevail over General Law**
2. **Goods Seized by Customs Officer, Magistrate has no Jurisdiction**
3. **Provisions of Customs Act will Prevail over the Provisions of Cr. P.C.**
4. **Special Act takes away the Power of the Court under section 452, Cr. P.C.**
5. **After Receipt of Intimation, the Jurisdiction of the Court Stands Ousted**
6. **Vehicle Seized**

Comments

1. Special Law Provision will Prevail over General Law

The anatomy of this saving section, *i.e.*, section 5 of the Cr. P.C is simple, yet subtle. Broadly speaking there are three components to be separated. Firstly the Criminal Procedure Code generally governs matters covered by it. Secondly, if a special or local law exists covering the same area this later law will be saved and will prevail. Thirdly if there is a specific provision to the contrary, then that overrides the special or local law, for example section 433A.[2]

1. *State of Karnataka* v. *Sir Janakusa Jeevansa Bakale,* 1999 (4) Crimes 382 (SC).
2. *Maru Ram Bhewana Ram* v. *Union of India,* AIR 1980 SC 2147: 1980 Cr LJ 1440.

2. Goods Seized by Customs Officer, Magistrate has no Jurisdiction

Cumulative effect of sections 124, 125, 110(2) is that a Magistrate has no jurisdiction to make orders with respect to the goods seized by the Customs Officer and liable to confiscation under the Customs Act, at least before launching of the criminal proceedings. Report of seizure of goods and arrest of accused does not give the magistrate jurisdiction, 1969 Cr LJ 1245 (Del) rel.[1]

3. Provisions of Customs Act will Prevail over the Provisions of Cr. P.C.

When the Customs Act, 1962 embodies elaborate provisions regarding confiscation and when the said provisions are independent of the provisions of Cr.P.C and are protected by provisions of section 5 of the Code, it was the duty of learned magistrate to deliver the cassettes seized in this case to the petitioner.[2]

4. Special Act takes away the Power of the Court under Section 452, Cr.P.C.

A plain reading of section 72 of the U.P. Excise Act, where it has been mentioned that whenever an offence punishable under this Act has been committed, it does not mean it should be committed by a person or group of persons. After going through the prosecution case it appears that for the contraband articles an offence under section 60 of the Act was committed. But for the reasons that none was caught red-handed or that no test-identification parade was held for the identification of the persons who fled away from the place of occurrence, the revisionists and co-accused were acquitted. That does not mean that no offence in respect of the excise material recovered from the car in question was committed. In these circumstances I must hold that even if when a particular person or a group of persons are acquitted for the same reason or other proceeding under section 72 of the Act can be started for confiscation of contraband articles, including the car in which those articles were being transported. The magistrate could have confiscated the articles under section 452 of the Cr. P.C. After acquitting the accused, the magistrate made the observations that the concerned authority may start proceeding under section 72 of the U.P. Excise Act if they so desire and they may issue further order of confiscation of the property.

Held: that when Special Act came into force, power under section 452 is abrogated and conferred it to the district magistrate to exercise it under section 72 of the U.P. Excise Act.[3]

5. After Receipt of Intimation, the Jurisdiction of the Court Stands Ousted

The jurisdiction of the magistrate to pass order regarding temporary custody or disposal of the property is taken away only in cases where confiscation proceeding is initiated followed by intimation in terms of section 52C of Indian Forest Act, 1927.

The intimation was received much after the order for temporary custody was passed by the magistrate. Under the circumstances, the order cannot be termed as

---

1. *Susanta Kumar Adhikary* v. *State of West Bengal,* 1983 Cr LJ 772 Cal: (1983) 1 Crimes 829 (Cal): 1983 Cal WN 287.
2. *Deputy Collector Enforcement* v. *Anoop Kumar,* 1986 (25) ELT 152 (P&H).
3. *Prem Nath Arora* v. *State of Uttar Pradesh,* 1997 Cr LJ 573 All: 1996 (3) All WC 1858: 1997 UP Cri R 46.

without jurisdiction and the learned Addl. Sessions Judge was also, therefore, right in upholding the order. However now that the intimation in terms of section 52C has been received by the learned Magistrate his jurisdiction to deal with the property any further stands ousted. He cannot, therefore, now pass any final order regarding disposal of the property. The Authorised Officer has now acquired jurisdiction to deal with such property.

For this purpose he is now free to direct production of the property before him and deal with the same in accordance with the provisions of section 52 of the Act.[2]

6. Vehicle Seized

The vehicle carrying liquor was seized in terms of section 55(a) of the Kerala Abkari Act. The application for the release of vehicle was rejected on the ground that the vehicle was entrusted to the Assistant Commissioner for the purpose of confiscation, who directed to furnish Bank Guarantee equal to the value of vehicle as fixed by the Mechanical Engineer. On appeal the High Court directed to release the vehicle on executing a bond with two sureties for the like amount.

In appeal the Apex Court held that the High Court ought not to have interfered in matter where statutory remedies are provided by way of revision to the Commissioner. Moreover the High Court has not indicated as to why that part of the order was interfered with and directed to furnish Bank Guarantee for the sum of Rs. 25,000.00 in addition to surety bond.[3]

62. Relevancy of statements under certain circumstances.—(1) A statement made and signed by a person before any gazetted excise officer, during the course of an inquiry or proceeding under this Act shall be relevant for the purpose of proving, in any prosecution for an offence under this Act, the truth of the fact which it contains,—

(a) when the person who made the statement is dead or cannot be found, or is incapable of giving evidence, or is kept out of the way by the adverse party, or whose presence cannot be obtained without an amount of delay or expense which, under the circumstances of the case, the Court considers unreasonable; or

(b) when the person who made the statement is examined as a witness in the case before the court and the court is of opinion that having regard to the circumstances of the case, the statement should be admitted in evidence in the interest of justice.

(2) The provisions of sub-section (1) shall, so far as may be, apply in relation to any proceeding under this Act, other than a proceeding before a court, as they apply in relation to a proceeding before a court.

CHAPTER VI

DETECTION, INVESTIGATION AND TRIAL OF OFFENCES

63. Power to obtain information.—The Excise Commissioner or any authorized excise officer may by order, require any person or any establishment deemed reasonably connected with any unlawful handling of any intoxicant to furnish to him such information as may be specified in the order.

64. Landholders, officers and others to give information.—(1) Whenever any liquor is manufactured, imported, exported, transported, collected, possessed or sold in contravention of this Act, the owner or occupier of the land or building or his agent, and every officer of police, land revenue department, local bodies and block development office shall, in the absence of reasonable excuse, be bound to give notice of the fact to an officer of the excise department as soon as the fact comes to his knowledge.

(2) Every person referred to in sub-section (1) shall be bound to assist the excise officers in carrying out the provisions of this Act.

(3) Every excise officer shall be bound to give immediate information to the Deputy Commissioner, of all breaches of any of the provisions of this Act, which may come to his knowledge under sub-section (1) or otherwise.

65. Power of arrest, search and seizures.—(1) Any excise officer may search any place, seize any article and arrest or detain any person if there is a reasonable doubt about them being involved in the commission of an offence under this Act:

Provided that no search shall be deemed to be irregular by reason only of the fact that witness for the search is not inhabitant of the locality in which the place searched is situated.

(2) Save as otherwise expressly provided in this Act, the provisions of the Code of Criminal Procedure, 1973 (2 of 1974) relating to search, seizure, arrest, detention, summons and investigation shall apply, as far as may be, to all actions taken in these respects under this Act.

SYNOPSIS

Comments

I. Arrest

1. Grounds of Arrest to be Given

If a policeman arrests without warrant upon reasonable suspicion of felony, or other crime of a sort, which does not require a warrant, he must in ordinary circumstances inform the person arrested of the true ground of arrest. He is not entitled to keep the reason to himself. In other words a citizen is entitled to know on what charges or on suspicion of what crime he is seized. The requirement that the person arrested should be informed of the reason why he is seized naturally does not exist if the circumstances are such that he must know the general nature of the alleged offence on which he is detained.[1]

2. *It is not Necessary that a Man in Order to get Arrested should be taken Prisoner*

Our legal system does not require that an arrest should be attended with any ritual or even that it should be ostentatious. It is not necessary that a man in order to get arrested should be taken prisoner; nor does the law regard as arrest only the ceremonial or hand-cuff or manacle. An authority is said to arrest another man if it prevents the latter from willing his movements and moving according to his Will. Under enlightened modern conditions it seldom becomes necessary for any police officer or other authority empowered to make arrests to actually seize or even touch a person's body with a view to his restraint. Utterance of a guttural word or sound, a gesture of the index finger or hand, the sway of the head or even the flicker of an eye are enough to convey the meaning to the person concerned that he has lost his liberty.

---

1. *Christie* v. *Leachinskey*, 1947 All ER 567: 1947 AC 573.

The petitioner was arrested by customs officials for his alleged involvement in smuggling. Thereafter, the petitioner was under the custody of Customs Department for 70 hours without interruption, and was detained in Customs House for investigation, without producing him before magistrate within 24 hours. The detention of petitioner by custom officials was, therefore, illegal.[1]

3. Initial Unlawful Detention, No Ground for Release

Accused person under judicial custody on the basis of valid remand order cannot be put to liberty solely on ground that his initial detention was in violation of Constitutional provision under article 20(1).[2]

4. Non-bailable Warrant can be Issued only by Name

A non-bailable warrant can be issued against a person only by name and not by mentioning the designation alone. The person who was the manager at the time of the commission of the offence alone can be proceeded against and not a person who happens to be manager at the time when the warrant is issued.[3]

The term 'arrest' has neither been defined in the Cr.P.C. nor in any other enactment dealing with offences. The word 'arrest' is derived from the French word "*arratrer*' meaning to stop or stay. It signifies a restraint of a person. 'Arrest' then can be defined as 'execution of the command of court of law or of a duly authorised officer'.[4]

II. Search

1. Local Witness – Witness of Non-respectable Person

An omission to get witness of the same locality will be at the most an act of irregularity and will not render the search as illegal.

The fact that the search was witnessed by non-respectable persons, namely two rickshawalas, would not affect the legality of the search, but would affect the weight of the evidence.[5]

2. Respectable Person

Respectable person is one who is impartial and whom the owner and the occupier of the premises searched can *prima facie* rely.[6]

3. Illegal Search

If the accused obstructs illegal search he commits no offence.[7]

4. Seizure of Articles not Vitiated by Illegal Search

So far as alleged illegality of the search is concerned, it is sufficient to say that even assuming that the search was illegal; the seizure of the articles is not vitiated.

---

1. *Kaiser Otmar* v. *State of Tamil Nadu,* 1981 Cr LJ (NOC) 208 (Mad DB): 1981 Mad LW Crl 158.
2. *Bal Mukand Jaiswal* v. *Supdt. District Jail,* 1998 Cr LJ 3343 All (FB).
3. *State of Uttar Pradesh* v. *Carew & Co. Ltd.,* II (1995) CCR 475 All.
4. *Union of India* v. *Pasam Narain Aggarwal,* (2008) 13 SCC 305.
5. *Sunder Singh* v. *State of Uttar Pradesh,* 1956 Cr LJ 801: AIR 1956 SC 411.
6. AIR 1959 Mad 450.
7. *State of Rajasthan* v. *Rehman,* AIR 1960 SC 210: 1960 All Cr R 175: (1960) 1 SCR 991: 1960 Mad LJ (Cri) 424: 1960 SCJ 521: 1960 (26) Cut LT 173: 1960 Cr LJ 286.

In such case the search could be resisted by the person, whose premises are sought to be searched. It may also be that because of the illegality of the search the court may be inclined to examine carefully the evidence regarding the seizure. But beyond these two consequences no further consequence ensues.[1]

5. Criminal Act or Obstruction not Justified, even if Search is Illegal

Even if the search is illegal, it does not justify any obstruction or other criminal acts committed against the person who had conducted the search.[2]

Search conducted by an officer without prior recording of the grounds for his belief that an offence under the Act was likely or being committed, held, illegal and without effect. Conviction based on such illegal search set aside.[3]

6. Grounds of Reasonable Belief to be Recorded before Making Search

The inspector who searched the car of the appellant had not made any record of any ground on the basis of which he had a reasonable belief that an offence under the Act was being committed, before proceeding to search the car and thus the provisions of section 54 of Karnataka Excise Act were not complied with.

Held: This rendered the entire search without jurisdiction and vitiated the conviction. Sections 53 and 54 of the Karnataka Excise Act contain valuable safeguards for the liberty of the citizen in order to protect them from ill-founded or frivolous prosecutions or harassment.[3]

7. Illegal Search will not Affect the Validity of Seizure and Trial

Assuming arguendo that the search was illegal, and then also, it will not affect the validity of the seizure and further investigation by the customs authorities or the validity of the trial, which followed on the complaint of the Assistant Collector of Customs.[4]

8. Conclusions on the Basis of the Reasoning and Discussions

That once an empowered officer or a duly authorised officer acting on prior information is about to search a person it is imperative for him to inform the concerned person of his right under sub-section (1) of section 50 of the NDPS Act of being taken to the nearest gazetted officer or the nearest magistrate for making the search. However, such information may not necessarily be in writing.

(ii) The failure to inform the concerned person about the existence of his right to be searched before gazetted officer would cause prejudice to the accused.

(iii) The search made by an empowered officer, on prior information, without informing the person of his right that if he so requires, he shall be taken before a

---

1. *Radha Kishan* v. *State of Uttar Pradesh,* AIR 1963 SC 822: 1963 All LJ 397: 1963 (2) Lab LJ 667: (1963) 1 Cr LJ 809: 1963 All Cr R 156: (1963) Supp 1 SCR 408.
2. *Shyam Lal Sharma* v. *State of Madhya Pradesh,* AIR 1972 SC 886: 1972 Cr LJ 638: 1972 SCD 423: 1972 (2) SCJ 291: 1972 SCA 181: (1972) 3 SCR 422: 1972 SCC (Cri) 470.
3. *K.L. Subbayya* v. *State of Karnataka,* AIR 1979 SC 711: 1979 Cr LJ 651: (1979) 2 SCC 115: 1979 SCC (Cri) 367: 1979 (1) Kant LJ 410.
4. *State of Maharashtra* v. *Natwarlal,* AIR 1980 SC 593: 1980 Cr LJ 429: 1980 UJ (SC) 171: 1980 Cr LR (SC) 105: (1980) 2 SCR 340.

gazetted officer or a magistrate, may not vitiate the trial, but would render the recovery of the illicit article suspect and vitiate the conviction and sentence of an accused where the conviction has been recorded only on the basis of the possession of the illicit article recovered from his person during search conducted in violation of the provisions of section 50 of the Act.

(iv) We do not express any opinion whether the provisions of section 50 are mandatory or directory, but hold that failure to inform the concerned person of his right as emanating from sub-section (1) of section 50 may render the recovery of the contraband suspect and the conviction and sentence of an accused bad and unsustainable in law.

(v) An illicit article seized from the person of an accused during search conducted in violation of the safeguards provided in section 50 of the Act cannot be used as evidence of proof of lawful possession of the contraband on the accused though any material recovered during that search may be relied upon by the prosecution, in other proceedings, against an accused, notwithstanding the recovery of that material during an illegal search.[1]

III. Investigation

Under the Code, investigation consists generally of the following steps (1) Proceeding to the spot, (2) Ascertainment of the facts and circumstances of the case (3) Discovery and arrest of suspected offender, (4) Collection of evidence relating to the commission of the offence which may consist of, (a) the examination of various persons (including accused) and the reduction of their statements into writing, if the officer thinks fit, (b) the search of places and seizure of things considered necessary for the investigation and to be produced at the trial, and (5) Formation of the opinion as to whether on the material collected there is a case to place the accused before a Magistrate for trial and if so, taking the necessary steps for the same by the filing of charge-sheet under section 173.[2]

1. Parallel Investigation by Excise and Police Officers

In the A.P. Excise Act, 1968 both excise officers and police officers have power to investigate.

Held: It may happen, in some cases, parallel investigations by police and excise officer. But this circumstance is no ground to hold that the police officers have no powers under the Act to file charge-sheet.[3]

Sections 55, 56, 57 and 60(b) of the Karnataka Excise Act make it clear that the investigation done by an Excise Officer empowered in regard to the offences under sections 32, 33 and so on, is recognised to be an investigation done by a police officer in charge of a police station and the report filed by such excise officer after investigation is deemed to be a report by a police officer for the purpose of section

---

1. *State of Punjab* v. *Baldev Singh*, AIR 1999 SC 2378: 1999 (3) Crimes 147: (1999) 6 SCC 172: (1999) SCC (Cri) 1080: 1999 (6) Supreme 159: (1999) 4 SCALE 144 (Constitution Bench).
2. *H.N. Nishbud* v. *State of Delhi*, AIR 1955 SC 196: 1955 Cr LJ 526: 1955 SCA 258: 1955 SCJ 283: 1955 SCR 1150.
3. *Banavath Lalu* v. *The State*, 1996 Cr LJ 1294.

190 of the Cr. P.C. (old) and the Magistrate shall take cognizance of the offence as per section 190(1)(b) of the Code (old), hence section 510 of the Cr. P.C. (old) applies and the chemical examiner's report of the samples is admissible.[1]

2. In a Summons Case Investigation can be Continued beyond Six Months

Magistrate has jurisdiction under section 167(5), the Cr. P.C. to permit the investigation to continue beyond a period of six months in a case triable as summons case, even if an application for this purpose is moved by the prosecution beyond this period. Even if permission is not granted it is open to the prosecution to file charge-sheet if the investigation conducted till then warrants such a course. Therefore, where the magistrate straightway acquits the accused because the investigation had continued beyond six months, the order of acquittal is illegal.

Section 167(5) cannot be read to mean that no permission could be sought from the magistrate once a period of six months has expired. It is evident, that before the magistrate will pass an order stopping further investigation he must give an opportunity to the police to satisfy him that there are any special reasons for continuing the investigation beyond a period of six months. This matter will thus come up for consideration only after six months have run out. If the provision is read to mean that he is powerless to grant permission after lapse of six months it would lead to a peculiar situation that he could not pass an order for continuing the investigation, even if he was of the view that it was in the interest of justice to do so. This would make section 167(5), the Cr. P.C. otiose an unacceptable situation.[2]

3. Effect of Non-examination of Investigating Officer

It is unfortunate that investigating officer has not stepped into the witness box without any justifiable ground. But this conduct of the investigating officer or other hostile witnesses cannot be a ground for discarding the evidence of PW5 and PW7 whose presence on the spot is established beyond reasonable doubt. They have suffered injuries and their evidence is corroborated by medical evidence. It is also in conformity with what has been stated in the FIR. In any case, investigating officer is not at all material witness for the purpose of establishing whether accused or the complainant party was aggressor. Non-examination of the investigating officer cannot be a ground for holding that injured witnesses should not be believed.[3]

66. Duty of police to accept seized articles.—Every officer-in-charge of a police station shall take charge of and keep in safe custody, pending the order of the Magistrate or the Deputy Commissioner, all articles seized under this Act which may be delivered to him and shall

1. *State of Karnataka* v. *Guruva Poojari*, ILR 1975 Kar 1616.
2. *State* v. *Jai Bhagwan*, 1985 Cr LJ 932 Del (DB): 1985 (2) Crimes 97: 1985 (28) DLT 77: 1985 (9) DRJ 4.
3. *Ambika Prasad* v. *Delhi Administration*, 82 (2000) DLT 476 (SC): AIR 2000 SC 718: (2000) 2 SCC 646: 2000 (2) SCJ 472: (2000) 1 SCALE 219: 2000 SCC (Cri) 522: 2000 (2) Supreme 633.

allow the excise officer who may accompany such articles, to affix his seal to such articles and to take samples of and from them.

67. Offences under this Act to be cognizable.—All major offences under this Act shall be cognizable and the provisions of the Code of Criminal Procedure, 1973 (2 of 1974) shall apply to them.

SYNOPSIS

Comments

1. Magistrate should Apply his Mind to the Contents

What is taking cognizance has not been defined in the Criminal Procedure Code and I have no desire to attempt to define it. It seems to me clear however that before it can be said that any Magistrate has taken cognizance of any offence under section 190(1)(a), the Criminal Procedure Code, he must not only have applied his mind to the contents of the petition but he must have done so for the purpose of proceeding in a particular way as indicated in the subsequent provisions of this Chapter – proceeding under section 200 and thereafter sending it for inquiry and report under section 202. When the magistrate applies his mind not for the purpose of proceeding under the subsequent sections of this Chapter, but for taking action of some other kind, *e.g.*, ordering investigation under section 156(3) or issuing a search warrant for the purpose of the investigation, he cannot be said to have taken cognizance of the offence.[1]

2. Cognizance is in Respect of an Offence

Once cognizance has been taken by the magistrate he takes cognizance of an offence, it is his duty to find out who the offenders really are and once he comes to the conclusion that apart from the persons set up by the police, some other persons are involved, it is his duty to proceed against those persons.[2]

3. Magistrate has to Apply his Mind to take Cognizance

Though the expression "taking cognizance" has not been defined in the Code, it can be said that before any magistrate takes cognizance of an offence he must have applied his mind for the purpose of proceeding in a particular way as indicated in the subsequent provisions. When a magistrate applies his mind not for the purpose of proceeding under the subsequent sections but for taking action of some other kind, *e.g.*, ordering investigation under section 156(3) or issuing a warrant for the purpose of such investigation, he cannot be said to have taken cognizance of the offence. AIR 1951 SC 207, Rel on.[3]

4. Both Cognizable and Non-cognizable Offence can be Investigated by Police Inspector

Where the offences committed by the petitioner are of such a nature that they are mingled with each other, the police inspector is justified in conducting investigation into a non-cognizable offence along with the principal offence of criminal breach of trust which is a cognizable offence and in such a case section 155(2) does not stand as a blanket ban in totally disabling the investigation officer from investigating into the other offences under sections 467 and 477A of the Penal Code.[4]

5. Application of Mind of Magistrate for Action under Chapter XV

The expression "taking cognizance of an offence" by the magistrate has not been defined in the Code. The ways in which such cognizance can be taken are set out in clauses (a), (b) and (c) of section 190(1). Whether the magistrate has or has not taken cognizance of the offence will depend on the circumstance of the particular case including the mode in which the case is sought to be instituted, and the nature of the preliminary action, if any, taken by the magistrate. Broadly speaking, when on receiving a complaint, the magistrate applies his mind for the purposes of proceeding under section 200 and the succeeding sections in Chapter XV of the Code of 1973, he is said to have taken cognizance of the offence within the meaning of section 190(1)(a). If instead of proceeding under Chapter XV, he has in the judicial exercise of his discretion, taken action of some other kind, such as issuing a search warrant for the purpose of investigation, or ordering

---

1. *Gopal Das Sindhi*, AIR 1961 SC 986: 1961 2 Cr LJ 39: 1961 Mad LJ (SC) 338: 1961 (1) SCJ 573: 1961 Andh LT 392.
2. *Raghubans Dubey* v. *State of Bihar*, AIR 1967 SC 1167: 1967 Cr LJ 1081: 1967 (2) Andh LT 23: (1967) 2 SCR 423: 1967 (2) SCJ 427: 1968 All LJ 33.
3. *Ajit Singh* v. *State*, 1970 Cr LJ 1075 Del (FB).
4. *In re* – Veerappan, Accused – petitioner, 1971 Cr LJ 1397.

investigation by the police under section 156(3), he cannot be said to have taken cognizance of any offence.[1]

6. Examination of Complainant under Section 200 is Essential

Where a police officer investigates a private complaint and thereafter submits a petition of complaint, he does so not as a public servant but as a complainant and as such his examination under section 200 was essential. Non-examination of the said complainant would affect the jurisdiction of the court to take cognizance and would vitiate the entire trial.[2]

7. Cognizance can be taken after the Expiry of Period of Limitation

Section 468 bars cognizance of certain offences after the period of limitation has expired. Naturally therefore if cognizance is taken against this provision of law, it will be an illegality which cannot be cured. The prosecution cannot be debarred from taking advantage of section 473, the Cr. P.C afterwards. It would not in fact be a case of curing of illegality but would rather be a case of removal of an illegality. Section 473 gives the court an additional power, to take cognizance after the expiry of the period of limitation not only in those cases where the delay has been explained but also in those cases where it is necessary so to do in the interest of justice.[3]

8. Cognizance

Whereas a magistrate orders investigation under section 156(3) of the Code and receives the report thereupon he can act on the report and discharge the accused straightway, issue process against the accused or apply his mind to the complaint filed before him and can take action under section 190.

When a magistrate applies his mind not for the purpose of taking cognizance but for the purpose of ordering investigation under section 156(3) of the Code or for issuing search warrant it cannot be said that the magistrate had taken cognizance.[4]

9. Report without Accompaniments not a Report

On the introduction of section 173 in its form in the Code, the police officer investigating into a cognizable offence is under a statutory obligation to submit alongwith its report under section 173(2) documents purporting to furnish evidence collected in the course of the investigation and the statements of the witnesses and the court before proceeding into the case, is under a duty to enquire whether the accused has been furnished with copies of all relevant documents received under section 173 by the court, a report under section 173(2) minus the accompaniments under section 173(5) cannot clearly be held to be a police report.[5]

---

1. *Devarapalli Lakshminarayana Reddy* v. *V. Narayana Reddy,* 1976 Cr LJ 1361 SC: (1976) 3 SCC 252: 1976 Cr LJ 1361: 1976 (2) SCJ 497: 1976 Supp SCR 524.
2. *Shyama Prasanna Das Gupta* v. *State,* 1976 Cr LJ 1517 Cal (DB).
3. *Roshan Lal* v. *State,* 1977 Cr LJ (NOC) 255 All.
4. *Tula Ram* v. *Kishore Singh,* AIR 1977 SC 2401: 1978 Cr LJ 8.
5. *Satya Narain Musadi* v. *State of Bihar,* AIR 1980 SC 506: 1980 Cr LJ 227: (1980) 3 SCC 152: 1980 SCC (Cri) 660.

10. Cognizance after the Period of Limitation, is to be taken with Care and Caution

A period of limitation has been prescribed under section 468 and the court is enjoined not to take cognizance of an offence specified in sub-section (2) of section 468, after the expiry of the period of limitation. Notwithstanding such a prohibition, in view of the language "except as otherwise provided" in section 468 which includes the one provided under section 473 and with the *non-obstante* clause in section 473, the court is invested with discretionary power to take cognizance of an offence despite the expiry of the period of limitation. The power is hedged with satisfaction of the court on the facts and circumstances of the case (1) that the delay has been properly explained; or (2) that it is necessary to take cognisance in the interest of justice. The court can go into the bar of limitation even after the cognizance was taken on the charge-sheet or complaint, the process was issued and trial was conducted. It is incumbent to give an opportunity to the accused at the time when the question of delay was being considered on the facts and circumstances and explaining the delay or if the court considers necessary in the interests of justice to take cognizance, though delay has not been properly explained.

In construing the delay it is not necessary to meticulously explain every day's delay but may be construed liberally to advance substantial justice when there is no wantom negligence, deliberate inaction or want of *bona fides* in pursuing the prosecution. How the discretion has to be exercised is left to the magistrate concerned depending on the facts and circumstances of each case. It is open to the accused to place the material in regard to want of *bona fides* or diligence in pursuing the prosecution. When the court is condoning the delay, by necessary inference, it is interfering with the right of the accused assuring him of the bar of limitation. Therefore, the court has to be circumspect to put harmonious interpretation of the relevant provisions and has to consider the facts and circumstances in each case and has to exercise the discretion reasonably assigning reasons therefor.[1]

11. Cognizance can be taken in the Absence of the Accused and also by Chief Judicial Magistrate in the Area of his Jurisdiction

Section 190(1)(a) read with sections 200, 202, 203 and 204, the Cr. P.C., leaves no manner of doubt that cognizance of an offence is taken at a stage when the accused is nowhere in the picture before the Magistrate and that, therefore, there is no question of taking cognizance of the offence in the presence of the accused. In other words, cognizance of an offence is not just a question of "can be", but it "has to be" taken in the absence of the accused.

Chief Judicial Magistrate is competent to take cognizance of any offence committed anywhere in his district in an area assigned to some other judicial magistrate subordinate to him, provided complaint or police report is presented in his court, instead of the court area of judicial magistrate.[2]

---

1. *K.Ch. Pandu Ranga Rao* v. *Secretary*, 1985 Cr LJ 176 AP (DB).
2. *Mahesh Chand* v. *State of Rajasthan*, 1985 Cr LJ 301 Raj (FB): AIR 1988 SC 2111: 1989 Cr LJ 121: JT 1988 (1) SC 618.

12. Informant must be given an Opportunity if the Magistrate Decides not to take Cognizance

When on a consideration of the report made by the officer-in-charge of a police station under sub-section (2)(i) of section 173, the Cr. P.C, the magistrate is not inclined to take cognizance of the offence and issue process, the informant must be given an opportunity of being heard so that he can make his submissions to persuade the magistrate to take cognizance of the offence and issue process.[1]

The exercise of the power under section 473, extending the period of limitation by condoning the delay in launching the prosecution, should precede taking cognizance of the offence. While so exercising such discretionary power, the court is obliged to record its order in writing, giving its reasons therefor. Any proceeding culminating in the conviction of a person in a criminal case, the cognizance of which has been taken after the expiry of the period of limitation as prescribed under section 468(2) without first resorting to section 473, is non-est in the eye of law.[2]

13. Magistrate must apply his Mind before taking Cognizance

When the challan is filed against any accused regarding certain offences and the magistrate is satisfied from the papers filed before him that a *prima facie* case is made out against the accused, there is no legal bar for him to take the cognizance against him under the law. Merely because the case against the co-accused is being re-investigated it cannot be said that the magistrate must await the result of the re-investigation before taking cognizance against the accused against whom challan has already been filed. What is necessary is that the magistrate must apply his mind to the challan papers before taking the cognizance.[3]

14. Cognizance can be taken by Magistrate even if Police Report says that No Case is made out

Upon receipt of a police report under section 173(2) a magistrate is entitled to take cognizance of an offence under section 190(1)(b) of the Code even if the police report is to the effect that no case is made out against the accused. The magistrate can take into account the statements of the witnesses examined by the police during the investigation and take cognizance of the offence complained of and order the issue of process to the accused. Section 190(1)(b) does not lay down that a magistrate can take cognizance of an offence only if the investigating officer gives an opinion that the investigation has made out a case against the accused. The magistrate can ignore the conclusion arrived at by the investigating officer and independently apply his mind to the facts emerging from the investigation and take cognizance of the case, if he thinks fit in exercise of his powers under section 190(1)(b) and direct the issue of process to the accused. The magistrate is not bound in such a situation to follow the procedure laid down in sections 200 and

---

1. *Bhagwant Singh* v. *Commissioner of Police*, 1985 Cr LJ 1521 SC: (1985) 2 SCC 537: 1985 (2) Andh LT 1: 1985 UJ (SC) 820.
2. *Kathamuthu* v. *Balammal*, 1987 Cr LJ 360 Mad (DB).
3. *Vardaram* v. *State of Rajasthan*, 1989 Cr LJ 724 Raj.

202 of the Code for taking cognizance of a case under section 190(1)(a) though it is open to him to act under section 200 or section 202 also.[1]

15. Extension of Time by the Court can be given after the Limitation Period is over without Hearing the Accused

Under section 167(5) if in any case triable as a summons case, investigation is not completed within a period of six months from the date on which the accused was arrested, the Magistrate shall order stopping further investigation of the offence unless the officer making investigation into the offence before the expiry of the said six months period satisfied the magistrate that for special reasons and in the interests of justice, the continuation of the investigation beyond the period of six months is necessary. The investigation conducted beyond the period of six months, without the permission of the magistrate as contemplated by the sub-section would be in clear breach of the direction given under the sub-section. The failure on the part of the magistrate to stop investigation on the expiry of six months as provided under the sub-section will not *ipso facto* be deemed to be an implied permission by the magistrate to the Investigating Officer to continue the investigation beyond the prescribed period as the continuation of the investigation beyond the prescribed period would be permitted by the Magistrate only for special reasons and in the interests of justice.

It is also well-settled that once a case is taken cognizance of by a competent court and the proceedings in the case are commenced, the antecedent illegality or irregularity in the investigation on the basis of which the final report has been filed will not invalidate or vitiate the proceedings, unless it is shown that prejudice has been caused thereby to the accused or any miscarriage of justice has resulted thereby. The failure on the part of the court to issue notice to the accused in view of the absence of incorporation of the rule of natural justice in section 473 of the code would not render the grant of extension of time after limitation period is over.[2]

Magistrate can take cognizance of offence if he is satisfied that material placed by the prosecution is sufficient for taking cognizance. He is not debarred from doing so merely because police filed an application, after submission of the charge-sheet, seeking permission to file supplementary charge-sheet. Power of magistrate not controlled by the investigating agency.

It cannot be said that if the investigating officer terms a police report as 'incomplete', it takes away the jurisdiction of the Magistrate to take cognizance of the offence, even if in the opinion of the Magistrate, the material is sufficient for him to be satisfied that it was a fit case for him to take cognizance of the offence.[3]

16. Cognizance means taking Judicial Notice of the Offence

Section 190 of the Cr. P.C talks of cognizance of offences by magistrate. This expression has not been defined in the Code. In its broad and literal sense, it means

1. *India Carat Pvt. Ltd.* v. *State of Karnataka,* 1989 Cr LJ 963 SC: (1989) 2 SCC 132.
2. *State of Karnataka* v. *Laxminarayana Bhat,* 1991 Cr LJ 2126 Kar: 1991 (2) Cr LC 787: 1991 (2) Crimes 251: 1991 (1) Kant LJ 257.
3. *State of Maharashtra* v. *Sharadchandra Vinayak Dongre,* 1995 SCC (Cri) 16: AIR 1995 SC 231: (1995) 1 SCC 42: 1994 AIR SCW 4301.

taking notice of an offence. This would include the intention to initiate judicial proceedings against the offender in respect of that offence or taking steps to see whether there is any basis for initiating judicial proceedings or for other purposes. The word "cognizance" indicates the point when a magistrate or a judge first takes judicial notice of an offence. It is entirely a different thing from initiation of preceding rather it is condition precedent to the initiation of proceedings by the magistrate or the judge. Cognizance is taken of cases and not of persons.[1]

17. Cognizance under section 468 is in Respect of the Offence Charged and not Proved. Period of Limitation would be with Reference to most Severe Offence

Sub-section (3) of section 468 which was added by the Code of Criminal Procedure (Amendment) Act, 1978, provides that in relation to offences which may be tried together, the period of limitation shall be determined with reference to the offence which is punishable with the more or most severe punishment. The language of sub-section (3) of section 468 makes it imperative that the limitation provided for taking cognizance in section 468 is in respect of the offence charged and not in respect of offence finally proved.[2]

18. Court should Apply its mind for the Purpose of Proceeding further in the matter

Taking cognizance would mean the action taken by the court for initiating judicial proceedings against the offender in respect of the offence regarding which the complaint is filed. Before it can be said that any magistrate or court has taken cognizance of an offence it must be shown, that he has applied his mind to the facts for the purpose of proceeding further in the matter at the instance of the complainant. If the magistrate or the court is shown to have applied the mind not for the purpose of taking action upon the complaint but for taking some other kind of action contemplated under the Code of Criminal Procedure such as ordering investigation under section 156(3) or issuing a search warrant, he cannot be said to have taken cognizance of the offence.[3]

19. Magistrate cannot take Cognizance, in Case Triable by Sessions Court against Persons who were not Named in Charge-sheet

Where offence was triable by sessions court the magistrate cannot take cognizance and issue process against those persons who may have been named in the FIR as accused persons, but not charge sheeted in the charge-sheet that was filed by the police under section 173 of the Cr.P.C.[4]

---

1. *State of West Bengal* v. *Mohd Khalid,* 1995 AIR SCW 559: (1995) 1 SCC 684.
2. *State of Himachal Pradesh* v. *Tata Dutta,* 2000 (1) Crimes 15 SC: AIR 2000 SC 297: (2000) 1 SCC 230: (1999) 7 SCALE 183: 2000 SCC (Cri) 125: 1999 (9) Supreme 421: 2000 (1) UJ (SC) 498.
3. *Narsingh Das Tapadia* v. *Goverdhan Das Partani,* 2000 (4) Crimes 12 (SC): 2000 AIR SCW 3268: 2000 (4) Civ LJ 840: 2000 (87) DLT 322: JT 2000 (10) SC 141: (2000) 7 SCC 183: 2001 (1) SCJ 48: 2000 (9) SRJ 36: (2000) 6 SCALE 299: 2000 SCC (Cri) 1326: 2000 (6) Supreme 205: 2001 (1) UC 50.
4. *Kishori Singh* v. *State of Bihar,* 2000 (4) Crimes 158 (SC): 2001 Cr LJ 123: AIR 2000 SCW 4166: 2000 (41) All Cri C 331: 2006 SCC (Cri) 275: 2000 (7) Supreme 182.

Order to SHO to investigate after taking cognizance by the magistrate is bad in law.[1]

20. Taking Cognizance

Cognizance requires intense application of mind to the facts. Mere numbering of application or registration of case is not cognizance.[2]

21. Opinion of Expert

The examination of typewriting and identification of typewriting on which the questioned document was typed is based on a scientific study of certain significant features of the typewriter peculiar to a particular typewriter and its individuality which can be studied by an expert having professional skill in the subject and, therefore, his opinion on that point relates to an aspect in the field of science which falls within the ambit of section 45 of the Indian Evidence Act. The opinion of typewriter expert in this context is admissible under section 45 of the Indian Evidence Act.[3]

68. Certain offences to be non-bailable.—All offences punishable under this Act with imprisonment of two years and more, shall be non-bailable and the provisions of the Code of Criminal Procedure, 1973 (2 of 1974) with respect to non-bailable offences, shall apply to those offences.

SYNOPSIS

1. **Cancellation of Bail under Inherent Power of High Court**
2. **Extension of Authorisation in Custody**
3. **Sessions Judge has No Powers to Stay Bail Order**
4. **Cancellation of Bail**
5. **Bailable and Non-bailable Offences**
6. **Anticipatory Bail – Jurisdiction where Arrest is Apprehended**
7. **Compulsive Bail**
8. **Anticipatory Bail where Arrest is Apprehended**
9. **Cognizance should also be taken within 60 or 90 days**
10. **After Filing of Chargesheet, Section 167 Ceases to Apply**
11. **Anticipatory Bail even after Issue of Process or Committal to Sessions**
12. **Remarkable Security in Bailable Offence**
13. **After Filing of Charge-sheet, Bail matter to be Dealt with by Regular Court**
14. **If Released on Compulsive Bail, automatic Re-arrest not Permissible on Filing Charge-sheet**
15. **Pending Application after Filing of Charge-sheet shall be Treated like Regular Bail Application**
16. **Condition in Bailable Offences**
17. **Forfeiture of Bail Bond**
18. **Delayed Action or Inaction of Court should not Deprive the Accused of his Indefeasible Right**

---

1. *Binoy Jacob* v. *The State,* 2001 VI AD (Del) 520.
2. AIR 2005 AP 274 FB.
3. *State* v. *S.J. Chaudhary,* 1996 (1) Crimes 96 (SC).

19. **Cognizance is taken in Respect of Offence Charged and not in Respect of Offence Finally Proved**
20. **Unreasonable Condition for Bail**
21. **Sureties can Discharge themselves Any time by Handing the Accused to the Custody of Law**
22. **Bail/Parole**
23. **Second Bail Application**
24. **No Second Appeal Against Order Passed by Magistrate under Section 446**
25. **Anticipatory Bail Application**

Comments

1. Cancellation of Bail under Inherent Power of High Court

Under section 561A (old), the High Court has inherent power to cancel the bail granted to a person accused of a bailable offence and in a proper case, such power can be exercised in the interest of justice.

Inherent power conferred on High Courts under section 561A has to be exercised sparingly carefully and with caution and only where such exercise is justified by the tests specifically laid down in the section itself.[1]

2. Extension of Authorisation in Custody

Extension of authorisation in any custody without the production of the accused does not make the order nullity. It introduces irregularity in the proceedings and such a procedure is not approved. Normally authorisation of detention in any custody should not be granted, unless the accused is produced before the magistrate. But in special circumstances, of course, if the court is satisfied in recording the satisfaction for non-production, it is open to the court to extend custody.[2]

3. Sessions Judge has No Powers to Stay Bail Order

Sessions Judge has no power to stay operation of bail order passed by the magistrate. Section 439(2) only empowers him to direct any person who has been released on bail to be arrested and committed to custody.[3]

The principle underlying section 437 is towards granting of bail except in cases where there appear to be reasonable grounds for believing that the accused has been guilty of an offence punishable with death or imprisonment for life and also when there are other valid reasons to justify the refusal of bail. From sub-section (1) to sub-section (7) the changes are from reasonable grounds for believing the accused guilty' to 'reasonable grounds for believing the accused not guilty'. At the stage of section 437(1) the limited enquiry before the magistrate relates to materials for basing the suspicion.

---

1. *Talab Haji Hussain* v. *Madhukar Purshottam Mondkar*, AIR 1958 SC 376: 1958 Mad LJ (Cri) 512: 1958 All Cri R 391: 1958 Cr LJ 701: 1958 SCJ 672: 1958 SCR 1226: 1959 SCA 321.
2. *Raj Narain* v. *Supdt. Central Jail, New Delhi*, AIR 1971 SC 178: 1970 SCD 108: 1971 Cr LJ 244: 1971 (2) SCJ 233: 1971 (2) SCA 458: (1971) 2 SCR 147.
3. *Rameshwar Prasad* v. *State*, 1975 Cr LJ 658 All.

Under section 439(1) the High Court or the court of sessions will have to exercise its judicial discretion in considering the question of granting of bail. The overriding considerations in granting bail which are common both in the case of section 437(1) and section 439(1) of the new Code are the nature and gravity of the circumstances in which the offence is committed; the position and the status of the accused with reference to the victim and the witnesses; the likelihood of the accused fleeing from justice; of repeating the offence; of jeopardizing his own life being faced with a grim prospect of possible conviction in the case; of tampering with witnesses; the history of the case as well as of its investigation and other relevant grounds which, in view of so many variable factors, cannot be exhaustively set out. Of these, on the two paramount considerations, *viz.*, likelihood of the accused fleeing from justice and his tampering with prosecution evidence relate to ensuring a fair trial of the case in a court of justice, due and proper weight should be bestowed.[1]

An order refusing an application for bail does not necessarily preclude another on a later occasion giving more materials, further developments and different considerations. While the court should set store by the circumstances that the bail application was once rejected it cannot be said that the court is barred from second consideration at a later stage.[2]

4. Cancellation of Bail

Very cogent and overwhelming circumstances are necessary for an order seeking cancellation of the bail. Even where a *prima facie* case is established, the approach of the court in the matter of bail is not that the accused should be detained by way of punishment but whether the presence of the accused would be readily available for trial or that he is likely to abuse the discretion granted in his favour by tampering with evidence.

In the present case the High Court completely overlooked the fact that it was not for it to decide whether the bail should be granted but the application was for cancellation of the bail. It was misdirected while examining the question of directing cancellation of bail by interfering with the discretionary order of the sessions court. The circumstance found by it that the victim attacked was a social and political worker cannot be considered to be so overriding as to permit such interference. The High Court was impressed by some of the most irrelevant considerations, overlooking the considerations relevant for deciding the question. The High Court's approach thus being erroneous must be set aside.[3]

5. Bailable and Non-bailable Offences

In non-bailable offence grant of bail in the discretion of court which is to be exercised judiciously.

An offence being non-bailable does not mean that bail can in no case be granted. A perusal of section 436 of the Code reveals that a person accused of a

1. *Gurucharan Singh* v. *State,* 1978 SCC (Cri) 41: AIR 1978 SC 179.
2. *Babu Singh* v. *State of Uttar Pradesh,* 1978 SCC (Cri) 133: 1978 Cr LR (SC) 86: 1978 Cr LJ (Cri) 69: 1978 Cr LJ 651: (1978) 1 SCC 579: 1978 (2) SCJ 135: (1978) 2 SCR 777.
3. *Bhagirathsinh* v. *State of Gujarat,* 1984 SCC (Cri) 63: AIR 1984 SC 372: (1984) 3 SCC 284: 1984 UJ (SC) 190.

bailable offence is entitled to bail as of right. However, where a person is accused of a non-bailable offence, it is not so. All that 'non-bailable' implies is that unlike the person accused of a bailable offence a person accused of non-bailable offence cannot claim bail as of right and the question of grant of bail to such a person is left by the legislature in the court's discretion to be exercised on a consideration of the totality of the facts and circumstances of a given case. The discretion has, of course, to be a judicial one informed by tradition methodized by analogy, disciplined by system and subordinated to the primordial necessity of order in social life.[1]

6. Anticipatory Bail – Jurisdiction where Arrest is Apprehended

Section 438(1) of the Criminal Procedure Code is wide enough to confer jurisdiction not only to the High Court or the court of sessions within whose territorial jurisdiction the offence has been committed and is to be enquired into and tried but also the High Court or the court of sessions where a person has reason to believe that he may be arrested in connection with the commission of non-bailable offence. By taking away the jurisdiction from the High Court or the court of sessions for the grant of anticipatory bail within the territorial jurisdiction in respect of a person who may be arrested in connection with non-bailable offence would be reading certain words in the section which are not to be found therein. Thus, no restriction whatsoever has been placed for exercise of power by the High Court or the court of sessions for the grant of anticipatory bail within whose territorial jurisdiction a person has reason to believe that he may be arrested in connection with non-bailable offence.[2]

7. Compulsive Bail

Once an accused is released on bail under section 167(2) he cannot be taken back in custody merely on the filing of a charge-sheet but there must exist special reasons for so doing besides the fact that the charge-sheet reveals the commission of a non-bailable crime.[3]

8. Anticipatory Bail where Arrest is Apprehended

Jurisdiction to grant bail does not arise with the offence only but with reference to the offender also. Pre-trial arrest has nothing to do with trial of the case and if there can be an extra territorial arrest, the jurisdiction to grant anticipatory bail may rest with the court, having jurisdiction over the place where arrest is apprehended. It cannot be said that only the court having jurisdiction to try the accused and if he is tried by any other court the court is corum non-judice. There is no trial at the stage, the anticipatory bail is asked for and hence there is no question of there being a corum non-judice.[4]

---

1. *Shantilal* v. *State of Madhya Pradesh*, 1989 Cr LJ 332 MP: (2007) 11 SCC 243].
2. *Capt. Satish Kumar Sharma* v. *Delhi Administration*, 1991 Cr LJ 950 Del (DB).
3. *Aslam Babalal Desai* v. *State of Maharashtra*, 1992 (III) Crimes 597 SC: 1992 Cr LJ 3712: 1992 AIR SCW 2621: JT 1992 (6) SC 21: (1992) 4 SCC 272: 1992 (3) SCJ 377: (1992) 4 SCR 545: 1992 SCC (Cri) 870.
4. *Jodha Ram* v. *The State of Rajasthan*, 1994 Cr LJ 1962 Raj.

9. Cognizance should also be taken within 60 or 90 days

The appellant was charged under section 302, etc. The matter was remanded to 12-11-93, charge sheet filed on 5-11-93, *i.e.*, 88th day from the date of arrest, *i.e.*, within 90 days. The accused was not produced before the court on 5-11-93, nor cognizance of the offence was taken. Applied for bail on 11-11-93. Held to be entitled for bail.[1]

10. After Filing of Charge-sheet, section 167 Ceases to Apply

"A careful consideration of the provisions of section 167 and the law laid down by the Supreme Court in *Lakshmi Brahmans'* case,[2] and the decision of Full Benches of Gujrat, Patna and Rajasthan High Courts makes it clear that an accused is entitled to right to bail under the proviso to section 167(2) only if the charge-sheet is not filed within 90 days or 60 days, as the case may be, from the date of the magistrate first authorised detention of the accused and that once the charge-sheet is filed within that period, section 167 ceases to apply and the accused cannot seek bail by virtue of proviso to section 167(2) on any other ground. In this case the fact that the charge-sheet was filed within the period of 90 days, the magistrate had not passed an order taking cognizance within that period does not entitle the accused to seek bail under proviso to section 167(2) without reference to the merit of the case."[3]

11. Anticipatory Bail even after Issue of Process or Committal to Sessions

Interim order restraining arrest (anticipatory bail) can be passed even after process has been issued or at the stage of committal of the case to the sessions court.[4]

12. Remarkable Security in Bailable Offence

The accused who allegedly committed an offence relating to illicit distilled liquor, which was a bailable offence was directed to deposit the cash security of Rs. 5000 with one surety in addition of bail bond.

Held: If a person accused of bailable offence is entitled to be released on bail, granting of such bail should not be harsh, oppressive and virtually in denial of bail. The court ordered to furnish proper security of Rs. 5000 with one surety and thereafter the cash deposit should be refunded. The court further observed that 'it is deplorable that even after the position relating to cash security has been elaborated by the Apex Court, learned JMFC, without any basis and without application of judicial mind has directed the accused petitioner to furnish cash security on presumptuous conclusions.[5]

13. After Filing of Charge-sheet, Bail matter to be Dealt with by Regular Court

While exercising jurisdiction under section 438, the Cr.P.C, the governing factor is that there was apprehension of arrest by a person accused of non-bailable

1. *Iqbal Zahoor Sheikh* v. *State of Maharashtra*, IV 1994 CCR 2607.
2. *State of Uttar Pradesh* v. *Lakshmi Brahman*, AIR 1983 SC 439: 1983 All LJ 419: 1983 Cr LJ 839: (1983) 2 SCC 372: 1983 (1) Crimes 797.
3. *Dori* v. *State of Karnataka*, IV (1994) CCR 2996 Kar.
4. *Nirbhay Singh* v. *State of Madhya Pradesh*, 1 (1995) CCR 497 MP (FB).
5. *Anwar Husain* v. *State of Orissa*, 1995 Cr LJ 863 (Ori).

offence but where charge-sheet has already been filed and non-bailable warrants had been issued, it should be left to the regular court to deal with the matter on an appreciation of evidence.[1]

14. If Released on Compulsive Bail, automatic Re-arrest not Permissible on Filing Charge-sheet

The proviso to section 167(2) of the Cr.P.C does not create indefeasible right on accused to exercise at any time. This right is applicable after the maximum time allowed by law till the charge-sheet is filed. This right is not available after the charge-sheet is filed. But on the other hand if he exercises the right within the time allowed by law and is released on bail under such circumstances, he cannot be re-arrested on the mere filing of the charge-sheet.[2]

15. Pending Application after Filing of Charge-sheet shall be Treated like Regular Bail Application

Thus to sum up it is clear:

The indefeasible right to be released on bail is created in favour of the accused, if the charge-sheet is not filed on the expiry of the statutory period as provided in proviso (a) to section 167(2) of the Code.

No doubt, said right is indefeasible right, but the life of that right is from the expiry of the period till the date the charge-sheet is filed; and

That right does not survive or remain enforceable on the charge-sheet being filed and the application filed during default period is pending for disposal, same is required to be decided like regular bail application, be it under the Code or any other Act, if it provides for bail like the Code."[3]

16. Condition in Bailable Offences

Under section 436, the Cr. P.C. there is no discretion left to court to impose condition while releasing a person on bail when he is accused of bailable offence.[4]

17. Forfeiture of Bail Bond

Forfeiture of a bond would entail the penalty against each surety for the amount, which he has undertaken in the bond executed by him. Both the sureties cannot claim to share the amount by half and half as each can be made liable to pay the amount of Rs. 25,000.[5]

18. Delayed Action or Inaction of Court should not Deprive the Accused of his Indefeasible Right

Proviso to section 167(2) of the 1973 Code under which indefeasible right to bail has been given to the accused should be given effect to in letter and spirit.

1. *P.V. Narasimha Rao* v. *C.B.I*, 1996 (4) Crimes 218 (DHC).
2. *Dr. Bipin Shanti Lal Panchal* v. *State of Gujarat*, AIR 1996 SC 2897: 1996 Cr LJ 1652: 1996 AIR SCW 734: (1996) 1 SCC 718: 1996 (2) SCJ 198: (1996) 1 SCR 193.
3. *Pramod Hari Prasad Tiwari* v. *State of Gujarat*, 1997 Cr LJ 1605 SC: 1997 (2) Cr CJ 95: 1997 (1) Guj LR 570: 1997 (3) Rec Cri R 451.
4. *Hanumanthe Gowda* v. *State of Karnataka*, 1997 (1) Crimes 303 Kar.
5. *Om prakash Shivprakash* v. *K.I. Kuriakose*, 1999 (4) Crimes 315 (SC): 2000 Cr LJ 26: JT 1999 (8) SC 569: 1999 (3) Ker LT 861: (1999) 8 SCC 633: 2000 (1) SCJ 518: 1999 (10) SRJ 452: (1999) 7 SCALE 8: 2000 SCC (Cri) 1: 1999 (9) Supreme 55.

Inaction or delayed action of the court in extending the benefit thereof would make it nugatory. Therefore, uninfluenced by the nature and gravity of the offence it is expected of the court to give the benefit of the default clause and release the accused forthwith if he is prepared to and does furnish bail. The maximum period of detention of an accused in custody as provided under section 167 should not be extended by court's order to enable the prosecution to file charge-sheet so that right for compulsive bail would be defeated. Justice must be rooted in confidence and confidence is destroyed when right-minded people go away thinking 'Judge was biased'.

To repeat with, in the present case after expiry of the prescribed period for filing charge-sheet, the petitioner moved for compulsive bail. The learned Special Judge instead of passing the orders on the very day adjourned the case to next day and on that day charge-sheet filed, he rejected the prayer.

In the result, I am inclined to give the benefit of the 'default' clause as envisaged in section 167(2) of the 1973 Code and admit the petitioner to bail.[1]

19. Cognizance is taken in Respect of Offence Charged and not in Respect of Offence Finally Proved

Sub-section (3) of section 468 which was added by the Code of Criminal Procedure (Amendment) Act, 1978, provides that in relation to offences which may be tried together, the period of limitation shall be determined with reference to the offence which is punishable with the more or most severe punishment. The language of sub-section (3) of section 468 makes it imperative that the limitation provided for taking cognizance in section 468 is in respect of the offence charged and not in respect of offence finally proved. Therefore, where the accused were charged under section 468 read with section 120B of the Penal Code, for which the imposable punishment is seven years and section 5(2) of the Prevention of Corruption Act, 1947, which is punishable with imprisonment for a term which may extend to seven years and for such offences no period of limitation having been provided for in section 468, the cognizance taken by the Special Judge cannot be said to be barred by limitation, when he convicted the accused for minor offences of sections 417 and 465 of the Penal Code on ground that cognizance for such minor offences was barred by limitation under section 468, the Cr. P.C.

After expiry of period of limitation, discretion by the court must be exercised by speaking order. In the absence of positive order, court cannot be deemed to have taken cognizance by condoning delay when cognizance was barred.[2]

20. Unreasonable Condition for Bail

Unreasonable condition cannot be imposed in granting bail. It would amount to refusal of bail.[3]

---

1. *Ramesh Das* v. *State of Orissa,* 1999 (4) Crimes 434 (Ori): 2000 (3) Cur Cri R 139: 1999 (88) Cut LT 487: 1999 (17) OCR 400: 1999 (2) Ori LR 451.
2. *State of Himachal Pradesh* v. *Tara Dutt,* AIR 2000 SC 297: 2000 Cr LJ 485: 1999 AIR SCW 4413: 2000 (1) Crimes 15: JT 1999 (9) SC 215: (2000) 1 SCC 230: (1999) 7 SCALE 183: 1999 (9) Supreme 421: 2000 (1) UJ (SC) 498.
3. 2002 VIII AD (Del) 768 (DB).

21. Sureties can Discharge themselves Anytime by Handing the Accused to the Custody of Law

The literal meaning of the word 'Bail' is surety. In *Halsbury's Laws of England'*, the following observation succinctly brings out the effect of bail:

> "The effect of granting bail is not to set the defendant (accused) at liberty but to release him from the custody of law and to entrust him to the custody of his sureties who are bound to produce him to appear at his trial at a specified time and place. The sureties may seize their principal at any time and may discharge themselves by handing him over to the custody of law and he will then be imprisoned."[1]

22. Bail/Parole

The effect of granting bail is to release the accused from internment though the court would still retain constructive control over him through the sureties – The word "parole" is in different lexicography – Parole is a form of temporary release from custody which does not suspend the sentence or the period of detention, but provides conditional release from custody and changes the mode of undergoing the sentence – During parole period there is no suspension of sentence but sentence is actually continuing to run during that period also. Both have different connotations in law – Bail is well-understood in criminal jurisprudence which is granted to a person who has been arrested in a non-bailable offence or has been convicted of an offence after trial. The respondent claims that he is entitled to remission of period during which he was on bail under orders of court. Therefore, taking in view of all provisions if it is to be held that he is entitled to such remission, the criminal justice system would be reduced to a mockery.[2]

23. Second Bail Application

Without the change in the circumstances second application would be deemed to be seeking review of the earlier judgment, which is not permissible under the Criminal Act.[3]

24. No Second Appeal Against Order Passed by Magistrate under Section 446

Appeal against imposing penalty on sureties passed by chief judicial magistrate before sessions court is maintainable. No second appeal would lie before High Court.

Forfeiture of bond entails penalty against each surety. Each surety is liable to pay entire surety amount. Surety cannot claim to share surety amount by half and half.

---

1. *Sunil Fulchand Shah* v. *Union of India*, (2000) 1 SCALE 660: AIR 2000 SC 1023: 2000 AIR SCW 582: 2000 (3) Crimes 44: (2000) 3 SCC 409: 2000 (1) SCJ 443: 2000 (4) Supreme 682.
2. *State of Haryana* v. *Nauratta Singh*, 2000 (2) JCC (SC) 429: AIR 2000 SC 1179: 2000 AIR SCW 817: 2000 (2) Crimes 6: (2000) 3 SCC 514: 2000 (3) SCJ 174: 2000 (4) SRJ 161: (2000) 2 SCALE 321: 2000 SCC (Cri) 711: 2000 (2) Supreme 249: 2000 (1) UJ (SC) 792.
3. *State of Madhya Pradesh* v. *Kajad*, 2001 VII AD (SC) 133: AIR 2001 SC 3317: (2001) 7 SCC 673: 2001 (3) SCJ 360: 2001 (9) SRJ 129: (2001) 6 SCALE 150: 2001 (6) Supreme 844: 2001 (2) UC 654.

For alternation of condition by Magistrate to the effect that accused was permitted to reside in another city bail-bond does not stand discharged. Surety is not absolved from his liability.

Offence charged against accused, foreign national under section 466, 471 and the Registration of Foreign Act and the Passport Act was not very serious. Accused slipped out of the country beyond reach of sureties. No allegation against surety that he has connived with accused jumping out the bail. Remission granted. Each of surety held liable to pay Rs. 5,000 instead of Rs. 25,000 as penalty.[1]

25. Anticipatory Bail Application

There is no bar in filing an application under section 438 after filing of charge-sheet or after issue of warrant of arrest in a complaint case.[2]

69. Power of court to try cases summarily.—Notwithstanding anything contained in the Code of Criminal Procedure, 1973 (2 of 1974), all offences under this Act punishable with fine or with imprisonment for a term not exceeding three years shall be tried in a summary way by a Metropolitan Magistrate and the provisions of sections 262 to 265 (both inclusive) of the said Code shall as far as may be, apply to such trial:

Provided that in the case of any conviction in a summary trial under this section, it shall be lawful for the Metropolitan Magistrate to pass a sentence of imprisonment for a term not exceeding one year:

Provided further that when at the commencement of, or in the course of, a summary trial under this section, it appears to the Metropolitan Magistrate that the nature of the case is such that a sentence of imprisonment for a term exceeding one year may have to be passed or that it is, for any other reason, undesirable to try the case summarily, the Metropolitan Magistrate shall, after hearing the parties, record an order to that effect and thereafter recall any witness who may have been examined and proceed to hear or rehear the case in the manner provided by the said Code.

SYNOPSIS

1. **Adopting Procedure of Warrant Case is Merely an Irregularity**
2. **Order should be Passed by the Judge, who Examined Witnesses**
3. **Irregularity of Trial of Summons Case as Warrant Case is Curable under Section 537**
4. **Maximum Punishment cannot be Deemed to be Governed by the Limit Period for a Particular Court**

---

1. *Mohammed Kunju* v. *State of Karnataka*, AIR 2000 SC 6: 2000 Cr LJ 165: 1999 (4) Crimes 320: JT 1999 (8) SC 487: 2000 (1) Ker LJ 55: 1999 (3) Ker LT 907: (1999) 8 SCC 660: (1999) 6 SCALE 693: 2000 SCC (Cri) 34: 1999 (9) Supreme 62.
2. *Shamim Ahmed* v. *State*, 2003 Cr LJ 2815 (FB): 2003 (3) All Cr LR 491: 2003 Cal Cri LR 419: 2003 (2) Cal LT 11: 2003 (3) Cur Cri R 450

5. **Summary Trial is Speedy Trial**
6. **Summons Case**

Comments

1. Adopting Procedure of Warrant Case is Merely an Irregularity

Omission to follow summary procedure in the initial stages of the case instead of following procedure meant for warrant trial would at best may amount to a mere irregularity and not illegality.

After the amendment of the Cr.P.C an offence under section 448 is triable as summons case and adopting the procedure prescribed for a case triable as a warrant case, is an irregularity which does not vitiate the proceedings and is curable by the provisions of section 537 as no prejudice to the accused has been established in the case.[1]

When the accused pleads guilty, the magistrate may not be obliged to write a judgment containing a brief statement of the reasons, but the magistrate is not absolved of the obligation to record the substance of the evidence. Otherwise, it would be difficult to conceive as to what could the accused have pleaded to. His plea of guilt is an admission to whatever factual data the prosecution lays before the court about the commission of the offence. Pleading guilty by the accused to the violation of a provision of law is no plea at all, as he would have to be confronted with the substance of the allegation, in order to enter upon a plea, one way or the order. When the substance of the allegations is not put to the accused, his entering any kind of plea is no plea legally, due to the non-observance of such procedural requirement of utmost importance.[2]

2. Order should be Passed by the Judge, who Examined Witnesses

Under section 326(3) whenever a summary trial case is dealt with by a Judge or a magistrate, who takes cognizance of the offence and records evidence, the judgment must be pronounced by the same Judge or the magistrate only; otherwise, the same will vitiate. The Judge or the magistrate, who tries the summary trial case must give his judgment and if he is transferred without pronouncing judgment, the succeeding Sessions Judge or the magistrate has to start the trial afresh and pronounce the judgment. Where the Sessions Judge who examined the witnesses was transferred and the succeeding Sessions Judge pronounced the judgment, the same is vitiated as per section 461(1).[3]

3. Irregularity of Trial of Summons Case as Warrant Case is Curable under Section 537

The procedure for summary trial is exactly the same as the procedure for trial of summons case. Warrant case procedure, being more elaborate, provides better opportunities to the accused to defend himself. It is open to the magistrate to convert summons case into a warrant case as per section 259 of the Code. The purpose of providing summons or summary procedure is to shorten the record and

---

1. *Gopal Das Sindhi* v. *State of Assam*, AIR 1961 SC 986: 1961 2 Cr LJ 39: 1961 (1) SCJ 573: 1961 Andh LT 392: ILR (1961) 13 Assam 432.
2. *Pawan Kumar* v. *State of Haryana*, 1996 SCC (Cri) 583: AIR 1996 SC 3300.
3. *Chandana Surya Rao* v. *State*, 1989 Cr LJ 2077 AP.

the work of the magistrate and save his time. Hence the procedure of section 16A of the Prevention of Food Adulteration Act cannot be regarded as mandatory in the sense that any departure shall vitiate the trial. The procedure adopted by the magistrate for offence triable under section 16A of summary trial would not vitiate the trial. The court relied on the judgment of Supreme Court in *Gopal Das* v. *State of Assam*,[1] wherein it was observed that the irregularity of a case triable as a summons case being triable as warrant case does not vitiate the proceedings and is curable under section 537 of the 1898 Code (section 465 of the 1973 Code).[2]

4. Maximum Punishment cannot be Deemed to be Governed by the Limit Period for a Particular Court

When appellant challenged the order by which the court took cognizance of the offence, the High Court proceeded on the assumption that the offence under section 7 of the Essential Commodities Act is punishable with imprisonment for a term not exceeding two years and, therefore, found that the period of limitation is three years from the date of offence. But the aforesaid assumption made by the High Court is on an erroneous basis because the offence under section 7(1)(a)(ii) is punishable with imprisonment which may extend upto seven years. That sub-clause is extracted below:

Penalties: (1) If any person contravenes any order made under section 3.

He shall be punishable, in the case of an order made with reference to clause (h) or clause (I) of sub-section (2) of the section, with imprisonment for a term which may extend to one year and shall also be liable to fine, and in the case of any other order, with imprisonment for a term which shall not be less than three months but which may extend to seven years and shall also be liable to fine.

Appellant endeavoured in the High Court to show that the said offence is punishable only up to two years, on the strength of the proviso to clause (f) in section 12AA (1) of the E.C. Act. That section stipulates that when a special court is constituted under section 12A for any area, thereafter all offences under the E.C. Act committed within that area shall be triable by that special court. Clause (f) of section 12AA(1) says that all such offences shall be tried in a summary manner. The proviso to that clause reads thus:

Provided that in the case of any conviction in a summary trial under this section, it shall be lawful for the special court to pass a sentence of imprisonment for a term not exceeding two years.

The contention is that the aforesaid limit fixed by the Parliament would have the effect of altering the extent of punishment for the offence under section 7 of the E.C. Act to imprisonment for a period of two years. We cannot agree that the effect of the said proviso was to amend section 7 by making the offence punishable only up to two years. The effect of the proviso is to limit the jurisdiction of the special court in awarding sentence. That is different from understanding the extent of the sentence, whether the offence had been reduced by Parliament through a process other than amendment of the provision. One has to look at the punishing provision

---

1. AIR 1961 SC 986.
2. *Jagdish Prasad* v. *State of Madhya Pradesh*, 1997 Cr LJ 27 MP (DB).

to know the extent of the sentence prescribed and not at the limit fixed for a particular court in the matter of awarding sentence, *e.g.*, section 326 of the Indian Penal Code deals with an offence punishable with imprisonment for life or with imprisonment for a term which may extend to 10 years. But that offence is triable by a magistrate of first class, the upper limit of whose powers in the matter of awarding sentence is restricted by section 29(2) of the Code as three years. By reason of that section it cannot be assumed that the offence under section 326, the IPC is punishable only with imprisonment for three years.[1]

5. Summary Trial is Speedy Trial

The term 'summary', when used in connection with legal proceedings, means a short, concise and immediate proceeding, without observance of the formalities of a full proceeding. Summary trial is one of the well-known and generally adopted procedure to achieve the objective and purpose of 'speedy trial'.[2]

6. Summons Case

Complaint under section 138 of the Negotiable Instruments Act is a summons case, not open for accused to seek discharge like in warrant case.[3]

70. Security for good conduct and abstaining from committing offences.—(1) Whenever any person is convicted of an offence punishable under this Act and the court convicting him is of opinion that such person habitually commits or attempts to commit, or abets the commission of any such offence and that it is necessary to require such person to execute a bond for abstaining from the commission of any such offence, the court may, at the time of passing sentence on such person, order him to execute a bond for a sum proportionate to his means, with or without sureties, for abstaining from the commission of such offence during such period, not exceeding three years, as it thinks fit to fix.

(2) The bond shall be in the prescribed form in terms of the provisions of the Code of Criminal Procedure, 1973 (2 of 1974) and shall insofar as they are applicable, apply to all matters connected with such bond to as if it were a bond to keep the peace ordered to be executed under section 106 of that Code.

(3) If the conviction is set-aside on appeal or otherwise, the bond so executed shall become void.

(4) An order under this section may also be made by an Appellate Court or by the High Court when exercising its power of revision.

---

1. *Nirmal Kanti Roy* v. *State of West Bengal*, II (1998) CCR 251 (SC): 1998 Cr LJ 3282: 1998 AIR SCW 2235: 1998 (2) Crimes 267: (1998) 4 SCC 590: (1998) 2 SCR 1147: (1998) 3 SCALE 232: 1998 SCC (Cri) 1100: 1998 (4) Supreme 209: 1998 (2) UJ (SC) 121.
2. *Mukesh* v. *State of Rajasthan*, 1998 Cr LJ 2439 Raj: 1998 (1) FAC 286: 1998 Raj Cri C 341.
3. *Ramaswamy* v. *Dhanalakshmi Bankers*, AIR 2007 (DOC) 258 (Mad): 2007 (1) NIJ 304.

CHAPTER VII

REVIEW, APPEAL AND REVISION

71. Review.—Any excise officer making an order under this Act may, within sixty days on his own motion or on an application, review his order, if the order contains some error or omission, apparent in such order:

Provided that order shall not be reviewed except after giving a reasonable opportunity of being heard to the person affected by that order.

SYNOPSIS

1. **No Review of the Order in Exercise of Powers under Section 482**
2. **Power of Review is Exercised to Correct a Mistake and not to Substitute a View**
3. **High Court cannot Review its Judgment Passed in Exercise of its Appellant, Revisional or Original Criminal Jurisdiction nor such Power can be Exercised under its Inherent Jurisdiction under Section 482**

Comments

1. No Review of the Order in Exercise of Powers under Section 482

The court is not empowered to review its own decision under the purported exercise of inherent power. The inherent power under section 482 is intended to prevent the abuse of the process of the court and to secure ends of justice. Such power cannot be exercised to do something which is expressly barred under the section 363 of the Code which expressly provides that no court when it has signed its judgment or final order disposing of a case, shall alter or review the same except to correct a clerical or arithmetical error save as otherwise provided by the Code. If any consideration of the facts by way of review is not permissible under the Code and is expressly barred, it is not for the court to exercise its inherent power to reconsider the matter and record a conflicting decision. If there had been change in the circumstances of the case, it would be in order for the High Court to exercise its inherent powers in the prevailing circumstances and pass appropriate orders to secure the ends of justice or to prevent the abuse of the process of the court. Where there is no such changed circumstances and the decision has to be arrived at on the facts that existed as on the date of the earlier order, the exercise of the power to reconsider the same materials to arrive at different conclusion is in effect a review, which is expressly barred under section 362.[1]

2. Power of Review is Exercised to Correct a Mistake and not to Substitute a View

The dictionary meaning of the word "re-view" is "the act of looking", offer something again with a view to correction or improvement. It cannot be denied that

1. *Mst. Simrikhia* v. *Dolley Mukherjee*, AIR 1990 SC 1605: 1990 Cr LJ 1599.

the review is the creation of a statute. The power of review can be exercised for correction of a mistake and not to substitute a view. Such powers can be exercised within the limits of the statute dealing with the exercise of powers. The review cannot be treated as an appeal in disguise. The mere possibility of two views on the subject is not a ground for review. Once a review petition is dismissed no further petition of review can be entertained.[1]

3. High Court cannot Review its Judgment Passed in Exercise of its Appellant, Revisional or Original Criminal Jurisdiction nor such Power can be Exercised under its Inherent Jurisdiction under Section 482

There is no provision in the Code of Criminal Procedure authorising the High Court to review its judgment passed either in exercise of its appellate or revisional or original criminal jurisdiction. Such a power cannot be exercised with the aid or under the cloak of section 482.

An application of review would lie, *inter alia* when the order suffers from an error apparent on the face of the record and permitting the same to continue would lead to failure of justice.

The power of review can also be exercised by the court in the event of discovery of new and important matter or evidence takes place which despite due diligence was not within the knowledge of the applicant or could not be produced by him at the time when the order was made. Furthermore, an application for review shall also lie for any sufficient reason.[2]

72. Appeal.—(1) Any person aggrieved by any decision or order passed under this Act by an excise officer, subordinate to the Deputy Commissioner, may appeal to the Deputy Commissioner.

(2) Any person aggrieved by any decision or order passed under this Act by the Deputy Commissioner may appeal to the Excise Commissioner.

(3) Any person aggrieved by any decision or order passed under this Act by the Excise Commissioner may appeal to the Financial Commissioner.

(4) Such appeal shall be filed within thirty days from the date of communication of such decision or order together with self-attested copy thereof:

Provided that a further period of thirty days may be allowed if the appellant establishes that sufficient cause prevented him from presenting the appeal within the aforesaid period of thirty days.

(5) At the hearing of an appeal, an appellant may be allowed to go into any ground not specified in the grounds of appeal or take

1. *Lily Thomas* v. *Union of India*, AIR 2000 SC 1650: 2000 Cr LJ 2433: 2000 AIR SCW 1760: (2000) 6 SCC 224: (2000) 4 SCALE 176: 2000 (3) Supreme 601: 2000 (2) UJ (SC) 1113.
2. *Inder Chand Jain* v. *Moti Lal*, (2009) DLT 734.

additional evidence if necessary, if it is established that such omission was not wilful or unreasonable.

(6) The appellate authority, after making such further inquiry as may be necessary, pass such order, as he thinks just and proper, confirming, modifying or annulling the decision or order as the case may be.

(7) The appeal shall be heard and decided within one year from the date on which such appeal is filed:

Provided that if an appeal is not decided within one year the relief prayed for in the appeal shall be deemed to have been granted.

73. Order of appellate authority.—(1) The order of the appellate authority disposing of the appeal shall be in writing and shall state the points for determination, the decision thereon and the reasons for the decision.

(2) The appellate authority shall communicate the order passed by him to the appellant and the excise officer whose order formed the subject-matter of appeal.

74. Deposit of excise revenue before filing appeal.—(1) Where the decision or order appealed against under this Chapter relates to any duty, fee or penalty levied under this Act, the person desirous of appealing against such decision or order shall produce satisfactory proof of the payment of the excise revenue before filing the appeal.

(2) Where in any particular case, the appellate authority is of opinion that the appellant has a *prima facie* case in his favour and deposit of duty, fee or penalty levied would cause undue hardship to such person, the appellate authority, on an application from the appellant, may dispense with such deposit and stay its recovery subject to furnishing such security and to such conditions as he may deem fit to impose, so as to safeguard the interest of revenue:

Provided that no appeal shall be entertained by the appellate authority, unless it is satisfied that such amount of excise revenue, as the appellant may admit to be due from him, has been paid.

(3) Where an application is filed for dispensing with the deposit of excise revenue levied under sub-section (2), the appellate authority shall, where it is possible to do so, decide such application within thirty days from the date of its filing.

(4) Notwithstanding anything contained in sub-section (1), no recovery action shall be initiated against the appellant until the application under sub-section (2) has been decided by the appellate authority.

75. Revision of orders by Excise Commissioner.—(1) The Excise Commissioner may, on his own motion, call for the record of any proceeding in which an officer subordinate to him has taken any decision or passed an order under this Act, including those related to the grant, issue or refusal to grant a licence, for the purpose of satisfying himself as to the legality or propriety of any such decision or order and may make such inquiry or cause such inquiry to be made and, subject to the provision of this Chapter, pass such order thereon as he thinks fit.

(2) No order, which is prejudicial to any person shall be passed under this section unless the person has been given an opportunity of being heard.

(3) The Excise Commissioner shall communicate the order passed by him under sub-section (1) to such person and the excise officer whose order formed the subject-matter of revision.

(4) No order under this section shall be passed by the Excise Commissioner in respect of any issue if an appeal against such issue is pending before the Deputy Commissioner.

(5) No order under this section shall be passed after the expiry of six months from the date on which the order sought to be revised has been passed.

SYNOPSIS

1. **Revision**
2. **Limitation Act Applicable though Copy is not Required to be Filed along with Memorandum of Appeal**

Comments

1. Revision

As regards the revisional jurisdiction of the High Court there is no provision similar to section 431. Nor is there any provision whether a revisional application can be or cannot be made in respect of an order of conviction when the convicted person is dead. There is the important distinction that while the appellate jurisdiction can be exercised only after an appeal is filed by the convicted person – or against an order of acquittal under section 411 or section 417, there is no such limitation on the court's revisional jurisdiction.[1]

2. Limitation Act Applicable though Copy is not Required to be Filed along with Memorandum of Appeal

Section 12(3) of Limitation Act applies even though copy is not required to be filed alongwith the memorandum of appeal or revision or review.[2]

---

1. *State of Kerala* v. *Narayani Amma Kamala Devi,* AIR 1962 SC 1530: (1962) 1 Ker LR 577: 1962 Ker LT (SC) 111: (1962) 2 Cr LJ 506: 1962 All LJ 846: 1962 (2) SCA 703: (1962) Supp 3 SCR 943: 1965 (2) SCJ 213.
2. *Addl. Collector, Customs* v. *Best & Co.,* AIR 1966 SC 1713: 1967 (1) SCA 238: 1967 SCD 354.

CHAPTER VIII

MISCELLANEOUS PROVISIONS

76. Power of Government to declare what shall be deemed to be liquor.—The Government may, by notification, declare as to what shall be deemed to be liquor for the purpose of this Act or the rules framed thereunder.

77. Power of Government to regulate drinking and to enforce prohibition.—The Government may issue such order and take such measures as may be deemed appropriate to regulate drinking or to enforce prohibition in whole or in any part of Delhi.

78. Power of Government to regulate molasses, black jaggery, mahua flower, etc., to prevent misuse.—The Government may frame rules to regulate movement, possession and sale of molasses, black jaggery, mahua flower, etc., indicating terms and conditions as are necessary and expedient to prevent their misuse for illicit distillation.

79. Power to regulate advertisement.—No advertisement, direct or surrogate, shall be made for promoting consumption of liquor. The Excise Commissioner may, however, at his discretion allow such advertisement which is educative and promotes responsible drinking.

80. Bar and limitation of certain suits.—No suit for damages shall lie in any civil court against the Government or any officer or person for any act done in good faith, in pursuance of this Act or of any other law for the time being in force relating to the excise revenue.

SYNOPSIS

Bar of Suit Against Government Servants

Comments

Bar of Suit Against Government Servants

Where the Legislature intends to restrict the limitation of suits, proceedings or prosecutions against the Government servants only the Legislature has chosen proper words of limitation to ensure the restricted operation of the provisions of the statute.[1]

81. Power of Government to make rules.—(1) The Government may by notification in the Official Gazette, make rules not inconsistent with the provisions of this Act to carry out the purposes of this Act.

1. *Public Prosecutor* v. *R. Raju*, 1972 SCC (Cri) 738: AIR 1972 SC 2504: 1972 Cr LJ 1699: (1973) 1 SCR 812.

(2) In particular and without prejudice to the generality of the foregoing power, such rules may provide for all or any of the following matters, namely:—

(a) prescribing the powers and duties of excise officers and delegation of power;

(b) prescribing the time and manner of presenting appeals and the procedure for prosecuting and dealing with review, appeal and revision;

(c) regulating import, export, transport, manufacture, collection, possession supply or storage of any intoxicant, mahua flower, black jaggery and molasses;

(d) regulating the sale and possession of toddy, neera or tari and tapping of trees for drawing toddy or tari;

(e) declaring the process of denaturation of spirit;

(f) regulating the wholesale or retail sale of intoxicants;

(g) regulating the time, place, rate and manner of payment of duty or fee and the taking of security for its due payment;

(h) prescribing the authority by which, the form and the manner in which, and the terms and conditions, subject to which any licence, permit or pass shall be granted;

(i) providing for the destruction or other disposal of any liquor deemed to be unfit for use;

(j) regulating disposal of confiscated articles;

(k) providing for the grant of reward to excise officers and informers;

(l) regulating the grant of expenses to witnesses;

(m) regulating the power of excise officer to summon witnesses;

(n) curbing activities of boot-leggers who distill, manufacture, store, transport, import, export, sell or distribute any intoxicant in contravention of any provision of this Act or the rules made thereunder;

(o) any other matter which is required to be, or may be prescribed under this Act.

(3) Without prejudice to any provision made in this behalf, any rule made under this Act may be made so as to be retrospective to any date not earlier than the date of commencement of this Act:

Provided that no rule shall be given effect retrospectively if it would have the effect of prejudicially affecting the interest of a person.

(4) Every rule made under this Act shall be laid, as soon as may be after it is made, before the Legislative Assembly while it is in session, for a total period of thirty days which may be comprised in one session or in two or more successive sessions, and if, before the expiry of the session immediately following the session or the successive sessions aforesaid the Legislative Assembly agrees in making such modifications in the rule or the Legislative Assembly agrees that the rule should not be made, the rules shall have effect only in such modified form or be of no effect, as the case may be; so, however, that any such modification or annulment shall be without prejudice to the validity of anything previously done or omitted to be done under that rule.

SYNOPSIS

Comments

I. Subordinate Legislation

No tax can be imposed by any bye-law or rule or regulation unless the statute under which the subordinate legislation is made specially authorises the imposition even if it is assumed that the power to tax can be delegated to the executive. The basis of the statutory power conferred by the statute cannot be transgressed by the rule making authority. A rule making authority has no plenary power. It has to act within the limits of the power granted to it.[1]

1. *Bimal Chandra Banerjee* v. *State of Madhya Pradesh,* AIR 1971 SC 517: 1971 MPLJ 168: 1971 (1) SCJ 678: (1971) 1 SCR 844.

It is a well-settled principle of interpretation of statutes that the conferment of rule-making power by an Act does not enable the rule-making authority to make a rule which travels beyond the scope of the enabling Act or which is inconsistent therewith or repugnant thereto.[1]

A subordinate legislation, if valid, and treated as if enacted in the Act has the same force as the Statute which enabled its making. When making of such a rule falls within the statutory purposes, the restrictions imposed by such a rule has to be held as the one imposed by the law made by the legislature. As, having regard to the language of section 7(3) of the Karnataka Excise Act and its effect, a valid rule made under the Act has to be treated, for all purposes, as a law made by the State legislature, it cannot be said that the rule under conferring the right of sole distribution of liquor on a Government company, being subordinate legislation, is not a restriction imposed by law as contemplated by article 304(b) of the Constitution.[2]

II. Retrospective Operation of Law

1. *Decision to be Based on Amended Law*

If the law, which the Tribunal seeks to apply to the dispute, is amended, so as to make the law applicable to the transaction in dispute, it would be bound to decide the question in the light of the law so amended. Similarly when the question has been referred to the High Court and in the meanwhile the law has been amended with retroactive operation, it would be the duty of the High Court to apply the law so amended if it applies. By taking notice of the law which has been substituted for the original provision, the High Court is giving effect to legislative intent and does no more than what must be deemed to be necessarily implicit in the question referred by the Tribunal, provided the question is couched in terms of sufficient amplitude to cover an enquiry into the question in the light of the amended law, and the enquiry does not necessitate investigation of fresh facts.[3]

2. *Rules have Effect Subject to the Act*

The proviso to article 309, clearly lays down that 'any rules so made shall have effect, subject to the provisions of any such Act'. Thus if the appropriate Legislature has passed an Act, under article 309, the rules framed under the proviso, will have effect, subject to that Act; but, in the absence of any Act, of the appropriate Legislature, on the matter, the rules, made by the President, or by such person as he may direct are to have full effect, both prospectively and, retrospectively. Apart from the limitations, pointed out above, there is none other, imposed by the proviso to article 227 regarding the ambit of the operation of such rules. In other words, the rules, unless they can be impeached on grounds such as breach of Part III, or any other Constitutional provision, must be enforced, if made by the appropriate authority.[4]

---

1. *State of Karnataka* v. *H. Ganesh Kamath,* 1983 SCC (Cri) 514: 1983 UJ (SC) 345: (1983) 2 SCC 402: 1983 SCC (Cri) 514: 1983 Cr LR (SC) 501.
2. *Jagadale* v. *State of Karnataka,* AIR 1990 Karn 251 (DB).
3. *Commissioner of Sales Tax, U.P.* v. *Bijli Cotton Mills,* AIR 1964 SC 1594: 1964 (2) SCJ 509: (1964) 7 SCR 383: (1964) 2 SCWR 204.
4. *B.S. Vadera* v. *Union of India,* AIR 1969 SC 118: 1970 (1) Lab LJ 499.

3. Retrospective Operation by Express Provision or Necessary Implication

It is open to a sovereign legislature to enact laws which have retrospective operation. Even when the Parliament enacts retrospective laws such laws are no doubt *prima facie* of questionable policy contrary to the general principles that legislation by which the conduct of mankind is to be regulated ought, when introduced for the first time, to deal with further acts, and ought not to change the character of past transaction carried on upon the faith of the then existing law. The courts will not, therefore, ascribe retrospectivity to new law affecting rights unless by express words or necessary implication, it appears that such was the intention of the legislature.[1]

4. Retrospective Effect cannot be given to a Law Enhancing Punishment for an Offence

The general principle as embodied in article 20(1) is that a statute can be made to operate retrospectively by express enactment to that effect or by necessary implication of law, *ex-post-facto* laws may be classified as follows: (a) every law that makes an action done before the passing of the law and which was innocent when done, and punishes that action; (b) every law that aggravates a crime or makes it greater than it was, when committed, (c) every law that changes the punishment and inflicts a greater punishment than the law annexed to the crime when committed; and (d) every law that alters the legal rules of evidence and receives less or different testimony than the law required at the time of the commission of the offence in order to convict the offender. Laws affecting rules of evidence and procedure are not covered by article 20(1). Hence, such rules may be made to operate retrospectively so as to apply to the prosecution for offences committed even before the passing of such rules.[2] Retrospective affect cannot be given to a law enhancing punishment for an offence, so as to cover offences committed prior to the making of the law.[3]

5. Retrospective Operation of Rules Possible, if Authorised by the Act

There is no doubt that unlike legislation made by a sovereign legislature, subordinate legislation made by a delegate cannot have retrospective effect, unless the rule-making power in the statute concerned expressly or by necessary implication confers power in this behalf.[4]

6. Harsh Operation of Retrospective Operation is Invalid

Retrospective operation of an Act, if harshly operates, is liable to be held as invalid.[5]

1. *I.T.O* v. *I.M.C. Ponnoose*, AIR 1970 SC 385: 1970 (1) SCJ 435: (1970) 1 SCR 678.
2. *Sajjan Singh* v. *State of Punjab*, AIR 1964 SC 464: 1964 Cur LJ (SC) 37.
3. *Commissioner of Wealth-tax, Amritsar* v. *Suresh Seth*, AIR 1981 SC 1106: 1981 (6) Taxman 35 (SC): 1981 Tax LR 786: 1981 SCC (Tax) 168: (1981) 2 SCC 790: 1981 UPTJ 941: 1981 UJ (SC) 555; and *Tiwari Kanhaiyalal* v. *Commissioner of Income-tax, Delhi*, AIR 1975 SC 902: 1975 Cr LJ 781: 1975 SCC (Cri) 312: 1975 SCC (Tax) 214: 1975 Tax LR 499: (1975) 4 SCC 401: 1975 (2) SCJ 34: (1975) 3 SCR 927.
4. *State of Madhya Pradesh* v. *Tikamdas*, AIR 1975 SC 1429 (3J): (1975) 2 SCC 100: 1975 SCC (Tax) 310: (1975) 2 SCWR 104.
5. *A.B. Abdul Kadir* v. *State of Kerala*, (1976) 25 CR 690: 1976 Tax LR 1293: (1976) 3 SCC 219: (1976) 2 SCR 690.

7. Unjust and Oppressive Rules Invalid

Rules are liable to be declared invalid if they are manifestly unjust or oppressive or outrageous or directed to an unauthorised end or violative of the general principles of the law of the land or so vague that it cannot be predicated with certainty as to what is prohibited by them or so unreasonable that they cannot be attributed to the power delegated or otherwise disclose bad faith. In the words of Lord Russell of Kilowen, C.J., in *Kruse* v. *Johnson*.[1]

> "If for instance, they were found to be partial or unequal in their operation as between different classes; if they were manifestly unjust; if they disclosed bad faith; if they involved such oppressive or gratuitous interference with the rights of those subject to them as could find no justification in the minds of reasonable men, the court might well say, 'parliament never intended to give authority to make such rules; they are unreasonable and *ultra vires*".[2]

8. Retrospectivity of Rules Permissible, when Authorised by Law

A careful reading of this sub-section makes it clear that any rule made under this sub-section shall operate retrospectively. Normally speaking a subordinate legislation cannot have retrospective effect because it is only the legislature which has the plenary power, which could legislate both prospectively and retrospectively having regard to the generally accepted principle of Delegates Non-Protest Delegate (a delegate cannot delegate). The solitary exception is where the Act itself authorises making of a rule retrospectively. That exactly is the position here. Therefore, one can have no quarrel with the proposition that the rule-making power under sub-section (3) of section 71 of the Karnataka Act could be exercised so as to make a rule retrospectively. This sub-section also lays down that when such a rule is made, the reasons for making the rule shall be specified in a statement laid before both Houses of the State Legislature. Therefore, here again in order that the legislature made aware of the reason, which prompted the Government to make a retrospective rule, the reasons will have to be stated.[3]

9. Enactment of Criminal Law with Retrospective Effect Possible, Except as Provided in Article 20(1) of the Constitution

A sovereign legislature has the power to enact prospective as well as retrospective laws. But article 20(1) sets two limitations upon the law-making power of every legislative authority in India as regards retrospective criminal legislation. It prohibits (i) the making of ex post facto criminal law, *i.e.*, making an act a crime for the first time and then making that law retrospective; (ii) the infliction of a penalty greater than that which might have been inflicted, under the law which was in force when the act was committed. What is prohibited under clause (i) is only conviction or sentence under an ex post facto law and not the

1. (1898) 2 QB 91 (99).
2. *Supreme Court Employees Welfare Association* v. *Union of India*, AIR 1990 SC 334: 1990 Lab IC 324.
3. *Ananthakrishna* v. *State of Karnataka*, ILR 1991 Kar 3582 (DB).

trial thereof. The prohibition is only against prescribing judicial punishment with retrospective effect.[1]

10. Retrospective Validation of Fee

Retrospective validity of fee is not valid since the High Court held that the fee was levied without providing *quid pro quo.* The legislature does not possess powers to reverse the decision rendered by the court in exercise of judicial powers.[2]

Retrospective operation of law does not apply to substantive statute unless expressly made retrospectively. However, in case of procedural laws, position is reverse, *i.e.,* they are of retrospective effect unless expressly said so otherwise.[3]

11. Retrospective Legislation

It cannot be said that vested right cannot be taken away by legislature by way of retrospective legislation. It will, however, be impermissible of violence of articles 14, 16 and any other constitutional provision.

It cannot be said that the effect of the writs issued by the court cannot be nullified by legislature by enacting a law with retrospective effect.[4]

Legislature, in exercise of plenary powers conferred on it by the Constitution render a judicial decision ineffective by enacting valid law on a topic within legislative field, fundamentally altering or changing with retrospective, curative or neutralizing effect, the condition on which such decision is based.[5]

12. Enabling Provision in the Act

Any legislation enacted outside the terms of the enabling provision will be vulnerable to judicial review and *ultra vires.*[6]

III. Gazette Notification

The Gazette-Extraordinary had been published dated May 15, 1995. In the notification issued finally approving the rules after consideration of the objections, it is stated that the Gazette containing draft rules was made available to public on 15th May, 1995. Considering the stakes involved in the matter and the urgency with which the State wanted to proceed, it is certainly possible for the State to make available to public the necessary notification of that very date on which it was issued by getting it published in the Gazette and when the State itself had made it clear that it was made available to the general public on 15th May, 1995 itself, there is no reason to doubt the correctness of the same. This procedure having been

---

1. *Ganga Ram Patel* v. *State of Orissa,* II (1995) CCR 678 (Ori).
2. *B. Krishna Bhat* v. *State of Karnataka,* (2001) 3 SCALE 175 SC: 2001 AIR SCW 1485: JT 2001 (4) SC 497: 2001 (4) Kant LJ 289: (2001) 4 SCC 227: 2001 (5) SRJ 356: 2001 (3) Supreme 136.
3. *Shyam Sunder* v. *Ram Kumar,* 2001 (V) AD (SC) 723: AIR 2001 SCW 2768: JT 2001 (6) SC 94: (2001) 8 SCC 24: 2001 (3) SCJ 291: (2001) 4 SCALE 710: 2001 (5) Supreme 492.
4. *Verender Singh Hooda* v. *State of Haryana,* AIR 2005 SC 137: 2005 Lab IC 4: 2004 AIR SCW 6386: (2004) 12 SCC 588: (2004) 9 SCALE 120: 2005 (1) Supreme 589.
5. *State Bank's Staff Union* v. *Union of India,* AIR 2005 SC 3446: 2005 Lab IC 4257: 2005 AIR SCW 4622: (2005) 7 SCC 584: 2005 (7) SCJ 368: 2006 (1) SCT 472: (2005) 7 SCALE 296: 2005 (6) Supreme 522.
6. *P.T.C. India Ltd.* v. *Central Electricity Regulatory Commission,* AIR 2010 SC 1338 (1361) (Cons. Bench).

followed by the Government, the matter having been examined at different levels and an institutional decision taken, no exception can be taken to the nature of consideration of the matter. There had been a detailed consideration made by the Excise Commissioner of the various objections raised by different persons and the reasons as to why they are enhancing also have been set forth. In the circumstances, it could not be contended that the respondents have not followed the due procedure in making the amendment to the rules.[1]

IV. Enforcement of Rules

1. Rules Laying before Legislature

In the case of a statute directing rules to be laid before the Parliament or the Legislature without any condition attached, the rule is only directory. Though the statute says that the rules shall be laid before the Parliament as the provision in the statute is conceived in public interest the dereliction of the duty by the Minister or other officer concerned in not following the procedure should not be made to affect the members of the public governed by the rules.

If the legislation intended to make that rule mandatory, they would have clearly mentioned the legal consequences of its non-compliance.[2]

Use of the word "shall" is not decisive whether it is mandatory or directory and the whole statute is to be considered of the rules. In the absence of contingency for non-compliance for laying of subordinate legislation before Legislature the rule will be directory.[3]

2. *Rules to be Effective from the Date they are Sought to be Enforced by the Government*

From the last portion of sub-section (4), it is quite evident that the intention of the Legislature was to make the rules effective from the date they are sought to be enforced by the Government and not from the date after the expiry of the 30 days after laying them before both the Houses. In case the rules were to become effective only after the expiry of 30 days after laying them before both the Houses, then making a provision that any modification or annulment made by the Legislature shall not prejudice or validly affect anything previously done under the rules would have no meaning.

Further, if the Legislature had intended that the rules should not take effect till they had the sanction of the two Houses, it would have expressly said so by employing negative language. The section does not say that the rule would not be effective till it is laid before the two Houses. What really it provides is that in the event of the two Houses modifying the rule, it is the modified rule, which would be effective and in the event of the two Houses annulling the rules, the rules would be ineffective. In this view of the matter the only irresistible conclusion that can be arrived at is that it is from the date on which the Government decides to make

---

1. *Karnataka Wine Merchants Association (Regd.), Bangalore* v. *State of Karnataka,* 1995 (4) Kar LJ 214(B).
2. *D.K. Krishnan* v. *Secretary, Regional Transport Authority, Chittoor,* AIR 1956 AP 1.
3. *Atlas Cycle Industries Ltd.* v. *State of Haryana,* 1979 SCC (Cri) 422: 1979 Cr LJ 927.

the rules effective, they come into force, and not after the expiry of 30 days after they are placed before both the Houses of the Legislature.[1]

3. Rules to be Effective from the Date of Enforcement

Rules become effective from date of its enforcement without a need to wait for its being placed before the Legislature; if Legislature modifies the rule, thereafter the modified rule shall be enforced and till then, whatever was done earlier under the unmodified rule remains valid.

Requirement of laying before the Legislature certainly, is a mandatory requirement, but, cannot e construed as a conditions precedent for the enforcement of the rules. Section 71 does not say that the rules could be enforced only after a laying of 30 days before the Houses of Legislature; it does not even provide for the withdrawal of or ceasing to have effect, of the rule, in case the rules are not so placed within any particular time.[2]

4. Rules-Making Powers

If the main Act is within the legislative competence of the State Legislature and the rules have been framed under a validly delegated authority and are within the scope of that authority, the rules cannot be challenged on the ground of lack of legislative competence. If the Act is valid, so are the rules.[3]

82. Power to remove difficulties.—(1) If any difficulty arises in giving effect to the provisions of this Act, the Government may, by order published in the Official Gazette, make such provisions, not inconsistent with the provisions of this Act, as may appear to be necessary for removing the difficulty:

Provided that no order shall be made under this section after the expiry of two years from the date of commencement of this Act.

(2) Every order made under this section shall be laid as soon as may be after it is made before the Legislative Assembly.

83. Repeal and savings.—Immediately with effect from the date on which this Act comes into force, the Punjab Excise Act, 1914 (1 of 1914) as in force in the National Capital Territory of Delhi shall stand repealed, provided that the repeal shall not affect—

(a) the previous operation of the Act under repeal;

(b) any penalty, forfeiture or punishment incurred in respect of any offence committed under the Act under repeal;

(c) any investigation or remedy in respect of any such penalty, forfeiture or punishment;

(d) any such investigation, legal proceeding or remedy may be instituted, continued or enforced and any such penalty,

1. *State of Karnataka* v. *Anjanappa & Co.*, 1988 (2) Kar LJ 118 (DB).
2. *Jagadale* v. *State of Karnataka*, AIR 1990 Karn 251 (DB).
3. *Khoday Distilleries Ltd.* v. *State of Karnataka*, (1996) 10 SCC 304: 1996 AIR SCW 308: AIR 1996 SC 911.

forfeiture or punishment may be imposed, as if this Act had not been passed:

Provided that subject to the preceding provisions, anything done or any action taken under the Act under repeal, shall be deemed to have been done or taken under the corresponding provision of this Act and shall continue in force accordingly, unless and until superseded by anything done or any action taken under this Act.

SYNOPSIS

1. **Repeal by Implication**
2. **Right of Renewal of Permit under the Old Act Stands Repealed with the Expiry of its Period**
3. **Effect of Repeal is to Obliterate the Act Completely from the Record of Parliament**
4. **Subsequent Legislation cannot Enhance the Punishment for the Offence Committed before its Commencement, it can Reduce the Same**
5. **Section 6 of General Clauses Act is not Applicable on Rules**

Comments

1. Repeal by Implication

Before coming to the conclusion that there is a repeal by implication, the court must be satisfied that the two enactments are so inconsistent or repugnant that they cannot stand together and the repeal of the express prior enactment must flow from necessary implication of the language of the later enactment.[1]

2. Right of Renewal of Permit under the old Act Stands Repealed with the Expiry of its Period

On the commencement of new Act, permit under the repealed Act continues to be operative till the expiry of its period. However, thereafter fresh application for grant of permit has to be made. Right of renewal of permit under old Act stands repealed with the expiry of its period.[2]

3. Effect of Repeal is to Obliterate the Act Completely from the Record of Parliament

Whenever an Act is repealed it must be considered, except to the transactions past and closed as if it had never existed. The effect thereof is to obliterate the Act completely from the record of Parliament as if it had never been passed by it, it never existed, except for the purpose of those actions which were commenced, prosecuted and concluded while it was existing law, legal fiction is one which is not actually a reality and which the law recognizes and court accepts a reality.

When there is a repeal and simultaneous re-enactment, section 6 of the General Clauses Act, 1897 would apply to such a case, unless certain intentions can be gathered from the repealing Act.[3]

---

1. *T.S. Baliah* v. *T.S. Rangachari,* AIR 1969 SC 701: (1969) 3 SCR 65.
2. *Secretary Q.DMTW Co-op. Society Ltd.* v. *Regional Transport Authority,* AIR 1995 SC 82: 1994 AIR SCW 4095: 1994 (24) All LR 360: JT 1994 (5) SC 426: 1994 (2) Ker LT 605: 1994 (3) SCJ 513.
3. *Gajraj Singh* v. *State Transport Tribunal,* AIR 1997 SC 412: 1996 All LJ 1767.

4. Subsequent Legislation cannot Enhance the Punishment for the Offence Committed before its Commencement, it can Reduce the Same

What is the jurisprudential philosophy involved in the second limb of clause (1) of article 20 of the Constitution? "No person shall be subjected to a penalty greater than that which might have been inflicted under the law in force at the time of commission of the offence." It is a fundamental right of every person that he should not be subjected to greater penalty than what the law prescribed, and no *ex post facto* legislation is permissible for escalating the severity of the punishment. But if any subsequent legislation would downgrade the harshness of the sentence for the same offence, it would be a salutary principle for administration of criminal justice to suggest that the said legislative benevolence can be extended to the accused who awaits judicial verdict regarding sentence.[1]

The position is well-known that at common law, the normal effect of repealing a statute or deleting a provision is to obliterate it from the statute book as completely as it had never been passed, and the statute must be considered as a law that never existed.[2]

5. Section 6 of General Clauses Act is not Applicable on Rules

At common law, the normal effect of repealing a statute or deleting a provision is to obliterate it from the statute-book as completely as if it had never been passed, and the statute must be considered as a law that never existed. To this rule, an exception is engrafted by the provisions of section 6(1). If a provision of a statute is unconditionally omitted without a saving clause in favour of pending proceedings, all actions must stop where the omission finds them, and if final relief has not been granted before the omission goes into effect, it cannot be granted afterwards. Savings of the nature contained in section 6 or in special Acts may modify the position. Thus, the operation of repeal or deletion as to the future and the past largely depends on the savings applicable. In a case where a particular provision in a statute is omitted and in its place another provision dealing with the same contingency is introduced without a saving clause in favour of pending proceedings then it can be reasonably inferred that the intention of the legislature is that the pending proceedings shall not continue but fresh proceedings for the same purpose may be initiated under the new provision.

Section 6 of the General Clauses Act, 1897 is applicable where any Central Act or regulation made after commencement of the General Clauses Act repeals any enactment. It is not applicable in the case of omission of a "rule".[3]

---

1. *State through CBI, Delhi* v. *Gian Singh,* (1999) 5 SCALE 497.
2. *Kolahpur Canesugar Works Ltd.* v. *Union of India,* (2000) 2 SC 536 Reported in 2001 VI AD (SC) 705.
3. *Kolhapur Canesugar Works Ltd.* v. *Union of India,* (2000) 2 SCC 536: AIR 2000 SC 811.

SCHEDULE

(*See* section 27)

S. No.	Description of intoxicants	Rate
(1)	(2)	(3)
1.	Indian Liquor and Foreign Liquor	400 per cent. of the wholesale price.
2.	Wine and Liquor (Indian and Foreign)	80 per cent. of the wholesale price.
3.	Beer and Cider (Indian and Foreign)	200 per cent. of the wholesale price.
4.	Country Liquor.	250 per cent. of the wholesale price.
5.	Spirituous Preparations, including essence, but other than Medicinal and Toilet preparations, as defined in the Medicinal and Toilet Preparations (Excise Duties) Act, 1955 (16 of 1955).	20 per cent. of the wholesale price.
6.	Bhang	Rs. 5.00 per kilogram.

THE DELHI EXCISE RULES, 2010[1]

In exercise of the powers conferred by section 81 of the Delhi Excise Act, 2009 (Delhi Act 10 of 2010), the Government of the National Capital Territory of Delhi hereby makes the following rules, namely:—

CHAPTER I

PRELIMINARY AND DEFINITIONS

1. Short title and commencement.—(1) These rules may be called the Delhi Excise Rules, 2010.

(2) These rules (other than the rules in Chapter X) shall come into force on the date of their publication in the Delhi Gazette. Chapter X shall be notified separately later. Till such date, the rates of duties, fees and price structure prescribed under the Punjab Excise Act, 1914 (as extended to the Natinal Capital Territory of Delhi) and rules made thereunder shall continue to be in force.

2. Definitions.—In these rules, unless the context otherwise requires.—

(1) "Act" means the Delhi Excise Act, 2009 (Delhi Act 10 of 2010);

(2) "alcopop" means flavoured alcoholic beverages having fruit juices or other flavourings with an alcoholic strength up to 5 per cent. v/v;

(3) "authorised agent" means any person authorised in writing by a licensee to appear on his behalf before any officer or before any court, empowered under the Act;

(4) "bhang" means the dried leaves of hemp plant, whether male or female, and whether cultivated or uncultivated;

(5) "bottle" means a bottle for excisable articles of such type or description as may be or as may have been permitted by the Excise Commissioner from time-to-time and includes can and pouch;

(6) "budget hotel" means a hotel approved by the Ministry of Tourism, Government of India which does not provide any room service of food or beverages of any kind;

(7) "bulk litre" means a litre with reference to the bulk or quantity of the contents;

(8) "chemical examiner" means the officer appointed by the Government as chemical examiner to the Excise Control Laboratory, Delhi Forensic Science Laboratory, the Central Revenues Control Laboratory or the Central Forensic Science Laboratory, and shall also include the deputy chemical examiners of the above laboratories or any other laboratory approved by the Excise Commissioner;

---

1. Came into force *vide* Notification No.F.10(8)/Fin(Rev.-I)/2010-11/SSF/104, dated 4th October, 2010.

(9) "customs area" means the area of a customs station and any area in which imported goods or exported goods are ordinarily kept before clearance by authorities under the Customs Act, 1962 (52 of 1962);

(10) "Customs bonded warehouse" means a public warehouse under section 57 or a private warehouse licensed under section 58 of the Customs Act, 1962 (52 of 1962);

(11) "defective bottle" means a sealed bottle containing less than the prescribed quantity of liquor, sedimented liquor, foreign object visible to the naked eye, material hazardous to health like dead insects, etc., any other defect which, in the opinion of the Deputy Commissioner, would render the liquor unfit for human consumption and a bottle whose date of validity has expired;

(12) "denatured spirit" means spirit having strength not less than 66 degree over proof or 94.85 per cent. volume by volume, negative methyl alcohol, positive methylene blue with 0.5 percent light caoutchoucine, 0.5 percent pyridine and 0.2 per cent. crotoualdehyde;

(13) "draught beer" means fresh beer contained in a keg not having more than 5 per cent. volume by volume (v/v) alcoholic contents;

(14) "economy Indian liquor" means low cost liquor as declared by the Excise commissioner;

(15) "family" means husband, wife, dependant sons, daughters and parents;

(16) "form" means a form appended to these rules;

(17) "gauge" means to determine the quantity of spirit contained in, or taken from any cask or other receptacle or to determine capacity of any cask or receptacle;

[1][(17A) "guest house" means a guest house approved by the Tourism Department, Government of National Capital Territory of Delhi;]

(18) "hop" means ripened cones of female hop plant used for giving flavour to malt liquor;

(19) "hostel" means a place used for lodging the students by an educational institution whether Government or private;

(20) "in bond" means to store intoxicant without payment of duty;

(21) "Inspector" includes – Sub-Inspector;

(22) "intoxicating spirituous preparations" means the intoxicating preparations containing more than 20 degrees proof alcohol, whether self generated or added as such;

(23) "keg" means a closed receptacle, made of wood or metal or such other substance, as may be designed for containing and carriage of beer by the brewery of the size of not less than twenty litres;

(24) "lahan" means a saccharine solution from which spirit is obtained by distillation and includes fermented wash;

(25) "leaked bottle" means a bottle of which the contents are not properly secured, resulting into leakage of contents thereof;

(26) "licensee" means a person licensed to manufacture, possess, import, export, transport, store, purchase, sale, or dispense any intoxicant;

1. Ins. by Notification No. F.10(12)/Fin(Rev-I)/2010-11/DS II/111, dated 21st March, 2011.

(27) "liqueur" means an alcoholic beverage, flavoured with fruits, herbs, nuts, spices, flowers, or cream and bottled with added sugar, alcoholic content is not a distinctive feature;

(28) "litre" means bulk litre of 1000 millilitres;

(29) "London Proof Spirit" means a mixture of ethyl alcohol and water which at a temperature of 15.5 degrees centigrade has a specific gravity of 0.91984 and contains 49.24 per cent. weight or 57.06 per cent. volume of alcohol;

(30) "malt" means the germinated barley;

(31) "medicated wine" means wine classified and assessed under item 22.05 of the Customs Tariff Act, 1975 (51 of 1975) containing not more than 42 degree proof alcohol;

(32) "military club" means a club admission to which is exclusively reserved for the members of the armed forces;

(33) "minimum stock" means such stock as may be fixed by the Excise Commissioner to be the minimum stock of liquor in bottles;

(34) "neutral spirit" means neutral spirit as defined by Bureau of Indian Standards;

(35) "over proof (o.p)" means spirit of a strength greater than that of London proof;

(36) "person" includes an individual, Hindu undivided family, partnership firm, co-operative society, and company incorporated under the Companies Act, 1956 (1 of 1956);

(37) "person interested in the business of a dealer" includes every person interested in such business as a proprietor, shareholder, member, director, partner, attorney or an agent;

(38) "plain spirit" means spirit to which no flavour has been communicated and to which no flavouring or colouring matter or other material or ingredient has been added;

(39) "prescription" means a prescription given by a registered medical practitioner to a *bona fide* patient;

(40) "proof with reference to spirit" means the strength or proof as ascertained by hydrometer or any other means authorized by the Excise Commissioner;

(41) "proper officer" means the Deputy Commissioner and any other officer of the Excise Department;

(42) "prove" means to test the spirit by hydrometer or any other method;

(43) "public place" means any place intended for use by or accessible to the public and includes any hostel and conveyance running or parked on public roads or parking area;

(44) "registered medical practitioner" means a medical practitioner in any state in India under any law registered as a medical practitioners;

(45) "restaurant" means any place to which the public are admitted for consumption of food and beverage for a consideration;

(46) "sacramental wine" includes wine, grape juice and such other liquor as may be approved by the Government from time-to-time for use for any *bona fide* religious purpose in accordance with ancient custom;

(47) "section" means the section of the Act;

(48) "special denatured spirit" means ethanol denatured with 0.2% crotonaldehyde and 4 grams denatonium benzoate/denatonium sacchride per 100 litres of ethanol;

(49) "spurious liquor" means liquor, which is fake, imitation or unauthentic;

(50) "under proof (u.p.)" means spirit of a strength less than that of London proof;

(51) "year" means the year beginning with 1st April or any subsequent date and ending with 31st March.

Words and expressions defined in the Act and not defined in these rules shall have the same meaning, respectively assigned to them in the Act.

Policy decision:

1. Grant of licence depends upon the policy prevailing as on the date of licence. The court would, therefore, not bind the Government with a policy, which was existing on the date of application as per the previous policy. A prior decision would not bind the Government for all times to come. When the Government is satisfied that the change in the policy was necessary in the public interest, it would be entitled to revise the policy and lay down a new policy; *PTR Transport (Madras) Private Ltd.* v. *Union of India,* (1996) 5 SCC 268.

2. It is well settled that the courts, in exercise of their power of judicial review, do not ordinarily interfere with the policy decisions unless such policy framed could be faulted on grounds of *mala fide,* unreasonableness, unfairness etc. The mere fact that it would hurt business interests of a party, does not justify validity of the policy; *Ugar Sugar Works Ltd.* v. *Delhi Administration,* (2001) 3 SCC 635.

3. In a case of this nature where the State has exclusive privilege and citizen has no fundamental right to carry on business in liquor, the policy, which was applicable, is the one, which is prevalent on the date of grant, and not the one, on which the application had been filed. If a policy decision had been taken on 16-9-2005 not to grant l-52 licence, no licence could have been granted after the said date; *Kuldeep Singh* v. *Government of N.C.T. of Delhi,* (2006) 5 SCC 702.

4. There cannot be any doubt whatsoever that a policy decision can be reviewed from time to time. It is also beyond any doubt the concessions granted can be withdrawn in public interest; *Kusumam Hotels (P) Ltd.* v. *Kerala Electricity Board,* (2008) 13 SCC 213.

5. The Court cannot strike down a policy decision taken by the government merely because it feels that another decision would have been fairer or would be fairer or wiser or more scientific or logical. The court can interfere only if the policy decision is patently arbitrary, discriminatory or *mala fide; R.K. Garg's* case, AIR 1981 SC 138.

CHAPTER II

IMPORT, EXPORT, TRANSPORT, POSSESSION, PERMITS AND PASSES OF INTOXICANTS

3. Passes and permits where not required.—Nothing in these rules shall apply to liquor imported, exported or transported.—

(1) for private consumption and not for sale, in any quantity not exceeding the maximum quantity prescribed for possession or retail sale, or

(2) by or on behalf of any Government officer in his official capacity.

4. All exports subject to other regulations.—All exports of liquor shall be subject, in addition to the provisions of these rules, to all regulations for its import into the State concerned.

5. Permission for re-export.—The permission to re-export of Indian Liquor, Foreign Liquor and Country Liquor to other States shall be granted by the Excise Commissioner.

6. Pass mandatory for import, export or transport of liquor.—No liquor shall be imported, exported or transported, except under a pass issued in accordance with the rules for the time being in force for such import, export and transport.

7. Liquor to be imported conforming to prescribed standards.—Liquor may be imported from any place in or outside India, provided it conforms to the specifications required in an order made by the Excise Commissioner with the prior approval of the Government or if no such order has been made, which conforms to the specifications laid down by the Bureau of Indian Standards regarding alcoholic strength.

8. Import of liquor from licensed sources.—Indian Liquor, Country Liquor, rectified spirit, denatured spirit and special denatured spirit shall not be imported, except from a licensed distillery, brewery, winery or bottling plant.

9. Payment of duty and fee on import, export and transport of liquor.—(1) No liquor on which the prescribed rate of duty and fee have not been paid or a bond has been executed in lieu thereof, may be imported, exported or transported.

(2) Excise Commissioner may allow re-export of Indian Liquor and Country Liquor without payment of duty in special cases for reasons to be recorded.

10. Grant of pass and permit.—(1) The licensee shall apply for the issue of transport pass and the same shall be issued in such form and manner as may be prescribed or as specified by the Excise Commissioner from time-to-time. Each application shall be accompanied by a receipted treasury challan showing the deposit of duty and fee, payable on the quantity of liquor for which transport pass is required, unless duty and fee have been paid at the time of import.

(2) The Assistant Commissioner shall cause the application to be scrutinized to see that the quantity applied is within the limit, if any, of the licensee and after satisfying himself that the duty has been paid and the application form is other wise in order, he shall issue the transport pass.

(3) The transport pass shall be in triplicate; the first copy shall be issued to the applicant, the second copy shall be given to the licensee of the warehouse, the third copy shall remain on record in the office in the form of compact disc or paper print. The quantity issued shall be indicated legibly both in figures and words on all the copies of the pass.

(4) No over-writing or cutting is permissible. If because of any reason some erroneous entries have been made in the pass, the Assistant Commissioner shall issue a fresh pass and shall cancel all the three copies of the defective pass.

(5) The signature of the excise official, by whom the pass is issued shall be in ink and his name and designation shall be written in capital letters on all the copies, whenever prepared manually.

(6) The liquor shall be issued from the warehouse on the basis of the transport passes. The record of transactions covered by such passes shall be maintained in Form 2.

(7) The record of such passes shall be maintained by the licensee or the excise officer, as the case may be, in register in Form 2.

(8) Before issuing the liquor, the licensee or the excise officer, as the case may be, shall make appropriate endorsements on the copies of the pass of the—

(a) pass-holder;

(b) warehouse licensee, and;

(c) copies to be retained by him in personal custody.

A monthly statement of all such passes shall be submitted to the Assistant Commissioner, who shall cause the entries made in the said statement to be compared with the relevant records in the office. The Assistant Commissioner, shall, after such comparison, submit his report to the Deputy Commissioner and shall make an endorsement to this effect on the statement aforesaid.

(9) The Assistant Commissioner shall maintain record showing the particulars of all such passes issued by him with a summary showing the total number of passes issued, names of the licensees to whom issued, total quantity of liquor and the total duty involved. The Assistant Commissioner shall append his signature below the summary.

11. Person licensed to import, export and transport of liquor and exception thereof.—No person except a licensed vendor may import, export or transport liquor, provided that—

(a) any person holding a permit for the possession of liquor may import and transport any quantity, not exceeding the quantity which he is permitted to possess under a permit on payment of prescribed duty and fee, if any;

(b) Defence Laboratory, Quarter Master General branch, may import, transport or possess Indian Liquor on the basis of an import permit for purposes of analysis without paying fee.

12. Conditions applicable on individual's possession limit.—No person shall have in his possession any quantity of intoxicant, except as per the limit of possession and retail sale prescribed and further on the condition that it shall not be—

(a) consumed in any public place;

(b) taken into or kept upon any premises used as a place to which the public are admitted for consumption of food or drink for consideration, unless such premises have been licensed for the consumption of liquor thereon under the Act or the rules made thereunder, or have been exempted by an order by the Government in writing from the provisions of these rules.

13. Possession of liquor not to extend to unlicensed civilian club.—(1) The possession of liquor of any kind by any person shall be restricted to the extent that it shall not be kept or possessed by or on behalf of such person on the premises of unlicensed civilian club.

14. Conditions applicable to grant of pass and permit.—(1) All passes and permits granted to cover import, export and transport of intoxicants shall be subject to the conditions—

(a) that bulk shall not be broken in transit;

(b) that copies of permits or passes shall be sent to the Excise Officer of the district of origin or destination, as the case may be, in the case of imports and exports:

Provided that a pass shall be sufficient to cover the transport of intoxicant to the premises where the importer is either licensed to sell or/and to possess intoxicants in Delhi.

(2) The export pass shall show in all cases the quantity and strength of intoxicants to be exported and that the duty at the rates prevailing in Delhi has been paid, or exemption has been granted, or a bond has been executed to safeguard excise revenue.

15. Import fee to be charged for import of liquor, if applicable.—In respect of permits granted for the import of liquor to the holders of L-1 licence, import fee, as prescribed, shall be charged.

16. Power of refusal to grant permit and pass.—The Excise Commissioner, the Deputy Commissioner or the Assistant Commissioner as the case may be, may refuse to grant any pass or permit for any sufficient reason to be recorded and shall not grant any such pass or permit, if he has reason to believe that the applicant has not paid any dues demanded from him.

17. Authority empowered to issue permit or pass.—Passes for the import, export or transport of liquor and permit for possession of liquor may be granted by the Deputy Commissioner or he may delegate his powers to any excise officer subordinate to him.

18. Extension of validity of permit or pass.—(1) No pass or permit shall be valid after the date of its expiry provided that the Deputy Commissioner, granting the permit or the authority to authorise the dispatch of any consignment under these rules may extend the period of currency thereof, if extension is applied for due to delay in transit of a consignment or for any other sufficient reason on payment of composition money, not exceeding twenty-five per cent. of the duty of the consignment, or otherwise, for reasons to be recorded.

(2) Where during the course of import of liquor, the delay occurs for reasons beyond the control of the licensee, he shall submit an application for re-validation of import permit to the Deputy Commissioner within three working days of the occurrence of the event and the Deputy Commissioner may re-validate the same.

(3) For transport permit, the application for such re-validation shall be made on the next working day from the date of expiry of validity.

(4) Where the application is not submitted within the stipulated period or the delay is for any other reason, the revalidation may be done on payment of composition money, which shall not exceed ten per cent. of the duty involved.

19. Condition for import of liquor for troops.—(1) Indian liquor may be imported from any State or Union territory of India for the use of troops, provided that such liquor does not suffer duty at a lower rate than that prevailing in Delhi and the import is covered by a permit in Form P-9, granted by the Deputy Commissioner or other authorized officer.

(2) For the import of liquor brands not registered in Delhi, the application made for the issue of the said permit, shall contain declaration of wholesale price of such brands for determination of duty as applicable for the brands registered in Delhi.

CHAPTER III

SALE AND LICENCE OF INTOXICANTS

20. Maximum limit for retail sale and individual possession of liquor.—The maximum quantities of intoxicants specified below, which for the purposes of the Act, may be sold by retail and possessed exclusively, by an individual not below the age of twenty-five years in Delhi, shall be as follows:—

(a)	(i) Indian Liquor and Foreign Liquor (Whisky rum, gin, vodka, and brandy), except wine liqueur, beer, cider and alcopop; (ii) wine, beer, liqueur, cider and alcopop; (iii) Indian Liquor or Foreign Liquor; (iv) Foreign Liquor	(i) nine litres; (ii) eighteen litres; (iii) one litre while entering into Delhi from other States; (iv) two litres while entering into Delhi from other countries.
(b)	Holder of licence in Form L-30	(i) licence in Form L-30 shall be issued by the Deputy Commissioner for specific limit (in excess of individual limit) to be determined in each case, on payment of prescribed fee for a year or part thereof for *bona fide* consumption by him, members of his family and his guests; (ii) the holder of licence in Form L-30 may purchase, transport and possess the quantity of liquor specified in the permit; (iii) the licence shall be renewed by the Assistant Commissioner on payment of requisite fee.
(c)	P-10 permit	P-10 permit may be issued by the Deputy Commissioner for specific occasion, for a specific limit to be determined in each case, on payment of prescribed fee. The holder of such permit shall be allowed to purchase, possess, transport and serve liquor at a place specified in the permit, subject to the following conditions:—

		(i) the area is screened off from public view; (ii) liquor is served only to adults above twenty-five years in age; (iii) liquor is procured from licensed source in Delhi and shall produce purchase voucher on demand; (iv) if liquor is served outside the residence, P-10 permit shall be obtained even if the quantity of liquor to be served is equal to or less than the possession limit of an individual specified in clause (a) of sub-rule (1): Provided that the Deputy Commissioner may delegate his power under this clause to any excise officer:

Provided that the above restrictions shall not apply in respect of sales to:—

(i) the members of the diplomatic missions in India, staying in Delhi;

(ii) the Hospitality Organisation, Ministry of External Affairs, Government of India:

Provided further that the Bishop of Delhi may, for *bona fide* church use for sacramental purpose, purchase, transport and possess sacramental wine up to 91 litres.

(2) Country liquor	3 litres
(3) Bhang or any preparation or admixture thereof	120 grams
(4) Rectified spirit	0.5 litre
(5) Denatured spirit	5 litres

(6) Defence personnel entering or passing through Delhi on leave may possess the quantity of intoxicants to the extent given below:

I	II	III	IV	V
S. No.	Ranks of officers	Whisky, brandy vodka, gin and rum (in litres)	Wine and liqueur, (in litres)	Beer and cider (in litres)
1.	Lieutenant General and his equivalent ranks in Navy and Air Force.	10	2	48
2.	Major General, Brigadier and their equivalent ranks in Navy and Air Force	5	2	48
3.	Other officers	3	2	15
4.	JCOs and their equivalent ranks in Navy and Air Force	2	—	—
5.	Other ranks	2	—	—

(7) Possession of lahan in any quantity is prohibited.

21. Period for which licence may be granted.—Unless the Government otherwise directs, licence shall ordinarily be granted for a period of one year.

Temporary licence may be given to provide for the sale of liquor on special occasions in such cases and on such occasions, as the Deputy Commissioner may determine.

All licences other than temporary licences shall, unless otherwise provided, determine on 31st March, next following the grant or renewal.

22. Determination of number of vends in any area.—(1) The number of liquor and bhang shops, which may be licensed in any area be the number which the Government considers necessary to meet the reasonable requirement of the population.

(2) The Deputy Commissioner may, at any time, in public interest order the transfer of any licensed liquor or bhang shop from one locality to the other.

23. Restriction on grant of licence to certain persons.—Persons to whom licences may not be granted.

In addition to the provisions contained in section 13, licence for the vend of intoxicant shall not be given to:—

(a) any person who does not have Permanent Account Number of the Income Tax Department or has not been assessed to income tax;

(b) any person who is not registered under the Delhi VAT Act, 2004;

(c) any person who has held a licence in Delhi for the sale of any intoxicant and has failed to pay due excise revenue and not exempted by an order of the Government from payment of duty.

24. Conditions for grant of licence for consumption "on" the premises.—(1) When it is proposed to grant a licence for retail vend of liquor for consumption "on" the premises on any premises which were not licensed in the preceding year, the Deputy Commissioner shall take all reasonable steps to ascertain the opinion of persons, who reside or have property in the neighbourhood and are likely to be affected by the proposal.

(2) The Deputy Commissioner shall cause pasting of notice of the proposal on or near the site proposed for the new licence and shall cause the proposal to be made known in the neighbourhood by means of loud speaker.

(3) If any objection is preferred to the proposal, the Deputy Commissioner or a gazetted officer deputed by him, shall enquire into it; the enquiry shall, if possible, be made on the spot. If it is not possible to make the enquiry on the spot, it shall be made in a formal proceeding at which evidence tendered for or against the proposal shall be recorded and the Deputy Commissioner shall decide accordingly. The date and place of the enquiry shall be mentioned in the notice of enquiry.

25. Restriction on employment of certain persons.—No licensee shall employ to assist him in his business in any capacity, whatsoever, any person whose employment, the Deputy Commissioner has, in his discretion forbidden.

26. Restriction on advertisement in print media.—No person shall print or publish in any newspaper, book, booklet, leaflet or any other publication or otherwise display or distribute any advertisement or other material soliciting the use of or offering any liquor or intoxicating drug or any product having nomenclature, similar to a liquor brand.

27. Prohibition on advertisement in electronic media.—No person shall advertise its liquor products or any products having similar nomenclature of a liquor product in electronic media, unless such advertisement conforms to the programme code and advertisement code as laid down in the Cable Television Networks (Regulation) Act, 1995 (7 of 1995) and the rules made thereunder.

Comments

Advertisement Code under Rule 7(2)(Viii) of the Cable Television Network Rules, 1994

No advertisement shall be permitted which promotes directly or indirectly or production, sale or consumption of cigarettes, tobacco products, wine, alcohol, liquor or other intoxicants:

Provided that a product that uses a brand name or logo which is also used for cigarettes, tobacco products, wine, alcohol, liquor or other intoxicants, may be advertised on cable service subject to certain conditions and such advertisements shall be previewed and certified by the Board of Film Certifications suitable for unrestricted public exhibition prior to telecast or transmission or retransmission.

28. Prohibition on circulation on material containing advertisement of liquor.—No person shall circulate, distribute or sell any newspaper, book, booklet, leaflet or other publication printed and published outside Delhi, which contains any advertisement or matter of the nature described in the preceding rule.

29. Foreign print media exempted from advertisement restriction.—The provisions of rules 26 and 28 shall not be applicable to any newspaper, book or magazine printed or published outside India.

30. Prohibition on show-casing of liquor.—No licensee shall display any bottle containing liquor or any empty liquor bottle or any specimen thereof in a show-window.

31. Advertisement material liable to confiscation.—Any bottle containing liquor displayed in any show-window and any newspaper, book, booklet, leaflet or other publication printed, published or otherwise displayed or distributed in contravention of the provision of these rules, besides taking any other action under the Act, shall be forfeited by the Government and such forfeited articles shall be disposed of in such manner as the Deputy Commissioner may direct.

CHAPTER IV

LICENSING OF LIQUOR

32. Class of licences and authorities to grant and renew licences.—(1) Subject to the provisions of sub-rule (2), the following classes of licences may be granted and renewed by authorities noted against each, on payment of prescribed fee:—

S. No.	Form	Details of Licences	Authority empowered to grant	Authority empowered to renew
1	L-1	Wholesale vend of Indian Liquor	Deputy Commissioner	Not renewable
2	L-1F	Wholesale vend of Foreign Liquor	Deputy Commissioner	Not renewable
3	L-2	Wholesale vend of Draught Beer	Deputy Commissioner	Not renewable
4	L-3	Wholesale vend of Country Liquor	Deputy Commissioner	Not renewable
5	L-4	Wholesale vend of Rectified Spirit.	Deputy Commissioner	Deputy Commissioner
6	L-5	Wholesale vend of Denatured Spirit including Special Denatured Spirit	Deputy Commissioner	Deputy Commissioner
7	L-6	Retail vend of Indian Liquor in public sector	Deputy Commissioner	Deputy Commissioner
8	L-6FG	Retail vend of Foreign Liquor in public sector to the holder of licence in Form L-6.	Deputy Commissioner	Deputy Commissioner
9	L-6FE	Retail vend of Foreign Liquor in public sector.	Deputy Commissioner	Deputy Commissioner
10	L-7	Retail vend of Indian Liquor in private sector	Deputy Commissioner	Deputy Commissioner
11	L-7FG	Retail vend of Foreign Liquor in private sector to the holder of licence in Form L-7.	Deputy Commissioner	Deputy Commissioner
12	L-7FE	Retail vend of Foreign Liquor in private sector	Deputy Commissioner	Deputy Commissioner
13	L-8	Retail vend of Country Liquor in public sector	Deputy Commissioner	Deputy Commissioner
14	L-9	Retail vend of Indian Liquor to holders of licence in Form L-1.	Deputy Commissioner	Deputy Commissioner

S. No.	Form	Details of Licences	Authority empowered to grant	Authority empowered to renew
15	L-10	Retail vend of Indian Liquor and Foreign Liquor in Shopping Malls	Deputy Commissioner	Deputy Commissioner
16	L-11	Retail vend of Beer, manufactured by Microbrewery.	Deputy Commissioner	Deputy Commissioner
17	L-12	Retail vend of Beer and Wine in Departmental Store.	Deputy Commissioner	Deputy Commissioner
18	L-12F	Retail vend of Foreign Beer and Wine in Departmental Store to the holder of licence in Form L-12.	Deputy Commissioner	Deputy Commissioner
19	L-13	Retail vend of Indian Liquor for home delivery	Deputy Commissioner	Deputy Commissioner
20	L-13F	Retail vend of Foreign Liquor for home delivery to the holders of licence in Form L-13.	Deputy Commissioner	Deputy Commissioner
21	L-14	Retail vend of economy Indian Liquor and Beer to holder of licence in Form L-8	Deputy Commissioner	Deputy Commissioner
22	L-15	Service of Indian Liquor in a hotel [1][or guest house] to residents in their rooms	Deputy Commissioner	Deputy Commissioner
23	L-15F	Service of Foreign Liquor in a hotel [1][or guest house] to residents in their rooms, to the holder of licence in Form L-15.	Deputy Commissioner	Deputy Commissioner
24	L-16	Service of Indian Liquor in a bar/ restaurant attached to a hotel	Deputy Commissioner	Deputy Commissioner
25	L-16F	Service of Foreign Liquor in a bar/ restaurant attached to a hotel to the holder of licence in Form L-16.	Deputy Commissioner	Deputy Commissioner
26	L-17	Service of Indian Liquor in independent restaurant	Deputy Commissioner	Deputy Commissioner
27	L-17F	Service of Foreign Liquor in independent restaurant to the holder of licence in Form L-17.	Deputy Commissioner	Deputy Commissioner
28	L-18	Service of Indian wine, beer and alcopop in independent restaurant	Deputy Commissioner	Deputy Commissioner
29	L-18F	Service of Foreign wine, beer and alcopop in independent restaurant to the holder of licence in Form L-18	Deputy Commissioner	Deputy Commissioner
30	L-19	Round the clock service of Indian Liquor in independent restaurant located either in arrival or departure area of International Airport.	Deputy Commissioner	Deputy Commissioner

1. Ins. by Notification No. F.10(12)/Fin(Rev-I)/2010-11/DS II/111, dated 21st March, 2011.

S. No.	Form	Details of Licences	Authority empowered to grant	Authority empowered to renew
31	L-19F	Round the clock service of Foreign Liquor in independent restaurant located either in arrival or departure area of International Airport to the holder of licence in Form L-19.	Deputy Commissioner	Deputy Commissioner
32	L-20	Service of Indian Liquor in a bar/ dining car in a luxury train.	Deputy Commissioner	Deputy Commissioner
33	L-20F	Service of Foreign Liquor in a bar/ dining car in a luxury train to the holder of licence in Form L-21.	Deputy Commissioner	Deputy Commissioner
34	L-21	Round the clock service/sale of Indian Liquor in a bar attached to a hotel located either in arrival or departure area of International Airport	Deputy Commissioner	Deputy Commissioner
35	L-21F	Round the clock service/sale of Foreign Liquor in a bar attached to a hotel located either in arrival or departure area of International Airport to the holder of licence in Form L-22	Deputy Commissioner	Deputy Commissioner
36	L-22	Retail vend of Indian Liquor in duty free shop for consumption "off" the premises located at departure Lounge of International Airport	Deputy Commissioner	Deputy Commissioner
37	L-23	Retail vend of Indian Liquor in military canteen	Deputy Commissioner	Deputy Commissioner
38	L-23F	Retail vend of Foreign Liquor in military canteen to the holder of licence in Form L-23.	Deputy Commissioner	Deputy Commissioner
39	L-24	Retail vend of Medicated Wine	Deputy Commissioner	Deputy Commissioner
40	L-25	Retail vend of Denatured Spirit including Special Denatured Spirit	Deputy Commissioner	Deputy Commissioner
41	L-26	Retail vend of Rectified Spirit	Deputy Commissioner	Deputy Commissioner
42	L-27	Retail vend of Bhang	Deputy Commissioner	Deputy Commissioner
43	L-28	Service of Indian Liquor in a club	Deputy Commissioner	Deputy Commissioner
44	L-28F	Service of Foreign Liquor in a club to the holder of licence in	Deputy Commissioner	Deputy Commissioner
		Form L-30.		

S. No.	Form	Details of Licences	Authority empowered to grant	Authority empowered to renew
45	L-29	Service of Indian Liquor at a club/ mess whose membership is exclusively for Government servants, retired Government servants, including members of armed forces, serving or retired and the club/ mess is not run on commercial lines	Deputy Commissioner	Deputy Commissioner
46	L-29F	Service of Foreign Liquor at a club/ mess whose membership is exclusively for Government servants, retired Government servants and the club/mess is not run on commercial lines to the holder of licence in Form L-31.	Deputy Commissioner	Deputy Commissioner
47	L-30	Licence for possession of liquor at home in excess of individual possession limit.	Deputy Commissioner	Assistant Commissioner
48	L-31	Licence for Warehouse for storage of Indian Liquor	Excise Commissioner	Not renewable
49	L-32	Licence for Warehouse for storage of Foreign Liquor	Excise Commissioner	Not renewable
50	L-33	Licence for Warehouse for storage of Country Liquor	Excise Commissioner	Not renewable
51	L-34	Licence for Warehouse for the storage of denatured spirit	Excise Commissioner	Excise Commissioner
52	L-35	Licence for Warehouse for the storage of rectified spirit	Excise Commissioner	Excise Commissioner
53	L-36	Licence to a registered medical practitioner, a chemist/druggist for sale of Intoxicating Spirituous Preparations.	Deputy Commissioner	Deputy Commissioner
54	L-37	Licence for Hotel Management Institutes for keeping liquor for the purpose of training	Deputy Commissioner	Deputy Commissioner

33. Classes of permits and authorities to grant and renew permit.—

S. No.	Form	Details of Licences	Authority empowered to grant	Authority empowered to renew
1	P-1	Permit for import of rectified spirit, denatured spirit and special denatured spirit	Deputy Commissioner	Deputy Commissioner
2	P-2	Permit for possession of denatured spirit exceeding five litres up to ten litres.	Deputy Commissioner	Deputy Commissioner

S. No.	Form	Details of Licences	Authority empowered to grant	Authority empowered to renew
3	P-3	Permit for possession of denatured spirit exceeding ten litres.	Deputy Commissioner	Deputy Commissioner
4	P-4	Permit for possession of special denatured spirit in bulk quantity.	Deputy Commissioner	Deputy Commissioner
5	P-5	Permit for possession of rectified spirit to educational institutions	Deputy Commissioner	Deputy Commissioner
6	P-6	Permit for possession of special denatured spirit by Industrial manufacturers	Deputy Commissioner	Deputy Commissioner
7	P-7	Permit for possession of intoxicating spirituous preparations	Deputy Commissioner	Deputy Commissioner
8	P-8	Permit for import or transport of intoxicating spirituous preparations	Deputy Commissioner	Deputy Commissioner
9	P-9	Permit for import of Indian Liquor and Country Liquor for troops.	Deputy Commissioner	Deputy Commissioner
10	P-10	Permit for service of Indian Liquor and Foreign Liquor at a place other than the licensed premises	Deputy Commissioner	Deputy Commissioner
11	P-11	Permit for liquor exhibitors.	Deputy Commissioner	Deputy Commissioner
12	P-12	Permit for import, export or transport of bhang.	Deputy Commissioner	Deputy Commissioner
13	P-13	Permit for service of Indian Liquor and Foreign Liquor at a temporary place at hotel, club and restaurant.	Deputy Commissioner	Deputy Commissioner
14	P-14	Import permit for import of liquor by holders of licence in Form L-1/L-1F/L-2/L-3	Assistant Commissioner	N.A.
15	P-15	Transport permit of transport of liquor	Assistant Commissioner	N.A.

(2) In cases where the yearly fee of a licence is determined by auction or tender, a licence shall be granted only to a person, who's tender or bid is accepted by the Government.

34. Grant of whole-sale and retail licence.—(1) Wholesale and retail licences of liquor shall be granted by the Deputy Commissioner in accordance with the terms and conditions, approved by the Government for each year.

(2) Notwithstanding anything contained in these rules, the Government may extend duration of any non-renewable licence expiring on 31st March in any year for such further period or periods as deemed fit on payment, in advance, of such fee as may be fixed:

Provided that any person holding such non-renewable licence, shall not be under any obligation to accept such offer to extend his licence.

Grant of licence:

State can adopt any mode of selling the licences for trade or business with a view to maximize its revenue so long as the method adopted is not discriminatory; *Khoday Distilleries Ltd.* v. *State of Karnataka*, (1995) 1 SCC 574.

35. Certain licences not to be granted in conjunction with other licences.—Except with the permission of the Government,—

(1) No person shall be granted more than one wholesale licence:

Provided that the holder of licence in Form L-1 may be granted licence in Form L-1F:

Provided further that for the purpose of licence in Forms L-1 and L-9, every distillery, brewery, winery and bottling plant shall be treated as a separate unit.

(2) No licence for retail sale of liquor for consumption "off" the premises and for consumption "on" the premises shall be granted to the holder of wholesale licence and *vice versa*:

Provided that the holder of L-1 licence may be granted licence exclusively for retail sale of the brands produced by him in Form L-9.

(3) No retail licence for consumption of liquor "off" the premises shall be granted to a person holding any other retail licence:

Provided that more than one licence in Forms L-6, L-8 and L-14 may be granted to a person.

36. Licence in Forms L-1 and L-3 to be granted to a distillery, brewery, winery or bottling plant.—Licences in Forms L-1 and L-3 shall only be granted to a distillery, brewery, winery or bottling plant in respect of such brands of Indian Liquor and Country Liquor, as are produced by distillery, brewery, winery or bottling plant.

37. Conditions for grant of licence.—(1) A licence shall be granted to,—

(a) an individual;

(b) a body incorporated under the Companies Act, 1956;

(c) a society registered under the Cooperative Societies Act;

(d) a partnership firm; or

(e) a limited liability partnership firm registered under Limited Liability Partnership Act, 2008.

(2) When a licence is granted to,—

(a) a partnership firm or a limited liability partnership firm, names of all the partners;

(b) a company incorporated under the Companies Act, 1956, names of all the directors;

(c) a co-operative society, names of the President, Secretary and the Treasurer,

shall be specified in the licence.

38. Addition and removal of a partner.—(1) On the application in writing of all the original partners, a partner may at any time be added, if the proposed partner is eligible under the rules, in which case he shall be responsible for all obligations incurred or to be incurred under the licence during the period of its currency as if it had originally been granted or renewed in his name:

Provided that the addition of the name of a new partner to a licence granted by auction or tender shall be permitted only on the death of an original partner in respect of a legal heir of the deceased partner.

On the application in writing of all the original partners, name of a partner may, at any time, be removed:

Provided that the removal of the name of a partner from a licence granted by auction or tender shall be permitted only in respect of the deceased partner.

(3) In case of removal, the retiring partner along with the continuing partner shall be jointly and severally responsible for all the excise liabilities incurred till the date of his retirement.

(4) In the case of proprietary licence, a partner may at any time be added with the prior approval of the Excise Commissioner, provided that he is a member of the family of the licensee.

39. Determination of licence by voluntary dissolution.—A licence granted to a partnership firm is determined by voluntary dissolution of the partnership subject to the liability of the partners jointly and severally for any loss caused to the Government thereby and for the performance of all obligations to the Government incurred by the partnership.

40. Licence to continue after its expiry, provided licence fee is paid.—(1) Where a licence is granted otherwise than by auction or tender it may be continued after the period of its expiry in respect of the same premises, with the permission of the licensing authority, provided that the requisite licence fee has been paid by the licensee. However, when any such licence has been determined by reason of surrender, cancellation or order of non-renewal or other cause or where it is proposed to issue licence in respect of the premises to persons not previously licensed, a new licence may be issued, provided—

(a) a new licence is not required on account of the addition of or removal of a partner on the application of all the partners or the change of a representative of a company or society;

(b) a licence continued to the legal heirs of a deceased licensee for the remaining period of the licence shall not be deemed to be a new licence;

(2) a new licence may not be required

(a) if the premises of a licence is changed during the period of its continuance, the authority competent to grant the licence may direct that the licence may be continued for the remaining period of the term on the existing fee.

(b) In case of death of licensee, the names of legal heirs may be substituted by the licensing authority.

(c) if the legal heirs of deceased are not interested to continue the licence, the same may be transferred by the authority competent to grant it, only for the remainder of its currency to a new licensee.

41. Application for the renewal of licence and permit to be received by February end along with licence fee.—All applications for the renewal of licences and permits shall be received in the office of the Deputy Commissioner before the end of February each year along with licence or permit fee, payable for the renewal of licence or permit. In case of delay, the Deputy Commissioner may admit such application before the expiry of the licence or permit, provided that there are good and sufficient reasons for the delay on payment of additional fee of twenty-five per cent. of the prescribed licence or permit fee:

Provided that the application for renewal of licence or permit may be admitted after the expiry of the licence or permit, if there are good and sufficient reasons for the delay on payment of double the amount of licence or permit fee payable, and the licence or permit may be renewed with the approval of the Excise Commissioner.

42. Notice to be issued when it is decided not to renew licence or permit.—Whenever it is proposed not to renew a licence or permit, which is renewable and granted on a fixed fee, the authority competent to renew it shall give notice to the holder of such licence or permit, record objections, if any, put forward by the licensee or the permit holder and pass an order in writing. The licensee or the permit holder may be given, an authenticated copy of such order free of cost.

43. Certain licences not to combine with any licence granted under clause (xiv) of section 2 of the Narcotic Drugs and Psychotropic Substances Act, 1985 (61 of 1985).—A licence under these rules, except a licence for the vend of medicated wines, denatured spirit and rectified spirit in Forms L-24, L-25 and L-26 respectively, may not be combined with any licence for any dealings with any dangerous drug as defined in clause (xiv) of section 2 of the Narcotic Drugs and Psychotropic Substances Act, 1985 without the sanction of the Excise Commissioner.

44. Grant of permits in Forms P-11 and P-13.—(1) Permit in Form P-11 for Liquor Exhibitors,—

(a) Total number of brands and their quantity shall be as approved by Excise Commissioner;

(b) the brands of Indian Liquor and Foreign Liquor registered in Delhi shall not be permitted during such exhibitions.

(2) Permit in Form P-13 for service of Indian Liquor and Foreign Liquor at bar, etc.—A permit in Form P-13 shall be granted by the Deputy Commissioner for service of Indian Liquor and Foreign Liquor at a bar, when temporary arrangements for the service of Indian Liquor and Foreign Liquor are required inside or outside but within the compound of the premises of licences in Forms L-15, L-16, L-17, L-28, L-29 on such terms and conditions as he may deem fit:

Provided that if the liquor is served in the open, the area shall be properly screened off from the public view:

Provided further that where the service of Indian Liquor or Foreign Liquor at a temporary bar at a place outside the compound of the licensed premises of holder of L-15 and L-16 licences when a temporary arrangement for service of India Liquor or Foreign Liquor is required in connection with National or International Conference, exhibition or function, the permit shall be issued with the prior approval of the Excise Commissioner, on such terms and conditions as the Excise Commissioner may deem proper.

(3) If a National or International Conference, exhibition or function is organized by an agency or organization other than the Ministry or Department of the Government, permit in Form P-13 for a temporary bar shall be granted by the Excise Commissioner on such terms and conditions as the Excise Commissioner may deem proper.

(4) Liquor may be served on dry days in the premises permitted in Form P-13 only to such foreigners and groups as may be sponsored by the Government of India and approved by an order of the Excise Commissioner:

Provided that no such approval or sponsorship shall be necessary in the case of service of liquor for the celebration of their respective national days by diplomatic missions, if such days happen to be on dry days;

(5) The permit holder is authorized to sell Indian Liquor and Foreign Liquor by retail to the residents of hotel, delegates to the conference, etc., with such restrictions as may be imposed by the Excise Commissioner at the time of grant of permit;

(6) The permit holder shall serve wine or beer in open bottles or in glasses and other Indian Liquor and Foreign Liquor only in glasses. Such bottles shall on no account be removed by any persons from the premises, except on an authority granted by the Excise Commissioner;

(7) Holders of P-13 permit may be permitted, if applied for, by the Deputy Commissioner to purchase and possess Indian Liquor and Foreign Liquor from licensed retail vends on such conditions as may be specified;

(8) In case of liquor provided by the guest, the permit holder may be required by the Excise Commissioner to keep the unconsumed stock out of the stock allowed under permit in Form P-13, if it exceeds the individual possession limit without a licence, in their safe custody pending disposal of the stock under orders of the Excise Commissioner.

45. Exemption of fee for permit in Form P-13 in certain cases.—The Excise Commissioner may, if satisfied that service of Indian Liquor and Foreign Liquor at a place inside or outside the licensed premises of the holders of licence in Forms L-15, L-15F, L-16, L-16F, I-17, L-17F L-28, L-28F, L-29 and L-29F is required to enable the Government of India to meet its obligations under any International agreement exempt, subject to such conditions as he may deem proper, any person applying for grant of P-13 permit from the payment of fixed fee as prescribed.

46. Name of the licensee to be intimated to the excise authority from where liquor is imported.—The name of the wholesale licensee of Country Liquor or Indian Liquor shall be intimated to the excise authority of the state wherefrom Country Liquor or Indian Liquor is to be imported as also to the excise officer in charge of the distillery concerned.

47. Auction and its procedure.—Unless otherwise prescribed, the Government shall, by order direct, whether licences in any form may be granted on fixed fee, or on a fee to be fixed by auction or tender in any year. The following procedure is prescribed for the grant of a licence by auction—

(1) The Excise Commissioner shall give at least ten days' notice of the date and place of the auction. This notice shall also specify—

(a) the conditions to which the auction shall be subject;

(b) the number and situation of the shops to be licensed on the basis of auction, where applicable;

(c) the occasions, if any, on which the shops are likely to be closed; and

(d) any other information which, in the opinion of the Excise Commissioner may be of use to intending bidders.

(2) The auction shall be held by the Deputy Commissioner or by such other gazetted officer, who shall be called the "Presiding Officer", as may be empowered in its behalf by the Government.

(3) Before the auction begins, the Presiding Officer shall read out the general conditions governing the auction and satisfy himself that the intending bidders have understood them.

(4) No person shall be allowed to bid for a licence unless—

(a) he has furnished a written statement and declaration;

(b) he has furnished the following documents:—

(i) documentary evidence to the satisfaction of the Presiding Officer that he is the *bona fide* representative of a distillery, brewery, winery or bottling plant which is not blacklisted in Delhi for the time being.

(ii) an attested photostat copy of the registered partnership deed or memorandum and articles of association, as the case may be, of the distillery, brewery, winery or bottling plant, referred to in sub-clause (i);

(iii) a sealed cover containing a statement of wholesale prices at which each bottle of Indian Liquor and Country Liquor of each brand and size is proposed to be sold by the intending bidder during the currency of the licence;

(iv) if the intending bidder is a sole proprietor, partnership firm, limited liability partnership firm, a private limited company or a society and did not hold a licence in Form L-1, or L-3 during the previous licensing period a certificate of solvency to the extent of rupees one lac or as specified by the Excise Commissioner, signed by a magistrate not below the rank of a Sub-Divisional Magistrate, having jurisdiction over the place where the intending bidder resides or the firm, company or society has its registered head office;

(v) a clearance certificate issued by the Income Tax Officer who assessed the intending bidder;

(vi) a no-dues certificate from the Deputy Commissioner in respect of dues realizable from the intending bidder up to the last date of the month preceding the date of auction, unless the intending bidder has specially been exempted from this requirement by the Government;

(vii) a no-dues certificate from the appropriate assessing authority if the intending bidder is or is interested in the business of a dealer, registered under the Delhi Value Added Tax Act, 2004 in respect of dues realizable under the Delhi Value Added Tax Act, 2004 up to the last date of the period preceding the date of auction for which such dealer has been assessed.

(c) he is allowed after scrutiny of his statement, declaration and documents by the Presiding Officer, to enter the bidding area which the Presiding Officer shall specify for intending bidders to assemble.

(5) (a) No person other than a Government servant on duty shall enter the bidding area, unless he is allowed entry by the Presiding Officer;

(b) only one person intending to bid on behalf of any person or firm shall be allowed to enter the bidding area.

(6) (a) The Presiding Officer shall put up each licence separately to auction after announcing its locality where necessary, and any other information that, in his judgment, is necessary to identify the licensee;

(b) the bids shall be made for the whole annual licence fee for the licence;

(c) the Presiding Officer shall cause the name of each person making the bid and the amount of the bid to be recorded and shall record the final bid accepted by him in his own hand;

(d) the Presiding Officer may refuse to record any bid if he has reason to believe that it has been made in the interest of any person who has not been allowed entry into the area marked for the assembly of intending bidders;

(e) the Presiding Officer may refuse to record any bid which he considers to be merely speculative or not made in good faith;

(f) if the Presiding Officer is of the opinion that the speculative or *mala fide* bidding is going on, he may, without prejudice to his power under clause (e), require an immediate deposit of the whole amount of bid. If such an order has been passed and announced to the assembly of bidders, all subsequent bids for the said licence shall be made subject to the condition that the whole amount of bid shall be immediately deposited on acceptance;

(g) all bids shall be in multiples of rupees one thousand;

(h) subject to the provisions of clause (f) above, the highest bidder shall pay a sum not less than twenty-five per cent. of the bid money in cash or by bank draft immediately on the conclusion of the auction;

(i) the person accepted as the auction purchaser shall sign his name or affix his thumb mark to the record of auction;

(j) the highest bidder shall also furnish a personal bond with a surety bond as specified in the terms and conditions of auction.

(7) The Excise Commissioner shall, on receipt of the report of the Presiding Officer, forward it to the Government with a report showing, if need be, the locality

for each licence auctioned and stating any other information that he may consider relevant.

(8) The Government may—

(a) accept the highest bid;

(b) reject the highest bid and accept any other bid;

(c) reject all or any of the bids on the ground that the highest bid is not adequate or for any other reason;

(d) where all the bids are rejected under clause (c) or where there were no bids, in its discretion, order a re-auction or direct that the licence may not be granted or may be granted by any other mode of fixing fee.

(9) A person whose bid is accepted under sub-rule (8) shall pay a sum not less than twenty-five per cent. of the fee prior to the grant of licence and shall pay the remainder of the fee in nine equal monthly instalments on or before the 7th of every month beginning from the second month of the currency of the licence:

Provided that any sum deposited by a successful bidder under clauses (f), (g) or (h) of sub-rule (6), shall be adjusted towards the first and, if need be, subsequent instalments of the licence fee.

(10) A person whose bid is accepted, shall take all requisite actions to complete all formalities required for grant of a licence within thirty days from the date of communication of acceptance of his bid and if he does not do so, all deposits made by him shall stand forfeited to the Government, and if the licence is re-auctioned, he shall not be entitled to any compensation.

48. Procedure for grant of licence by tender.—In case the licence is decided to be granted by tender, the following procedure shall be followed:—

(1) Tenders for the grant of licence shall be invited by the Excise Commissioner after giving not less than ten days' notice specifying *inter alia*—

(a) the conditions to which the tender shall be subject;

(b) the number and situation of the shops to be licensed on the basis of tender where applicable;

(c) in the case of licences in Form L-3, the minimum and the maximum quantities of liquor required to be made available for sale either during the currency of the licence or during any specified shorter period;

(d) any other information which in the opinion of the Excise Commissioner may be of use to the intending bidders.

(2) No tender shall be considered unless the earnest money, as specified by the Excise Commissioner, has been deposited in a Government Treasury or a Scheduled Bank in favour of the Excise Commissioner or bank draft is attached to each tender.

(3) No tender shall be entertained from any person whose name is on the black list, against whom any demand is pending or who is otherwise debarred from holding such licence.

(4) Tenders may be invited for licence fee or, in the case of licence in Form L-3 for rates or prices at which the licensee shall supply liquor.

(5) A tender shall specify the whole annual licence fee and not the amount of monthly instalment in which it is payable.

(6) A tender from a partnership firm shall contain the names of all the partners. No such tender shall be entertained unless it is signed by all the partners and is accompanied by an attested copy of the partnership deed. Such attestation shall be done by a gazetted officer.

(7) The Excise Commissioner may, in his discretion, reject any tender where, in his opinion, the tenderer or any of his partners, has formed a pool tending to create an undesirable monopoly of interest.

(8) The Excise Commissioner is not bound to accept the highest tender or any tender at all. When the highest tender is not accepted, and a lower tender is proposed to be accepted, the Excise Commissioner shall record his reasons therefor. No tender shall be accepted without the approval of the Government.

(9) If in the opinion of the Government, it is necessary for the purpose of achieving uniformity in the rates, negotiations may be made with the tenderers. It may for that purpose, appoint an officer or a committee of officers to negotiate with the tenderers, whose tenders are otherwise in order. The officer or the committee shall then negotiate with the tenderer in the ascending order of the tender rates but no tenderer shall have a vested right to be called for such negotiation. The negotiations made by the officer or the committee of officers shall be subject to the final decision of the Government.

(10) The deposits made by unsuccessful tenderer shall be refunded to him.

(11) (a) Where tenders have been invited for licence fee, the successful tenderer whose tender has been accepted by the Excise Commissioner with the approval of the Government, shall pay the whole amount and the earnest money deposited by him shall be adjusted towards the satisfaction of dues payable by him as aforesaid or as security amount wherever such security is provided;

(b) any person whose tender is accepted, whether for licence fee or for rates, shall take all requisite action to complete all formalities required for grant of a licence within seven days from the date of communication of acceptance of his tender and if he does not do so, all deposits made by him shall stand forfeited to the Government and while the licence may be re-tendered or granted in any other manner, he shall not be entitled to any compensation.

(12) (a) If any person, whose tender has been accepted, fails to make the deposits of twenty five per cent. of annual fee or if he refuses to accept the licence, the Excise Commissioner may call for fresh tenders, and any deficiency in fee arising as a result thereof together with all expenses incurred in inviting tenders shall be recoverable from the defaulting tenderer in the manner laid down in section 29;

(b) it shall also be lawful for the Excise Commissioner to forfeit the earnest money of the defaulting tenderer either in part or in full, deposited by the said tenderer.

(13) Where tenders are invited for licence fee, a licensee shall, by the 7th of the month in which he begins his business under his licence and thereafter by the 7th of every subsequent month, pay in advance one-twelfth of the annual fee till the whole fee is paid. The twenty-five per cent. advance paid under sub-rule (2) shall

be adjusted at close of the year. He may, however, at any time, pay the whole amount due if he so wishes.

(14) Where tender money exceeds rupees one lac, it shall be in multiple of rupees five thousand and for lesser amount it shall be a multiple of rupees five hundred.

(15) Where tenders have been invited for licence fee, if the Excise Commissioner is of the opinion that no suitable tender is forthcoming, he shall, with the previous sanction of the Government resell the licence by auction.

(16) If it is not considered expedient to accept the highest or the lowest tender, as the case may be, the Excise Commissioner shall refer the matter to the Government as to whether—

(a) the licence be auctioned; or

(b) the shop to which the licence relates be closed either permanently or till a person willing to take it up at the minimum fee comes forward; or

(c) the vend to which the licence relates be carried on by a vendor who may be paid commission on sales.

(17) When a licence has been cancelled, the Deputy Commissioner may re-sell it by public auction or by inviting fresh tenders or by private contract and any deficiency in fee and all expenses incurred on such resale or attempted re-sale shall be recoverable by the defaulting licensee in the manner laid down in section 29. The Deputy Commissioner shall communicate the result of such re-sale in a statement in duplicate to the Excise Commissioner. If the amount realized from the original licensee including the initial deposit of one-fourth of the annual fee and the amount bid by the incoming licensee together are less than the amount previously tendered by the original licensee together with the expenses incurred, if any, in connection with resale, the deficiency shall be recovered from the original licensee. If these amounts together are more than the amount previously tendered, no refund shall be made to the original licensee.

49. Refund of licence fee when delay is not attributable to licensee.—(1) If the licence fee for any licence is of an annual character and the licence is granted after the commencement of the financial year, the Government may, if it is satisfied that the delay was not attributable to the licensee, remit the fee payable by a sum not exceeding the proportional amount for the quarter before the licence was granted.

(2) When a licence is cancelled for a cause other than a breach of conditions of licence, the licensee may be excused payment of the fee due to remainder of the term of the licence and if the fee has been paid in advance, proportionate fee for the un-expired period of licence shall be refunded.

50. General Conditions applicable to all licences.—Every licence under these rules shall be granted subject to the condition that the licensee shall comply with the provisions of the Act, the rules framed thereunder, terms and conditions of his licence and the orders issued by the Excise Commissioner from time-to-time and for such observance give security in such form, manner and amount as may be specified. In addition, if the authority granting the licence so requires, shall give a personal bond with or with without surety in such amount as may be required to the satisfaction of such authority.

51. Conditions dealing with licensed premises.—(1) No retail vend of Indian Liquor, Foreign Liquor or Country Liquor shall be located within one hundred meters from the following, namely:—

(a) major educational institutions;

(b) religious places;

(c) hospitals with fifty beds and above:

Provided that the condition mentioned in clause (c) above shall not apply for retail vend of liquor for consumption "on" the premises:

Provided further that the condition of hundred meters shall apply for the licences granted after the commencement of these rules:

Provided also that if any major educational institution, religious place or hospital with fifty beds or above comes into existence subsequent to the establishment of the retail vend of Indian Liquor, Foreign Liquor or Country Liquor, the aforesaid distance restrictions shall not apply.

Explanation I—For the purpose of clause (a) above major educational institutions would mean middle and higher secondary schools, colleges and other institutions of higher learning recognized by the Government.

Explanation II—For the purpose of clause (b) above, a religious place would imply a religious place having a pucca structure with a covered area of more than 400 square feet.

Explanation III—The measurement of distance shall be the shortest traversable distance, from the mid point of the actual main entrance/door of the premises proposed for licence to mid point of the actual main door/entrance of the building of the places mentioned in clauses (a), (b) and (c) above.

(2) The licensee shall not carry on any business connected with his licence, or store any liquor to be sold or otherwise deal with under his licence, except in the premises specified in his licence, hereinafter called the 'licensed premises'. The Excise Commissioner, may however, grant in an exceptional case, permission to store liquor at a place other than the licensed premises. This permission shall be granted on payment of an extra fee as prescribed and only in cases where it is impracticable to store the required stock in the licensed premises. Before the grant of permission, the Excise Commissioner shall satisfy himself that the proposed place is adequately guarded and that there is no means of access to it by the public.

(3) The licensed premises shall be established and maintained by the licensee at his own cost.

(4) No licensed premises for sale and storage of liquor shall be used for any other business, except with the permission of the Excise Commissioner. Persons or institutions holding more than one licence must have separate premises for their business. Separate accounts shall be maintained for sale conducted under such licences:

Provided that this sub-rule, except the provision relating to maintenance of separate accounts for sale conducted under the liquor licence, shall not apply to departmental store holding licence in Form L-12.

(5) If a licensee holds a licence in Form L-16, L-16F in conjunction with a licence in Form L-15, L-15F, he shall not, in pursuance of the licence in Form

L-15, L-15F, sell any liquor after the hours fixed as the closing hours for the licence in Form L-16, L-16F in any part of the licensed premises to which persons not residents in the hotel are admitted or in any room or bar adjoining or opening into any room to which persons not residents in the hotel are admitted.

(6) Licensed premises shall be the premises owned or leased by the licensee, provided that where local conditions render it necessary, sites for liquor shops may be leased or bought for Government under the special orders of the Government in each case.

(7) Where the premises have been specially provided by the Government for any shop, the licensee shall be bound to carry on his business in those premises, and to pay to the Government, in addition to his licence fee, such rent for the premises as may be fixed by the Excise Commissioner.

(8) In the case of dining car licence in the Form of L-20 and L-20F the licensed premises are every dining car authorised by the railway administration and any other premises licensed shall be for the purpose of storage only.

(9) Retail licences for consumption "off" the premises shall be permitted at sites or premises, located in a pucca building, the land use of which is commercial approved and shall conform to the orders and instructions issued by the Excise Commissioner from time-to-time.

(10) Retail licences for consumption "on" the premises, shall be granted at a site, duly approved by the local authority concerned, provided that the following documents have been furnished, issued by the agencies concerned:-

(a) Eating House Licence;

(b) Lodging House Licence in the case of L-15 only;

(c) Health and Trade Licence;

(d) Certificate by the Tourism Department, Government of Delhi, in the case of licences in Forms L-17 , L-28 and L-29; or the one which fulfils the following conditions:—

(i) that the building should be well constructed and the approach should be suitable for restaurant;

(ii) that there should be adequate arrangements for service to the customers;

(iii) that the restaurant should, at all times adhere to good maintenance and service. The rates should be fixed in accordance with the rules, if any, prescribed by the local authorities and submitted to the Excise Department for concurrence. The rates should be prominently displayed on the menu cards. These should also include VAT, service charges etc;

(a) certificate from the Tourism Department, Government of India in the case of licences in Forms L-15 and L-16;

(b) registration certificate under the Delhi Value Added Tax Act, 2004;

(c) site plan including the store room, area for the bar and the area for the service of liquor, prepared by registered architect;

(d) No objection Certificate from the Fire Department.

[1][(e) Certificate from the Tourism Department, Government of India for grant of licence in Form L-15 and L-16 in case of hotels and Certificate

---

1. Ins. by Notification No. F.10(12)/Fin(Rev-I)/2010-11/DS II/111, dated 21st March, 2011.

from the Tourism Department, Government of National Capital Territory of Delhi for grant of licence in Form L-15 in case of guest houses.]

(11) The licensed premises of all kinds of licences shall have adequate storage facility, proper electrical fittings and shall be duly insured against fire and other natural hazards. The licensee shall keep the premises thoroughly clean and dry and shall comply with the orders issued by the Deputy Commissioner for the removal of defects in the building.

(12) In case of Indian Liquor and Country Liquor vends, the licensed premises shall be used for the storage and sale of liquor as licensed and no other business shall be transacted from such premises, except with the approval of the Excise Commissioner.

(13) The licensee shall maintain conspicuously, above the main outer door of the licensed premises, a signboard exhibiting in conspicuous painted letters, his name, address and the class of licence held by him. The information shall be in Hindi, Urdu and Gurumukhi for country liquor and in Hindi, Urdu, Gurumukhi and English for Indian Liquor and Foreign Liquor Licence.

(14) The retail licensee for sale of liquor for consumption "off" the premises shall display at a conspicuous place in the licensed premises a list showing the retail price inclusive of VAT of each size of bottle of each brand of liquor on sale and the retail price, if any, fixed by the Excise Commissioner.

(15) Except during the licensed hours, the licensee shall permit no person except employees or members of his family to enter or remain on the licensed premises:

Provided that this clause shall not apply to departmental stores holding licences in Form L-12.

52. Declaration of dry days and conditions applicable thereto.—(1) No licensee shall sell liquor on the days, which are notified as dry days by the Excise Commissioner, with the previous approval of the Government from time-to-time:

Provided that this restriction shall not apply to the service of liquor by the holder of a licence in Form L-15 to a resident in his room:

Provided further that this restriction shall not apply to the service/sale of liquor by the holders of licence in the Forms L-16, L-17, L-19, L-20, L-21, , L-22, L-28, L-29, P-10 and P-13 on all dry days except Republic Day, Independence Day and Mahatma Gandhi's Birthday:

Provided also that the Excise Commissioner, with the prior approval of the Government, may—

(i) delete any day from or add any day to the list of dry days notified under this rule;

(ii) permit consumption of liquor on any licensed premises on any dry day.

(2) No licensee shall be entitled to any compensation on account of any addition to the list of dry days in accordance with clause (a) of proviso three to sub-rule (1).

(3) The business premises of a licensee shall be kept closed on all dry days:

Provided that the Assistant Commissioner may, by order in writing permit a licensee to deposit liquor in his premises, or to open the premises for any work other than sale, on a dry day on prescribed fee.

53. Conditions relating to conduct of business.—(1) The licensee shall neither give concession, rebate or discount on the sale price of liquor nor shall he give liquor as a gift.

(2) Any transaction of the nature of gift or loan between the licensee and an excise officer is prohibited.

(3) The licensee shall not receive anything in barter for any intoxicant.

(4) The licensee shall not permit any professional entertainment or dancing, or the playing of musical instruments or singing by professionals, to be carried on his premises in such a way as to attract the general attention of his customers:

Provided that this condition shall not apply to a hotel or a restaurant or a club licensed in Forms L-15, L-16, L-17, L-28 and L-29, except insofar it is imposed by the Deputy Commissioner by general or special order. However, in the case of L-17 licensee only live singing /playing of instruments by professionals shall be allowed.

(5) Every licensee shall, in respect of liquor sold by him, issue a cash memo and keep a counter-foil or duplicate copy thereof. Such cash memos shall be serially numbered, and bound in a book of hundred cash memos each and shall be signed by the licensee or his duly authorised agent and shall show the quantity and the name of the article sold by him or any other information as specified by the Deputy Commissioner.

(6) (a) Every licensee shall maintain the registers, as prescribed or as specified by the Excise Commissioner, for the class of business carried on by him, and on the expiry of his licence, shall make them over to the Deputy Commissioner or some other excise officer empowered by him in this behalf under a valid receipt. The licensee shall maintain and submit all the prescribed returns punctually and maintain true accounts of transaction from day to day in ink. He shall enter all the figures in English numerals and other particulars in Hindi, English, Gurumukhi or Urdu characters unless the Deputy Commissioner, by special order noted on the licence, permits the use of other numerals or characters;

(b) If a licensee deals in liquor of more than one brand, he shall maintain accounts and submit returns brand-wise.

(7) The licensee shall not permit the resort to his licensed premises of persons, whom there is reason to believe to be habitual criminals. He shall prevent gaming and disorderly conduct therein and shall give information to the excise officer or the nearest police officer of the resort to his licensed premises of any person suspected of having committed an offence or habitually committing offences for which under the Code of Criminal Procedure, 1973, warrant would ordinarily issue, and of every irregularity committed therein, tending to disturb the public peace and he shall, at all times for police purposes, permit free access to the police to all parts of his licensed premises.

(8) The licensee shall, at any time, produce for inspection on demand of any excise officer of the rank of Excise Inspector and above, his licence and his accounts and shall allow the inspection of his registers, stock and premises by the said officer.

(9) The licensee shall maintain an inspection note-book with the pages numbered consecutively and hand it over on demand to any excise officer, of the

rank of Excise Inspector and above, on a receipt being given therefor. Any punishment or warning incurred by the licensee, without forfeiture or cancellation of his licence, shall be recorded in the said note-book.

(10) The licensee shall furnish to the Deputy Commissioner every year in the month of April a list of the persons employed or proposed to be employed in his licensed business. The licensee shall not employ any person whose employment has been objected by the Deputy Commissioner.

54. Fixation of price.—(1) The criteria for fixation of wholesale or MRP of liquor for each licensing year shall be decided by the Excise Commissioner, with the approval of the Government. Thereafter, the Excise Commissioner may, after giving an opportunity of being heard to the person licensed to sell such liquor, fix the price of liquor in wholesale or in retail or in both.

(2) The Excise Commissioner, for reasons to be recorded, may increase or decrease the existing wholesale or retail prices, at any time, after giving an opportunity to the licensee of being heard.

(3) Where the price of any liquor is fixed under sub-rule (1) or sub-rule (2), the licensee shall be bound to sell such liquor at such price.

(4) In case of Foreign Liquor, the Excise Commissioner may, if he deems fit, fix prices. However, MRP, as arrived at, by adding various components of price structure, shall be displayed on each bottle by L-1F licensee by way of affixing retail price stickers.

(5) While fixing the MRP of liquor, the same shall be rounded off to the next multiple of:

(a) rupees ten in the case of quart and above;

(b) rupees five in the case of pint and nip;

(c) rupees five in the case of beer of all sizes whether in bottle or can.

(6) The amount so increased shall be added in the duty.

55. Working hours and conditions relating to sale of liquor.—(1) The hours for the sale of liquor shall be such as may be specified in an order made by the Excise Commissioner and different orders may be specified for different categories of licences.

(2) The licensee, except a chemist or druggist holding a licence in Form L-26, shall not sell or keep on his licensed premises any chloral hydrate, butyl chloral hydrate or para aldehyde, any caramel, or colouring matter or any essence or material used for flavouring beverages or any rectified spirit.

(3) The licensee shall not, except under the orders of the Excise Commissioner or in accordance with the terms and conditions of his licence, compound, blend, colour, flavour or rectify any liquor sold by him or store in his licensed premises.

(4) The licensee shall not alter or tamper with the labels and capsules on bottles containing liquor for sale.

(5) The licensee shall not deteriorate, adulterate or dilute any liquor to be sold by him, or sell the same knowing it to have been deteriorated, adulterated or diluted, or stored or permit to be stored in his licensed premises, any liquor in a deteriorated, adulterated or diluted state.

(6) No sale of liquor, whether in wholesale or retail shall be made by any measures other than standard stamped measures, approved by the Excise Commissioner. The standard measures shall be the proof litre or bulk litre and the multiple. The licensee shall keep such stamped standard fractional measures of proof or bulk litres as are available in the market and have been approved by the Excise Commissioner.

(7) The licensee shall not allow any person to conduct sales on his behalf, unless the name of such person has previously been submitted to the Deputy Commissioner for approval:

Provided that this condition shall not apply to.—

(a) the licensee of a hotel, restaurant and club;

(b) a licensee, holding licence in Forms L-25 and L-26 or;

(c) licence for retail sale of denatured spirit.

(8) Subject to the provisions of these rules, every licensee shall, in respect of liquor, which he is licensed to sell, meet the demand of every customer entitled to be served, who tenders payment, for what is required by him, and the licensee shall maintain sufficient stock of liquor, in which he is licensed to deal, to meet the probable demand. This rule does not compel a licensee to meet the demand of a customer even if accompanied by a tender of payment if the customer owes payment for liquor, previously sold under the licence on credit, in case where a sale of credit is permissible.

(9) The licensee shall not sell liquor except of the following strength and subject to the following conditions:—

(a) a licensee for the sale of country liquor shall not sell liquor in the bottles and of the strength, otherwise than, as may be specified by the Excise Commissioner;

(b) a licensee for the sale of Indian Liquor and Foreign Liquor shall not sell Indian Liquor and Foreign Liquor of the strength less than 25 degrees under proof in the case of brandy, whisky or rum or of a liquor intended to pass as, whisky, brandy or rum or of a strength less than 35 degrees under proof in the case of gin, vodka or of liquor intended to pass as gin or vodka:

Provided that the minimum strength of 25 degrees or 35 degrees under proof shall not be enforced in case of liqueur, wine, beer, cider and alcopop;

(c) the licensee shall not store for sale or sell any liquor which does not conform to the specifications required in an order made by the Excise Commissioner and if no such order has been made, which does not conform to the specifications laid down by the Bureau of Indian Standards with regard to the strength of liquor;

(d) the licensee may be permitted to sell beer of alcoholic strength up to 5 per cent. volume by volume and strong beer with alcoholic strength of above 5 per cent. volume by volume up to 8.25 per cent. volume by volume;

(e) the permissible variation in the liquor contents of any bottle of liquor shall be plus or minus one per cent.

56. Procedure dealing with left over stock.—If any person, who has held a licence under these rules, has in his possession, on the expiry, or determination of his licence, any intoxicant, he shall take action for its disposal in the following manner:—

(a) he shall submit to the Deputy Commissioner the list of such intoxicants within fifteen days from the expiry of the licence indicating therein the sale price of each brand. The Deputy Commissioner may allow him time, not exceeding 15 days for the disposal of such stocks to the existing licensees:

Provided that if duty has not been paid on such stocks and the purchaser does not hold a licence permitting him to possess them in bond, the duty on such stocks at the rates in force on the date of sale shall be recovered from the purchaser before the possession thereof is taken;

(b) in case the licensee is unable to dispose of such stocks, in part or in full, within the stipulated time, he shall immediately surrender the same to the Deputy Commissioner alongwith a list mentioning the quantity and brand of undisposed stock on the following day. It shall be open to the licensee to reduce subsequently the sale price earlier intimated by him. If no sale price is intimated to the Deputy Commissioner at the time of surrendering the stocks, it shall be lawful for the Deputy Commissioner to dispose of such stocks to the existing licensees on a price determined by him;

(c) the Deputy Commissioner shall arrange to dispose of the surrendered stock at the price intimated by the outgoing licensee or determined by him. Whenever such price is reduced by the out-going licensee, the Deputy Commissioner shall dispose of the remaining stocks at such reduced price, as may be intimated to him by the former licensee from time-to-time or as determined by him. In case the stocks remain unsold for a period of two months from the date of the determination of the licence, it shall be lawful for the Deputy Commissioner to destroy the stocks, after obtaining the approval of the Excise Commissioner. No compensation shall be payable for such destruction to the outgoing licensee. No refund of duty, if paid, shall be allowed on stocks of liquor which ultimately remained unsold and are destroyed:

Provided that if duty has not been paid on such stock, the Deputy Commissioner shall not order its destruction but may require in writing any person holding a licence to acquire the stock, or any part thereof, by purchase from the former licensee within six weeks of service of the requisition after payment of duty at the rates in force on the date of the requisition, at such price as may have been indicated by the former licensee or such price as the Excise Commissioner may fix after hearing the parties;

(d) in case the out-going licensee fails to surrender the stock of liquor as provided in clause (b) to the Deputy Commissioner it shall be lawful for the Deputy Commissioner to destroy the same.

57. Conditions when the sole licensee dies and his licence is not continued.—When a sole licensee dies and the Deputy Commissioner does not continue the licence to the legal heirs of the licensee or other person for the remainder of the period , the legal heirs shall not be entitled for the refund of licence fee paid by the deceased licensee.

58. Surrender of licence when it is cancelled.—On revocation, cancellation or determination of any licence, the licensee or his representative shall cease to carry on his business under it, and shall return his licence to the Deputy Commissioner.

59. No compensation in certain cases.—No compensation shall be paid to a licensee for any closure made under section 25 or on account of opening of a new shop or the issue of any special licence or on account of any change during the currency of a licence in the conditions thereof, or in the rate at which duty is charged on liquor or in any other matter connected with the excise administration and dealt with under the powers conferred by the Act or the rules framed thereunder.

60. Refund of duty when liquor is unfit for human consumption.—If the Excise Commissioner is satisfied that any liquor manufactured or imported was not an excisable article, being unfit for human consumption at the time of such manufacture, import or subsequently and that duty on such liquor has been paid by the licensee, he shall order the refund of such duty. In case the duty has not been paid, no duty shall be charged on such liquor.

61. Maintenance of record.—(1) The licensee shall maintain Stock Register, Daily Sale Register, Inspection Book and other Registers in such form and manner as may be specified by the Excise Commissioner from time-to-time.

(2) Unless surrendered to the Assistant Commissioner, such record shall be preserved for a period of three years from the close of the licensing period for which the licence was last granted or renewed:

Provided that if any case is pending either before the Departmental officers or in the court of law, the record shall be preserved till the final proceedings are over.

62. Reference to Excise Commissioner in matters not provided for.—In all matters not expressly provided for in these rules, the same shall be referred to the Excise Commissioner, whose decision shall be binding on the licensee.

Administrative Instructions

Guidelines and administrative instructions can supplement gaps in enactments and rules framed under it though not supplement their contents.

Where there are no statutory rules or regulations or the provisions of the Act are silent, the authorities conferred with the powers can form valid notifications or administrative instructions which would govern the field; *State of Uttar Pradesh* v. *Daulat Ram,* (2002) 4 SCC 98.

Order

An order would be deemed to be Government order as and when it is issued and publicized. Internal communication while processing a matter cannot be said to be order issued by the competent authority; *Union of India* v. *Kartick Chandra Mondal,* I (2010) SLT 475.

63. Sale of approved brands only.—The licensee shall not sell liquor of any brand, not approved by the Deputy Commissioner and the Deputy Commissioner shall be under no obligation to permit the sale of any brand of liquor.

64. Pictures of national leaders and gods, etc., not to be displayed on licensed premises.—Pictures and photographs of prominent national leaders, saints, Gods, Goddesses or any other religious symbol shall not be exhibited on any premises licensed for sale and service of liquor.

65. Sensitising public against consumption of liquor at public place.—The licensee shall exhibit prominently in the licensed premises notice drawing the attention of the public to the provisions of section 40 that consumption of liquor in a public place is punishable with fine and/or imprisonment.

66. Special conditions.—Licences in different forms prescribed in the rules shall, in addition to the conditions prescribed elsewhere, be subject to the special conditions prescribed as under—

(1) Licence in Form L-1 for wholesale vend of Indian Liquor to the trade.—

(a) the licensee shall sell liquor to the holders of licence for consumption "on" and "off" the premises or as directed by the Excise Commissioner;

(b) licensee shall have Warehouse duly licensed by the Excise Commissioner;

(c) no licensee shall sell any brand of liquor of which he is not the manufacturer, or its agent, unless permitted by the Excise Commissioner;

(d) duty on Indian Liquor imported into Delhi shall be payable by the licensee before grant of import pass at such rates as may be notified, unless the liquor is to be kept, after import in a bonded warehouse, established or licensed by the Excise Commissioner.

(2) Licence in Form L-1F for the wholesale vend of Foreign Liquor to the trade.—

(a) the licensee shall not supply Foreign Liquor for retail sale to any person other than the holder of a licence in Forms L-6FG, L-6FE, L-7FG, L-7FE, L-12F, L-13F L-15F, L-16F, L-17F, L-17FE , L-20F, L-20FE, L-21F, L-23F L-28F, L-29F;

(b) the licensee shall have bonded warehouse duly approved by the Excise Commissioner in addition to the Customs approved bonded warehouse;

(c) the licensee shall affix the sticker containing the statutory requirements of retail price, label and hologram or any other security feature as decided by the Excise Commissioner in the godown approved by the Excise Commissioner;

(d) the licensee shall furnish authorization letter from the manufacturer or the importer in India for every brand;

(3) The licence in Form L-2 for vend of draught beer.—

(a) Before any licence for draught beer is granted, the licensee shall satisfy the following conditions:—

(i) the draught beer shall be imported in kegs only;

(ii) there should be proper refrigeration arrangements for the safe storage of draught beer;

(iii) it shall be the duty of the licensee to ensure that no stale or deteriorated beer is sold;

(iv) the draught beer once imported into Delhi, shall not be allowed to be exported for any reason whatsoever;

(v) mixing of CO_2 may be done within the permissible limits to provide necessary fizz;

(b) If after import of draught beer, it is found to have been deteriorated either during the transport of the kegs from the brewery to the licensed premises or the licensee has subsequently found that such stocks have deteriorated during the storage prior to sale, the same shall be destroyed, after the receipt of the report from the Chemical Examiner, with the permission of the Deputy Commissioner.

(4) Licence in Form L-3 for the wholesale vend of Country Liquor.—

(i) the licensee shall not sell Country Liquor to any person other than the holder of licence in Form L-8;

(ii) the Government may fix the wholesale price (exclusive of duty, retail margin, local transport charges and VAT) of Country Liquor and may fix different prices for different types of Country Liquor:

Provided that the Government may authorize any officer or committee of officers, to negotiate with the tenderer with a view to arrive at a uniform lowest price for supply of country liquor in bottles of different sizes. No tenderer shall have any right to be called for negotiation:

Provided further that having once fixed the price, the Government shall not vary it to the disadvantage of the licensee during the currency of his licence and that he shall not vary the price, if licence has been granted on the basis of prices quoted in competitive tenders;

(iii) the licensee shall not bottle, case, capsule or label country liquor on the premises of his licence, unless specially permitted to do so by the Excise Commissioner;

(iv) the licensee shall, in addition to any quantities which he may be required to make available for sale under clause (f) always keep in his licensed premises such minimum stock as may be laid down from time-to-time by the Excise Commissioner; .

(v) the licensee shall, during the currency of his licence, acquire and make available for sale such quantities of country liquor in different sizes of bottles in a year as may be required by an order of the Excise Commissioner and the Excise Commissioner shall not be under any obligation to guarantee the sale of all the country liquor so required to be made available;

(vi) the licensee shall make supplies as may be required in the terms and conditions under which licence is granted;

(vii) subject to the provisions contained in clauses (d) and (f), the licensee shall make available for sale in his licensed premises so much of country liquor as can be manufactured out of extra neutral alcohol, if allocated to him, by the Excise Commissioner and shall, for this purpose take all necessary actions, including action to obtain allocation orders from the Excise Commissioner and release orders from other Excise Authorities;

(viii) the licensee shall render a true and correct account of the quantities of extra neutral alcohol, If allocated and released to him, utilised and supplied by him in the form of country liquor and remaining in balance with him so as to reach the Deputy Commissioner on or before the 3rd day after the close of the fortnight to which the statement pertains.

(5) Licences in Forms L-6, L-6FG, L-6FE, L-7, L-7FG, L-7FE ,L-10, L-12, L-12F, L-14 for retail sale of Indian Liquor and Foreign Liquor for consumption "off" the premises:—

(a) the licensee shall not sell liquor to any person for consumption "on" the premises.

(b) the licensee shall not sell liquor to any other licensee:

Provided that in case of licensees holding more than one licences, the transfer of stock from one licensed premises to another may be made with the prior approval of the Deputy Commissioner or any other excise officer authorized by him.

(6) Licence in Form L-8 for the retail vend of country liquor for consumption "off" the premises.—

(a) the licence for retail vend of country liquor shall be granted by tender, auction or fixed fee;

(b) the licensee shall, unless otherwise permitted by the Excise Commissioner in exceptional cases, get his requirement of country liquor from a person licensed to sell country liquor by wholesale in Delhi;

(c) the licensee may, if no arrangement is made in Delhi, obtain his supplies of country liquor up to 20 per cent. of his sale of country liquor from any distillery or bottling plant, approved for this purpose by the Excise Commissioner:

Provided that in the case of the import of country liquor in bulk, beyond the limits of Delhi, the licensee shall not break bulk until the consignment has reached Delhi and has been compared by an Excise Inspector with the pass, covering the consignment;

(d) the licensee shall not sell or expose for sale country liquor in bottles of such shape or colour or bearing such figures, words or marks as are reasonably made to lead persons to believe that such liquor is other than country liquor;

(e) the licensee shall sell country liquor at such rates as may, from time-to-time, be fixed by the Government;

(f) the licensee shall maintain account of receipt and sale in Form F-6 and shall at the end of each month prepare and submit to the Excise Department a monthly true abstract of receipt and sales;

(g) the licensee shall not store in the licensed premises—

(i) any empty liquor bottle, cork, capsule, pilfer proof seal, bottle neck, etc., except as provided under the rules;

(ii) any bottle of soda water or any other soft drink;

(iii) rectified spirit and denatured spirit;

(iv) any other intoxicant.

(7) Licence in Form L-9 for retail vend of Indian liquor to holders of licence in Form L-1.—

(a) the licensee shall not sell liquor to any person for consumption "on" the premises;

(b) the licensee shall not sell liquor to any other licensee:

Provided that in case of licensees holding more than one licences, the transfer of stock from one licensed premises to another may be made with the prior approval of the Deputy Commissioner or any other excise officer authorized by the Deputy Commissioner.

(8) Licence in Form L-13 for home delivery of Indian liquor by ordering through e-mail or by fax (not on telephone).—

(a) the licensee shall make delivery of liquor at the residences only if order is received through e-mail or by Fax (not on telephone) and no delivery shall be made to any hostel, office, and institution;

(b) the licensee shall not sell liquor to any person for consumption "on" the premises;

(c) the licensee shall not sell liquor to any other licensee:

Provided that in case of licensees holding more than one licences, the transfer of stock from one licensed premises to another may be made with the prior approval of the Deputy Commissioner or any other excise officer authorized by the Deputy Commissioner.

(9) Licences in Forms L-15, L-15F for service of Indian Liquor and Foreign Liquor in a hotel [1][or guest house] to the residents in their rooms.—

(a) no liquor shall be served by the licensee to any person except to the order of a *bona fide* resident;

(b) no liquor shall be served by the licensee at any place other than the room in which the person ordering it resides for the time being;

(c) the licensee shall possess a certificate of recommendation from the Department of Tourism, Government of India [2][in case of Hotels and certificate from Tourism Department, Governemnt of National Capital Territory of Delhi, in case of Guest Houses];

(d) no licensee shall purchase any liquor from any person other than a person holding a licence in Forms L-1 and L-1F, without the permission of the Excise Commissioner.

(10) Licences in Forms L-16 and L-16F for service of Indian liquor and Foreign Liquor in a bar attached to a hotel.—

---

1. Ins. by Notification No. F.10(12)/Fin(Rev-I)/2010-11/DS II/111, dated 21st March, 2011.
2. Added by Notification No. F.10(12)/Fin(Rev-I)/2010-11/DS II/111, dated 21st March, 2011.

(a) the licensee shall not serve any Indian Liquor and Foreign Liquor at any premises of his hotel other than the premises of the bar and restaurants, if any, specified and endorsed on his licence:

Provided that liquor may be served in additional area including lawns of hotels and reception rooms on special request with the conditions that:

(i) the permission for the additional area shall be granted on payment of additional licence fee as prescribed;

(ii) the service of liquor in the additional area shall be allowed only from the main bar counter;

(iii) seat covers in additional area shall not be more than the seat covers of main licence;

(iv) additional area shall be screened off from the public on roads and adjoining areas.

(b) the licensee shall not store Indian Liquor and Foreign Liquor at any premises other than the store-room and bar specified and endorsed on his licence on payment of additional fee as prescribed;

(c) the licensee shall serve wine or beer in open bottles or in glasses and other Indian Liquor and Foreign Liquor only in glasses:

Provided that service of Indian Liquor and Foreign Liquor in a glass other than wine or beer shall not be less than 30 millilitres before the addition of any other liquid;

(d) no licensee shall purchase liquor from any person other than the person holding licences in Forms L-1 and L-1F without the permission of the Excise Commissioner.

(11) Licences in Forms L-17, 17F, L-18, L-18F, L-19, L-19F and L-21,L- 21F for service of Indian Liquor and Foreign Liquor for consumption "on" the premises in independent restaurant.—

(a) the licensee shall not serve Indian Liquor and Foreign Liquor at a premises other than the one specified and endorsed on the licence:

Provided that special permission may be granted to the holder of the above licences for service of liquor in additional area on the following terms and conditions, namely.—

(i) the permission for the additional area shall be granted on payment of additional licence fee as prescribed;

(ii) the service of liquor in the additional area shall be allowed only from the main bar counter and the additional area means the area located adjacent to the existing bar;

(iii) seat covers in additional area shall not be more than the seat covers of main licence;

(iv) additional area shall be screened off from the public view;

(b) the licensee shall not store Indian Liquor and Foreign Liquor at a place other than the store room and bar specified and endorsed on the licence;

(c) the licensee shall serve beer and wine in open bottles or in glasses and other Indian Liquor and Foreign Liquor only in glasses:

Provided that service of Indian Liquor and Foreign Liquor in a glass other than wine or beer shall not be less than 30 millilitres before the addition of any other liquid;

(d) no licensee shall purchase Indian Liquor and Foreign Liquor from any person other than the one holding licences in Forms L-1 and L-1F, without the permission of the Excise Commissioner.

(12) Licences in Forms L-20 and L-20F for service of Indian Liquor and Foreign Liquor in a bar or a dining car in a luxury train.—

(a) the licensee shall be India Tourism Development Corporation, a State Tourism Development Corporation, its units or any other agency, approved by the Excise Commissioner;

(b) the licensee shall not serve Indian Liquor and Foreign Liquor at any premises other than the premises of the bar or dining car specified and endorsed on the licence;

(c) the licensee shall serve wine or beer in open bottles or glasses and Indian Liquor and Foreign Liquor only in glasses:

Provided that service of Indian Liquor and Foreign Liquor in a glass other than wine or beer shall not be less than 30 milliliters before the addition of any other liquid;

(d) the licensee shall serve Indian Liquor and Foreign Liquor for consumption "on" the premises only to *bona fide* passengers boarding the train;

(e) the licensee shall not serve Indian Liquor and Foreign Liquor to persons employed in railway service on train;

(f) the licensee shall be required to take licence for service of Indian Liquor and Foreign Liquor from the excise authorities of those states through which the train passes;

(g) the licensee shall not purchase liquor from any person other than the person holding licence in Forms L-1 and L-1F without the permission of the Excise Commissioner;

(h) in the event of dismantling of bar in the train for any reason, whatsoever, the licensee shall intimate the stock position of liquor to the Excise Commissioner and it may be disposed of in the manner as decided by him.

(13) Licence in Form L-22 for the retail vend of Indian Liquor in duty free shop for consumption "off" the premises.—

(a) the licensee shall sell Indian Liquor in retail for consumption 'off' the premises to *bona fide* passengers going out of India, against foreign exchange;—

(b) the licensee shall not sell Indian Liquor to persons employed at air-port except under the rules framed by the administration concerned.

(14) Licence in Form L-23 and L23F for the vend of Indian Liquor and Foreign Liquor in military canteen approved by the competent military authority.—

(a) licence in Form L-23 shall be granted on the basis of dependency certificate issued by the Area Manager of the Canteen Stores Department, Delhi for sale of Indian Liquor and Foreign Liquor only in military unit;

(b) the licensee shall not sell liquor, except such liquor as he may be permitted to sell;

(c) notwithstanding anything contained in sub-rule (2) of rule 51, the licensee shall establish separate places of vend without taking separate licences in cases where a portion of a unit is detached for training and other purposes or is left behind;

(d) the licensee shall not sell liquor of any description to persons other than those attached to the regiment for which his licence is granted or duly authorised by the competent military authority to use such canteens.

(15) Licence in Form L-24 permitting sale of medicated wines.—

(a) the licensee shall not sell under this licence any wine, except the wines which are classified as medicated wines;

(b) the licensee shall not sell any article covered by his licence except for medicinal purpose;

(c) the licensee shall not sell to any person at any one time any article covered by his licence in greater quantity than 9 litres or twelve quart bottles, provided that sale in larger quantities may be made to persons holding a chemist's licence and to Government and charitable dispensaries;

(d) except upon the order of a medical practitioner, the licensee shall not knowingly sell or supply any article covered by his licence for consumption by a minor or a person of unsound mind;

(e) no licence shall be required for the sale of medicated wine, containing up to 20 degree proof spirit.

(16) Licence in Form L-28 and L-28F for service of Indian Liquor and Foreign Liquor at a club.—

(a) the licensee shall be authorised to sell Indian Liquor and foreign liquor by retail for consumption on the club premises to its members, but he shall not sell liquor to the persons below twenty-five years of age even if they are members of the club;

(b) the licensee shall serve wine or beer in open bottles or in glasses and other Indian Liquor and Foreign Liquor only in glasses. Such bottles shall on no account, be removed by the members of the club from the premises:

Provided that service of Indian Liquor and Foreign Liquor in a glass other than wine or beer shall not be less than 30 millilitres before the addition of any other liquid;

(c) the licensee shall purchase liquor from the holders of licence in Forms L-1 and L- 1F;

(d) the licensee is authorized to avail thirty guest nights per month;

(e) Excise Commissioner may permit guest nights exceeding thirty per month;

(f) the licensee shall obtain permit in Form P-13 from the Deputy Commissioner for holding guest nights;

(g) liquor may be served in additional area including lawns of club on special request with the conditions that—

(i) the permission for the additional area shall be granted on payment of additional licence fee as prescribed;

(ii) the service of liquor in the additional area shall be allowed only from the main bar counter;

(iii) seating capacity in additional area shall not be more than the seating capacity of main licence;

(iv) additional area shall be screened off from the public view on roads and adjoining areas.

(17) Licence in Form L-29, L-29F for retail vend of Indian Liquor and Foreign for consumption "on" the premises at club or mess whose members are exclusively Government servants and retired Government servants, including the members of armed forces serving or retired and such a club or mess is not running on commercial lines.—

(a) the licensee shall sell Indian Liquor and Foreign Liquor by retail for consumption "on" the premises to its members only but he shall not sell liquor to a person below 25 years of age even if he is the member of the club;

(b) the licensee shall serve wine or beer in open bottles or in glasses and other Indian Liquor and Foreign Liquor only in glasses . Such bottles shall, on no account, be removed by the members from the premises;

(c) the licensee shall purchase liquor from the holders of licences in Forms L-1 and L-1F;

(d) the licensee is authorized to avail thirty guest nights per month;

(e) Excise Commissioner may permit guest nights exceeding thirty per month;

(f) the licensee shall obtain permit in Form P-13 from the Deputy Commissioner for holding guest nights;

(g) liquor may be served in additional area including lawns of club on special request with the conditions that—

(i) the permission for the additional area shall be granted on payment of additional licence fee as prescribed;

(ii) the service of liquor in the additional area shall be allowed only from the main bar counter;

(iii) seating capacity in additional area shall not be more than the seating capacity of main licence;

(iv) additional area shall be screened off from the public view on roads and adjoining areas.

(18) Licence in Form L-37 for Hotel Management Institutes for keeping liquor for the purpose of training.—

(a) the licence shall be issued to Hotel Management Institute or other teaching institute recognized by the Government;

(b) the liquor shall be used for teaching purpose only;

(c) the liquor shall be purchased from licensed retail vends only;

(d) the limit of liquor shall be decided by the Excise Commissioner.

(e) the licensee shall obtain permit in form P-13 from the Deputy Commissioner for holding guest nights;

(f) liquor may be served in additional area including lawns of club on special request with the conditions that—

(g) the permission for the additional area shall be granted on payment of additional licence fee as prescribed;

(h) the service of liquor in the additional area shall be allowed only from the main bar counter;

(i) seating capacity in additional area shall not be more than the seating capacity of main licence;

(k) additional area shall be screened off from the public view on roads and adjoining areas.

(19) Licence in form L-37 for Hotel Management Institutes for keeping liquor for the purpose of training.—

(a) the licence shall be issued to Hotel Management Institute or other teaching institute recognized by the Government;

(b) the liquor shall be used for teaching purpose only;

(c) the liquor shall be purchased from licensed retail vends only;

(d) the limit of liquor shall be decided by the Excise Commissioner.

67. Duty.—Duty, unless such duty has been paid by the wholesaler at the time of import, shall be payable by each licensee before the grant of transport pass for the liquor purchased by him.

68. Security and bond.—The amount of security, personal surety and bond which any licensee shall be required to furnish, shall be as specified by the Excise Commissioner.

Non-refund of Security Deposit

PUDA had retained security deposit of Rs. 4,000.00 from 10-3-1989 till 19-1-1997 without any reasonable cause, which amounted to deficiency in service by PUDA. Not having asked for such refund, the respondents cannot take advantage of their lapse. Supreme Court reduced the rate of interest from 18% granted by the National Commission to 10% from the date of deposit till the date of actual payment; *Punjab Urban Planning and Development Authority* v. *Bhupinder Singh*, (2008) 13 SCC 572.

69. Specification of bottles.—(1) (a) The bottles containing Indian Liquor, the pilfer-proof seals and the capsules used hereon, to be sold in Delhi, shall be of specification, as approved by the Excise Commissioner.

(b) The bottles used for bottling country liquor for sale in Delhi shall be of such shape as may be approved by the Excise Commissioner and shall contain the following particulars:—

(i) Dilly Abkari (in Hindi, Urdu and Gurumukhi) or Delhi Excise in English;

(ii) bonded liquor or duty paid in Delhi as the case may be;

(iii) the name and registered monogram of the factory manufacturing the bottles and shall not bear any other visible markings.

(2) ***Capsules or seals to be used on bottles of Indian Liquor and country liquor.***— All bottles containing Indian Liquor or country liquor shall, unless otherwise required by the Excise Commissioner, be securely sealed with pilfer proof seals in such a way as to make it impossible to remove the seal without its being cut or broken.

(3) Labels to be used on the bottles of Indian Liquor and country liquor,—

(a) all labels required to be used on bottle of spiced country liquor shall bear the words "masaledar" in Hindi, Urdu and Gurmukhi characters and the words "Spiced country liquor" in English;

(b) no label shall be allowed if the design is of an objectionable nature or conveys the impression that the label is intended to be imitation of labels used on Foreign Liquor or in the case of country liquor in imitation of Indian liquor;

(c) labels must be affixed to the bottles as to be easily distinguishable. No label shall be pasted over the words showing the quantity of liquor, moulded on the bottles.;

(d) labels on each bottles of Indian Liquor and country liquor sold by the licensee, shall bear the following particulars:—

(i) batch no;

(ii) date of bottling;

(iii) a phrase "for sale in Delhi only";

(iv) a warning in bold letters in Hindi, Urdu, Gurmukhi and English to the effect that, 'Consumption of liquor is Injurious to health';

(v) retail price;

(vi) ingredients; details;

(vii) consumer care detail, *i.e.*, name and designation, address and telephone number of concerned person;

(viii) name of the licensed bottler and the place of bottling in full in Hindi or English;

(ix) contents/quantity;

(x) bar code;

(xi) bonded liquor or duty paid in Delhi as the case may be;

(xii) strength in proof and volume by volume;

(xiii) best before use (in case of beer):

Provided that mono-cartons or any other form of single packing shall also be required to bear the particulars as at (i), (iii), (v), (ix), (xii) and (xiii) above where the bottles are supplied in mono-cartons or in any other form of single packing;

70. Excise Black List, manner of blacklisting.—(1) Any licensee, tenderer, bidder, manufacturer or supplier, whose products are sold in Delhi, may be blacklisted by the Deputy Commissioner for violation of the provisions of the Act and the rules framed thereunder or for any other reason which may be considered detrimental to the interest of revenue or public health. No such order shall be passed without giving reasonable opportunity of hearing to the person concerned.

(2) Any person whose name is mentioned in the black list shall be debarred from applying for or holding any excise licence within Delhi for such period, not exceeding five years, as may be specifically indicated in the blacklisting order.

(3) The name of the blacklisted persons shall be circulated by the Deputy Commissioner to the Excise Authorities of the neighbouring States.

CHAPTER V

LICENCE AND PERMIT FOR SALE OF DENATURED, SPECIAL DENATURED AND RECTIFIED SPIRIT

71. Grant of permit for import of rectified spirit, denatured spirit and special denatured spirit.—(1) In respect of permits in Form P-1 granted for the import of rectified spirit, denatured spirit and special denatured spirit, the prescribed import fee shall be charged.

(2) The Excise Commissioner may, with the prior approval of the Government and subject to such conditions as he may deem necessary, exempt any denatured spirit and special denatured spirit imported for use in any of the specified alcohol based industry from the levy of import fee.

(3) The denatured spirit and special denatured spirit not meant for sale but for use of officers of the Government in their official capacity, hospitals dispensaries run by the Government, statutory corporations, local bodies and other hospitals/dispensaries recognised under Medical Attendance Rules may be exempted by the Excise Commissioner from payment of import fee.

72. Application for grant of licence for denatured, special denatured and rectified spirit.—An application for the grant of licence for dealings in denatured spirit, special denatured spirit or rectified spirit in whole sale or retail, shall contain the particulars as prescribed in Form F-1

73. Enquiries to be made by Deputy Commissioner before grant of licence.—On receipt of an application, the Deputy Commissioner shall make such enquiries for verification of the particulars of application and also such other enquiries as he may deem necessary and if he is satisfied that there is no objection to the grant of licence applied for, he shall, unless the application requires the orders of the Excise Commissioner, issue a licence in the appropriate form and subject to conditions and on payment of prescribed fee.

74. Sanction of Excise Commissioner required in certain cases.—(1) Application for licence to a manufacturer, requiring the order of the Excise Commissioner for fixation of quantities, shall be submitted to the Deputy Commissioner, who shall forward it to the Excise Commissioner, with his recommendations. The Excise Commissioner may pass such orders as he may deem necessary for fixation of possession limit, annual as well as one-time basis.

(2) The licence shall be granted by the Deputy Commissioner.

75. Licence in Form L-4 for the wholesale vend of rectified spirit.—All the provisions of rule 82 laid down for a licence in Form L-26 shall apply to this licence. The licensee shall sell rectified spirit only to a person holding a licence for sale of rectified spirit or to persons holding permit for purchase of alcohol in Form P-5.

76. Licence in Form L-5 for wholesale vend of denatured spirit including special denatured spirit, to trade only.—(1) All the provisions of rule 81 laid down for a licence in Form L-25 except sub-rules (4) and (5) shall apply to this licence and the licensee shall observe the same.

(2) The licensee shall sell denatured spirit only to a person holding a licence for sale of denatured spirit or to person holding permits for purchase and possession of denatured spirit more than ten litres.

(3) The licensee shall sell denatured spirit in quantities more than 10 litres and every such sale shall be covered by a permit in Form P-3 granted by the Deputy Commissioner or any other officer authorised to issue such passes.

(4) The licensee shall keep standard measures of one litre and five litres, approved by the Controller of Weights and Measures, Delhi. Unless otherwise permitted, he shall cause all receptacles in which denatured spirit is kept, to be gauged, numbered giving their capacity and shall have dip rods prepared for such receptacles.

(5) Every drum or other vessel, containing denatured spirit received or kept for sale in the licensed premises or approved godown, shall be conspicuously labelled or branded with the words "Manufactured and denatured at (name of the distillery)".

(6) The licensee shall maintain a correct account of each and every transaction of receipt and sale of denatured spirit in a register in Form F-9. Such account and stock shall be produced immediately on demand for inspection by an excise officer not below the rank of Excise Inspector. He shall also produce, in support of his accounts of receipt, the export or transport passes and in respect of his accounts of issue, the bill or cash memos along with such transport passes.

(7) The licensee shall not sell any denatured spirit from the consignment received, unless Assistant Commissioner gives him permission to do so after verifying the quality, quantity and strength of the denatured spirit. No such permission shall be given, unless the denatured spirit is found, on examination by the Chemical Examiner to contain specified quantity of denaturants.

(8) The licensee shall, notwithstanding that he may be required to submit any other return of sale, furnish a monthly statement of receipt and sale of denatured spirit, together with the details of payment of permit fee in Form F-31, not later than the 7th of every month to the Assistant Commissioner.

(9) The monthly statement in Form F-31, on receipt from the licensee, shall be checked from entries made in a register in Form F-10. If on checking, any omission or error in any statement is discovered, the same shall be brought to the notice of the Assistant Commissioner for such action as he may deem necessary.

(10) After the close of the financial year, the licensee shall prepare a statement in Form F-32, in duplicate, showing the details of monthly receipt of denatured spirit and the fee paid thereof and shall submit the original to the Assistant Commissioner by 15th April, each year.

(11) If no statements are furnished by the licensee in respect of any month by the prescribed date or if the Assistant Commissioner is not satisfied about the correctness of the statements, furnished and it appears necessary for him to make assessment, the Assistant Commissioner shall serve a notice calling upon the

licensee to produce his stock and sale registers along with other relevant records and documents and proof of payment of import fee, which he wishes to examine. In the notice, he shall state the period in respect of which such assessment is proposed and shall fix a date giving reasonable time to the licensee for producing such documents and accounts, etc., and for considering any objections, which the licensee may raise.

77. Procedure for grant of permit for rectified spirit to educational institution, homoeopathic chemists and practitioners in Form P-5.—(1) The following procedure shall be observed before a permit for rectified spirit in Form P-5 is granted by the Deputy Commissioner in the case of an educational institution, homoeopathic practitioners and chemists,—

(a) an application for rectified spirit required for use in research and teaching, should be made by the governing body or the representative of the university, college or other educational institution to the Deputy Commissioner. In the application the situation of the particular university, college or educational institution for research or teaching, the number of laboratories therein, the purpose to which the spirit is required, the bulk quantity likely to be required in the course of the year;

(b) the Deputy Commissioner may grant permit in Form P-5 in favour of the representative of the educational institution concerned;

(c) the spirit received at any one institution must only be used in the laboratories of that institution and must not be distributed for the use in the laboratory of any other institution or used for any other purpose than that authorized;

(d) the stock of spirit in each institution must be kept under separate lock in a special compartment under the control of the permit holder;

(e) the spirit received may be distributed by the permit holder undiluted to any of the laboratories belonging to the same institution;

(f) the quantity of spirit in stock at any one time must not exceed half the estimated quantity required in a year.

(2) The following procedure shall be observed for the grant of a permit for rectified spirit in Form P-5 by the Deputy Commissioner to a homoeopathic chemist, practitioner or for the manufacture and sale of homoeopathic medicines:

(a) an application for the possession of rectified spirit by a homoeopathic chemist or practitioner shall be made in writing to the Deputy Commissioner giving the following particulars—

(a) name and address of the applicant;

(ii) the quantity of rectified spirit in litres likely to be possessed by the applicant at any one time;

(iii) the maximum quantity of rectified spirit in litres required by the applicant in a year;

(iv) the amount of the security which the applicant is prepared to furnish as a guarantee for the performance of the conditions of the permit and the rules;

(v) a list of preparations which are to be manufactured;

(b) if the application is accepted, the Excise Commissioner shall determine—

(i) the quantity of rectified spirit in litres to be possessed at any time;

(ii) the quantity of rectified spirit in litres to be obtained during the year;

(iii) the nature and amount of the security to be furnished for the performance of the conditions of the permit and the rules; and

(iv) the preparations to be manufactured by the applicant hereinafter referred to as the approved homoeopathic chemist or practitioner;

(c) the permit in Form P-5 shall be granted for a period not exceeding one year. It shall be renewed from year to year, by the Deputy Commissioner who may, however, on sufficient cause shown, refuse to renew it or at any time determine it;

(d) before the permit in Form P-5 is granted the approved homoeopathic chemist or practitioner shall execute a bond for such amount as may be specified by the Excise Commissioner;

(e) the approved homoeopathic chemist or practitioner shall be required to maintain the accounts in Form F-20.

78. Grant of permit in Form P-6 for possession of special denatured spirit by industrial manufacturers.—The procedure prescribed for grant of permit in Form P-5 shall be applicable here also.

79. Licence in Form L-25 for retail sale of denatured spirit up to five litres without permit and to the holder of permit in Form P-2.—(1) (a) The possession limit of the licensee shall be fixed by the Deputy Commissioner on annual or one time basis or both up to ten thousand litres from time-to-time;

(b) no licensee shall have in his possession at any time, denatured spirit in a quantity in excess of ten thousand litres without the prior sanction of the Excise Commissioner.

(2) The licensee shall sell denatured spirit up to five litres without permit and up to ten litres to person holding permit in Form P-2 authorising him to purchase and possess denatured spirit exceeding five litres up to ten litres.

(3) (a) The licensee shall, in particular, satisfy himself about the *bona fide* of the purchaser to ensure that the denatured spirit is required for genuine use;

(b) the licensee, before selling denatured spirit by retail to any individual for private home use, shall use all reasonable diligence to ascertain the requirement and shall maintain proper record of such transactions;

(c) likewise the licensee shall ensure that the denatured spirit to be sold to an educational and research institution or a furniture, polish dealer, private hospital, dispensary or registered medical practitioner does not exceed ten litres. In all such cases the licensee shall obtain a written requisition in which, *inter alia*, the quantity already in possession of the applicant shall be mentioned. Particulars of all such sales shall be entered in a separate register and all such requisitions and the register shall be checked by the Inspector of the area;

(d) the sales of denatured and special denatured spirit in excess of ten litres shall be made against the special permit issued by the Deputy Commissioner in Form P-3.

(4) The licensee shall keep an account of each and every transactions of receipt and sale of denatured spirit in a register in Form F-8 and shall submit such periodical returns, as may be specified by the Excise Commissioner:

(a) Unless otherwise permitted by the Excise Commissioner, the licensee shall store all his stock of denatured spirit in the licensed premises. In case the Deputy Commissioner has permitted the storage of denatured spirit in a godown under sub-rule (2) of rule 51, the licensee shall maintain an account of receipt and issue of denatured spirit at the godown separately in a register in Form F-6. The godown shall be used only for the storage of denatured spirit for issue to the licensed premises. The sale of denatured spirit from the godown on any pretext is strictly prohibited.

(b) Transport of denatured spirit from licensed premises to the godown and from godown to the licensed premises shall be regulated on the basis of a challan in Form F-18, issued by the licensee himself or by his authorized agent.

(c) The licensee shall neither sell denatured spirit of a lesser strength than 50 degree over proof, nor shall he mix denatured spirit with any other spirit.

(d) The licensee shall not adulterate or dilute denatured spirit to be sold by him or sell the same knowing it to have been adulterated or diluted or store or permit to be stored in his licensed premises or the licensed godown, denatured spirit in an adulterated or diluted state.

(e) The licensee shall keep denatured spirit in corked bottles or in a drum securely closed. All bottles, jars, drums or casks, etc., containing denatured spirit shall bear a label printed in red and containing skull and cross bones with a warning "not to be taken internally" written in Hindi, Urdu, Gurumukhi and English.

(f) The licensee shall procure his supplies of denatured spirit by purchase from other vendors licensed to sell denatured spirit or by removal from licensed distilleries or warehouse licensed to store denatured spirit after obtaining permit/pass required under the rules.

(g) The licensee shall allow any excise officer, not below the rank of Excise Inspector, to take samples of denatured spirit, imported or lying in storage with him free of cost, for the purpose of verification and analysis of the denaturants and contents of spirit thereof.

(h) The licensee shall comply with all directions and instructions issued by the Excise Commissioner from time-to-time.

(i) In the event of the enhancement of import fee leviable on denatured spirit, the difference of import fee shall be levied, on the balance of the stock, and the licensee shall pay such difference within thirty days of the date on which the enhanced rates come into force.

(j) The licensee shall maintain conspicuously above the main outer gate of the licensed premises, a signboard bearing his name and the words 'Licensed vendor of denatured spirit' written in Hindi, Urdu, Gurumukhi and English. The board shall be of the size not less than

1 meter x 30 centimeter and shall be painted in white with red letters. A board of similar size, exhibiting in conspicuous printed letters, the name of the licensee and the words "Approved godown, for storage, and not for sale of denatured spirit" written in Hindi, Urdu, Gurumukhi and English, shall be fixed at the outer gate of the godown, if any, approved by the Deputy Commissioner.

(k) (a) Every licensee shall display at a conspicuous place of the licensed premises the sale price and opening stock of denatured spirit in such manner as to be easily accessible to the customers visiting the premises;

(b) the retail price fixed by the licensee for every consignment, having regard to the cost of spirit, incidental charges and the fee levied, shall be intimated to the Deputy Commissioner within three days of the receipt of the consignment.

(l) No licensee shall withhold from sale any denatured spirit kept for sale.

(m) No licensee shall obtain denatured spirit fraudulently in excess of the monthly or annual quota fixed for him by the Deputy Commissioner.

(n) In case the licensee wants to sell denatured spirit in bottles, he shall use standard size bottles. The capacity of the bottles shall be clearly indicated on the label affixed on the bottle itself.

80. Licence in Form L-26 for the retail vend of rectified spirit.—(1)(a) No licensee shall have in his possession at any time rectified spirit in a quantity in excess of the prescribed possession limit, without the prior sanction of the Excise Commissioner. The Excise Commissioner may permit the possession of rectified spirit by a licensee up to 50,000 litres. Permission to licensee to possess more than 50,000 litres of rectified spirit at any time shall be granted with the previous sanction of the Government;

(b) The licensee shall satisfy himself about the *bona fide* of the purchaser to ensure that the rectified spirit is required for the genuine use and the purchaser is not a person of ill-repute or bootlegger or an agent of a bootlegger. In all cases where a person comes to purchase spirit repeatedly, the licensee shall be bound to inform the Deputy Commissioner.

(2) The licensee shall not reduce the strength of rectified spirit below what it was when he purchased it.

(3) The licensee shall not sell rectified spirit except for *bona fide* medicinal, industrial and scientific purposes.

(4) Except with the sanction of the Deputy Commissioner the licensee shall not sell rectified spirit in any one transaction more than the quantity, which the purchaser is permitted to possess at any one time.

81. Grant of permit for possession of denatured spirit exceeding ten litres.—(1) The grant of permit for possession for more than ten litres of denatured spirit for the purpose of business on payment of prescribed fee in P-3, granted by the Deputy Commissioner shall be restricted to the following persons:—

(a) *bona fide* dealers in furniture, chemists, varnish makers or other persons engaged in any business who require denatured spirit for purpose of their business;

(b) manufactures requiring denatured spirit for industrial purpose duly recommended by the Commissioner of Industries;

(c) medical institutes registered with the Directorate of Health Services, Ayush, Directorate of Ayush, educational institutions registered with the Directorate of Education, and the Universities located in Delhi;

(d) hospitals/dispensaries under the control of the Government/local authority;

(e) any other person with the permission of the Excise Commissioner.

(2) A permit for the possession of denatured spirit shall be granted to the following categories of consumers by Deputy Commissioner or authorised excise officer in Form P-2 up to the limit of 10 litres at one time on payment of prescribed fee:

(a) an educational and research institution;

(b) a furniture dealer, polish dealer or painter;

(c) a private hospital, dispensary or registered medical practitioner;

(d) an individual requiring denatured spirit for use in polishing.

(3) A permit for the possession of rectified spirit granted to any chemist, medical practitioner, scientific body, superintendent of a hospital, manufacturing chemist, any local fund hospital, dispensary or educational institution which requires rectified spirit shall be granted by the Deputy Commissioner in Form P-5 on payment of prescribed fee.

(4) (a) The Deputy Commissioner may, on payment of prescribed fee, grant a permit for the possession of special denatured spirit in excess of the limit specified for retail sale, to any manufacturer of alcohol based industry for use in his business. Such permit shall be in the Form P-4;

(b) persons holding such permit shall pay, unless exempted by the Excise Commissioner, supervision charges on the total quantity of industrial spirit consumed at the prescribed rate.

CHAPTER VI

ESTABLISHMENT OF WAREHOUSES FOR LIQUOR

82. Grant of Licence.—(1) No licence for a warehouse, whether bonded or otherwise for storage of liquor, shall be granted by the Excise Commissioner, unless the applicant possesses a licence for wholesale of liquor in Delhi.

(2) Licence for a warehouse for storage of Liquor shall be granted on payment of prescribed fee:

(a) in Form L-31 for storage of Indian Liquor;

(b) in Form L-32 for storage of Foreign Liquor;

(c) in Form L-33 for storage of Country Liquor

(d) in Form L-34 for storage of denatured spirit;

(e) in Form L-35 for storage of rectified spirit.

83. Storage of liquor.—(1) Liquor, imported for the purpose of wholesale vending, shall be stored in the premises, licensed by the Excise Commissioner and in the case of Foreign Liquor, premises for the storage of Foreign Liquor after removal from Customs Bonded Warehouse for further transport or export.

(2) No liquor shall be removed from the warehouse without payment of duty levied under the Act, if not paid at the time of import;

(3) All the licensees, authorised to establish warehouses for storage of liquor, shall be permitted to import liquor on payment of duty or execution of a bond for payment of duty under the Act.

(4) No licensee shall store in the warehouse any class or brand of liquor other than that permitted by the Deputy Commissioner.

(5) The licensee shall transport liquor to his licensed premises and store therein such manner as the Excise Commissioner may, by order, specify and the Excise Commissioner may, specify different kinds of packaging of bottles for different categories of liquor.

84. Right of inspection.—The Excise Commissioner or any other excise officer may inspect and examine the warehouse and liquor stored there at any time and licensee shall render all proper assistance in making such inspection and examination.

85. Establishment.—The Excise Commissioner may post excise officer, not below the rank of Excise Inspector and as many excise constables, as he may deem sufficient for ensuring the due observance of the Act, rules, regulations and the directions issued by the Excise Commissioner or the Deputy Commissioner. Their establishment shall, unless otherwise directed by the Excise Commissioner be subject to the control of the Deputy Commissioner.

86. Building.—(1) The building for the warehouse shall be arranged by the applicant. He shall furnish a correct plan of the premises, which he proposes to use for the purpose of his business under his licence and of the entire building. The plan shall be submitted in duplicate, showing the plan and elevation of the premises and the position of various rooms, cupboards, racks and all-important details connected with the warehouse. A No Objection Certificate from the landlord with regard to the premises for the storage of liquor, if it is not owned by him, shall also be necessary. The Deputy Commissioner, after making such enquiries of the details of the building, submitted by the applicant; furnish a report to the Excise Commissioner. The Excise Commissioner shall, if he is satisfied that the condition of the proposed building for the warehouse is suitable for the storage and supply of liquor to the liquor vends, accord his approval.

(2) The building of the warehouse shall be *pucca* with suitable locking arrangements and sufficient storage capacity but not less than 500 square feet located in approved commercial or industrial area.

(3) The Excise Commissioner may allow licensee to have additional warehouse for the storage of liquor on a prescribed fee.

87. Closure of warehouse.—The Excise Commissioner may order the closure of warehouse during the currency of the licensing period and the Government shall not be liable to pay any compensation in lieu thereof or make good any loss which the licensee may suffer on this account.

88. Locks.—(1) In case of bonded warehouse, it shall be under the lock and key of the officer-in-charge and of the licensee jointly.

(2) When the officer-in-charge is absent from duty in the warehouse on account of leave, he shall hand over the keys of the bonded warehouse to the excise officer, appointed in his place by the Deputy Commissioner, who shall discharge all the functions of the officer-in-charge.

89. Stocks.—The licensee shall always be bound to keep a minimum stock of liquor as may be laid down from time-to-time by the Excise Commissioner. Failure to build up and to maintain the minimum stock of liquor and failure to maintain its regular supplies as specified by the Excise Commissioner, from time-to-time and/or failure to, supply liquor within time, which the Excise Commissioner deems reasonable, shall render the licensee liable to pay such penalty as prescribed.

90. Samples.—(1) Any Excise Officer authorised by the Deputy Commissioner or the Excise Commissioner may take samples of liquor for analysis. Samples shall be taken in three sealed quart, pint or nip bottles, in the presence of the licensee or his authorised representative and such bottle shall be immediately and securely sealed in the presence of the excise officer and the licensee or his authorised representative. Both of them shall sign the label which shall be fixed to the bottle and describe the contents thereof as accurately as possible. One bottle shall then be made over to the licensee or his representative, the second bottle shall be dispatched to the chemical examiner for analysis and the third bottle shall be kept in store of the excise office.

(2) If the sample conforms to the prescribed specifications, the samples kept in the warehouse and in the excise office shall be released to the licensee by the Assistant Commissioner, who shall then take them in stock.

(3) Where the sample does not conform to the prescribed specifications, the samples shall be preserved till the disposal of the case and thereafter they shall be destroyed by the order of the Assistant Commissioner, in the presence of the Excise Inspector.

(4) In the case of country liquor, at least one sample shall be drawn from each batch received in the warehouse for analysis.

91. Employees.—(1) The licensee shall furnish to the Assistant Commissioner a list containing the names of the Manager or Assistant Manager, employed by him and of all the employees whose duties require them to enter into the warehouse premises. The Assistant Commissioner shall forward a copy of the list to the Deputy Commissioner for his approval and the licensee shall not employ persons to whom the Deputy Commissioner may object.

(2) If the licensee desires to employ any person temporarily, requiring him to enter into the warehouse premises to replace an employee, who is absent, on leave to perform any duty in the warehouse, he shall inform the Assistant Commissioner who shall add the name of such person to the list mentioned in sub-rule (1).

(3) If any employee leaves the service of the licensee or is no longer employed on duty requiring him to enter into the warehouse, the licensee shall inform the Assistant Commissioner, who shall inform the Deputy Commissioner accordingly.

92. Entry to warehouse.—No person shall be allowed to enter into the warehouse except:

(a) licensee;

(b) any director, or partner of the company owning the warehouse licence;

(c) any excise officer;

(d) any person authorised by the licensee;

(e) any employee and such other person as may be authorised in writing by the Excise Commissioner.

93. Search before entering warehouse.—(1) Every person entering the warehouse or leaving it, may be searched at the gate by the excise staff.

(2) All the consignments, on their arrival as well as at the time of issue from the bonded warehouse, shall be checked by the excise staff deputed at the warehouse.

94. Permission to open warehouse beyond prescribed working hours.—The Excise Commissioner, on the request of the licensee, may permit the licensee to open the warehouse beyond the prescribed hours on payment of prescribed fee in advance.

95. Arrival of consignment.—(1) On arrival of the consignment the Assistant Commissioner shall be informed immediately and the consignment shall not be opened until the same has been examined and verified with the pass by the Assistant Commissioner, who shall also note the results in the prescribed register and also on the pass covering the consignment. One copy of the pass with entries of receipt shall be immediately returned to the officer-in-charge who issued the pass, and other copy with entries thereon shall be kept in the warehouse.

(2) The consignment issued from the warehouse and received into the warehouse may be checked at the gate by the excise staff.

(3) Any discrepancy noticed by the excise staff shall be reported to the Assistant Commissioner, who shall further report to the Deputy Commissioner for further necessary action.

96. Import permit.—(1) The liquor shall be imported by the licensee against the import permit valid for the specified period, issued by the Assistant Commissioner or any other officer authorised by the Excise Commissioner.

(2) In the case of country liquor, it shall be the duty of the licensee to obtain necessary allocation, if required, from the state or Union territory where the distillery or the bottling plant is situated within the time prescribed in the contract. The Excise Commissioner shall not accept any responsibility in this behalf.

97. Loss due to fire, etc.—Government shall not be held liable for the loss or damage by fire, theft or due to any other cause whatsoever, occurring to any quantity of liquor stored in the warehouse. In case of fire or other accident, the Assistant Commissioner shall immediately attend and open the warehouse during the day or night.

98. Enquiry.—If fire, theft or any other accident, causing loss or damage to liquor, stored in the warehouse takes place, the Excise Commissioner shall immediately cause an enquiry to be held by a Gazetted Officer and if in such enquiry, it is found that theft or fire has occurred due to connivance or negligence of the licensee, the Excise Commissioner shall determine his liability to pay the duty on the wasted liquor. On receipt of the enquiry report and on the basis of the evidence before him, the Excise Commissioner may if he is satisfied, that the theft has occurred due to connivance or negligence of the licensee, take necessary action against the licensee:

Provided that before any liability is determined, the licensee shall be given an opportunity of being heard after giving him a copy of the enquiry report.

99. Breaching of Act and rules by employees.—If it comes to the notice of the licensee that any person, employed by him has committed any breach of the Act, the rules framed thereunder or of the agreement entered into by him, it shall be his duty to report the matter to the Assistant commissioner and to comply with his direction. The Assistant commissioner shall report the matter together with the action taken by him to the Deputy Commissioner.

100. Wastage due to breakage in transit or warehouse.—(1) Wholesale licensee shall not be liable to pay duty on liquor which is or has been contained in bottles found damaged in transit upto the extent of 0.2 per cent. of the volume of consignment and to pay duty as applicable for breakage in transit beyond that or found broken or defective at the warehouse.

101. Sorting of consignments.—(1) The liquor consignments shall be sorted out by the licensee at the time of issuing liquor to the retail vends with a view to ensure that no defective or leaked bottles are issued. Such bottles shall be separated and be dealt with in prescribed manner.

(2) The licensee shall submit report to the Assistant Commissioner daily of all the leaked, broken and defective bottles, detected each day. The Assistant Commissioner shall keep an account of such bottles and shall report the same to the Deputy Commissioner.

(3) The licensee shall keep the necks of the broken bottles separately from the defective and leaked bottles. Such necks shall be preserved in containers, which shall be made over to the officer-in-charge of the warehouse at the time of the closure of the warehouse. Such containers shall thereafter be sealed date-wise, indicating the quantity therein and the labels pasted thereon shall bear the signatures of both the licensee or his representative and the Assistant Commissioner, who shall be responsible for the safe-custody of such containers. The remnants, after destruction, shall be removed from the warehouse on the same day. The empty bottles, of which the contents have been destroyed, shall also be removed by the warehouse licensee on the same day.

(4) The provisions of sub-rules (2) and (3) shall not apply where duty paid liquor is stored in the warehouse and the accounting of the leaked, broken and defective bottles shall be maintained by the licensee under intimation to the Assistant Commissioner.

CHAPTER VII

SUPPLY AND SALE OF HEMP DRUGS (BHANG)

102. Form of licence.—There shall be only one type of licence in Form L-27 for the retail vend of hemp drugs (bhang) or its preparation or any admixture thereof.

103. Licence to be granted by auction or tender.—Licence shall be granted by Deputy Commissioner through auction or tender separately and not in groups, and the fee payable for the licence shall be fixed at the time of auction or tender.

104. Manner of disposal of stock of hemp drug on expiry of licence.—If any person, who has held a licence under the rules, has in his possession, on the expiry or determination from any other cause, *i.e.*, by cancellation of his licence, any hemp drugs which he was unable to dispose of during the time when his licence was current, under the provisions of these rules to any person licensed or authorized to purchase them, he shall dispose them of in such manner as the Deputy Commissioner may direct.

105. Licensee is bound to take left over stock.—Any person who is granted a retail licence, shall be bound if so desired by the Deputy Commissioner, to take over the surplus stock of the person who held the retail licence for the same place in the preceding year at a price fixed by the Deputy Commissioner.

106. Licensee to meet demand of customers.—The licensee shall, in respect of hemp drugs, which he is licensed to sell, meet the demand of all the customers entitled to be served.

107. Licensee to maintain accounts.—The licence holder shall maintain an account of receipt and sale made by him under his licence in such form as the Excise Commissioner may, from time to time, direct.

108. Licensee not to keep certain chemicals.—The licensee shall not keep in stock, or sell, either mixed with the hemp drugs which he is authorized to sell or separately, any chloral hydrate, butyl chloral hydrate, or para-aldehyde.

109. Licensee not to hold any other licence.—The licensee shall not hold directly or indirectly through an agent, any other licence granted under the Act, nor shall he act as the agent of any person, holding such a licence.

110. Consequences of licensee infringing rules or conditions of licence.—In the event of licence-holder infringing rules or any of the conditions, he shall be liable to be deprived of his licence at the Deputy Commissioner's discretion, in addition to any other penalty to which he may be liable under the penal provisions of the Act.

111. Surrender of licence on cancellation.—On the termination of the period for which licence is granted or on the licence being cancelled by the Deputy Commissioner as provided under rule 110, the licence holder shall forthwith surrender the licence to the Deputy Commissioner.

112. Conditions for grant of licence.—Licence in Form L-27 for the retail vend of hemp drugs or its preparation or admixture thereof shall be granted under the following conditions:—

(a) If the licensee makes default in paying any monthly instalment on the first day of the month in respect of which it is due, it shall be in the discretion of the Deputy Commissioner to cancel the licence forthwith and recover any loss caused to the Government by such default in the manner provided in section 29;

(b) the licensee shall not, in any case, be entitled to demand refund of any fee paid to the Government in respect of his licence;

(c) the licensee shall not sell hemp drugs or its preparation or admixture thereof in quantity more than 120 grams to one person at one time;

(d) the licensee shall not permit hemp drugs or its preparation or admixture thereof to be consumed on the premises of his shop;

(e) the licensee shall not permit hemp drugs or its preparation or admixture thereof to any insane person or a minor;

(f) the licensee shall not allow any person to conduct sales on his behalf unless the name of such person has been previously submitted to the Deputy Commissioner for approval and endorsed by him on the licence;

(g) the licensee shall maintain daily account of his hemp drug sales and of his balance in store in the following form and shall submit an abstract of such account to the Deputy Commissioner at the end of every month—

Month and date	Balance of previous date	Today's receipts		Total	Today's sale in quantity	Balance in store at the end of the day
		Qty.	Source of supply			
1	2	3	4	5	6	7

(h) the licensee shall, on demand, by an excise officer, produce the licence and his sale accounts for inspection by such officer;

(i) no alteration, addition or deletion in the names of partners shall be made except in accordance with rule 38. Any contravention of this condition may entail the cancellation of the licence, besides such penal action as may be deemed necessary;

(j) the licensee shall be bound to pay all Government dues in time;

(k) the licensee shall open his shop for purposes of sale during the hours as specified by the Excise Commissioner.

113. Hemp drugs not to be sold on dry days.—The licensee shall not sell hemp drugs on dry days as declared by the Excise Commissioner from time-to-time.

114. Hemp drug to be imported exported or transported under a pass.—Hemp drugs shall not be imported, exported or transported except under a pass in Form P-12 issued in accordance with the rules for the time being in force for such import, export or transport. Such import or export shall be made between persons licensed to do so.

CHAPTER VIII

IMPORT, EXPORT, TRANSPORT, POSSESSION AND SALE OF INTOXICATING SPIRITUOUS PREPARATIONS

115. Possession.— No person shall have, except to the extent permitted by rule 116, in his possession any quantity of any intoxicating spirituous preparation without the authority and in accordance with the terms and conditions of a licence or permit granted under the rules.

116. Possession without permit.—The following intoxicating spirituous preparations may be possessed without a licence or permit by the persons and to the extent noted against each:—

(1) Allopathic, Homoeopathic, Ayurvedic and Unani Preparations:—(a) a patient on the authority and up to the extent of a prescription issued by a registered medical practitioner and dispensed either by the registered medical practitioner himself or by a licensee;

(b) a registered medical practitioner up to one litre of each such preparation at any one time;

(c) a registered medical practitioner in managing or supervising charge of a hospital or dispensary, clinic run by private individual, organisation, Government, Municipal Corporation, other local body, or a charitable organisation up to the requirement of such hospital or dispensary or clinic for a year.

(2) Toilet preparations:—A *bona fide* consumer up to 0.3 litres of each variety.

(3) Essences:

(a) a *bona fide* consumer up to 0.2 litres of each variety;

(b) a manufacturer of aerated water, up to 5 litres of each variety at any one time.

(4) All kinds of intoxicating spirituous preparations:—An excise officer acting in his official capacity up to any quantity.

117. Import, export and transport.—A licensee, a registered medical practitioner or a permit-holder may, subject to rule 115, import, export or transport intoxicating spirituous preparations on the authority of a permit or a pass under these rules.

118. Import, export or transport by certain institutions.—A registered medical practitioner, in managing or supervising charge of a Government, Municipal Corporation, any other local body, charitable hospital, dispensary, clinic or that run by private individual or organisation duly approved by the Deputy Commissioner, may import and transport such quantity of intoxicating spirituous preparations, as may be specified on the indent, not exceeding the requirements for one year, duly counter-signed by the officer in the Directorate of Health Services or the Directorate of Ayurveda, Unani, Sidha and Homoeopathy Delhi as the case may be, and in the case of veterinary hospital and dispensary, by the Deputy

Superintendent of Civil Veterinary Hospital. A copy of the indent shall be furnished, in advance, to the Deputy Commissioner for record and for such action as he may deem expedient in relation to the indent in regard to the quantity to be imported or transported.

119. Sale.—A manufacturer or a licensee shall, subject to the conditions of his licence, sell intoxicating spirituous preparations to:—

(a) a registered medical practitioner;

(b) a licensee as specified;

(c) a permit holder as specified;

(d) a person holding a prescription of a registered medical practitioner; and

(e) any person in any quantity which he is permitted to possess without permit or licence under the rules or as may be specified in his licence or permit.

120. Registered medical practitioner to dispense on prescription.—A registered medical practitioner shall sell intoxicating spirituous preparations only for dispensing his own prescription or the prescription of another registered medical practitioner.

121. Unless otherwise provided, the preparations to be sold only once on the prescription.—Unless the prescription bears an indication by registered medical practitioner that it is to be repeated and at what interval of time it is to be repeated and how many times it is to be repeated, the licensee or the registered medical practitioner shall sell the intoxicating spirituous preparations only once on the prescription. After noting the date on the prescription and making an entry in the sale register, the prescription shall be returned to the patient or his representative. If the prescription bears an indication as aforesaid, the licensee or the registered medical practitioner, dispensing the prescription, shall enter on the prescription the date of sale and shall sign and affix his seal on the prescription and return the prescription to the patient or his representative.

122. Grant of licence by Deputy Commissioner.—The Deputy Commissioner may grant a licence in Form L-36 to any registered medical practitioner, chemist or druggist holding a licence under the Drugs and Cosmetics Act, 1940, any person running a general stores, toilet preparations, essences, or ayurvedic or unani medicines, not exceeding in aggregate to one thousand litres in a year.

123. Licence to be granted by the Excise Commissioner.—The Excise Commissioner is to grant licence for the possession and sale of intoxicating spirituous preparations or any class of such preparations in any quantity exceeding in aggregate to one thousand litres in a year.

124. Licence fee.—The licence fee shall be yearly as prescribed.

125. Form of application for grant of licence.—A person desirous of obtaining a licence may apply to the Deputy Commissioner, provided that the Deputy Commissioner may, for reasons to be recorded, refuse to grant the licence.

126. Person and quantity in respect of which permit may be granted.—(1) No permit for the possession of intoxicating spirituous preparations, in excess of the quantities specified in rule 116 shall be granted except in respect of such kinds thereof, as are described in column 1 of the schedule below to the persons specified in column 2, to the extent specified in column 3, and for the purpose specified in column 4 of the said schedule:

(a) Allopathic medicinal preparations	(i) manufacturer of homoeopathic dilutions. (ii) any person	2.5 litres each 0.5 litre each	for manufacturing some other preparations for private home consumption
(b) Toilet preparations	(i) institution (ii) any person	2.5 litres each variety 0.5 litre of each variety	for external use. for private home consumption
(c) Essences	(i) manufacturer of aerated water (ii) manufacturer of ice cream (iii) any person for *bona fide* private consumption	9 litres each 2.5 litres each 0.5 litre each	for manufacture of aerated water for manufacture of ice cream for private home consumption
(d) Intoxicating spirituous preparations	(i) Institution (ii) any person	As fixed by Deputy Commissioner	for *bona fide* consumption.

(2) A permit in Form P-7 may be granted by the Assistant Commissioner to any person mentioned in sub-rule (1) on payment of fee, as prescribed:

Provided that no such fee shall be payable if the permit is required for personal use.

127. Grant of permit in Form P-8.—The Assistant Commissioner shall grant permit in Form P-8 for the import of intoxicating spirituous preparations.

128. Issue of export and transport passes.—The Assistant Commissioner shall issue export and transport passes as specified by the Excise Commissioner.

129. Maintenance of accounts.—(1) The licensee or the permit holder shall maintain true account of his daily transactions and submit a monthly return to the Deputy Commissioner:

(2) The Excise Commissioner, in his discretion, may relax in full or in part, the provision for the maintenance of accounts in the case of an individual or certain class of licences.

130. Duty payable on intoxicating spirituous preparations.—Duty on intoxicating spirituous preparations, not leviable under the Medicinal and Toilet Preparations (Excise Duties) Act, 1955 (16 of 1955) shall be paid as prescribed.

131. Rules not to apply in certain cases.—These rules shall not apply to the intoxicating spirituous preparations:

(a) imported into India;

(b) as are considered by the Excise Commissioner, from time-to-time, to be incapable of being misused for potable purposes and declared as such by him, by issue of notification.

CHAPTER IX

MISCELLANEOUS

132. Manner of disposal of confiscated goods.—The goods, vehicle or animal, confiscated by the Deputy Commissioner, may be disposed of by him in the following manner.—

(1) Indian Liquor and Foreign Liquor, if it is in sealed bottles the contents of which may reasonably be believed not to have been tampered with, after getting the clearance from the Chemical Examiner, shall be disposed of through L-6 Licensees or in any other manner, deemed fit by the Excise Commissioner, at a price fixed by him.

(2) Country Liquor, liquor not fit for human consumption, rectified spirit, denatured spirit, intoxicating drugs, medicinal and toilet preparations containing alcohol, perfumed spirit and alcoholic essences, stills, implements and apparatus for the manufacture of liquor and intoxicating drugs, shall be destroyed.

(3) Vehicles and animals shall be put to auction and sold to the highest bidder with in a period of one month or such extended period as deemed fit by the Excise Commissioner.

(4) A notice may also be issued to the owner of liquor, animal or vehicle to attend the auction, in case he so desires:

Provided that if delay occurs in disposal of carrier vehicle at the instance of the owner of the vehicle, a parking fee at the rate of rupees one hundred per day shall be charged from the owner of the vehicle as the case may be.

133. Destruction to be done in presence of Assistant Commissioner.—(1) Whenever any confiscated goods has to be destroyed in conformity with these rules, it shall be destroyed in the presence of the Assistant Commissioner.

134. Action when order of confiscation of goods and its sale is reversed in appeal.—If an order of confiscation and sale of liquor, animal or vehicle be reversed on appeal, such liquor, animal or vehicle or the sale proceeds thereof, if sold and the balance of the amount, if any, deposited for feeding upkeep or safe custody thereof after deduction of the expenditure, if any, incurred in its maintenance shall be returned along with interest at the rate of six per cent. per annum, to the owner thereof, or his duly authorised agent, if claimed within two months from such order.

135. Action when offender is not known.—Liquor, animal, vehicle or other goods, in respect of which an offence has been committed and the offender is not known or cannot be found and intoxicants which are found unclaimed in railways, other transport and in the post office shall, when forwarded to the Excise Commissioner be dealt with under these rules.

136. Disposal of goods when offence is compounded.—Any liquor, animal or vehicle confiscated in a case compounded under section 57, shall be disposed of in accordance with these rules.

137. Grant of reward.—(1) In a case, where confiscation is ordered by the Deputy Commissioner, the Excise Commissioner shall grant in such proportion, as he thinks fit, to any excise officer, who may have contributed to the seizure of the property so confiscated, a reward equal to twenty per cent. of the proceeds of the liquor, animal or vehicle.

(2) Where a sentence of imprisonment and/or fine is imposed, reward may, in the discretion of the Excise commissioner, be granted to the excise officers responsible for such conviction:

Provided that the aggregate amount of the reward thus granted in any one case, shall not exceed rupees fifty thousand, if the reward is given by the Excise Commissioner.

(3) In all cases where the proposed reward exceeds the amount mentioned in sub-rule (2), previous sanction of the Government shall be necessary.

(4) Twenty five per cent. of the amount of reward shall be given to the informer, if any, and the remainder to the persons actually involved in the seizure of goods.

(5) (a) Recommendation rolls for payment of rewards shall be submitted to the Excise Commissioner after the case has ended in conviction of the offender or the proceeds of confiscated goods have been realized and where an appeal has been preferred, after the order of sale is confirmed and where no appeal is filed, after the limitation period for filing the appeal has expired. The rolls or bills shall clearly indicate the amount realized from disposal of confiscated goods or order passed in conviction;

(b) on receipt of the recommendation rolls or bills, the amount sanctioned or passed by the Excise Commissioner or the Government, as the case may be, be drawn on abstract contingent bills and forwarded to the officers concerned.

(6) Class 1 and Class 2 Excise Officers shall be eligible for the reward.

(7) The decision of the Excise Commissioner in the distribution of reward, if it is as a result of team work, shall be final.

138. Form of appeal.—(1) Every appeal under section 72 shall be made in the form of a petition addressed to the authority to whom the appeal lies; shall be drawn up in concise and intelligible language; shall bear the signature or mark of the appellant or his duly authorised agent and shall also file the receipt showing the payment of fee as prescribed.

(2) The petition of appeal shall contain the following particulars:

(a) the name, father's name, occupation and place of residence or business address of the appellant;

(b) the date of order appealed against;

(c) a brief and precise statement of facts;

(d) the grounds of objection to the order appealed against.

(3) The petition shall be accompanied by the order appealed against in original or a self authenticated copy thereof.

(4) The appellant shall deposit a sum as ordered by the appellate authority and shall furnish a surety of the balance amount.

(5) The deposit of amount may be dispensed with at the discretion of the appellate authority for reasons to be recorded.

Appeal: Right of appeal is a creation of statute. It is never an inherent right. While conferring such right, statute may impose restrictions like limitations or pore-deposit of penalty or it may limit the area of appeal to question of law or some times substantial question of law; *Raj Kumar Shivehare* v. *Assistant Director, Directorate of Enforcement*, AIR 2010 SC 2239.

139. Method of presentation of appeal.—The petition of appeal shall either be presented to the appellate authority by the appellant or his agent or be forwarded to such authority by registered post.

140. Hearing of appeal.—(1) If the appellate authority does not reject the appeal under rule 141, it shall fix a date for regular hearing.

(2) The appellate authority may at any stage adjourn the hearing of an appeal to any other date.

(3) If, on the date fixed for hearing or any other date to which the hearing is adjourned, the appellant does not appear before the said authority either in person or through an agent, the said authority may decide the appeal *ex parte* on the basis of material available on record.

141. Rejection of appeal.—(1) If the petition of appeal does not comply with the requirements of rule 138, it may be rejected:

Provided that no appeal shall be rejected under this rule, unless the appellant is given such opportunity, as the appellate authority thinks fit, so as to enable him to comply with the requirements of the said rule.

(2) An appeal may also be rejected on other grounds, which shall be reduced to writing by the appellate authority:

Provided that if an order rejecting an appeal under this sub-rule is passed, the appellant shall be given an opportunity of being heard.

142. Copy of order to be supplied.—A copy of order passed in appeal shall be supplied free of cost to the appellant and another copy shall be sent to the officer whose order forms the subject-matter of appeal.

143. Procedure to be followed for filing review and revision.—The procedure prescribed for appeal shall also be applicable for filing review and revision.

144. Powers to summon witnesses and grant expenses.—The Excise Officers have the same powers to summon witnesses and grant expenses as provided in the Code of Civil Procedure, 1908.

145. Establishment of excise out-post.—The Excise Commissioner, may establish Excise out-posts at such places as he may think fit on any road, for the prevention of smuggling of intoxicants and may depute excise officer to be in charge of such out-post.

146. Driver of vehicle or animal to stop it until the search is conducted.—The driver of any vehicle or laden animal arriving at an excise post shall stop his vehicle or animal on arrival at the out-post until the excise officer has conducted his search.

The excise officer in-charge of the out-post shall permit the vehicle or animal to proceed unless he has reasons to exercise any of his powers of search.

147. Complaints to be recorded in a book.—Complaints of wrongful detention may be recorded in a book kept for the purpose with the excise officer, in-charge of the outpost. This book shall be submitted to the Deputy Commissioner at the end of each month for his perusal.

148. Classes of Excise Officers.—There shall be two classes of Excise Officers, designated as Class 1 and Class 2. These shall be as follows:—

(1) (a) Class I Excise Officers:

(i) Deputy Commissioner;

(ii) Assistant Commissioner;

(iii) Superintendent Excise;

(iv) Inspector (Excise).

(2) (b) Class 2 Excise Officers

(i) Excise Clerk;

(ii) Excise Constable.

(3) The persons mentioned below are invested with the powers of Excise Officers of Class 1 and Class 2 respectively:

(a) To exercise the powers of Class 1 Excise Officer:

(i) Deputy Commissioner of Police;

(ii) Assistant Commissioner of Police

(iii) Inspector Police;

(iv) Sub-Inspector Police;

(v) Officers posted in the Excise Intelligence Bureau of the above ranks;

(vi) Sub-Divisional Magistrate;

(vii) Tehsildar;

(viii) Naib Tehsildar.

(b) To exercise the powers of Class 2 Excise Officer:

(i) Assistant Sub-Inspector Police;

(ii) Head Constable;

(iii) Police Constable;

(iv) Officers posted in the Intelligence Bureau of the above ranks.

149. Powers of Class 2 Excise Officer.—(a) Power under section 65 of the Act, to arrest without warrant any person found committing an offence under sections 33 and 40 of the Act.

(b) Power under section 65 to seize and detain intoxicants or other articles liable to confiscation in connection with any of the aforesaid offences and to detain and search person upon whom and any vessel, raft, vehicle, animal, package, receptacle or covering in or upon which he may have reasonable cause to suspect any such article to be.

150. Power of Class 1 Excise Officer.—(a) All powers of Class 2 Excise Officers;

(b) All powers not included in the foregoing and conferrable under section 65 of the Act;

(c) Powers to grant bail under section 68 of the Act, for offence punishable with imprisonment of less than two years

151. Repeal and savings.—(1) Immediately with effect from the date on which these Rules come into force, (i) the Delhi Excise Liquor Definitions, 1973, (ii) the Delhi Excise Duty Orders, 1976, (iii) the Delhi Powers and Appeal Orders, 1952, (iv) the Delhi Intoxicants License and Sale Rules, 1976, (v) the Delhi Liquor License Rules, 1976, (vi) the Delhi Liquor Import, Export, Transport and Possession Rules, 1976, (vii) the Delhi Liquor Permit and Pass Rules,... (viii) the Delhi (Intoxicants) Confiscation Orders, 1933, (ix) the Delhi Chemical Works Rules, 1933, (x) the Delhi Supply and Sale of Hemp Drugs Rules, 1976, (xi) the Delhi Import, Export, Transshipment and Possession (in bond) of Rectified Spirit Orders, 1960, (xii) the Delhi Intoxicating Spirituous Preparations, Import, Export, Transport, Possession and Sale Rules, 1953, (xiii) the Delhi (Sale of Duty Free Indian Made Foreign Liquor to Diplomats/Foreign Embassies/United Nations and other allied agencies in Delhi) Bonded Warehouse Rules, 1975, (xiv) the Delhi Draught Beer Rules, 1977, (xv) the Delhi Excise Barriers Rules, 1955, (xvi) the Delhi Excise Bottle Rules, 1943, (xvii) the Delhi Beer Bottle Rules, 1943 (xviii) the Delhi Country Liquor Bonded Warehouse Rules, 1976, (xix) the Delhi Country Liquor Retail Vend Rules, 1976, (xx) the Delhi Import of Ganja Orders, 1915, (xxi) the Delhi Import and Possession of Charas Orders, 1943 , (xxii) the Delhi Charas Permit and Pass Rules, 1943 and (xxiii) the Delhi Charas Warehouse Rules, 1943, shall stand repealed:

Provided that till the rules under Chapter X are notified, the rates of duties, fees and price structure prescribed under the Punjab Excise Act, 1914 (as extended to the National Capital Territory of DelhI) and rules made thereunder shall continue to be in force.

(2) Notwithstanding any such repeal, any thing done or any action taken or purported to have been taken or any licence granted, under the rules repealed by sub-rule (1), shall, insofar as these are not inconsistent with these rules or the Delhi Excise Act, 2009, be deemed to have been done, taken or granted under the corresponding provisions of these rules.

CHAPTER X

FISCAL MEASURES

[1][**152. Rate of Duty.**—Duty on all excisable articles shall be *ad-valorem* on wholesale price at the following rates, namely:—

(1) Indian Liquor and Foreign Liquor

(i) Indian Liquor (Whisky, Rum, Gin, Vodka, Brandy)—

Wholesale price (WSP) slab	Wholesale price (WSP) per Quarts of 750 ml (in Rupees)	Duty @ of wholesale price
1.	Up to 24	250 per cent.
2.	Above 24 to 50	Duty for maximum WSP in slab 1 + 170 per cent. of amount by which WSP exceeds Rs. 24.
3.	Above 50 to 250	Duty for maximum WSP in slab 2 + 80 per cent. of amount by which WSP exceeds Rs. 50.
4.	Above 250 to 750	Duty for maximum WSP in slab 3 + 65 per cent. of amount by which WSP exceeds Rs. 250.
5.	Above 750	Duty for maximum WSP in slab 4 + 30 per cent. of amount by which WSP exceeds Rs. 750

(ii) Indian Wine and Liquor—

Wholesale price (WSP) slab	Wholesale price (WSP) per Quarts of 750 ml (in Rupees)	Duty @ of wholesale price
1.	Up to 100	65 per cent.
2.	Above 100 to 250	Duty for maximum WSP in slab 1 + 40 per cent. of amount by which WSP exceeds Rs. 100.
3.	Above 250	Duty for maximum WSP in slab 2 + 30 per cent of amount by which WSP exceeds Rs. 250.

1. Ins. by Notification No. F.10(8)/Fin(Rev-I)/2010-11/DS-II/247, dated 7th June, 2011 (w.e.f. 1-7-2011).

(iii) Indian Beer, Cider and Alcopop—

Sl. No.	Category	Duty @ of wholesale price
1.	Beer, Cider and Alcopop containing 5 per cent. or less alcohol v/v having Maximum Retail Price (MRP) up to Rs. 100 per quarts of 650 ml	110 per cent.
2.	Beer, Cider and Alcopop containing more than 5 per cent. alcohol v/v but not exceeding 8 per cent. alcohol having Maximum Retail Price (MRP) up to Rs. 100 per quarts of 650 ml	120 per cent.
3.	Beer having Maximum Retail Price (MRP) more than Rs. 100 per quarts of 650 ml.	120 per cent.

(iv) Foreign Liquor (Whisky, Rum, Vodka, Gin, Brandy)—

Wholesale price (WSP) slab	Wholesale price (WSP) per Quarts of 750 ml (in Rupees)	Duty @ of wholesale price
1.	Up to 1000	85 per cent.
2.	Above 1000	Duty for maximum WSP in slab 1 + 50 per cent. of amount by which WSP exceeds Rs. 1000.

(v) Foreign Liquor (Wine, Liqueur, Beer and Cider)—

Wholesale price (WSP) slab	Wholesale price (WSP) per Quarts of 750 ml (in Rupees)	Duty @ of wholesale price
1.	Up to 1000	65 per cent.
2.	Above 1000	Duty for maximum WSP in slab 1 + 50 per cent. of amount by which WSP exceeds Rs. 1000.

Provided that the amount of duty payable shall be subject to the provisions of rule 54 of the Delhi Excise Rules, 2010:

Provided further that the duty payable in respect of packings other than quarts *i.e.*, 750 ml/700 ml/650 ml as applicable, shall be levied proportionately.

(2) **Country Liquor** – Duty @ 200% of Wholesale Price.

(3) **Spirituous Preparations, including essence but other than Medicinal and Toilet preparations** – Duty @ 20% of Wholesale Price.

(4) **Bhang** – Duty @ Rs. 5 per Kilogram]

[1][153. **Rate of duty for consumption "on" the premises and for sale through Canteen Stores Department (CSD).**—(1) For consumption "on" the premises of Licences in Forms L-17, L-18, L-19, L-20, L-28, L-29, an additional duty at the rate of twenty per cent. of wholesale price over and above the duty prescribed for Indian Liquor as in Clauses (i), (ii) and (iii) of sub-rule (1) of rule 152 shall be levied subject to the maximum rates as set forth in the Schedule under section 27 of the Act.

(2) For consumption "on" the premises of Licences in Forms L-15, L-16, L-21, an additional duty at the rate of thirty per cent. of wholesale price over and above the duty prescribed for Indian Liquor as in clauses (i), (ii) and (iii) of sub-rule (1) of rule 152 shall be levied subject to the maximum rates as set forth in the Schedule under section 27 of the Act.

(3) For sale of Indian Liquor and Foreign Liquor through the Canteen Stores Department (holders of licence in Form L-23/L-23F), the rate of duty shall be fifty per cent. of the rate of duty prescribed in clauses (i), (ii) and (iii) and seventy-five per cent. of the rate of duty mentioned in clauses (iv) and (v) of sub-rule (1) of rule 152.]

[1][154. **Rates of fee.**—The following shall be the rates of licence fee, label registration fee and other fees leviable in respect of excisable articles for various categories of licences—

(1) *Licence Fee for wholesale vend of Indian Liquor, wholesale vend of Foreign Liquor and wholesale vend of Country Liquor*—

(a) The license fee for the licenses in Form L-1, L-1F, L-3, L-31, L-32 and L-33 shall be prescribed in the terms and conditions approved by the Government for each year as provided under rule 34(1) of the Delhi Excise Rules, 2010.

(b) The licence fee for each additional sourcing for the approved brands of Indian Liquor shall be Rs. 5 Lacs per brand in addition to the prescribed licence fee.

(2) *Licence Fees for Other Category of Licences*—

Sl. Nos.	Reference of rule	Forms of Licence	Description of Licences	Annual Licence fee (in Rs)
1	2	3	4	5
1.	32(1)	L-2	Wholesale vend of Draught Beer	50,000
2.	32(1)	L-4	Wholesale vend of Rectified spirit	25,000
3.	32(1)	L-5	Wholesale vend of Denatured spirit including special denatured spirit	25,000
4.	32(1)	L-6	Retail vend of Indian Liquor in public sector	2,50,000
5.	32(1)	L-6FG	Retail vend of Foreign Liquor in public sector to the holders of licence in Form L-6.	Ten per cent. of licence fee applicable for L-6 licence

1. Ins. by Notification No. F.10(8)/Fin(Rev-I)/2010-11/DS-II/247, dated 7th June, 2011 (w.e.f. 1-7-2011).

1	2	3	4	5
6.	32(1)	L-6FE	Retail vend of Foreign Liquor in public sector.	2,00,000
7.	32(1)	L-7	Retail vend of Indian Liquor in private sector	8,00,000
8.	32(1)	L-7FG	Retail vend of Foreign Liquor in private sector to the holders of licence in Form L-7.	Ten per cent. of licence fee applicable for L-7 licence
9.	32(1)	L-7FE	Retail vend of Foreign Liquor in private sector	6,00,000
10.	32(1)	L-8	Retail vend of Country Liquor in public sector	1,00,000
11.	32(1)	L-9	Retail vend of Indian Liquor to holders of licence in Form L-l.	10,00,000
12.	32(1)	L-10	Retail vend of Indian licence and Foreign Liquor in Shopping Malls	6,00,000
13.	32(1)	L-11	Retail vend of Beer, manufactured by Microbrewery.	2,50,000
14.	32(1)	L-12	Retail vend of Beer and Wine in Departmental Stores.	2,00,000
15.	32(1)	L-12F	Retail vend of Foreign Beer and Wine in Departmental Stores to the holders of licence in Form L-12.	Ten per cent. of licence fee applicable for L-12 licence
16.	32(1)	L-14	Retail vend of economy Indian Liquor and Beer to holders of licence in Form L-8	2,00,000
17.	32(1)	L-15	Service of Indian Liquor in a hotel or a guest house to residents in their rooms	Hotels and Guest Houses having rooms — Licence Fee (in Rs.) Up to 25 — 75,000 26 to 50 — 1,00,000 51 to 100 — 2,00,000 101 to 200 — 3,00,000 201 to 300 — 4,00,000 301 to 400 — 5,00,000 401 and above — 6,00,000

<table>
<tr><th>1</th><th>2</th><th>3</th><th>4</th><th colspan="3">5</th></tr>
<tr><td>18.</td><td>32(1)</td><td>L-15F</td><td>Service of Foreign Liquor in a hotel or a guest house to residents in their rooms to the holders of licence in Form L-15</td><td colspan="3">Ten per cent. of licence fee applicable for L-15 licence</td></tr>
<tr><td rowspan="8">19.</td><td rowspan="8">32(1)</td><td rowspan="8">L-16</td><td rowspan="8">Service of Indian Liquor in a bar/restaurant attached to a hotel</td><td>Category</td><td>Upto 75 covers (in Rs.)</td><td>Above 75 covers (in Rs.)</td></tr>
<tr><td>Budget Hotels</td><td>4,00,000</td><td>5,50,000</td></tr>
<tr><td>1 Star</td><td>4,25,000</td><td>6,25,000</td></tr>
<tr><td>2 Star</td><td>5,25,000</td><td>7,25,000</td></tr>
<tr><td>3 Star</td><td>5,75,000</td><td>8,00,000</td></tr>
<tr><td>4 Star</td><td>6,25,000</td><td>8,50,000</td></tr>
<tr><td>5 Star</td><td>7,50,000</td><td>10,50,000</td></tr>
<tr><td>Above 5 Star</td><td>9,00,000</td><td>12,00,000</td></tr>
<tr><td></td><td></td><td></td><td colspan="4">Fee for service of liquor for round-the-clock in a restaurant attached to hotel of 5 Star and above category shall be twice the amount of fee applicable L-16 licence.</td></tr>
<tr><td>20.</td><td>32(1)</td><td>L-16F</td><td>Service of Foreign Liquor in a bar/restaurant attached to hotel to the holders of licence in Form L-16</td><td colspan="3">Ten per cent. of Licence fee applicable for L-16F licence</td></tr>
<tr><td rowspan="5">21.</td><td rowspan="5">32(1)</td><td rowspan="5">L-17</td><td rowspan="5">Service of Indian Liquor in independent restaurant</td><td>having seat covers:</td><td colspan="2">Licence Fee</td></tr>
<tr><td>up to 50</td><td colspan="2">4,75,000</td></tr>
<tr><td>51 to 100</td><td colspan="2">6,75,000</td></tr>
<tr><td>101 to 200</td><td colspan="2">9,00,000</td></tr>
<tr><td>201 and above</td><td colspan="2">11,50,000</td></tr>
<tr><td>22.</td><td>32(1)</td><td>L-17F</td><td>Service of Foreign Liquor in independent restaurant to the holders of licence in Form L-17</td><td colspan="3">Ten per cent. of licence fee applicable for L-17 licence</td></tr>
<tr><td>23.</td><td>32(1)</td><td>L-18</td><td>Service of Indian wine/beer and alcopop in independent restaurant</td><td>Having seat covers</td><td colspan="2">Licence Fee</td></tr>
<tr><td rowspan="4"></td><td rowspan="4"></td><td rowspan="4"></td><td rowspan="4"></td><td>Upto 50</td><td colspan="2">2,50,000</td></tr>
<tr><td>51-100</td><td colspan="2">3,50,000</td></tr>
<tr><td>101-200</td><td colspan="2">4,50,000</td></tr>
<tr><td>201 and above</td><td colspan="2">5,50,000</td></tr>
</table>

1	2	3	4	5
24.	32(1)	L-18F	Service of Foreign wine, beer and alcopop in independent restaurant to the holders of licence in Form L-18.	Ten per cent. of licence fee applicable for L-18 licence
25.	32(1)	L-19	Round the clock service of Indian Liquor in independent restaurant located either in arrival or departure area of International Airport.	Having Seat Covers: up to 50 — 9,50,000 51 to 100 — 13,50,000 101 to 200 — 18,00,000 201 and above — 23,00,000
26.	32(1)	L-19F	Round the clock service of Foreign Liquor in independent restaurant located either in arrival or departure area of International Airport to the holders of licence in Form L-19.	Ten per cent. of licence fee applicable for L-19 licence
27.	32(1)	L-20	Service of Indian Liquor in a bar/dining car in a luxury train.	1,00,000
28.	32(1)	L-20F	Service of Foreign Liquor in a bar/dining car in a luxury train to the holders of licence in Form L-20.	Ten per cent. of licence fee applicable for L-20 licence
29.	32(1)	L-21	Round the clock service/ sale of Indian Liquor in a bar attached to a hotel located either in arrival or departure area of International Airport	Category / Upto 75 covers / Above 75 covers 4 star / 14,00,000 / 18,00,000 5 star and above / 15,00,000 / 20,00,000
30.	32(1)	L-21F	Round the clock service/ sale of Foreign Liquor in a bar attached to a hotel located either in arrival or departure area of International Airport to the holders of licence in Form L-21	Ten per cent. of licence fee applicable for L-21 licence

1	2	3	4	5	
31.	32(1)	L-22	Retail vend of Indian Liquor in duty free shop for consumption "off" the premises located at departure Lounge of International Airport	2,50,000	
32.	32(1)	L-23	Retail vend of Indian Liquor in military canteen	NIL	
33.	32(1)	L-23F	Retail vend of Foreign Liquor in military canteen to the holders of licence in Form L- 23	NIL	
34.	32(1)	L-24	Retail vend of Medicated Wine	1000	
35.	32(1)	L-25	Retail vend of Denatured Spirit including Denatured Spirit	for possession limit up to 1000 BL	2000
				for possession limit more than 1000 BL	5000
36.	32(1)	L-26	Retail vend of Rectified Spirit		5000
37.	32(1)	L-27	Retail vend of Bhang		5000
38.	32(1)	L-28	Service of Indian Liquor in a club	having membership: (a) up to 800 (b) 801 to 1,500 (c) More than 1,500	 75,000 1,00,000 2,00,000
39.	32(1)	L-28F	Service of Foreign Liquor in a club to the holders of licence in Form L-28	Ten per cent. of licence fee applicable for L-28 Licence	
40.	32(1)	L-29	Service of Indian Liquor at a club/mess whose membership is exclusively for Government servants, retired Government servants, including	7,500	

1	2	3	4	5
			members of armed forces, serving or retired and such a club/mess is not run on commercial lines.	
41.	32(1)	L-29F	Service of Indian Liquor at a club/mess whose membership is exclusively for Government servants, retired Government servants, including members of armed forces, serving or retired and such a club/mess is not run on commercial lines to the holders of licence in Form L-29.	Ten per cent. of licence fee applicable for L-29 Licence
42.	66(10), (11), (16), and (17)		Additional area for the holders of licence in Form L-16, L-16F, L-17, L-17F, L-18. L-18F, L-19, L-19F, L-21, L-21F, 28, L-28F, L-29, L-29F	Additional seventy-five per cent. of the regular licence fee for the corresponding licences.
43.	32(1)	L-30	Licence for possession of liquor at home in excess of individual possession limit.	3,000
44.	32(1)	L-34	Licence for Warehouse for storage of denatured spirit	20,000
45.	32(1)	L-35	Licence for Warehouse for storage of rectified spirit	30,000
46.	51(2)		Additional storage space for holder of licences of retail vend of Indian Liquor, Foreign Liquor and Country Liquor.	Ten per cent. of the correspon-ding licence fee per month.
47.	32(1)	L-36	Licence to a registered medical practitioner, chemist/druggist for sale of Intoxicating Spirituous Preparations.	5,000

1	2	3	4	5
48.	32(1) and 66 (18)	L-37	Licence for Hotel Management Institutes for keeping liquor for the purpose of training	25,000

(3) The 'label registration fee' for the brands of Indian Liquor, Foreign Liquor and Country Liquor shall be prescribed in the terms and conditions approved by the Government for each year as provided under sub-rule (1) of rule 34 of the Delhi Excise Rules, 2010.

(4) *Other fees (Permit/Pass/Import/Export)*—

Sl. No.	Rule	Form of Permit/ Pass	Description	Fee (in Rs)
1	2	3	4	5
1.	71	P-1	Permit for Import of rectified spirit, denatured spirit and special denatured spirit	(a) Rs. 5 per 20 bulk litres of rectified spirit. (b) Rs. 2 per bulk litre of denatured spirit and special denatured spirit.
2.	79(2)	P-2	Permit for possession of denatured spirit exceeding five litres up to ten litres	100
3.	81(1)	P-3	Permit for possession of denatured spirit exceeding ten litres.	500
4.	81(4)	P-4	Permit for possession of special denatured spirit in bulk quantity	2,000
5.	77	P-5	Permit for possession of rectified spirit to educational institutions etc.	250
6.	78	P-6	Permit for possession of special denatured spirit by Industrial manufacturers	50,000

1	2	3	4	5
7.	126(2)	P-7	Permit for possession of intoxicating spirituous preparations	5,000
8.	127	P-8	Permit for Import or transport of intoxicating spirituous preparations	Rs. 1 per litre
9.	19	P-9	Permit for Import of Indian Liquor and Country Liquor for troops	250
10.	20(1)(c)	P-10	Service of Indian Liquor and Foreign Liquor at a place other than the licensed premises	5,000
11.	44(1)	P-11	Permit for liquor exhibitors	25,000
12.	114	P-12	Permit for import, export or transport of bhang	Rs. 3 per kg. or part thereof
13.	44(2)	P-13	Service of Indian Liquor and Foreign Liquor at a temporary place at hotel, club and restaurant	5,000
14.	15	P-14	(a) Fee for Import of Indian Liquor (other than economy) for holder of L-1 licence, excluding beer	Rs. 5.00 per Litre
			(b) Fee for Import of Indian Liquor having MRP upto Rs. 120 for holder of L-1 licence excluding beer	Rs. 1.25 per litre
15.	94		Fee for opening of warehouse beyond prescribed hours or on dry days	Rs. 5,000 per occasion
16.	138 and 143		Fee for filing Appeal, Review and Revision	Rs. 500 per occasion

FORMS

FORM L-1

[*See* rules 32 & 66(1)]

1.	Category of Licence	:	L-1 (Licence for wholesale vend of Indian Liquor)
2.	Registration number	:	
3.	Name and style of company/firm, etc.		
4.	Name of director	:	
5.	Address of office	:	....
6.	Address of Warehouse	:	....
7.	Hours of sale	:	
8.	Licence fee	:	
9.	Licence valid up to	:	31-03-20....
10.	Brands registered	:	As annexed
11.	Date of Issue of Licence	:	

Conditions:

This licence is granted subject to observance of the provisions of the Delhi Excise Act, 2009 the Rules framed thereunder; terms and conditions of licence and the instructions issued by the licensing authority from time-to-time.

Deputy Commissioner

FORM L-1F

[*See* rules 32 & 66(2)]

1. Category of Licence	:	L-1F (Licence for wholesale vend of Foreign Liquor)
2. Registration number	:	
3. Name and style of Firm	:	
4. Name of director/ proprietor/partner	:	
5. Address of office	:	....
6. Address of Warehouse	:	....
7. Hours of sale	:	
8. Licence fee	:	
9. Licence valid upto	:	31-03-20...
10. Brands registered	:	As annexed
11. Date of Issue of Licence	:	

Conditions:

This licence is granted subject to observance of the provisions of the Delhi Excise Act, 2009, the Rules framed thereunder; terms and conditions of licence and the instructions issued by the licensing authority from time-to-time.

Deputy Commissioner

FORM L-2

[*See* rules 32 & 66(3)]

1. Category of Licence	:	L-2 (Licence for Whole-sale vend of Draught Beer)
2. Registration number	:	
3. Name and style of company/firm, etc.	:	
4. Name of director/ partner/proprietor	:	
5. Address of office	:	....
6. Address of Warehouse	:	....
7. Hours of sale	:	
8. Licence fee	:	
9. Licence valid up to	:	31-03-20...
10. Brands registered	:	As annexed
11. Date of Issue of Licence	:	

Conditions:

This licence is granted subject to observance of the provisions of the Delhi Excise Act, 2009 the Rules framed thereunder; terms and conditions of licence and the instructions issued by the licensing authority from time-to-time.

Deputy Commissioner

FORM L-3

[*See* rules 32 & 66(4)]

1. Category of Licence	:	L-3 (Licence for Wholesale vend of Country Liquor)
2. Registration number	:	
3. Name and style of company/firm etc.	:	
4. Name of director/ partner/proprietor	:	
5. Address of office	:	....
6. Address of Warehouse	:	....
7. Hours of sale	:	
8. Licence fee	:	
9. Licence valid up to	:	31-03-20...
10. Brands registered	:	As annexed
11. Date of Issue of Licence	:	

Conditions:

This licence is granted subject to observance of the provisions of the Delhi Excise Act, 2009 the Rules framed thereunder; terms and conditions of licence and the instructions issued by the licensing authority from time-to-time

Deputy Commissioner

FORMS L-4 & 5

(WHOLESALE VEND OF RECTIFIED SPIRIT/DENATURED SPIRIT)

[*See* rules 75 & 76]

LICENCE FOR POSSESSION OF RECTIFIED SPIRIT/DENATURED SPIRIT

No.

The licence authorising the possession of rectified spirit/denatured spirit in the premises specified below and for the period from to .... is granted to...

This Licence is granted subject to the provisions of the Delhi Excise Act, 2009 the Rules framed thereunder; terms and conditions of licence and the instructions issued by the licensing authority from time-to-time

Deputy Commissioner

Description of licensed premises...

Supplementary condition, if any:—

One time possession limit in litres

ENDORSEMENT OF RENEWAL

This licence is hereby renewed on the condition herein before stated for the period state below:—

Period from....................................to................... ....fee Rs. ....

Deputy Commissioner

FORM L-6

[*See* rules 32 & 66(5)]

1. Category of licence		L-6 (Retail vend of Indian Liquor in public sector
2. Registration number		
3. Name of Company/ Firm/Individual	:	
4. Name of the director/ proprietor/ partner	:	
5. Address of L-6 vend	:	
6. Hours of sale	:	
7. Licence fee	:	
8. Validity upto	:	31-03-20...
Date of Issue	:	

Conditions:

This Licence is granted subject to the provisions of the Delhi Excise Act, 2009 the Rules framed thereunder; terms and conditions of licence and the instructions issued by the licensing authority from time-to-time

Deputy Commissioner.

FORM L-6FE

[*See* rules 32 & 66]

1. Category of licence	:	L-6FE (Retail vend of Foreign Liquor in public sector)
2. Registration number	:	
3. Name of company/firm/ individual	:	
4. Name of the director/ proprietor/ partner	:	
5. Address of L-6FE vend	:	
6. Hours of sale	:	
7. Licence fee	:	
8. Validity up to	:	31-03-20...
9. Date of Issue	:	

Conditions:

This Licence is granted subject to the provisions of the Delhi Excise Act, 2009 the Rules framed thereunder; terms and conditions of licence and the instruction issued by the licensing authority from time-to-time

Deputy Commissioner.

FORM L-6FG

[*See* rules 32 & 66(5)]

1. Category of licence	:	L-6FG (Retail vend of Foreign Liquor in public sector to the holder of licence in Form L-6)
2. Registration number	:	
3. Name of company/firm/ individual	:	
4. Name of the director/ proprietor/ partner	:	
5. Address of L-6FG vend	:	
6. Hours of sale	:	
7. Licence fee	:	
8. Validity upto	:	31-03-20...
9. Date of Issue	:	

Conditions:

This Licence is granted subject to the provisions of the Delhi Excise Act, 2009 the Rules framed thereunder; terms and conditions of licence and the instructions issued by the licensing authority from time-to-time

Deputy Commissioner.

FORM L-7

[*See* rules 32 & 66(5)]

1. Category of licence	:	L-7 (Retail vend of Indian Liquor in private sector)
2. Registration number	:	
3. Name of company/firm/ individual	:	
4. Name of the director/ proprietor/partner	:	
5. Address of L-7 vend	:	
6. Hours of sale	:	
7. Licence fee	:	
8. Validity upto	:	31-03-20...
9. Date of issue	:	

Conditions:

This Licence is granted subject to the provisions of the Delhi Excise Act, 2009, the Rules framed thereunder; terms and conditions of licence and the instructions issued by the licensing authority from time-to-time.

Deputy Commissioner

FORM L-7FE

[*See* rules 32 & 66(5)]

1. Category of licence	:	L-7 FE (Retail vend of Foreign Liquor in private sector)
2. Registration number	:	
3. Name of company/ firm/individual	:	
4. Name of the director/ proprietor/partner	:	
5. Address of L-7FE vend	:	
6. Hours of sale	:	
7. Licence fee	:	
8. Validity upto	:	31-03-20...
9. Date of issue	:	

Conditions:

This Licence is granted subject to the provisions of the Delhi Excise Act, 2009, the Rules framed thereunder; terms and conditions of licence and the instructions issued by the licensing authority from time-to-time.

Deputy Commissioner

FORM L-7FG

[*See* rules 32 & 66(5)]

1. Category of licence	:	L-7 FG (Retail vend of Foreign Liquor in private sector to the holder of licence in Form L-7)
2. Registration number	:	
3. Name of company/ firm/individual	:	
4. Name of the director/ proprietor/ partner	:	
5. Address of L-7 FG vend	:	
6. Hours of sale	:	
7. Licence fee	:	
8. Validity upto	:	31-03-20...
9. Date of issue	:	

Conditions:

This Licence is granted subject to the provisions of the Delhi Excise Act, 2009, the Rules framed thereunder; terms and conditions of licence and the instructions issued by the licensing authority from time-to-time.

Deputy Commissioner

FORM L-8

[*See* rules 32 & 66(6)]

1. Category of licence	:	L-8 (Retail vend of Country Liquor in public sector)
2. Registration number	:	
3. Name of company/firm/ individual	:	
4. Name of the director/ proprietor/partner	:	
5. Address of L-8 vend	:	
6. Hours of sale	:	
7. Licence fee	:	
8. Validity upto	:	31-03-20...
9. Date of issue	:	

Conditions:

This Licence is granted subject to the provisions of the Delhi Excise Act, 2009, the Rules framed thereunder; terms and conditions of licence and the instructions issued by the licensing authority from time-to-time.

Deputy Commissioner

FORM L-9

[*See* rules 32 & 66(7)]

1. Category of licence	:	L-9 (Retail vend of Indian Liquor to holders of licence in Form L-1)
2. Registration number	:	
3. Name of company/ firm/individual	:	
4. Name of the director/ proprietor/partner	:	
5. Address of L-9 vend	:	
6. Hours of sale	:	
7. Licence fee	:	
8. Validity upto	:	31-03-20...
9. Date of issue	:	

Conditions:

This Licence is granted subject to the provisions of the Delhi Excise Act, 2009, the Rules framed thereunder; terms and conditions of licence and the instructions issued by licensing authority from time-to-time.

Deputy Commissioner

FORM L-10

[*See* rules 32 & 66(5)]

1. Category of licence	:	L-10 (Retail vend of Indian Liquor and Foreign Liquor in Shopping Malls)
2. Registration number	:	
3. Name of company/ firm / individual	:	
4. Name of the director/ proprietor/ partner	:	
5. Address of L-10 vend	:	
6. Hours of sale	:	
7. Licence fee	:	
8. Validity upto	:	31-03-20...
9. Date of issue	:	

Conditions:

This Licence is granted subject to the provisions of the Delhi Excise Act, 2009, the Rules framed thereunder; terms and conditions of licence and the instructions issued by the licensing authority from time-to-time.

Deputy Commissioner

FORM L-12

[*See* rules 32 & 66(5)]

1. Category of licence	:	L-12 (Retail vend of Beer and Wine in Departmental Stores)
2. Registration number	:	
3. Name of company/ firm/individual	:	
4. Name of the director/ proprietor/partner	:	
5. Address of L-12 vend	:	
6. Hours of sale	:	
7. Licence fee	:	
8. Validity upto	:	31-03-20...
9. Date of issue	:	

Conditions:

This Licence is granted subject to the provisions of the Delhi Excise Act, 2009, the Rules framed thereunder; terms and conditions of licence and the instructions issued by licensing authority from time-to-time.

Deputy Commissioner

FORM L-12F

[*See* rules 32 & 66(5)]

1. Category of licence	:	L-12F (Retail vend of Foreign Beer and Wine in Departmental Store to the holder of licence in Form L-12)
2. Registration number		
3. Name of company/ firm/individual	:	
4. Name of the director/ proprietor/partner	:	
5. Address of L-12F vend	:	
6. Hours of sale	:	
7. Licence fee	:	
8. Validity upto	:	31-03-20...
9. Date of issue	:	

Conditions:

This Licence is granted subject to the provisions of the Delhi Excise Act, 2009, the Rules framed thereunder; terms and conditions of licence and the instructions issued by the licensing authority from time-to-time.

Deputy Commissioner

FORM L-13

[*See* rules 32 & 66(8)]

1. Category of licence	:	L-13 (Retail vend of Indian Liquor for home delivery)
2. Registration number	:	
3. Name of company/ firm/individual	:	
4. Name of the director/ proprietor/partner	:	
5. Address of L-13 vend	:	
6. Hours of sale	:	
7. Licence fee	:	
8. Validity upto	:	31-03-20...
9. Date of issue	:	

Conditions:

This Licence is granted subject to the provisions of the Delhi Excise Act, 2009, the Rules framed thereunder; terms and conditions of licence and the instructions issued by the licensing authority from time-to-time.

Deputy Commissioner

FORM L-13F

[*See* rule 66(8)]

1. Category of licence	:	L-13F (Retail vend of Foreign Liquor for home delivery to the holders of licence in Form L-13)
2. Registration number	:	
3. Name of company/firm/ individual	:	
4. Name of the director/ proprietor/partner	:	
5. Address of L-13F vend	:	
6. Hours of sale	:	
7. Licence fee	:	
8. Validity upto	:	31-03-20...
9. Date of issue	:	

Conditions:

This Licence is granted subject to the provisions of the Delhi Excise Act, 2009, the Rules framed thereunder; terms and conditions of licence and the instructions issued by the licensing authority from time-to-time.

Deputy Commissioner

FORM L-14

[*See* rules 32 & 66(5)]

1. Category of licence	:	L-14 (Retail vend of economy Indian Liquor and Beer to holder of licence in Form L-8)
2. Registration number	:	
3. Name of company/ firm/individual	:	
4. Name of the director/ proprietor/ partner	:	
5. Address of L-14 vend	:	
6. Hours of sale	:	
7. Licence fee	:	
8. Validity upto	:	31-03-20...
9. Date of issue	:	

Conditions:

This Licence is granted subject to the provisions of the Delhi Excise Act, 2009, the Rules framed thereunder; terms and conditions of licence and the instructions issued by the licensing authority from time-to-time.

Deputy Commissioner

FORMS L-16, L-16F, L-20, L-20F

[*See* rules 32 & 66(10)(12)]

1. Registration No. :
2. Name of the hotel
3. Constitution of hotel :
4. Names of the proprietor/ partners/directors :
5. Address :
6. No. of L-16 bars :
7. No. of L-16F bars
8. Hours of sale :
9. Licence fee (T.R. No., date and amount) :
10. Date of issue :
11. Validity of licence :

Conditions:

This Licence is granted subject to the provisions of the Delhi Excise Act, 2009, the Rules framed thereunder; terms and conditions of licence and the instructions issued by the licensing authority from time-to-time.

Deputy Commissioner

DETAILS OF RENEWAL

Period Signature and seal of Renewing Authority	Fee paid T.R. no., date and amount

FORMS L-23/L-23F

[*See* rules 32 & 66(14)]

1. Category of Licence	:	Retail vend of Indian Liquor and Foreign Liquor in Military Canteen
2. Registration number		
3. Name and Style of Unit	:	
4. Name and designation of the applicant	:	
5. Address	:	
6. Address of godown, if any	:	
7. Hours of sale	:	
8. Licence fee/secutity money	:	
9. Period for which licence is valid	:	
10. Date of issue	:	

Conditions:

This licence is valid subject to the provisions of the Delhi Excise Act, 2009, the Rules framed thereunder; terms and conditions of licence and the instructions issued by the licensing authority from time-to-time.

Deputy Commissioner

Special Conditions:—

1. The sale of liquor is to be confined to the military personnel only.
2. The canteen shall be run by the unit itself and not by a private contractor.
3. The sale statement must be submitted to the Excise Department by the 10th of every month.

FORMS L-25 & 26

[*See* rules 32, 79 & 80]

LICENCE FOR RETAIL VEND OF DENATURED SPIRIT AND RECTIFIED SPIRIT

1. Category of licence..
2. Registration No. ....
3. Name and style business concern...
4. Name(s) of proprietor/partners (i) ....
   (ii) ....
   (iii) ....
   (iv) ....
5. Address...
6. Address of godown (s), if any (i) ....
   (ii) ....
7. Hours of sale..
8. Licence fee...
9. Date of issue...
10. Period for which licence is valid...

Conditions:

This licence is valid subject to the provisions of the Delhi Excise Act, 2009, the Rules framed thereunder; terms and conditions of licence and the instructions issued by the licensing authority from time-to-time.

Deputy Commissioner

FORM L-27

FORM OF LICENCE FOR RETAIL VEND OF HEMP DRUGS (BHANG) OR ANY PREPARATION OR ANY ADMIXTURE THEREOF

(*See* rules 32 & 102)

Register No.

Name and description of licensed vendor.

Locality of shop.

Whereas......................son of......................has stressed to pay the sum of Rs. ....for the right of selling hemp drugs (bhang) or any preparation or any admixture thereof in retail at ....during the term of......................and has paid into the Government Treasury at ....the sum of Rs. ....being one-sixth of such sum.

Therefore, the Deputy Commissioner hereby grants the said ....hereinafter called the licensee, a licence to sell hemp drugs (bhang) or any admixture thereof in accordance with retail at....................during the terms above specified and subject to the conditions hereinafter stated. The licence is granted personally to.......................hereinafter named, and is not transferable.

In the event of his dying during the currency of licence, it shall immediately lapse.

This licence is valid subject to the provisions of the Delhi Excise Act, 2009, the Rules framed thereunder; terms and conditions of licence and the instructions issued by the licensing authority from time-to-time.

Signature of licensee Deputy Commissioner

Conditions of Licence

1. The balance of fee due by the licensee in respect of this licence shall be paid in equal monthly instalments commencing from ....20...... Each instalment shall be paid on the first day of the month in respect of which it has to be paid and is due.
2. (i) The licensee shall, for the purpose of selling hemp drugs, under this licence maintain a shop at ....in ....and nowhere else, nor shall he sell hemp drugs or any preparation or admixture thereof under this licence elsewhere than at such shop.

   (ii) so long as he holds this licence, he shall keep at the shop above named supply of hemp drugs for sale to the public;

   (iii) the licensee shall sell hemp drugs to anyone offering to pay ready money for the same.

Note.—The number of instalments will be here entered according to the term. If the licence is being granted for the whole year, then the payment shall be made in ten equal instalments commencing from April 1st 20.....

Signature of licensee Deputy Commissioner

FORMS L-28, L-28F, L-29, L-29F

[*See* rules 32 & 66(16), (17)]

LICENCE FOR CONSUMPTION OF LIQUOR "ON" THE PREMISES IN A CLUB

1. Category of licence..
2. Registration No. ....
3. Name and style of the Club...
3. Constitution of the Club: Company/Cooperative Society/Society/ Partnership/Proprietorship...
4. Names of the Directors/Secretary/President/ Partners/Proprietor...
5. Address of the Club...
6. Address of godown, if any..
7. Hours of sale..
8. Licence fee...
9. Date of issue...
10. Period for which licence is valid...

Conditions:

This licence is granted subject to the provisions of the Delhi Excise Act, 2009, the Rules framed thereunder, terms and conditions of licence and the instructions issued by the licensing authority from time-to-time.

RENEWALS:

Period	Amount of fee deposited	Challan No. and date	Signature Licensing Authority

FORM L-30

LICENCE FOR POSSESSION OF LIQUOR AT HOME IN EXCESS OF INDIVIDUAL POSSESSION LIMIT

[*See* rules 32 & 20(1)(b)]

Stamp size S. No Permit No.L-32/

Date of issue

Valid up to 31-3-20...

Photo Name..

Father's/husband's name..

Occupation..

Address...

Quantity in Litres..

Indian Liquor Foreign Liquor Wine Liqueur Beer Cider.......................

Conditions:

This licence is granted subject to the provisions of the Delhi Excise Act, 2009, the Rules framed thereunder , terms and conditions of licence and the instructions issued by the licensing authority from time-to-time.

Signature of licence holder Deputy Commissioner

Conditions:

1. The licence is not transferable.

2. The licence shall be valid for the premises for which permission has been granted.

3. The licence may be withdrawn, suspended or cancelled at any time by the Deputy Commissioner for reasons to be recorded

4. The licence may be renewed from year to year ending 31st March following on payment of prescribed fee.

5. The licence holder shall purchase the stock of liquor only from authorised sources in Delhi.

6. The possession is for self/family consumption and not for sale.

7. The violation of the conditions will not only lead to the cancellation of the licence but may also attract the penal provisions of the Delhi Excise Act, 2009 and the Rules framed there-under for illegal vending of liquor.

Stamp Size

Photo

FORM L-31, L-32, L-33, L-34, L-35

LICENCE FOR WAREHOUSE FOR STORAGE OF INDIAN LIQUOR/FOREIGN LIQUOR/COUNTRY LIQUOR/DENATURED SPIRIT/RECTIFIED SPIRIT

(*See* rules 32 & 82)

The under mentioned premises belonging to Shri/Sarvashri.............. of.....................(the licensee are hereby licensed subject to the provisions of the Delhi Excise Act; the Rules framed thereunder and any orders issued , as a Warehouse for the storage of Indian Liquor/Foreign Liquor on which duty has/has not been paid.

(1) Situation and description of the premises.

(2) The licence is granted to Shri/Sarvashri...................................who has/have paid the prescribed licence fee.................. It is not transferable to any person and will remain in force....................., unless revoked, until 31st March............................

(3) The licence holder shall be held responsible for the safe custody of the liquor and for the observance of law.

(4) Minimum stock as specified should be maintained.

(5) The packages shall be stocked in the warehouse in such manner as the Assistant Commissioner may direct so as to facilitate inspection from time-to-time.

(6) The licence holder shall maintain such stock books as may be prescribed/specified by the Excise Commissioner so as to enable any easy check to be made that the provisions of the excise law and the conditions of the licence are being satisfactorily complied with by the licence holder.

(7) The licence shall cease to be valid whenever there is a change in the constitution of the firm.

(8) That the licensee shall receive the payment from his clients in the manner approved by the Excise Commissioner for the purpose.

(9) This licence may be revoked or suspended or its renewal may be refused if any declaration made or information given in the application therefor is found to be false or if any undertaking given in such application is not carried out or for violations of (i) terms and conditions of the licence of (ii) the rules governing the licence or (iii) any direction issued by the Excise Commissioner.

Conditions:

This licence is valid subject to the provisions of the Delhi Excise Act, 2009, the Rules framed thereunder; terms and conditions of licence and the instructions issued by the licensing authority from time-to-time.

Date Excise Commissioner

Renewal of the Licence

Date of renewal	*Year for which renewed*	*Signature of Excise Commissioner*

FORM L-36

LICENCE FOR THE SALE OF INTOXICATING SPIRITUOUS PREPARATIONS

(*See* rules 32 & 122)

Licence No. .... Date......................

Licence for the sale of intoxicating spirituous preparations mentioned on the reverse is granted to Shri..................................proprietor/manager of M/s................................ having place of business at..for the period from ....to 31st March, 20.... on payment of annual fee of Rs. ....paid into the treasury on.....................................

This licence is granted subject to the Delhi Excise Act, 2009; the Rules framed thereunder and to the terms and conditions specified below.

Description of the licensed premises...

Dated.....................................

Licensing Authority

Conditions:

1. On the termination or the cancellation of the licence, the licensee shall surrender the licence, stock and account books to the competent authority. The Licensing Authority may, after such enquiry as may be deemed necessary, direct any licensee to whom the stock s transferred, to pay such price of the stock, as he/it may deem fit. The stock, unfit for human consumption, shall be liable to destruction at the cost of the licensee whose licence is terminated or cancelled.

2. The licensee shall permit the Excise Officer, to enter the premises and examine the stock and accounts connected with the licence.

3. The licensee shall not import from other States any intoxicating spirituous preparations except under an import permit granted by the Licensing Authority. Such an import permit shall, however, not be necessary in case supplies of intoxicating spirituous preparations are obtained in bond, from a licensed manufactory or bonded warehouse in accordance with the Medicinal and Toilet Preparations (Excise Duties) Rules, 1956.

4. As soon as the consignment of the intoxicating spirituous preparations is received by the licensee, he shall inform the Licensing Authority,, who shall depute an officer of the Department to check and verify the contents with the pass covering the consignment. The licensee shall then enter the receipt in his sales register before making sale.

5. The licensee shall maintain all permits, passes and copies of the prescriptions and produce them before the inspecting officer in order to enable him to check the receipts and sales of such preparations.

6. The licensee shall keep the stock of such preparations separately at the licensed premises and nowhere else.

7. The licensee shall maintain accounts in the prescribed form and shall submit the prescribed returns monthly.

8. The licensee shall not possess and sell any intoxicating spirituous preparations except the following:—

Name of intoxicating spirituous preparations.	Quantity allowed to be possessed and sold during the year

FORM L-15 & L-15F

[*See* rules 32 & 66(9)]

1. Registration No. :
2. Name of the hotel
3. Constitution of the licensed firm/Co. :
4. Names(s) of the proprietor/ partners/Directors(s) :
5. Address :
6. Whether holds L-15F or not :
7. Hours of sale :
8. Licence license fee (T.R. No., date and amount) :
9. Date of issue :
10. Period for which licence is valid :

This Licence is valid subject to the provisions of the Delhi Excise Act, 2009, the Rules framed thereunder; terms and conditions of licence and the instructions issued by the licensing authority from time-to-time.

Deputy Commissioner

DETAILS OF RENEWAL

Period	*Detail of fee (T.R. no., date and amount)*	*Signature and seal of the Renewing Authority*	*Period*	*Detail of fee (T.R. no., date and amount)*	*Signature and seal of the Renewing Authority*

FORMS L-17/L-17F, L-18/L-18F, L-19/L-19F, L-21/L-21F

[*See* rules 32 & 66(11)]

LICENCE FOR SERVICE OF INDIAN LIQUOR AND FOREIGN LIQUOR FOR CONSUMPTION "OFF" THE PREMISES IN INDEPENDENT RESTAURANT

1. Category of Licence :
2. Registration No.
3. Name of the restaurant :
4. Constitution of the licensee firm/Co. :
5. Name(s) of the proprietor/partners/ director(s)
6. Address :
7. Address of godown, if any :
8. Hours of sale :
9. Details of licence fee (TR No., date and amount) :
10. Date of issue :
11. Seat covers approved :
12. Period for which license is valid :

This licence is valid subject to the provisions of the Delhi Excise Act, 2009, the Rules framed thereunder; terms and conditions of licence and the instructions issued by the licensing authority from time-to-time.

Deputy Commissioner

DETAILS OF RENEWAL

Periods	Details of fee (TR. no., date and amounts)	Seats covers	Signature and seal of the Renewing Authority	Periods	Details of fee (TR. no., date and amounts)	Seats covers	Signature and seal of the Renewing Authority

FORM-L-22/L-22F

[*See* rules 32 & 66(13)]

1. Category of Licence	:	L-22 (Retail vend of Indian Liquor in duty free shop for consumption "off" the premises)
2. Registration number	:	
3. Name of firm/Individual	:	
4. Name of the director/ propriter/partner	:	
5. Address	:	
6. Hours of sale	:	
7. Licence fee	:	
8. Validity upto	:	
9. Date of issue	:	

Conditions:

This licence is valid subject to the provision of the Delhi Excise Act, 2009, the Rules framed thereunder; terms and conditions of licence and the instructions issued by the licensing authority from time-to-time.

Deputy Comissioner

Special Conditions:—

1. That they shall only make sale to passengers in transit or going out of India.
2. That the entire sale shall be against foreign currency.
3. That cash memos/vouchers shall be in the name of the passengers with ticket No. and other particulars.
4. That monthly sale statement should be submitted by the 5th day of the month following to which it relates.
5. That they will procure the Indian Liquor direct from the distillery or against import passes issued by the excise office.

FORM L-37

(LICENCE FOR HOTEL MANAGEMENT INSTITUTE FOR KEEPING LIQUOR FOR THE PURPOSE OF TRAINING)

[*See* rules 32 & 66(19)]

Licence No. .... Validity.........................

1. Category of licence:	....
2. Licence no.	....
3. Name and address of the Hotel Management Institute/Teaching Institute	....
4. Name of the person authorised by the Institute with designation	....
5. Registration number allotted by Government/Any other number for recognition by the Government	....
6. Licence is valid up to:	....
7. Licence fee	Rs. 50,000
8. Quantity of liquor allowed in litres	Whisky
	Rum
	Gin
	Vodka
	Wine
	Others

Conditions:

This licence is valid subject to the provisions of the Delhi Excise Act, 2009, the Rules framed there-under; terms and conditions of licence and the instructions issued by the licensing authority from time-to-time.

Deputy Commissioner

Conditions:

1. The Institute must be recognized by the Government and in case the recognition is withdrawn the licence shall be deemed to be cancelled from that date.
2. The Institute must inform the Excise Department in case of de-recognition of the Institute within seven days and the balance stock should be surrendered to the Deputy Commissioner for disposal as per Excise Laws.
3. The liquor shall be used for teaching purpose only.
4. The liquor shall be purchased from licensed liquor vend only.
5. The licensee Institute must keep a true account of liquor purchased and used for teaching purpose on day-to-day basis.

FORM P-1

[*See* rule 15(1)]

Book No.................... S. No................

(IMPORT PERMIT FOR RECTIFIED/DENATURED/
SPECIAL DENATURED SPIRIT/ABSOLUTE ALCOHOL)

Permit No....................

Date of issue .... Valid up to.............

M/s.............. to whom a licence in Form L-4/L-5 has been granted for the wholesale of rectified/denatured/special denatured spirit/absolute alcohol is hereby authorised to import from M/s............... rectified/denatured/special denatured spirit/absolute alcohol on the above noted premises as per details given below:

Kind of spirit	Quantity in litres	Import fee	Amount of fee with challan No. and date	Remarks

1. The above quantity of spirit shall be imported in one consignment and shall not be opened in transit.

2. Mode of transport: By truck/rail/..................................

This permit is granted subject to observance of the provisions of the Delhi Excise Act, 2009 the Rules framed thereunder; terms and conditions of licence and the instructions issued by the licensing authority from time-to-time.

Deputy Commissioner

Copy to:

1. Officer-in-charge (Excise), ...Distillery.
2. Area Excise Inspector.
3. Concerned licence holder.......................... /Delhi/New Delhi.

Deputy Commissioner

FORM P-2

[*See* rules, 33 & 79(2)]

PERMIT FOR THE POSSESSION OF DENATURED SPIRIT IN THE LIMIT OF ONE TIME POSSESSION OF 10 (TEN) LITRES

No. P-2/*Ad hoc*/.......................... Dated................................

Valid up to.........................

This permit authorizes the possession of denatured spirit up to the limit of 10 litres at a time in the premises herein specified under the Delhi Excise Act, 2009 and the Rules framed therein:—

....

....

....

Special Conditions:

1. This permit authorizes the holder only for the possession and use of denatured spirit, rendered permanently and effectively unfit for human consumption and not for sale.

2. The permit holder may purchase denatured spirit from any L-27 licensee against entries in this permit.

3. Denatured spirit shall be kept in the premises specified above and shall be used only for the following purposes:..

4. The permit holder shall maintain account of the use of denatured spirit in the following form:

S. No.	Name of the place and address where denatured spirit is used	Date and use of denatured spirit	Signature of Head where denatured

This permit is granted subject to observance of the provisions of the Delhi Excise Act, 2009 the Rules framed there under; terms and conditions of licence and the instructions issued by the licensing authority from time-to-time.

Assistant Commissioner

FORM P-3

PERMIT FOR THE POSSESSION OF DENATURED SPIRIT EXCEEDING THE LIMIT OF RETAIL SALE

[*See* rules 33 & 79(3)(d)]

No. of permit...................................

Date of permit.................................

The permit authorises the possession of denatured spirit exceeding ten litres only in the premises herein specified, *viz.* ....and for the period from 20.....to 20....is granted to.........................of ....subject to the conditions prescribed under the Delhi Excise Act, 2009; Rules framed thereunder and the special conditions below:

Special conditions:

This exemption extends only to the possession and use of the holder of the permit not for sale of spirit rendered effectually and permanently unfit for human consumption. The permit holder may purchase denatured spirit from any licensed vendor or may remove such spirit from a licensed distillery. The spirit shall be kept on the premises specified above and shall be used only for the following purposes:—

This permit is granted subject to observance of the provisions of the Delhi Excise Act, 2010 the Rules framed there under; terms and conditions of licence and the instructions issued by the licensing authority from time-to-time.

Dated

Deputy Commissioner

FORM P-4

PERMIT FOR POSSESSION OF SPECIAL DENATURED SPIRIT BY INDUSTRIAL MANUFACTURERS

[*See* rules 33 & 81(4)(a)]

No. of permit..................................

Date of permit..................................

This permit is for authorising the possession of special denatured spirit..................................for the period from..................................to..................................is granted to............................ subject to the provisions of Delhi Excise Act, 2009; the Rules made thereunder and also the conditions mentioned framed from time-to-time..

Purpose for which special denatured spirit is allowed to be used:—

Endorsement of renewal

RENEWAL

Period Fee

This permit is granted subject to observance of the provisions of the Delhi Excise Act, 2009 the Rules framed thereunder; terms and conditions of licence and the instructions issued by the licensing authority from time-to-time.

Deputy Commissioner

FORM P-5

PERMIT FOR THE POSSESSION OF RECTIFIED SPIRIT EXCEEDING THE LIMIT OF RETAIL SALE

[*See* rules 33 &77]

No. of permit....................................

Date of permit...................................

This permit authorises the possession of rectified spirit in privileged quantities to be used in drugs, medicines or chemicals only at the premises herein specified *viz:* ....or for purposes of teaching and research at an educational institution or homoeopathic chemist, practitioner or for manufacture and sale of homoeopathic medicines for the period from........................to..........................is granted to........................ of...............................in the district of..................................subject to the conditions prescribed under the Delhi Excise Act, 2009, the Rules framed thereunder and the special conditions below:—

Special Conditions:

1. The permit holder is authorized to possess rectified spirit for use in the manufacture of drugs, medicines and chemicals, except in the case of educational institution where rectified spirit shall be kept for teaching and research purposes.
2. The permit holder shall not have in his possession more than.................................. litres of rectified spirit. No sale of rectified spirit is permitted.
3. This permit is granted subject to observance of the provisions of the Delhi Excise Act, 2009 the Rules framed thereunder; terms and conditions of licence and the instructions issued by the licensing authority from time-to-time.

Delhi

Dated

Deputy Commissioner

FORM P-6

(PERMIT FOR POSSESSION OF SPECIAL DENATURED SPIRIT BY INDUSTRIAL MANUFACTURERS)

(*See* rules 33 & 78)

No. of permit:.....................................

Date of permit....................................

This permit authorizes the possession of special denatured spirit (ethanol-denatured with 0.2 per cent. crotonaldehyde and 4 grams of denatonium benzoate/denatonium sacchride per 100 litres of ethanol) to....................................at....................................for admixture with petrol for the period....................................to....................................subject to the provisions of the Delhi Excise Act, 2009, the rules framed thereunder and the conditions mentioned overleaf.

This permit is granted subject to observance of the provisions of the Delhi Excise Act, 2009 the Rules framed there under; terms and conditions of licence and the instructions issued by the licensing authority from time-to-time.

Deputy Commissioner

Special conditions:

1. The total quantity of special denatured spirit stored in the said premises shall not exceed 1896 kilo litres at one time.
2. The annual authorised possession limit of the permit holder has been fixed at 24,000 kilo litres;
3. The strength of special denatured spirit shall not be less than 60 degree over proof to which prescribed denaturants have been added.
4. It shall be the personal responsibility of the permit holder to ensure that the special denatured spirit imported/stocked by him contains prescribed denaturants in appropriate quantity.
5. The permit holder shall not obtain special denatured spirit from any source other than a distillery, without the prior approval of the Excise Commissioner
6. No special denatured spirit shall be used in the premises for the manufacture of any substance other than that mentioned in the permit.
7. No special denatured spirit shall be removed from the premises without the prior sanction of the Excise Commissioner.
8. The permit holder shall comply with the directions of the Excise Commissioner/ Deputy Commissioner as to the manner in which the special denatured spirit shall be stored and disposed of.
9. It shall be the personal responsibility of the permit holder to ensure that no attempt is made or allowed to be made which may have the effect of reducing the effectiveness of denaturants or their quality in special denatured spirit or other wise which would render the special denatured spirit reasonably potable.
10. The authorised excise officers shall have the authority to enter and inspect the premises.
11. No special denatured spirit shall be taken away from the premises by any person other that the duly authorized excise officer or under specific authorisation of the Excise Commissioner.
12. The keys of all vessels, which are required to be locked, shall be kept in the personal custody of the permit holder or any person duly authorized by him in writing with the prior approval of Deputy Commissioner.

13. Particulars of the quantity and strength of every consignment of specially denatured spirit must be entered in a book on the day of receipt. The book shall be accessible to the excise officers, who visit the premises and every pass, which accompanied special denatured spirit received, shall be available for comparison with the book by the Excise Officer concerned.

14. The permit holder shall notify to the Deputy Commissioner any loss of special denatured spirit, resulting from theft or any other reason whatsoever. No remission of refund of duty shall be allowed for such loss.

Endorsement For Renewal

FORM P-7

PERMIT FOR THE POSSESSION OF INTOXICATING SPIRITUOUS PREPARATIONS

[*See* rules 33 & 126(2)]

No. of permit...................................... Date of permit......................................

Permit authorising the possession of intoxicating spirituous preparations in privileged quantities only in the premises herein specified *viz*..........................and for the period from................... to 31st March, 20.... is granted to.................of ....subject to the provisions of the Delhi Excise Act, 2009; the Rules framed thereunder and the conditions specified below:—

Conditions

1. The permit holder may possess such of the intoxicating spirituous preparations and in such quantities as are mentioned below.
2. The permit-holder shall use in one year only such quantities of intoxicating spirituous preparations as are mentioned against each.
3. The permit-holder shall, in regard to such matters as are not specifically prescribed, carry out the directions of the authority granting the permit or superior in rank.
4. The permit-holder shall keep up-to-date accounts of receipt and consumption of intoxicating spirituous preparations and in such manner as may be required by the authority granting the permit.
5. The permit-holder shall permit the excise officers to enter the premises and examine the stock and accounts connected with the permit.

This permit is granted subject to observance of the provisions of the Delhi Excise Act, 2009 the Rules framed thereunder; terms and conditions of licence and the instructions issued by the licensing authority from time-to-time.

Dated Deputy Commissioner

FORM P-8

FORM OF PERMIT FOR THE IMPORT/TRANSPORT OF INTOXICATING SPIRITUOUS PREPARATION

(*See* rules 33 & 127)

Number of permit

Date of permit

Name of licensee ....

(Registered Medical Practitioner)

Licensed to sell intoxicating spirituous preparations at.................................In the.......................................district, is hereby permitted to import/ transport the intoxicating spirituous preparations as below from manufacturer/ licensee at........... ....to his vend premises.

This permit is valid up to the.......................day......................of.................20...

This permit is granted subject to observance of the provisions of the Delhi Excise Act, 2009 the Rules framed thereunder; terms and conditions of licence and the instructions issued by the licensing authority from time-to-time.

Deputy Commissioner

Name of the intoxicating spirituous preparations	Quantity	Rate of duty to be charged before issue (if any)	Remarks

(To be prepared in duplicate, one copy to be given to the applicant)

FORM P-9

PERMIT FOR THE IMPORT, EXPORT OR TRANSPORT OF LIQUOR FOR THE USE OF TROOPS

(*See* rules 33 & 19)

PERMISSION is hereby given for the removal of ....litres of country liquor and.....................................litres of Indian Liquor/Foreign Liquor/Country Liquor from the..............................distillery/brewery/winery/bottling plant to the office of the ....at...................It is valid up to

This permit is granted subject to observance of the provisions of the Delhi Excise Act, 2009 the Rules framed thereunder; terms and conditions of licence and the instructions issued by the licensing authority from time-to-time.

Deputy Commissioner

Delhi

FORM P-10

PERMIT FOR SERVICE OF LIQUOR IN DELHI AT UN-LICENSED PREMISES

[*See* rules 33 & 20(1)(a)(c)]

(To be filled by the applicant)

1. (i) Name of the applicant
   (ii) Father/husband's name
   (iii) Address/telephone/mobile no.
2. Whether individual/company/partnership firm/society, etc.
   (Specify the status of the applicant)
3. (i) Name and complete address of the premises
   (ii) Place where the function is proposed to be held
4. Occasion (Specify if it is a marriage birthday etc.)
   also enclose a copy of invitation card, if available
5. Date and time of the function (Specify the starting time as well as the ending time)
6. Approximate number of persons likely to attended the function
7. (i) Quantity of liquor required. (Indian Liquor/Foreign Liquor, beer separately)
   (ii) Details of the outlet from where the liquor has been purchased/is proposed to be purchased.
8. Date and number of TR-5.

It is certified that the information give above is correct. It is further certified that the liquor to be served in the party would not exceed the quantity fixed by the competent authority and would be purchased from authorized sources in Delhi.

Signature of applicant

Date:

For office use only:—

P-10 is granted for the above event. The holder of this licence is entitled to procure the quantity of liquor specified in this licence from authorised sources in Delhi and is also authorised to possess, transport and serve this quantity of liquor for consumption of his guests at the premises/place specified above subject to the following conditions.

(a) the applicant shall carry the bill in original issued by the retail liquor vend in Delhi from where the liquor has been procured;

(b) the area where the liquor is to be served shall be screened off from public view;

(c) liquor shall be served only to adults above 25 years in age.

This permit is granted subject to observance of the provisions of the Delhi Excise Act, 2009 the Rules framed thereunder; terms and conditions of licence and the instructions issued by the licensing authority from time-to-time.

Deputy Commissioner

Office Seal

FORM P-11

(PERMIT FOR LIQUOR EXHIBITORS/IMPORTERS OF LIQUOR SAMPLES)

[*See* rules 33 & 44(1)]

Permit No: .... (Fee of Rs. 25,000/per event of exhibition)

1. Name and the address of the permit holder ....
2. Name and address of the authorised representative of the permit holder ....
3. Premises/place where the exhibition is proposed to be held ....
4. Date and time of the exhibition during which date the permit is valid (a) Date of start Date of closing (b) Time of start Time of closing
5 Details of brands and quantity as approved List enclosed

Deputy Commissioner

Conditions:

1. The holder of this permit is entitled to exhibit only those Indian Liquor/Foreign Liquor brands which not registered in Delhi and quantity of liquor as specified against each brand in this permit.
2. The holder is also authorised to possess, transport and sample the above mentioned brands and quantity of liquor in Delhi.
3. This permit is granted subject to observance of the provisions of the Delhi Excise Act, 2009 the Rules framed thereunder; terms and conditions of licence and the instructions issued by the licensing authority from time-to-time.

DETAILS OF BRANDS AND QUANTITY AS APPROVED

(list as at serial No. 5 of the permit)

S. No	Category	Brand	Quantity permitted per day

FORM P-12

IMPORT/TRANSPORT/PERMIT FOR BHANG

(*See* rules 33 & 114)

Permit No..................
Date of issue
Valid up to.................

M/s...........................to whom licence in Form P-12 for retail vend of bhang and admixtures thereof has been granted is hereby authorized to import Bhang through rail/ road transport from M/s...as per details given below:

Quantity of bhang	Rate of duty	Amount of duty paid with challan and date	Remarks

Note:—The above quantity of bhang shall be imported in one consignment and shall not be opened in transit.

Deputy Commissioner

Copy to:

1. ....The District Excise and Taxation Officer (Concerned District Excise and Taxation Officer from where Bhang has been imported)...
2. The Area Excise Inspector
3. The contractor concerned.

This permit is granted subject to observance of the provisions of the Delhi Excise Act, 2009 the Rules framed thereunder; terms and conditions of licence and the instructions issued by the licensing authority from time-to-time.

Deputy Commissioner

FORM P-13

APPLICATION FOR GRANT OF P-13 PERMIT

(*See* rules 33 & 44)

1. Name of the hotel, restaurant or club and location of the premises where the party is proposed to be held

2. Name, address and telephone number of the host

3. Purpose

4. Date and timing of the party

5. Approximate number of persons to attend the party

6. Whether the host is the regular member of the club, in case the party is proposed to be held in a club, if yes, mention the membership number

7. If the entertainment programme is organized, mention the details

8. Date and serial number of T.R.S.

9. If the liquor of hotel, restaurant or club is not to be used, indicate the quantity and source of liquor(documentary evidence to be retained) Certified that the above party has been fixed in our hotel, restaurant or club and the particulars given above are correct. Only authorized liquor shall be served after P-13 is granted.

This permit is granted subject to observance of the provisions of the Delhi Excise Act, 2009 the Rules framed thereunder; terms and conditions of licence and the instructions issued by the licensing authority from time-to-time.

Date...........................

Signature of the representative
Name in Capital letters
Designation

For office use only

P-13 is granted for the above event

Dated..........

Deputy Commissioner
Official seal

FORM P-14
PERMIT OF IMPORT OF LIQUOR

(*See* rule 33)

Permit No................Indian Liquor/Foreign Liquor Valid upto...................Date of Issue M/s................................(Address).............................whom licence in Form L-1/L-1F/L-2/ L-3 has been granted for the wholesale vend of liquor is hereby authorised to import on the abovesaid premises Indian Liquor/Foreign Liquor from M/s.......................................
....
as per details given below:—

Kind of liquor	Strength	Quantity in proof litres/ in bottles	Quantity in bulk litres	Rate of import pass fee, if any TR 5 No. and date	Amount of import pass fee paid with
1	2	3	4	5	6

Notes: 1. The above quantity shall be imported in one consignment and shall not be opened in transit.

2. Mode of Transport: By Truck/Rail

3. This permit is granted subject to observance of the provisions of the Delhi Excise Act, 2009 the Rules framed thereunder; terms and conditions of licence and the instructions issued by the licensing authority from time-to-time

FORM P-15

TRANSPORT PERMIT PASS FOR THE TRANSPORT OF ALL KINDS OF LIQUOR FROM LICENSED PREMISES

(*See* rule 33)

Transport Permit No..................Order No. ....Date.........................

This permit is issued for transport of liquor of the following description from the licensed premises of M/s...
to the licensed premises of M/s...
for possession and sale within Delhi. Valid upto..

S. No.	Description of liquor (Brands)	Quantity required Cases			Batch No.	Remarks
1	2	3			4	5
					(Excise Inspector)	
Total						

Notes: 1. Not valid for dry days.

2. Transport passes are to be prepared in duplicate. One copy to be retained by the licensee.

3. Column no. 4 and if necessary, column no. 5 will be filled by the licensee from whose premises liquor is transported.

4. This permit is granted subject to observance of the provisions of the Delhi Excise Act, 2009 the Rules framed thereunder; terms and conditions of licence and the instructions issued by the licensing authority from time-to-time.

Signature of Inspector/
Wholesale Licensee

Vehicle No. ....Cases.................................Invoice No. ....
Date...................Time of issuance..

Representative of the licensee Godown Incharge/Excise Inspector

Note.—Hologram nos./Seamilised bar code to be mentioned overleaf.

No. of Holograms Affixed.

S. No. From S. No To Total Nos.

(Signature of Bond Manager/Incharge) (Signature of Bond Inspector)

FORM F-1

APPLICATION FOR LICENCE FOR DEALING IN DENATURED SPIRIT, SPECIAL DENATURED SPIRIT AND RECTIFIED SPIRIT

(*See* rule 72)

1. Name of the applicant.

2. Business address.

3. Residential address (s)

4. Whether the applicant is a partner with any other person holding a licence for vend of denatured spirit, rectified spirit or country liquor?

5. Details of premises to be used for storage of spirit to be given.

6. Whether the premises are owned or leased? In case of later, name of the landlord and monthly rent, if any, to be given. (Rent receipt or no objection certificate from the landlord to be attached).

7. Whether the premises are being used for any other purpose? If so, details of the business for which the premises are being used, to be given.

8. Whether the premises are fire proof? If so, whether the same have been approved by the Delhi Fire Service or other Local Authority.

9. Quantity of spirit required to be possessed at one time; and during the course of the year ending 31st March.

10. Whether the applicant has any other licence under the Delhi Excise Act, 2009 and the rules framed there-under? If so details thereof to be given.

11. A declaration in writing as to whether the applicant has been convicted or not at any time, of an offence punishable under the provisions of the Delhi Excise Act, 2009, its predecessor Act or any law in force on the subject in any part of India.

Dated:

Signature of the Applicant
with stamp, if any

FORM F-2

REGISTER TO BE MAINTAINED BY EVERY PERSON HOLDING LICENSE L-1, L-6 FOR THE WHOLESALE AND RETAIL VEND OF INDIAN LIQUOR

[*See* rules 10(6) & (7)]

	All entries to be of quantities in litres								Signature and date of the Excise Inspector on comparison of receipt entries with passes.	No. and date of passes under which issued.	Name, address and licences of person to whom each issue is made	All entries to be of quantities in litres							Remarks
		Daily total receipts										Daily total receipts							
							Beer										Beer		
Month and date	No. and date of pass under which received	Imported whisky, rum, brandy and gin	Whisky, brandy and gin made in India	Coloured rum made in India]	Other spirits and liquor	Wine	Imported	Indian				Imported whisky, brandy, rum and gin	Whisky, brandy and gin made in India	Coloured rum made in India	Other spirits and liquor	Wine	Imported	India	
1	2	3	4	5	6	7	8	9	10	11	12	13	14	15	16	17	18	19	20

The monthly returns to be submitted to the Excise Inspector are the totals of column 3 to 9 and 13 to 19 with the balance at the end of each month.

At the end of each day's business, the totals of the day's transaction should be entered in columns 13 to 19; the totals of the issue columns should be copied under the totals of the corresponding receipt columns 3 to 9 and the daily balance should then be entered under them in the receipt column.

FORM F-3

(ACCOUNT TO BE MAINTAINED BY EVERY PERSON HOLDING A LICENCE IN FORM L-6 FOR THE RETAIL VEND OF INDIAN LIQUOR)

[*See* rules 53(6)(a)]

All entries to be of quantities in litres

Daily total of receipts										Daily total of issues		
								Beer				
Month and date	Name of L-1 licensee from whom received	Transport pass no. and date	Imported whisky, brandy, rum and gin	Whisky, brandy and gin made in India	Coloured rum made in India	Other spirits and liquors	Wine	Imported	Indian	Imported whisky, brandy, rum and gin	Whisky brandy and gin made in India	Coloured rum made in India
1	2	3	4	5	6	7	8	9	10	11	12	13

				Daily Balance							
		Beer							Beer		
Other spirits and liquors	Wine	Imported	Indian	Important whisky, brandy, rum and gin	Whisky, brandy, rum and gin	Coloured rum made in India	Other spirits and liquors	Wine	Imported	Indian	Remarks
14	15	16	17	18	19	20	21	22	23	24	25

The monthly returns to be submitted to the Excise Inspector are the total of columns 4 to 17 with the balance shown in columns 18 to 24 at the end of each month.

FORM F-5

DAILY STOCK REGISTER OF LIQUOR IN THE LICENSED WAREHOUSE NAME OF THE DISTILLERY/BOTTLING PLANT...............

[*See* rule 61(1)]

Date	Import pass no. and date	Quantity received			Quantity issued					Balance			Wastage				
		Dozen bottles					Dozen bottles			Dozen bottles							
		750 ml.	375 ml.	Bulk litres	Name of retail licensee	Transport pass no. and date	750 ml.	375 ml.	Bulk litres	750 ml.	375 ml.	Bulk litres	Breakage	Leakage	Defective	Samples	Bulk litres
1	2	3	4	5	6	7	8	9	10	11	12	13	14	15	16	17	18

FORM F-6

REGISTER TO BE MAINTAINED BY EVERY PERSON HOLDING LICENCE IN FORM L-8 & L-27 FOR RETAIL VEND OF COUNTRY LIQUOR AND DENATURED SPIRIT

[*See* rules 66(6)(f) & 79(5)]

Month and date	Name and address of the distillery from whom received	Transport pass no. and date	Transport note no. and date	Quantity received			Issued			Particulars of the Cash memos against which sold	Balance			Remarks
				In dozen of bottles		Quantity in litres	No. of bottles sold (in dozen)		Quantity in litres		Dozen bottles		Quantity. in litres	
				750 ml	375 ml		750 ml	375 ml						
1	2	3	4	5		6				7			8	9

FORM F-7
(REGISTER TO BE MAINTAINED BY EVERY PERSON HOLDING LICENSE L-26 FOR VEND OF MEDICATED WINES)

[*See* rule 66(16)]

No register is prescribed for detailed entries of stocks and sales, but each licensee must submit at the end of each month to the Excise Inspector of his district a statement in the following form showing sales during the month, *viz:*

Name of licensee...licensed at...

Sales of medicated wines during the month of..

Medicated wine   Number of bulk litres sold

....

FORM F-8

REGISTER TO BE MAINTAINED BY L-27 (RETAIL LICENSEE OF DENATURED SPIRIT)

[*See* rule 79(4)]

Receipt

1. Month and date
2. Opening balance
3. Name and address of L-5 wholesale dealer from whom received
4. Pass no. and date
5. Quantity in litres
6. Progressive total

Issue

7. Name and address of the purchaser
8. Occupation or trade
9. Quantity issued
10. Price charged
11. Signature of the purchaser
12. Balance

FORM F-10

REGISTER TO BE MAINTAINED BY L-4 AND L-5 (WHOLESALE LICENSEE OF RECTIFIED OR DENATURED SPIRIT RESPECTIVELY)

[*See* rule 76(9)]

Receipts

1. Date and month
2. Name and address of the distillery from where received
3. Pass No. and date
4. Quantity in litres
5. Rate fixed
6. Progressive total

Issue

7. Pass no. and date
8. Name and address of the dealer L-27 or L-28 (retail) to whom issued.
9. Quantity in litres
10. Price charged
11. Balance at the close of the month
12. Signature of the purchaser
13. Remarks

FORM F-11

(MONTHLY STATEMENT OF INTOXICATING SPIRITUOUS PREPARATIONS TO BE SUBMITTED TO THE DEPUTY COMMISSIONER)

[*See* rule 129(1)]

Name of the Licensee

Particulars of licensed premises

Name of the month	Total quantity of intoxicating spirituous preparations in hand at the close of the preceding month	Total quantity received during the month	Total quantity sold during the month	Balance in hand at the close of month	Remarks

Date Signature of licensee

(To be submitted by the 7th of the following month)

FORM F-12

(*See* rule-6)

IMPORT PERMIT FOR INDIAN LIQUOR/FOREIGN LIQUOR

Book No................................ S. No........................

Permit No. ....

Date of Issue................................ Valid upto................................

M/s..to whom a licence in Form L......has been granted for the wholesale trade of Indian Liquor/ Foreign Liquor/Country Liquor is hereby authorized to import on the above said premises India Liquor/ Foreign Liquor/Country Liquor from M/s................................as per details given below:—

Kind of – foreign liquor/ beer	In case of Indian Liquor/ Foreign Liquor/ Country Liquor its strength	Quantity in proof litres/in bottles	Rate of with duty challan no. and date	Amount of duty paid	Remarks

Notes: (1) The above quantity shall be imported in one consignment and shall not be opened in transit.

(2) Mode of transport: By truck/rail/air...

Signature of permit issuing authority

Copy to:

1. The Officer-in-charge (Excise)................................Distillery.
2. The area Inspector................................Delhi/New Delhi.
3. The licence holder concerned.

Signature of permit issuing authority

FORM F-13

IMPORT PERMIT FOR COUNTRY LIQUOR

(*See* rule 6)

No. of permit................................

Date of permit...............................

M/s.................................licensed to sell Country Liquor wholesale at...........................in Delhi is hereby permitted to import one consignment of liquor as below from the ....to his licensed premises (Warehouse)................................by road in truck................................ This permit is valid up to the.......................day of.........................

(................................)

Signature of the officer granting the permit

Description of country liquor	Strength of country liquor	Quantity in	
		Dozen bottles (in figures and words)	Bulk litres (in figures and words)

Copy to:—

1. The Officer-in-charge (Excise)....................Distillery.
2. The Excise Officer (W.H.), Delhi.
3. The A.C.P. (E.I.B.), Delhi
4. The Excise Commissioner (UP), Allahabad.

....

Signature of Permit Issuing Authority

Book No.........................

Sl. No.............................

FORM F-14

REGISTER CONTAINING THE NAMES AND OTHER PARTICULARS OF EMPLOYEES IN THE WAREHOUSE

(*See* rule 91)

(To be maintained by the Officer-in-charge)

Name of licensee with address..

S. No.	Name	Age	Residence	Employed as

FORM F-15

TRANSPORT PASS FOR RECTIFIED /DENATURED SPIRIT/ABSOLUTE ALCOHOL

(*See* rule 6)

Pass. No. ……………..

Date of Issue of pass.............................. Valid up to……………

M/s ....who is a holder of licence in form L..................... is hereby permitted to transport, for retail sale/consumption, rectified/denatured spirit/ absolute alcohol from the licensed premises of M/S..on the above-said address, as per details given below:—

Kind of spirit	Quantity (in litres)	Rate of duty	Amount of duty paid with challan No. and date	Remarks

1. Mode of transport: truck/tempo/
2. This pass is valid only for 3 days unless extended.

Signature of the permit issuing authority

Copy to:—

1. Concerned licence holder
2. Wholesale licensee from where spirit is to be obtained.
3. Area Inspector

Signature of the permit issuing authority

FORM F-16
TRANSPORT PASS
(*See* rule 6)

Book No. .... Date of issue..................

Serial no. ....

M/s Shri ...., Country Liquor vend licensee is hereby authorized to obtain the under-mentioned quantity of Country Liquor from the Warehouse of M/s...situated at................................ and transport the same to his licensed vend premises at...............................

S. No.	Type of Country Liquor	Quantity in		Special duty paid (in figures and words)	Rate of duty
		Dozen (in figures and words)	Bulk litres (in figures and words)		
1	2	3	4	5	6

Notes: (1) The Country Liquor shall be transported by road.

(2) This pass is valid for three days unless extended.

(3) The pass-holder shall obtain the necessary transit note from excise officer, Warehouse.

Signature of Assistant Commissioner

PART II

The above mentioned quantity of country liquor has been issued in my presence.

Date...................................

Time.................................. Signature of Excise Officer Warehouse

FORM F-17

TRANSPORT PASSES OF INDIAN LIQUOR AND FOREIGN LIQUOR

(*See* rule 6)

Pass No.................................. Book No.............................

Dated..................................

For the transport/export of liquor of the following description from the premises of ....licensed for the sale of Indian Liquor/ Foreign Liquor to the premises of..licensed for the sale/ possession of..............................in the..on the authority of permit No. ....dated........................granted by............................ valid up to......................

S. No.	Kind of Liquor	Quantity in terms of quart/ bottle equivalent to 750 ml.	Strength	Description of vessel
(1)	(a) Indian Liquor (b) Foreign Liquor (c) Country Liquor			

(1) Mode of transport: truck/tempo

(2) This Pass is valid only for 3 days.

Signature of licensee Signature of Excise Inspector

Note.—This permit shall be in triplicate. One copy shall be retained in the office of issue, another given to exporter or transporter and the third copy in the care of exporter be sent to the Collector of the district of destination.

FORM F-18

[*See* rule 79(6)]

Sl. No. .... Dated

Pass for the transport of denatured spirit/special denatured spirit from the licensed premises/godown, licensed premises of the person holding licence for the sale of denatured spirit/special denatured spirit.

<table>
<tr><td colspan="6">Name of the licensee..........................Licensed at.................Godown situated at....................</td></tr>
<tr><td rowspan="2">Serial No.</td><td rowspan="2">Date</td><td colspan="2">Quantity of spirit transported</td><td colspan="2">Transported</td></tr>
<tr><td>No. of drums</td><td>Bulk litre</td><td>From</td><td>To</td></tr>
<tr><td>1</td><td>2</td><td>3</td><td>4</td><td>5</td><td>6</td></tr>
<tr><td colspan="6">Signature of the licensee</td></tr>
</table>

Notes: (1) This form shall be printed in duplicate having printed serial number in column 1.

(2) The name of the licensee, as well as the place of the licensed premises and godown shall also be printed.

(3) Original copy shall accompany the consignment while second copy shall be kept at the place of issue.

(4) In case any form gets spoilt both the copies shall be kept intact and produced for inspection whenever asked for.

FORM F-19

DIARY OF OFFICER-IN-CHARGE WAREHOUSE

(To be maintained by the Officer-in-charge of each Warehouse in duplicate)

Name of the Officer-in-charge Name of the licensee

S. No.	Date	Brief account of the work in the Warehouse	Remarks by the Assistant Commissioner/ Deputy Commissioner visiting the Warehouse

N.B.:—One copy shall be retained by the Officer-in-charge and the other copy shall be forwarded to the Assistant Commissioner/Deputy Commissioner every fortnight.

FORM F-20

APPLICATION FOR LICENCE OF WAREHOUSE FOR THE STORAGE OF INDIAN LIQUOR/FOREIGN LIQUOR/COUNTRY LIQUOR UNDER THE DELHI EXCISE RULES, 2010

[*See* rule 77(2)(e)]

To

The Excise Commissioner,

Delhi.

Sir,

I/We.......................................residing at.......................................request that I/We may be granted a licence for the use of my/our premises described as accompanying.

Overleaf as a Warehouse during the year ending 31st March, 20..... may be renewed.......................................for.......................................

2. I/We agree to abide by the terms and conditions of the licence which may be granted/ renewed.

3. I/We have verified that the surety/ sureties specified in the bonds/in case of renewal executed by me/us in form..(s) under rule.......................................is/are above and is/are solvent.

5. I/We hereby declare that no excise licence previously held by me/ us has been revoked or suspended or has failed to be renewed owing to a breach of the Act and/ or rules governing the grant of excise licence.

6. Description of premises are as under:—

Description of each main division or sub-division of the Warehouse	Distinguishing letter or number of letter and number of each	Detailed description of each	Purpose of each

1. Situation
2. Area and total storage capacity.
3. Varieties of dutiable goods to be stored.
4. Quantities of each variety of such goods stored during the previous year.
5. Estimated quantity of each variety of such goods to be stored during the period of licence applied for.

I/We declare that to our knowledge, the information furnished herein is true and complete.

Signature of the Applicant(s)

Place..........................

Date..........................

FORM F-21

(FORM OF APPLICATION FOR THE GRANT OF A LICENCE FOR THE SALE OF INTOXICATING SPIRITUOUS PREPARATIONS)

(*See* rule 125)

1. Name of the applicant
2. Father's name
3. Resident of
   (1) House no.
   (2) Ward
   (3) Police Station
   (4) Delhi/New Delhi
4. Brief history of the previous business.
5. Locality of the premises to be licensed (Full particulars to be given).
6. Name of the shop or establishment (whether firm, society, partnership or company)
7. Details of the sales of intoxicating spirituous preparations made during the three years prior to application.
8. Particulars of the intoxicating spirituous preparations for which a licence is required and quantity of each such preparation.

I do hereby declare that I shall abide by the law in force in respect of the import, export, transport, possession and sale of intoxicating spirituous preparations.

Signature of the applicant

Dated.....................20...

(This application is to be submitted to the Deputy Commissioner).

FORM F-22

APPLICATION FOR THE TRANSPORT PERMIT OF DENATURED SPIRIT/RECTIFIED SPIRIT

The Assistant Commissioner
National Capital Territory of Delhi, L and N Block,
Vikas Bhawan, New Delhi

Sir,

I/we hold a possession permit in Form P-3/P-5 and licence in Form L-27 as per details given below:—

1. Name and address of the permit holder, telephone/mobile no., if any:—
 ....
 ....
2. Permit/licence No. ....
3. Possession limit of the permit/licence holder..
 (a) Annual assessed requirement: ....
 (b) One time possession limit...
4. Details of the stock with the permit holder/licence:—
 ....
5. Details of last transport permit issued with pass no; date and quantity.
 ....
6. Quantity of denatured spirit applied for (both in figures and words):
 ....
7. Name of the wholesale licensee:
 from whom the spirit is to be drawn
 Name of the person who received the transport permit, *i.e.,* the whole sale dealer or any representative.

It is requested that we may be granted a transport permit for........................litres of denatured sprit.

Signature of the permit/licence holder
with full address

Description of licensed premises..

Supplementary conditions, if any..

ENDORSEMENT FOR RENEWAL

This licence is hereby renewed on the conditions hereinbefore stated for the period stated below:—

Period from..........................to..........................Fee..........................

Deputy Commissioner

FORM F-23

APPLICATION FOR RENEWAL OF (P-2, P-3, P-4 AND P-5, P-6 POSSESSION PERMIT) AND L-4; L-5; L-27; AND L-28 LICENCES

1. Name of licence/possession permit holder.

   Address of business premises

2. Total consumption of spirit during the preceding year showing receipt and consumption/sale of spirit month wise as per stock register duly verified by the Excise Inspector should be enclosed.

3. Whether the prescribed renewal fee has been paid (Original receipt in Form F.R.S. for payment of renewal fee from the S.O. accounts should be enclosed).

   Original receipt no. ....

   Date...

   N.B. Application to be accompanied by

   Licence/possession permit.

Signature of the applicant with stamp

II. Recommendation of the Assistant Commissioner (Spirit)

III. Order of the Deputy Commissioner

FORM F-24

APPLICATION FOR GRANT OF POSSESSION PERMIT IN FORM P-3 (FOR DENATURED SPIRIT), P-5 (FOR RECTIFIED SPIRIT/ABSOLUTE ALCOHOL), P-6 (FOR SPECIAL DENATURED SPIRIT)

1. Name of the applicant : ....
2. Father/husband's name : ....
3. Residential address : ....
4. Business address : ....

   N.B.—Attested copy of house tax/rent receipt/proof of lawful possession of premises should be attached.

5. Trade/occupation/profession of the applicant : ....
6. Whether the applicant is already engaged in any manufacturing industries, if so, the location of premises and the nature of trade : ....
7. Whether the applicant is registered under the Shops Establishment Act, if so, attested copy to be filed : ....

N.B.—If the applicant is registered with the Commissionerate of Industries, the application should be accompanied by their recommendation indicating the actual one time and annual requirement, and the remaining columns of this form may be left blank but the aforesaid requirement should be enclosed.

9. Whether the applicant is registered with value added tax department, if so, state the number : ....
10. Whether the applicant is payer of income tax, if so, his permanent account no. : ....
11. Type of permit P-3 for denatured spirit, P-5 for rectified spirit (delete whichever not applicable)
12. Annual quota and one time limit required, state separately for rectified spirit, absolute alcohol, denatured spirit
13 Address of premises to be used for manufacturing purposes : documents as in column 4 above should be attached, however, the premises for the purpose of this column are the same as for col. 4 this space may be left blank.
14. Nature: whether proprietorship/partnership/society/company, if partnership an attested copy of the partnership deed on rupees three

stamp papers; if private limited company; copy of memorandum and articles of association; if society, copy of bye laws and list of members should be enclosed.

15. Any other information considered relevant.

Place:

New Delhi/Delhi Signature of the applicant

Dated...................... Stamp

N.B.—An affidavit should be attached covering the following points from the applicant and where relevant from each partner:

(1) That I have not been declared insolvent by any court of law in India and am not below 25 years.

(2) That I have not been convicted by a criminal court for any non-bailable offence or of any offence punishable under any law relating to any tax payable during a period of five years preceding the date of application.

(3) That I have not be convicted for any offence punishable under the Delhi Excise Act, 2009 or its predecessor Act; Narcotics Drugs and Psychotropic Substances Act, 1985 or the Medicinal and Toilet Preparations (Excise Duties) Act, 1955, during a period of five years preceding the date of application.

(4) That I am not interested, whether as proprietor; partner; employee; shareholder or agent in the business against whom any dues to the excise department in Delhi are outstanding.

(5) Verification:

Verified on this.............day of..............20.... that the contents of the above application are true and correct to my knowledge and nothing material has been concealed therefrom.

Applicant

FORM F-25

REGISTER SHOWING THE ACCOUNT OF DAILY TRANSACTION OF EACH KIND OF INTOXICATING SPIRITUOUS PREPARATIONS

(*See* rule 129)

Name of Licensee

Particulars of the licensed premises

Number of licence.

Receipt					Issue		
Date	Opening balance	No. and date of pass	Name of the licensee/ manufacturer from whom purchased	Quantity	No. and date of pass, if any	Particulars of the purchaser	Quantity sold
Balance in hand (Quantity)			Initial of licensee		Remarks		

Note.—Entries relating to each intoxicating spirituous preparation will be made on a separate page.

FORM F-26

APPLICATION FOR REMOVAL/ CLEARANCE OF INDIAN LIQUOR/ FOREIGN LIQUOR/COUNTRY LIQUOR FROM THE WAREHOUSE

(*See* rule 10)

To

The Deputy Commissioner,

The Officer-in-charge,

I/We..apply for leave to remove/clear the undermentioned Indian Liquor/Foreign Liquor from the Warehouse situated at..

(1) Description of each kind of Indian Liquor/Foreign Liquor/Country Liquor proposed to be removed. Name of Indian Liquor/Foreign Liquor/ Country Liquor and quantity in both bulk and proof litres.

(2) Name and address of the person to whom to be supplied.

(3) Cost of liquor...................................... In rupees................................in foreign currency concerned.

(4) Particulars of Exemption Certificate issued by the Ministry of External Affairs.

Dated............................... Signature of the licensee.

I hereby certify that the consignment has been issued only after verifying Exemption Certificate of Ministry of External Affairs *vide* their authority no. ....for the use of the Officer-in-Charge of the Warehouse:—

No. ....dated.....................................

(i) Total no. of cases.

(ii) Quantity of Indian Liquor/Foreign Liquor/Country Liquor in bulk as well as proof litre.

Dated......................... Officer-in-Charge.

FORM F-27
TRANSIT NOTE

Book No. .... Serial No. ....

1. Time of issue of stock from the Warehouse
2. No. and date of transport pass.
3. Truck/tempo/vehicle no.
4. Name of the driver of the tempo/truck/vehicle
5. No. of bags/crates carried
6. No. of bottles in dozens/bulk litres.
7. Name of the licensee's representative escorting the truck/tempo
8. Name and place of the vend.
9. Signature of the licensee or his representative
10. Signature of the Warehouse licensee or his representative.

Date................................ Countersigned

Time................................ Office-in-charge, Ware House

PART II

For use of the vend

1. The above noted stock has been received and duly entered in the stock register being maintained at page no. ....
2. Time of receipt of stock
3. Quantity received.

Signature of the Country Liquor Vend
Licensee or his representative

PART III

(To be returned to the Officer-in-charge Warehouse)

1. The above noted stock has been received and duly entered in the stock register being maintained at page no. ....
2. Time of receipt of stock
3. Quantity received

Signature of Area Inspector

FORM F-28
STATEMENT OF TRANSPORT PASSES

S. No.	Date	Transport pass no. and date	Name of the pass-holder	Quantity in		Amount of duty paid as per transport pass	Valid upto	Quantity issued in		Transit note no. and date	
				B..L.	Dozen			B.L.	Dozen		
1	2	3	4	5	6	7	8	9	10	11	12

FORM F-29

DAILY STOCK REGISTER OF COUNTRY LIQUOR IN THE WAREHOUSE

	Receipts						Issue					Wastage			Destruction					Balance			
Date	No. and date of the consignment	Export Pass no. and date issued by the excise authorities of exporting State	Covering Pass no. and date issued by Delhi Excise Department	Dozen			Transport Pass no. and date	Name of CLV licensee	Dozen			Dozen			Dozen					Dozen			
				750 ml	375 ml.	Bulk litres			750 ml	375 ml	Bulk litres	750 ml.	375 ml.	Bulk litres	Breakage	Leakage	Defective	Samples	Bulk litres	750 ml.	375 ml.	Bulk litres	Remarks
1	2	3	4	5			6	7	8			9			10					11			12

FORM F-30
DAILY SALE REGISTER
[*See* rule 61(1)]

Date	Name of the Warehouse	Total sale in			Price per bottle	Cash memo no.	Total sale proceeds
		bulk litres	dozens	bottles			
1	2	3	4	5	6	7	8

FORM F-31

MONTHLY RETURN OF PAYMENT OF PERMIT FEE AND RECEIPT AND SALE OF DENATURED SPIRIT/SPECIAL DENATURED SPIRIT

[*See* rule 76(8)]

(To be submitted to Assistant Commissioner by the licensed vendors not later than 7th of every month)

Name of the licence.................................. Licensed at...

For the sale of...................................

Month/ date	Quantity received	Permit fee paid		No. of import permit/ pass	Quantity sold	Balance
		T.C.	Dated and no.			
1	2	3	4	5	6	7
Total for the month:						

Signature of licensee.

Checked and entered in the register in Form F-31 at serial No...............page..........

FORM F-32

YEARLY RETURN OF PAYMENT OF PERMIT FEE, RECEIPT AND SALE OF DENATURED SPIRIT/SPECIAL DENATURED SPIRIT

[*See* rule 76(10)]

(To be submitted to the Assistant Commissioner by licensed vendors not later than 15th April, each year)

Name of the licensee................................ Licensed at....................

for the sale of..

Month (April to March)	Total quantity of denatured spirit/ special denatured spirit	Details of payment of permit fee	Total quantity sold during the month	Balance
1	2	3	4	5
Total				

Remarks by the Assistant Commissioner

Checked with the monthly statement in Form F-31 received from the licensee with the following variations, if any.

Excise Clerk

The statement has been personally checked by me with the monthly statements in Form F-31 and entries in the register in form and the treasury challan in respect of payment received from the treasury and I am satisfied/not satisfied for the reasons as under:

Superintendent of Excise

FORM F-34

PERSONAL BOND WITH SURETY BOND

[*See* rule 47(6)]

(To be executed by the highest bidder in auction)

Whereas M/s ....bid at an auction under rule 48 of the Delhi Excise Rules, 2010 in order to get a licence in form.........................has been required to and deposited a sum of Rs. ....; And whereas the aforesaid M/s........... ....has also been required to furnish a personal bond with a surety bond conditioned on taking all requisite action to complete all formalities required for granting a licence in form..with in seven days from the date of communication of acceptance of his bid.

Now, therefore, the aforesaid M/s .... (herein after known as the bidder) and M/s.. (herein after known as the surety) hereby bind themselves jointly and severally to the President of India and agree that the aforesaid bidder shall take all requisite actions to complete all formalities required for the grant of a licence in form.....................................with in seven days from the date of the communication of acceptance of his bid and that if he does not do so, all deposits made by him shall stand forfeited to the President of India and that a further sum of Rs. ....shall also stand forfeited to the President of India

It is also declared that this bond is given under the orders of the Government for the performance of an act in which the public are interested.

Witnesses:—

1. Signature.......................................	Signature..
Name and address.....................	Name of the bidder................................
	Stamp of the firm represented by the bidder.
2. Signature.....................................	Signature..
Name and address.....................	Name of surety and complete address

FORM F-38

PASS FOR THE EXPORT/ TRANSPORT OF INTOXICATING SPIRITUOUS PREPARATION

(*See* rule 128)

Pass No. .... Dated ....

For the export/ transport of the intoxicating spirituous preparations from the premises of...........................at...................................to the premises of M/s............................... at.....................on the authority of permit No.....................date......................signed by the competent authority of.....................District.

S. No.	Name of preparation	Batch No.	No. of containers	Quantity	Strength	Proof itres contents	Rate of duty
Amount of duty				Remarks			

Deputy Commissioner

This pass is valid up to.......................................

The Licensee shall not open the bulk unless it has been checked by excise officer.

(To be prepared in triplicate-one part will accompany the consignment, another will be sent to the Excise Office of the district issuing the permit against which supply is being made, the counterfoil to be kept by the office issuing this pass).

THE PUNJAB EXCISE ACT, 1914

WHEREAS it is expedient to consolidate and amend the law in, [1][Punjab] relating to import, export, transport, manufacture, sale and possession of intoxicating liquor and of intoxicating drugs; it is hereby enacted as follows:—

CHAPTER I

PRELIMINARY AND DEFINITIONS

1. Short title.—(1) This Act may be called the Punjab Excise Act, 1914 and

(2) **Extent and commencement.**—It extends to the whole of Punjab.

(3) It shall come into force on such date as the State Government may be notification direct.

2. Repeal of enactments.—The enactments, mentioned in Schedule (1) are repealed to the extent specified in the fourth column thereof.

3. Definitions.—In this Act and the rules made under it unless there is some-thing repugnant in the subject or context:—

(1) "Beer" includes ale, porter, stout and all other fermented liquors made from malt.

(2) "to bottle" means to transfer liquor from a cask or other vessel to a bottle, jar, flask or similar receptacle whether any process of manufacture be employed or not, and bottling including re-bottling.

(3) "Collector" includes any revenue officer in independent charge of district and any official appointed by the State Government to discharge through out any specified local area, the functions of a Collector under this Act.

(4) "Commissioner" means the chief officer incharge of the revenue administration of a division.

(5) "denatured" means effectually and permanently rendered unfit for human consumption.

(6) "Excisable article" means:—

(a) any alcoholic liquor for human consumption; or

(b) any intoxicating drug;

[(6a) "excise bottle" means a bottle of such type or description as may be or may have been at any time permitted for the bottling of liquor or beer by rules made under this Act].

[(6b) "excise duty" and "countervailing duty" means any such excise duty or countervailing duty as the case may be as in mentioned in entry[2] 51 of list II in the Seventh Schedule to the Constitution.

[(7) "Excise Commissioner" means the Excise Commissioner appointed as such by the State Government under section 9 and includes any other officer appointed by the State Government to discharge the functions of the Excise Commissioner under this Act.][3]

---

1. Subs. for "East Punjab" which had been substituted for the "Punjab" by Indian Independence (Adaptation of Bengal and Punjab Acts) Order, 1948 by Adaptation of Laws (3rd Amendment) Order, 1951.
2. Subs. for the word and figure "item 40" by Adaptation of Laws (3rd Amendment) Order, 1951.
3. Subs. *vide* Punjab Act No 20 of 1998.

(8) "Excise Officer" means any officer or person appointed or invested with powers under this Act.

(9) "Excise revenue" means revenue derived or derivable from any payment, duty, fee, tax confiscation or fine imposed or ordered under the provisions of this Act, or of any other law for time being in force relating to liquor or intoxicating drugs, but does not include a fine imposed by a court of law.

(10) "Export" means to take out of Punjab otherwise than across a customs frontier as defined by the Central Government.

(11) "Financial Commissioner" shall when there are more Financial Commissioners than one be construed as meaning one or more of the Financial Commissioners.

(12) "Import" (except) in the phrase "import into India means to bring into Punjab otherwise than across a custom frontier as defined by the Central Government.

(12a) "intoxicant" means any liquor or intoxicating drug.

(13) "intoxicating drugs" mean:

(i) the leaves, small stalks and flowering or fruiting tops of the Indian hemp plant (Canabis Sativa L.) including all forms known as bhang, siddhi or ganja.

(ii) Charas, that is the resin, obtained from the Indian hemp plant, which has not been submitted to any manipulations other than those necessary for packing and transport.

(iii) any mixture with or without natural materials of any of the above forms of intoxicating drug or any drink prepared therefrom; and

(iv) any other intoxicating or narcotic substance which the State Government may by notification declare to be an intoxicating drug such substance not being opium coca leaf, or a manufactured drug as defined in section 2 of the Dangerous Drugs Act, 1930.

[1][(13A) "Lahan" means any solution made from any kind of gur or molasses or both:

(i) to which a fermentation agent has been added to promote fermentation; or

(ii) which has undergone the process of fermentation; and from which spirit can be obtain by distillation; and]

(14) "Liquor" means intoxicating liquor and includes [1][Lahan and] all liquid consisting of or containing alcohol; also any substances which the State Government may by notification declare to be liquor for the purposes of this Act.

(15) [***][2]

(16) "manufacture" includes every process, whether natural or artificial by which any intoxicant is produced or prepared and also re-distillation, and every process for the rectification, reduction flavouring, blending or colouring of liquor.

[(16A) "Offender" means any person, who in contravention of any provision of this Act, the rules framed thereunder, any notification issued or any order made

1. Added by Punjab Act 36 of 1973.
2. Clause (15) was omitted by the Punjab Separation of Judicial and Executive Functions Act, 1964 (Punjab Act No. 25 of 1964).

or any licence, permit or pass granted under this Act, imports or exports or transports or possession any liquor.][1]

(17) "place" includes a building, shop, tent, enclosure, booth, vehicle, vessel, boat and raft.

(18) "Sale" expression referring to "sale" include any transfer otherwise than by way of gift.

(19) "spirit" means any liquor containing alcohol obtained by distillation whether denatured or not.

(20) "tari" means fermented or unfermented juice drawn from any kind of palm tree.

(21) "transport" means to move from one place to another within Punjab.

4. 'Country Liquor' and 'Foreign liquor'.—The State Government may by notification declare what for the purposes of this Act or any portion thereof shall be deemed to be "country liquor" and "foreign liquor".

5. Power of State Government to declare limit of sale by retail and by whole-sale.—The State Government may by notification declare with respect either to the whole of Punjab or to any local area comprised therein, and as regards purchasers generally or any specified class of purchasers and generally or for any specified occasions the maximum or minimum quantity or both of any intoxicant which for the purposes of this Act may be sold by retail and by whole sale.

6. Power to limit application of notifications, permits, etc., made under this Act.—Where under this Act any notification is made any power conferred, any appointment made or any license, pass or permit granted, it shall be lawful to direct:—

(a) that it shall apply to the whole of Punjab or to any specified local area or areas;

(b) that it shall apply to all or any specified intoxicant or intoxicants or class thereof;

(c) that it shall apply to all or any class or classes of persons or officers;

(d) that it shall be in force only for some special period or occasion.

7. Saving of enactments.—Save as provided by the Schedule I nothing contained in this Act shall effect the provisions of the [2][*See* Customs Act, 1887] (VII of 1878) the Cantonments Act, 1910] or the Indian Tariff Act, 1894 or any rule or order made thereunder.

CHAPTER II

ESTABLISHMENT AND CONTROL

8. Superintendence and control of excise administration and excise officers.—(a) Subject to the control of the State Government and unless the State Government shall by notification otherwise direct, the general superintendence and administration of all matters relating to excise shall vest in the Financial Commissioner.

(b) Subject to the general superintendence and control of the Financial Commissioner and unless the State Government shall by notification otherwise direct, the Commissioner shall control all other excise officers in his division.

(c) Subject as aforesaid and to the control of the Commissioner and unless the State Government shall by notification otherwise direct the Collector shall control all other excise officers in his district.

1. Ins. *vide* Punjab Act 10 of 2003.
2. *See* now the Customs Act, 1962.

9. Excise Commissioner.—The State Government may by notification appoint an Excise Commissioner and subject to such conditions and restrictions as it may deem fit may invest him with all or any of the powers conferred on the Financial Commissioner by this Act.

10. (a) Other classes of excise officers.—There shall be such other classes of excise officers as the State Government may by notification declare and the State Government may appoint as many person as it deems fit to be excise officers of these classes.

(b) Their powers.—The State Government shall by notification declare what powers under this Act shall be exercised by excise officers of each class.

(c) Mode of conferring powers.—In conferring powers under this Act the State Government may empower persons by name or in virtue of their office or classes of official generally by their official title.

11. Power to invest persons with special powers under this Act.—The State Government may by notification invest any person, not being an excise officer, with power to perform all or any of the functions of an excise officer, under this Act, and such person shall in the exercise of these functions be deemed to be an excise officer.

12. Local limits of jurisdiction.—The jurisdiction of the Financial Commissioner and of the Excise Commissioner shall extend to Punjab the jurisdiction of Commissioners shall extend to their divisions and the jurisdiction of Collectors and other excise officers shall unless, the State Government shall otherwise direct, extend to the districts in which they are for the time being employed.

13. Delegation:—(a) The State Government may by notification delegate to the Financial Commissioner or Commissioners all or any of its powers under this Act, except the powers conferred by sections 14, 21, 22, 31, 56 and 58 of this Act.

(b) The State Government may by notification permit the delegation by the Financial Commissioner, Commissioner or Collector to any person or class of persons specified in such notification of any powers conferred by this Act or exercised in respect of excise revenue under any Act for the time being in force.

14. Appeal.—An appeal shall lie from an original or appellate order of any excise officer in such cases or classes of cases and to such authority as the State Government shall by notification declare.

[1][**15. Revision and review.**—(1) The Excise Commissioner may, *suo moto,* at any time or on an application made to him, call for the record of any proceedings which are pending before, or have been disposed of, by any excise officer subordinate to him for the purpose of satisfying himself as to the legality or propriety of such proceedings or of any order made therein and may pass such order in relation thereto as he may deem fit:

Provided that the application shall be made within a period of one hundred and eighty days of the date of taking of the proceedings or of passing of the order, as the case may be.

(2) The State Government may by notification also confer upon any excise officer the powers of the Excise Commissioner under sub-section (1) to be exercised subject to such conditions, and in respect of such areas, as may be specified in the notification.

(3) The Excise Commissioner or the Excise Officer on whom powers of the Excise Commissioner have been conferred under sub-section (2) may review his own order.

(4) The Financial Commissioner may, *suo moto,* at any time or on an application made to him, call for the record of any case decided under the proceeding sub-sections and if

1. Subs. by Punjab Act 8 of 1965, section 2.

in his opinion the final order contains an erroneous decision on any question of law, he may pass such order on the case as he may deem fit.

(5) No order shall be made under this section which adversely effect the rights of any person upon whom an obligation is imposed by or under this Act, without giving such persons a reasonable opportunity of being heard].

CHAPTER III

IMPORT, EXPORT AND TRANSPORT

16. Import, export and transport of intoxicants.—No intoxicant shall be imported, exported or transported except:—

(a) after payment of any duty to which it may be liable under this Act or execution of a bond, for such payment, and

(b) in compliance with such conditions as the State Government may impose.

17. Power of State Government to prohibit import, export and transport of intoxicants.—The State Government may by notification—

(a) prohibit the import or export of any intoxicant into or from Punjab, or any part thereof; or

(b) prohibit the transport of any intoxicant.

18. Passes necessary for import, export and transport.—Except as otherwise provided by any rule made under this Act, no intoxicant exceeding such quantity as the State Government may prescribe by notification shall be imported, exported or transported except under a pass issued under the provisions of the next following section:

Provided that in the case of duty paid foreign liquor such passes shall be dispensed with unless the State Government shall by notification otherwise direct:

Provided further, that on such conditions as may be determined by the Financial Commissioner, a pass granted under the excise Law in force in another State may be deemed to be a pass granted under this Act.

19. Grant of passes for import, export and transport.—Passes for the import, export and transport of intoxicants may be granted by the Collector:

Provided that passes for the import and export of such intoxicant as the Financial Commissioner may from time-to-time determine shall be granted only by the Financial Commissioner.

CHAPTER IV

MANUFACTURE, POSSESSION AND SALE

A. MANUFACTURE

20. Manufacture of intoxicants prohibited except under the provisions of this Act.—(1) (a) No intoxicant shall be manufactured or collected;

(b) no hemp plant shall be cultivated;

(c) no tari-producing tree shall be tapped;

(d) no tari shall be drawn from any tree, and

(e) no person shall use, keep or have in his possession, any materials, still, utensil, implement or apparatus whatsoever for the purpose of manufacturing any intoxicant other than tari.

Except under the authority and subject to the terms and conditions of a licence granted in that behalf by the Collector.

(2) No distillery or brewery shall be constructed or worked except under the authority and subject to the terms and conditions of a licence granted in that behalf by the Financial Commissioner under section 21.

21. Establishment or licensing of distilleries and breweries.—The Financial Commissioner, subject to such restriction or condition as the State Government may impose may,—

(a) establish a distillery in which spirit may be manufactured under a licence granted under section 20.

(b) discontinue any distillery so established.

(c) licence the construction and working of a distillery or brewery.

(d) make rule regarding—

(1) the granting of licences for distilleries, stills or breweries.

(2) the security to be deposited by the licencee of a distillery or brewery;

(3) the period for which the licence shall be granted;

(4) the inspection and examination of such distillery or brewery and the warehouses connected there with and of the spirit or fermented liquor made and stored therein;

(5) the management and working of the distillery or brewery;

(6) the form of accounts to be maintained and the returns to be submitted by the licencee;

(7) the upkeep of buildings and plant;

(8) the size and description of stills and other plants;

(9) the manufacture, storing and passing out of spirit and contents of passes;

(10) the prices to be charged by the licencee;

(11) any other matters connected with the working of distilleries or breweries.

22. Establishment or licensing of warehouses.—The Financial Commissioner, subject to such restrictions or conditions as the State Government may impose, may:—

(a) establish or licence a warehouse wherein any intoxicant may be deposited and kept without payment of duty.

(b) discontinue any warehouse so established.

23. Removal of intoxicants from the distillery etc.—No intoxicant shall be removed from any distillery, brewery, warehouse or other place of storage, established or licensed under this Act, unless the duty if any (payable under Chapter V) has been paid or a bond has been executed for the payment thereof.

B. POSSESSION

24. Possession of intoxicants.—(1) No person shall have in his possession any quantity of any intoxicants in excess of such quantity as the State Government has, under section 5, declared to be the limit of retail sale, except under the authority and in accordance with the terms and conditions of—

(a) a licence for the manufacture, sale or supply of such article; or

(b) in the case of intoxicating drugs, a licence for the cultivation or collections of the plants from which such drugs were produced; or

(c) a permit granted by the Collector in that behalf;

(2) *Exceptions.*—Sub-section (1) shall not apply to—

(a) any intoxicant in the possession of any Excise Officer, common carrier or warehouse man as such or;

(b) Omitted by East Punjab Act 12 of 1949.

(3) A licensed vendor shall not have in his possession at any place, other than that authorised by his licence, any quantity of any intoxicant in excess of such quantity as the State Government has under section 5 declared to be the limit of sale by retail except under a permit granted by the Collector in that behalf.

(4) **Prohibition and restriction of possession of intoxicant in certain cases.**—Notwithstanding anything contained in the forgoing sub-sections the State Government may by notification prohibit the possession of any intoxicant or restrict such possession by such conditions as it may prescribe.

[1][**24A. Possession of unused and printed labels, corks, etc., by certain persons to be punishable.**—No person shall have in his possession any unused and printed label, cork, capsule or seal, duly approved by any authority under this Act or under any rule or order made thereunder for use by a person licensed to establish or work a distillery or brewery or to bottle liquor, or any other label, cork, capsule or seal which is an imitation of such un used and printed label, cork, capsule or seal, as the case may be:

Provided that nothing herein shall apply to—

(a) a person licensed to establish or work a distillery or brewery or to bottle liquor; or

(b) a person who, in execution of an order received from a person specified in clause (a) manufactures or prints any such label, cork, capsule or seal.

25. Prohibition of possession of intoxicant unlawfully manufactured, imported etc.—No person shall have in his possession any quantity of any intoxicant knowing the same to have been unlawfully imported, transported, manufactured, cultivated or collected or knowing the prescribed duty not to have been paid thereon.

C. SALE

26. Sale of intoxicants.—No liquor shall be bottled for sale and no intoxicant shall be sold except under the authority and subject to the terms and conditions of a licence granted in that behalf provided that—

(1) a person licensed under section 20 to cultivate the hemp plant may sell without a licence those portions of the plant from which any intoxicating drug can be manufactured to any person licensed under this Act to deal in the same or to any officer whom the Financial Commissioner may appoint in this behalf;

(2) a person having the right to the tari drawn from any tree may sell the same with out a licence to a person licensed to manufacture or sell tari under this Act;

(3) on such conditions as the Financial Commissioner may determine a licence for sale under the Excise Law for the time being in force in other parts of the whole of the India Except Part B States may be deemed to be a licence granted in that behalf under this Act;

(4) nothing in this section applies to the sale of any foreign liquor lawfully procured by any person for his private use and sold by him or on his behalf or on behalf of his representatives in interest upon his quitting a station or after his decease.

27. Grant of lease of manufacture etc.—(1) The State Government may lease to any man not below the age of twenty-five years, on such conditions and for such period as it may deem fit, the right—

(i) of manufacturing or of supplying by wholesale, or of both, or

(ii) of selling by wholesale or by retail, or

1. Subs. by Punjab Act 31 of 1963, section 2.

(iii) of manufacturing or of supplying by wholesale, or of both and of selling by retail;

any [Excisable article][1] within any specified local area.

(2) The Collector shall grant to a lessee under sub-section (1) a licence in the terms of his lease; and, when there is no condition in the lease which prohibits sub-letting, may, on the application of the lessee, grant a licence to any sub-lessee approved by the Collector.

28. Manufacture and sale of liquor in military Cantonments.—Within the limits of any military cantonment and within such distance from those limits as the Central Government in any case may prescribe, no licence for the manufacture or sale of liquor and no lease of the retail vend of liquor, such as is described in section 27, shall be granted unless with the consent of the Commanding Officer.

29. Prohibition of sale to persons under the age twenty-five years.—No licensed vendor and no person in the employ of such vendor or acting on his behalf shall sell or deliver any liquor or intoxicating drug to any person apparently under the age of twenty-five years whether for consumption by such person or by another person and whether for consumption on or off by the premises of such vendor.

30. Prohibition of employment of men under the age of twenty-five years and of women.—No person who is licensed to sell any liquor or intoxicating drug for consumption on his premises shall during the hours in which such premises are kept open for business, employ or permit to be employed either with or with out remuneration any man under the age of 25 years or any women in any part of such premises in which such liquor or intoxicating drug is consumed by the public.

CHAPTER V

DUTIES AND FEES

31. Duty on excisable articles.—An excise duty or a countervailing duty as the case may be at such rate or rates as the State Government shall direct, may be imposed either generally or for any specified local area, on any excisable article.

(a) imported, exported or transported in accordance with the provisions of section 16; or

(b) manufactured or cultivated under any licence granted under section 20; or

(c) manufactured in any distillery established or any distillery or brewery licensed under section 21:

Provided as follow:—

(i) duty shall not to be so imposed or any article which has been imported into India and was liable on importation to duty under the Indian Tariff Act, 1894, or the[2] See Customs Act, 1878;

(ii) *Explanation.*—Duty may be imposed under this section at different rates according to the places to which any excisable article is to be removed for consumption, or according to the varying strength and quality of such article.

32. Manner in which duty may be levied.—Subject to such rules regulating the time, place and manner as the Financial Commissioner may prescribe, such duty shall be levied rateably, on the quantity of excisable article imported, exported, transported, collected or manufactured in or is sued from a distillery brewery or warehouse:

---

1. Subs. *vide* Punjab Act No. 20 of 1998, for "country liquor or intoxicating drug".
2. *See* now the Customs Act, 1962.

Provided that duty may be levied:—

(a) on intoxicating drugs by an acreage rate levied on the cultivation of the hemp plant or by a rate charged on the quantity collected.

(b) on spirit or beer manufactured in any distillery established or any distillery or brewery licensed, under this Act in accordance with such scale or equivalents calculated on the quantity of materials used, or by the degree of attenuation of the wash or wort, as the case may be, as the State Government may prescribe;

(c) on tari, by a tax on each tree from which the tari is drawn:

Provided further that where payment is made upon issue of an excisable article for sale from a warehouse established or licensed under section 22(a) it shall be made—

(a) if the State Government by notification so directs, at the rate of duty which was in force at the date of import of that article, or

(b) in the absence of such direction by the State Government, at the rate of duty which is in force on that article on the date when it is issued from the warehouse.

33. Payment for grant of leases.—Instead of or in addition to any duty leviable under this chapter the State Government may accept payment of a sum in consideration of the lease of any right under section 27.

33A. Saving for duties being levied at commencement of the Constitution.—(1) Until provision to the contrary is made by Parliament, the State Government may continue to levy any duty which it was lawfully levying immediately before the commencement of the Constitution under this chapter as then in force.

(2) The duties to which this section applies are:—

(a) any duty on intoxicants which are not excisable articles within the meaning of this Act; and

(b) any duty on an excisable article produced outside India and imported into Punjab whether across a customs frontier as defined by the Central Government or not.

(3) Nothing in this section shall authorise the levy by the State Government of any duty which as between goods manufactured or produced in the State and similar goods not so manufactured or produced, discriminates in favour of the former or which, in the case of goods manufactured or produced out side the State, discriminates between goods manufactured or produced in one locality and similar goods manufactured or produced in another locality.

CHAPTER VI

LICENCES, PERMIT AND PASSES

34. Fees for terms, conditions and form of, and duration of licences, permits and passes.—(1) Every licence, permit or pass granted under this Act shall be granted—

(a) on payment of such fees, if any,

(b) subject to such restrictions and on such conditions,

(c) in such form and containing such particulars,

(d) for such period.

As the Financial Commissioner may direct.

(2) **Security.**—Any authority granting a licence under this Act may require the licensee to give such security for the observance of the terms of his licence, or to make such deposit in view of security, as such authority may think fit.

35. Grant of licence for sale.—(1) Subject to the rules made by the Financial Commissioner under the power conferred by this Act, the Collector may grant licences for the sale of any intoxicant within his District.

(2) **Ascertainment of public opinion.**—Before any licence is granted in any year for the retail sale of liquor for consumption on any premises which have not been so licensed in the preceding year, the Collector shall take such measure in accordance with rules to be made by the State Government in this behalf, as may best enable him to ascertain local public opinion in regard to the licensing of such premises.

(3) A licence for sale in more than one district of the Punjab shall be granted by the Financial Commissioner only.

36. Power to cancel or suspend licences, etc.—Subject to such restrictions as the State Government may prescribe, the authority granting any licence, permit or pass under this Act may cancel or suspend it.

(a) If it is transferred or sublet by the holder thereof without the permission of the said authority; or

(b) if any duty or fee payable by the holder thereof be not duly paid; or

(c) in the event of any breach by the holder of such licence, permit or pass or by his servants, or by any one acting on his behalf with his express or implied permission, of any of the terms or conditions of such licence, permit or pass; or

(d) if the holder thereof is convicted of any offence punishable under this Act or any other law for the time being in force relating to revenue, or of any cognizable and non-bailable offence, or of any offence punishable under the Dangerous Drugs Act, 1930, or under the Merchandise Marks Act, 1889, or of any offence punishable under sections 482 to 489 (both inclusive) of the Indian Penal Code; or

(e) if the holder thereof is punished for any offence referred to in clause (8) of section 197 of the [1][See Customs Act, 1878; or]

(f) where a licence permit or pass has been granted on the application of the grantee of a lease under this Act, on the requisition in writing of such grantee; or

(g) at Will, if the conditions of the licensee or permit provide for such cancellation or suspension.

37. Power to cancel any other licence.—When a licence, permit, or pass held by any person is cancelled under clause (a), (b), (c), (d) or (e) of section 36, the authority aforesaid may cancel any other licence, permit or pass granted to such person by or by the authority of the State Government, within the same district under this Act or under any other law for the time being in force relating to excise revenue or under the Opium Act, 1878, and the Financial Commissioner may cancel any such licence, permit or pass granted to such person in any district to which this act applies.

38. Power to recover fee.—In the case of cancellation or suspension of licence under clause (a), (b), (c), (d) or (e) of section 36, the fee payable for the balance of the period for which any licence would have been current but for such cancellation or suspension, may be recovered from the ex-licensee as excise revenue.

39. Power of collector to take grants under management or to re-sell.—If any holder of a licence granted under this Act, or any person to whom a lease has been granted under section 27, makes default in complying with any condition imposed upon him by such licence or lease, the collector may take the grant under the management at the risk

1. *See* now the Customs Act, 1962.

of the person who has so defaulted or may resell it and recover in the manner laid down in section 60 of this Act any deficiency in price and all expenses of such resale.

40. No compensation or refund claimable for cancellation or suspension of licence, etc., under this section.—When a license permit or pass is cancelled or suspended under clause (a), (b), (c), (d) or (e) of section 36 or under section 37 the holder shall not be entitled to any compensation for its cancellation or suspension nor to the refund of any fee paid or deposit made in respect thereof.

41. Powers to withdraw licenses.—(1) Whenever the authority which granted a licence, permit or pass under this Act considers that such licence permit or pass should be withdrawn for any cause other than those specified in section 36, it may on remitting a sum equal to the amount of the fees payable in respect thereof for fifteen days, withdraw the license either:—

(a) on the expiration of fifteen days notice in writing of its intention to do so; or

(b) forthwith without notice.

(2) **Compensation in the case of withdrawal.**—If any licence, permit or pass be withdrawn under clause (b) of sub-clause (1) in addition to the sum remitted as aforesaid there shall be paid to the licensee such further sum (if any) by way of compensation as the Financial Commissioner may direct;

(3) **Refund of fee of deposit.**—When a licence, permit or pass is withdrawn under this section, any fee paid in advance or deposit made by the licensee in respect thereof shall be refunded to him after deducting the amount (if any) due to the State Government.

42. Technical irregularities in license etc.—No licence, permit or pass granted under this Act shall be deemed to be invalid by reason merely of any technical defect, irregularity or omission in the license or in any proceedings taken prior to the grant thereof.

(2) The decision of the Financial Commissioner as to what is a technical defect, irregularity or omission shall be final.

43. No claim in consequence of refusal to renew a licence etc.—No person to whom a license permit or pass may have been granted shall be entitled to claim any renewal thereof and no claim shall lie for damages or otherwise in consequence of any refusal to renew a licence, permit or pass on the expiry of the period for which it remains in force.

44. Surrender of license.—(1) No holder of a licence granted under this Act to sell an intoxicant shall surrender his licence except on the expiration of one month's notice in writing given by him to the Collector of his intention to surrender the same and on payment of the fee payable for the license for the whole period for which it would have been current but for the surrender:

Provided that, if the Collector is satisfied that there is sufficient reason for surrendering, the licence, he may remit to the holder thereof the sum so payable on surrender or any portion thereof.

(2) Sub-section (1) shall not apply in the case of any licence granted under section 27(2).

Explanation.—The words "holder of a licence" as used in this section include a person whose tender or bid for a license has been accepted although he may not actually have received the licence.

CHAPTER VII

POWERS AND DUTIES OF OFFICERS, ETC.

45. Power to enter and inspect places of manufacture and sale.—Any excise officer not below such rank as the State Government may prescribe to:—

(a) enter and inspect at any time by day or by night, any place in which any licensed manufacturer carriers on the manufacture of or stores any intoxicant;

(b) enter and inspect at any time within the hours during which sale is permitted, and at any other time during which the same may be open, any place in which any, intoxicant is kept for sale by any person holding a license under this Act;

(c) examine accounts and registers, test, measure or weigh any materials, stills, utensils, implements, apparatus or intoxicant found in that place;

(d) seize any account, registers, measures, weights, or testing instruments which he has reason to believe to be false.

46. Power of Excise Officers to investigate offences punishable under this Act.—(1) The [1][State] Government may by notification invest any excise officer, not below the rank of [Inspector][2] with power to investigate any offence punishable under this Act, committed within the limits of the area in which the officer exercises jurisdiction.

(2) Every officer so empowered may within those limits exercise the same powers in respect of such investigation as an officer incharge of a police station may exercise in a cognizable case under the provisions of [Chapter XII of the Code of Criminal Procedure 1973.][3]

47. Powers of arrest, seizure and detention.—Any officer of the excise, police, salt, or land revenue department, not be low such rank and subject to such restrictions as the State Government may prescribe, any other person duly empowered by notification by the State Government in this behalf, may arrest with out warrant any person found committing an offence punishable, under section 61, or section 63, and may seize and detain any intoxicant or other article which he has reason to believe to be liable to confiscation under this Act or other law for the time being in force relating to excise revenue; and may detain and search any person upon whom, and any vessel, raft, vehicle, animal, package, receptacle or covering in or upon which he may have reasonable cause to suspect any such article to be.

48. Power of Magistrate to issue warrant for search or arrest.—A Magistrate having reason to believe that n offence under section 61 or 63, has been, is being or is likely to be committed, may:—

(a) issue a warrant for search of any place in which he has reason to believe that any intoxicant, still, utensil, implement, apparatus or materials, in respect which such offence has been, is being or is likely to be committed, are kept or concealed; and

(b) issue a warrant for the arrest of any person whom he has reason to believe to have been, to be or to be likely to be engaged in the commission of any such offence.

49. Powers of Excise Officer to search without warrant.—(1) Whenever any excise officer not below such rank as the State Government may by notification prescribe, has

1. Subs. for the word "Provincial" by the Adaptation of Laws Order, 1950.
2. Subs. *vide* Punjab Act No. 20 of 1998 for "sub-inspector".
3. Subs. *vide* Punjab Act No. 20 of 1998.

reason to believe that an offence punishable under sections, 61, 62, 63 or 64, has been, is being or is likely to be committed in any place, and that a search warrant cannot be obtained without affording the offender an opportunity of escape or of concealing evidence of the offence, he may, at any time, by day or night enter and search such place.

(2) **Further powers of seizure, detention, search and arrest.**—Every excise officer as aforesaid may seize any thing found in such place which he has reason to believe to be liable to confiscation under this Act and may detain, and search and, if he thinks proper, arrest any person found in such place whom he has reason to believe to be guilty of such offence as aforesaid.

49A. Powers of excise officer to obtain information.—(1) Any excise officer not below such rank as the State Government may by notification prescribe, may by order require any person to furnish to any specified authority or person any such information in his possession concerning any unlawful import, transport, manufacture or possession of any intoxicant, or any materials, still, utensil, implement or apparatus whatsoever, for the purpose of manufacturing any intoxicant, or any unlawful cultivation of any plants from which an intoxicating drug can be produced as may be specified in the order.

(2) Any person upon whom an order is served under sub-section (1) shall be bound, in the absence of reasonable excuse, to furnish correct information.

50. Procedure relating to arrests, searches etc.—Save as in this Act otherwise expressly provided, the provisions of the [Code of Criminal Procedure 1973][1] relating to arrests, detentions in custody, searches, summonses warrants of arrests, search warrants, production of persons arrested and investigation of offences shall be held to be applicable to all actions taken in these respects under this Act, provided that:—

(1) any offence under this Act may be investigated by an officer empowered under section 46 without the order of a Magistrate.

(2) whenever an excise officer below the rank of Collector makes any arrest, seizure or search he shall within twenty-four hours thereafter make, a full report of all the particulars of the arrest, seizure or search to his immediate official superior and shall unless bail be accented under section 73 take or send the person arrested or the article seized, with all convenient dispatch to a [2][Judicial Magistrate] for trial or adjudication.

51. Police to aid excise officer.—All police officers are required to aid the excise officers in the due execution of this Act, upon request made by such excise officers.

52. Duty of landholders and others to give information.—

(a) every owner or occupier of land or any building and the agent of any owner or occupier of land or any building on which,

(b) every lambardar, village headman, village accountant, village watchman, village policeman and every officer employed in the collection of revenue or rent of land on the part of Government or the court of wards in whose village:—

there shall be any manufacture or illegal import or collection of any intoxicant not licensed under this Act, or any unlawful cultivation of any plants from which an intoxicating drug can be produced, shall be bound, in the absence of reasonable excuse, to give notice of the same to a Magistrate or to an officer of the excise, police or land revenue department as soon as the fact comes to his knowledge.

---

1. Subs. *vide* Punjab Act No. 20 of 1998.
2. Subs. for the word "Magistrate" by the Punjab Separation of Judicial and Executive Functions Act, 1963 (Punjab Act No. 25 of 1964).

53. Duty of officer in-charge of police station to take charge of articles seized.—Every officer incharge of a police station shall take charge of and keep in safe custody, pending the orders of a Magistrate, or of the Collector or of an officer empowered under section 46(1) to investigate the case, all articles seized under this Act which may be delivered to him, and shall allow any excise officer who may accompany such articles to the police station, or may be deputed for the purpose by his superior officer to affix his seal to the articles and to take samples of and from them. All samples so taken shall also be sealed with the seal of the officer incharge of the police station.

54. Power to close shops for the sake of public peace.—(1) The District Magistrate or sub-Divisional Magistrate by notice in writing to the licensee; may require that any shop in which any intoxicant is sold shall be closed at such times or for such period as he may think necessary for the preservation of the public peace.

(2) If a riot or unlawful assembly is apprehended or occurs in the vicinity of any such shop, [1][an Executive Magistrate] of any class may require such shop to be kept closed for such period as he may think necessary:

Provided that where any such riot or unlawful assembly occurs the licensee shall, in the absence of, a Magistrate, close his shop without any order.

(3) When any sub-Divisional Magistrate makes a direction under sub-section (1) or [1][any Executive Magistrate] makes a direction under sub-section (2) he shall forthwith inform the Collector of his action and his reasons thereof.

CHAPTER VIII

GENERAL PROVISIONS

55. Measures weights and testing instruments.—Every person who manufactures or sells any intoxicant under a license granted under this Act shall be bound;

(a) to supply him self with such measures, weight and instruments as the Financial Commissioner may prescribe, and to keep the same in good condition; and

(b) on the requisition of any excise officer, duly empowered by the Collector in that behalf at any time to measure, weight or test any intoxicant in his possession in such manner as the said excise officer may require.

56. Power of State Government to exempt intoxicants from the provision of the Act.—The [1][State] Government may by notification, either wholly of partially and subject to such conditions as it may think fit to prescribe, exempt any intoxicant from all or any of the provisions of this Act.

57. Bar of certain suits.—No suit shall lie in any civil court against the Government or any officer or person for damages for any act in good faith done, or ordered to be done, in the pursuance of this Act or of any other law for the time being in force relating to the excise revenue.

58. Power of State Government to make rules.—(1) The State Government may by notification make rules for the purpose of carrying out the provisions of this Act or any other law for the time being in force relating to excise revenue.

(2) In particular and without prejudice to the generality of the foregoing provisions, the State Government may make rules:—

(a) prescribing the duties of excise officers;

(b) regulating the delegation of any power by the Financial Commissioner, Commissioner or Collector, under section 13, clause (b);

---

1. Subs. for the words "a Magistrate" by the Punjab Separation of Judicial and Executive Functions Act, 1964 (Punjab Act No. 25 of 1964).

(c) prescribing the time and manner of presenting and the procedure for dealing with appeals from orders of excise officers;

(d) regulating the import, export, transport or possession of any intoxicant or Excise bottle and the transfer, price or use of any type of description of such bottle;

(e) regulating the period and localities for which, and, the persons, or classes of persons, to whom licenses, permits and passes for the vend by wholesale or by retail of any intoxicants may be granted and regulating the number of such licenses which may be granted in any local area;

(f) prescribing the procedure to be followed and the matters to be ascertained before any licence is granted for the retail vend of liquor for consumption on the premises;

(g) for the prohibition of the sale of any intoxicant to any person or class of persons;

(h) regulating the power of excise officers to summon witnesses from a distance;

(i) regulating the grant of expenses to witnesses and compensation to persons charged with offences under this Act and subsequently released, discharged or acquitted;

(j) for the prohibition of the employment by a license holder of any person or class of persons to assist in his business in any capacity what so ever;

(k) for the prevention of drunkness, gambling and disorderly conduct in or near any licensed premises and the meeting or remaining of persons of bad character in such premises;

(l) Prohibiting the printing, publishing or otherwise displaying or distributing any advertisement or other matter commending or soliciting the use of, or offering any intoxicant calculated to encourage or incite any individual or class of individuals or the public generally to commit an offence under this Act, or to commit a breach or evade the provisions of any rule or order made thereunder, or the conditions of any license, permit or pass obtained thereunder:—

(m) prohibiting within the State the circulation, distribution or sale of any newspaper, book, leaflet, booklet, or other publication printed and published outside the State which contains any advertisement or matter of the nature described in clause (1):

(n) declaring any newspaper, book, leaflet, booklet, or other publication, wherever printed or published, containing any advertisement or matter [1][of the nature described in clause (1)] to be forefeited to the State Government; and

(o) implementing generally the policy of prohibition.

(3) **Previous publication of rules.**—The power conferred by this section of making rules is subject to the condition that the rules be made after previous publication:

Provided that any such rules may be made without previous publication if State Government consider that they should be brought into force at once.

59. Powers of Financial Commissioner to make rules.—The Financial Commission may, by notification, make rules.

(a) regulating the manufacture, supply, storage or sale of any intoxicant, including:—

1. Subs. for the words "commending or soliciting the use of, or offering any intoxicant, by Punjab Act 18 of 1955, section 2.

(i) the character, erection, alteration, repair, inspection, supervision, management and control of any place for the manufacture, supply storage or sale of such article and the fittings, implements apparatus and registers to be maintained therein;

(ii) the cultivation of the hemp plant and the collection of spontaneous growth of such plant and the preparation of any intoxicating drug.

(iii) the tapping of drawing of tari from any tari producting tree.

(b) regulating the bottling of liquor for purposes of sale.

(c) regulating the deposit of any intoxicant in a warehouse and the removal of any intoxicant from any warehouse or from any distillery or brewery.

(d) prescribing the scale of fees or the manner of fixing the fees payable in respect of any licence, permit or pass or in respect of the storing of any in toxicant;

(e) regulating the time, place and manner of payment of any duty or fee;

(f) prescribing the authority by, the restrictions under, and the conditions on, which any licence, permit or pass may be granted including provision for the following matters:—

(i) the prohibition of the admixture with any intoxicant of any substance deemed to be noxious or objectionable;

(ii) the regulation or prohibition of the reduction of liquor by a licensed manufacturer or licensed vendor from a higher to a lower strength;

(iii) the fixing of strength or price below which any intoxicant shall not be sold, supplied or possessed;

(iv) the prohibition of sale of any intoxicant except for cash;

(v) the fixing of the days and hours during which any licensed premises may or may not be kept open, and the closure of such premises on special occasions;

(vi) the specification of the nature of the premises in which any intoxicant may be sold, and the notice to be exposed at such premises;

(vii) the form of the accounts to be maintained and the return to be submitted by licence-holders; and

(viii) the prohibition or regulation of the transfer of licences;

(g) (i) declaring the process by which spirit shall be denatured;

(ii) for causing spirits to be denatured through the agency or under the supervision of its own officers;

(iii) for ascertaining whether such spirit has been denatured;

(h) providing for the destruction or other disposal of any intoxicant deemed to be unfit for use;

(i) regulating the disposal of confiscated articles;

(j) prescribing the amount of security to be deposited by holders of leases, licences, permits or passes for the performance of the conditions of the same.

60. (1) Recovery of dues.—The following moneys namely:—

(a) all excise revenue.

(b) any loss that may accrue, when in consequence of default a grant has been taken under management by the Collector or has been resold by him under section 39; and

(c) all amounts due to the Government by any person on account of any contract relating to the excise revenue;

may be recovered from the person primarily liable to pay the same, or from his surety (if any), by distress and sale of his moveable property or by any other process for the recovery of arrears of land revenue due from land holders or from farmers of land or their sureties.

(2) When a grant has been taken under management by the Collector or has been resold by him under section 39 the Collector, may recover in any manner authorised by sub-section (1) any money due to the defaulter by any lessee or assignee.

(3) In the event of default by any person licensed or holding a lease under this Act all his distillery, brewery, warehouse or shop premises, fittings or apparatus and all stocks of intoxicants or materials for manufacture of the same held in or upon any distillery, brewery, warehouse or shop premises shall be liable to be attached in satisfaction of any claim for excise revenue or in respect of losses incurred by State Government through such default and to be sold to satisfy such claim which shall be a first charge upon the sale proceeds.

CHAPTER IX

OFFENCES AND PENALTIES

61. [Penalty for offences triable by a court][1]—(1) Whoever in contravention of any section of this Act, or of any rule, notification is sued or given thereunder or order made, or of any license, permit or pass granted under this Act:—

[(a) manufactures or collects any intoxicant; or

(aa) imports, exports, transports or possession intoxicants, namely, lahan or all liquid consisting of or containing alcohol manufactured otherwise than in a licensed distillery, brewery or bottling plant in the State of Punjab; or][2]

(b) constructs or works any distillery or brewery; or

(c) uses, keeps or has in his possession any materials, still, utensil, implements or apparatus whatsoever for the purpose of manufacturing any intoxicant other than tari,

shall be punishable for every such offence with imprisonment for a term which may extends to three years [3][and with fine upto to [4][twenty-five thousand rupees] [5][***]

[6][Provided that in the case of an offence relating to the possession of:—

(i) a working still for the manufacture of any intoxicant, such imprisonment shall not be less than one year and such fine shall not be less than five thousand rupees;

(ii) Lahan, such imprisonment shall not be less than six months and such fine shall not be less than one thousand rupees;

(iii) country liquor manufactured otherwise than in a licensed distillery in Punjab, in a quantity not exceeding ten bottles, each bottle containing

1. Subs. *vide* Punjab Act 10 of 2003.
2. Subs. *vide* Punjab Act 32 of 2006.
3. Subs. for the words "or with fine which may extend two thousand rupees or with both", by the Punjab Act 35 of 1956, section 2(i).
4. Subs. *vide* Punjab Act No. 20 of 1998.
5. Words "if found in possession of a working still for the manufacture of any intoxicants, shall be punishable with minimum sentence of six months' imprisonment and fine of two hundred rupees," omitted by Punjab Act 36 of 1973.
6. Proviso added by Punjab Act 31 of 1976, section 2.

750 milliliters, such imprisonment shall not be less than three months and such fine shall not be less than five hundred rupees; and in a quantity exceeding ten bottles of the aforesaid capacity, such imprisonment shall not be less than six months and such fine shall not be less than one thousand rupees;

(iv) foreign liquor other than—

(a) manufactured in a licensed distillery or brewery in India; or

(b) imported into Indian on which custom duty is leviable under the Indian Tarrif Act, 1934 or the Customs Act, 1962.

(c) such imprisonment shall not be less than six months and such fine shall not be less than two thousand rupees.

[(v) foreign liquor manufactured in a distillery or brewery in India, in quantity exceeding ten bottles on which the excise duty or any other levy payable under this Act, has not been paid, such imprisonment shall not be less than six months and such fine shall not be less than two thousand rupees.][1]

(2) **Penalty for unlawful import, export, transport, manufacture, possession, sale etc.**—Whoever in contravention of any section other than sections 29 and 30 of this Act or of any rule, notification issued or given thereunder or order made or of any license, permit or pass granted under this Act—

(a) sells any intoxicants; or

(b) cultivates the hemp plant; or

(c) removes any intoxicant from any distillery, brewery or warehouse established or licensed under this Act; or

(d) bottles any liquor for the purposes of sale; or

(e) taps or draws tari form any tari producing tree,

shall be punishable with imprisonment for a term which may extend to [2][two years and fine which may extend two thousand rupees].

[61A. Penalty for offences not triable by a court.—(1) Whosoever, in contravention of any provision of this Act, the rules framed thereunder, any notification issued or any order made or any license, permit or pass granted under this Act, imports, exports, transports or possesses any intoxicants other than those, specified in clause (aa) of sub-section (1) of section 61 (hereinafter referred to as such intoxicants) shall, along with such intoxicants and means of transport, except the passenger buses, owned by the Central Government or the State Government or any of their undertaking, be detained by an Excise Officer, who shall make a report to the Assistant Excise and Taxation Commissioner, in-charge of the district within a period of twenty-four hours of such detention. The Excise Officer shall forward such intoxicants and the means of transport along with the necessary documents to the Assistant Excise and Taxation Commissioner in-charge of the district.

(2) On the receipt of the report to in sub-section (1), the Assistant Excise and Taxation Commissioner in-charge of the district, shall record the statements of the offender and the officers, concerned with the case, and release the offender.

(3) The Assistant Excise and Taxation Commissioner in-charge of the district, may by an order impose the following penalties after providing the offender a reasonable

1. Added *vide* Punjab Act No. 20 of 1998.
2. Subs. for the words "one year or with fine which may extend to two thousand rupees or with both" by Punjab Act 35 of 1956, section 2(ii).

opportunity of being heard in case, such intoxicants detained are licit, on which the excise duty and other levies have been paid in the State of Punjab, namely:—

(a) rupees five thousand in case, the detection of such intoxicants, does not exceed two cases *i.e.* 18 bulk litres; and

(b) rupees ten thousand in case, the detection of such intoxicants, exceeds than two cases *i.e.* 18 bulk litres.

(4) The Assistant Excise and Taxation Commissioner in-charge of the district, may confiscate such intoxicant and may also by an order impose the following penalties after providing the offender a reasonable opportunity of being heard in case such intoxicants detained is illicit, on which the excise duty and other levies have not been paid in the State of Punjab, namely:—

(a) rupees twenty-five thousand in case of detection of such intoxicants, does not exceed five cases *i.e.* 45 bulk litres;

(b) rupees fifty thousand in case of detection of such intoxicants, exceeds five cases *i.e.* 45 bulk litres, but not exceed 450 bulk litres; and

(c) rupees one lac in case of detection of such intoxicants exceeds fifty cases *i.e.* 450 bulk litres.

(5) If the penalty referred to in sub-section (4), is not paid within a period of one week from the date of the order, the Assistant Excise and Taxation Commissioner in-charge of the district shall pass a speaking order for confiscation of the means of transport and the liquor after giving an opportunity of being heard to the offender and the owner of the means of transport. In case, the owner of such intoxicants and the means of transport are not available, then the order for confiscation may be passed by the Assistant Excise and Taxation Commissioner in-charge of the district by affording an opportunity of being heard to the offender, who has been caught with the goods. The confiscated such intoxicants shall thereafter, be destroyed under the supervision of the Assistant Excise and Taxation Commissioner in-charge of the district and an authenticated copy of the said order shall be supplied to the affected person free of costs.

(6) The Assistant Excise and Taxation Commissioner incharge of the district, shall put to auction the confiscated means of transport within a period of thirty days from the date of the order of confiscation passed under sub-section (5). The amount received from auction after deducting the expenditure incurred on it, shall be adjusted towards the payment of penalty by the owner. The unrecovered amount of penalty, if any, shall be recoverable as arrears of land revenue.][1]

62. Penalty for unlawful selling to person under twenty-five or employing them or women.—If any licensed vendor, or any person in his employ or acting on his behalf:—

(a) in contravention of section 29 sells or delivers any liquor or intoxicating drug to any person apparently under the age of twenty-five years, or

(b) in contravention of section 30 employs or permits to be employed, on any part of his licensed premises referred to in that section any man under the age of twenty-five years or women, or,

(c) sells any intoxicant to a person who is drunk or intoxicated; or

(d) permits drunkness, intoxication, disorderly conduct or gaming the licensed premises of such licensed vendor; or

(e) permits any person whom he know or has reason to believe to have been convicted of any non-bailable offence or any reputed prostitute to frequent

1. Subs. by Punjab Act No. 32 of 2006.

his licensed premises whether, for the purposes of crime or prostitution or not.

he shall in addition to any other penalty to which he may be liable be punishable with a fine which may extend to five hundred rupees.

When any licensed vendor or any person in his employ or acting on his behalf is charged with permitting drunkness or intoxication on the licensed premises of such vendor and it is proved that any person was drunk or intoxicated on such premises, it shall lie on the person charged to prove that the licensed vendor or the person employed by him or acting on his behalf took all reasonable steps for preventing drunkness or intoxication on such premises.

63. Penalty for rendering or attempting to render denatured spirit fit for human consumption.—Whoever renders or attempts render fit for human consumption any spirit, whether manufactured in India or not, which has been denatured, or has in his possession any spirit rendered fit for human consumption in respect of which he knows or has reason to believe that any such attempt has been made, shall be punishable with imprisonment for a term which may extend to one year [1][and with fine which may extend to one thousand rupees.]

[2][**63.A. Penalty for possession of unused and printed lables, corks etc., in contravention of section 24A.**—Whoever in contravention of the provisions of section 24A has in his possession any unused and printed lable, cork, capsule or seal or an imitation there of, shall be punishable with imprisonment for a term which may extend to six months and with fine.

64. Penalty for fraud by licensed manufacturer or vendor or his servant.—If any licensed manufacturer or licensed vendor or any person in his employ or acting on his behalf;

(a) sells, or keeps or exposes for sale, as foreign liquor any liquor which he knows or has reason to believe to have been manufactured from rectified spirit or country liquor; or

(b) marks any bottle, case, package or other receptacle containing liquor so manufactured from rectified spirit or country liquor, or the cork of any such bottle or deals with any bottles, case package or other receptacle containing such liquor with the intention of causing it to be believed that such bottle, case, package, or other receptacle contains foreign liquor;

he shall be punishable with imprisonment for a term which may extend to three months, [3][and with fine which may extend to five hundred rupees.]

65. Penalty for certain acts by licence or his servant.—Whoever being the holder of a licence, permit or pass granted under this Act or being in the employ of such holder or acting on his behalf:—

(a) fails wilfully to produce such licence, permit or pass on the demand of any excise officer or of any other officer duly empowered to make such demand; or

(b) in any case not provided for in section 61 wilfully contravenes any rule made under section 58 or section 59; or

1. Subs. for the words "or with fine which may extend to one thousand rupees, or with both" by Punjab Act 35 of 1956, section 3.
2. Ins. by Punjab Act 31 of 1963, section 3.
3. Subs. for the words "or with fine which may extend to five hundred rupees, or with both," by Punjab Act 35 of 1956, section 4.

(c) wilfully does or omits to do anything in breach of any of the conditions of the license, permit or pass not otherwise provided for in this Act

[shall be punishable with a fine which may extend to five thousand rupees.][1]

66. Penalty for consumption in chemists shops etc.—(1) If any chemist, druggist, apothecary or keeper of a dispensary allows any intoxicant which has not been *bona fide* medicated for medicinal purposes to be consumed on his business premises by any person not employed in his business, he shall be punishable with imprisonment for a term which may extend to three months [2][and with fine which may extend to one thousand rupees.]

(2) If any person not employed as aforesaid consumes any such intoxicant on such premises, he shall be punishable with fine which may extend of two hundred rupees.

67. Manufacture, sale or possession by one person on account of another.—(1) When any intoxicant has been manufactured or sold or is possessed by any person on account of any other person and such other person known or has reason to believe that such manufacture or sale was, or that such possession is, on his account, the article, shall for the purpose of this Act be deemed to have been manufactured or sold by or to be in the possession of such other person.

(2) Nothing in sub-section (1) shall absolve any person who manufactures, sells or has possession of an intoxicant on account of another person from liability to any punishment under this Act for the unlawful manufacture, sale or possession of such article.

68. Penalty for offences not otherwise provided for.—Whoever is guilty of any act or intentional omission in contravention of any of the provisions of this Act; or of any rule, notification or order made, issued or given, thereunder and not otherwise provided for in this Act, shall be punishable for every such act or omission with a fine may extend to [3][five thousand rupees.]

[4][**68A. Enhanced punishment for certain offences after previous conviction.**—Whoever having been convicted for an offence punishable under sub-section (1) of section 61 of this Act, is again convicted of an offence punishable under the said sub-section shall:—

(a) for a second offence be punished with not less than twice the punishment awarded to him on his first conviction; and

(b) for a third or subsequent offence be punished with not less than twice the punishment awarded to him on his second conviction or immediate last conviction:

Provided that the enhanced punishment does not exceed the imprisonment of three years and a fine of two thousand rupees:

Provided further that if on a previous conviction the sentence awarded was that of fine only, a sentence of imprisonment for a term which may extend to three years shall also be awarded on subsequent conviction and such sentence of imprisonment shall be in addition to the enhanced penalty of fine:

---

1. Subs. *vide* Punjab Act No. 20 of 1998.
2. Subs. for the words "or with fine which may extend to one thousand rupees, or with both", by Punjab Act 35 of 1956, section 5.
3. Subs. by Punjab Act 20 of 1998 for the words "five hundred rupees".
4. Subs. by Punjab Act 22 of 1963, section 2, previously inserted by Punjab Act 35 of 1956, section 6.

Provided further that the enhanced punishment would not in any way affect the minimum sentence prescribed for the offence of possession of a working still for the manufacture of any intoxicant.]

69. Attempt to commit offences punishable under the Act.—Whoever attempts to commit or abets any offence punishable under this Act shall be liable to the punishment provided for the offence.

69A. Security for abstaining from commission of certain offences.—(1) Whenever any person is convicted of an offence punishable under sections 61, 63 and 69 and the court convicting him is of the opinion that it is necessary to require such person to execute a bond for abstaining from the commission of offences punishable under these sections, the Court may, at the time of passing sentence on such person, order him to execute a bond for a sum proportionate to his means, with or without sureties, for abstaining from the commission of such offences during such period, not exceeding three years, as it thinks fit to fix.

[(2) The bond shall be in the form contained in Schedule II and the provisions of the Code of Criminal Procedure, 1973, shall, insofar as they are applicable, apply to all matters connected with such bond, as if it were a bond to keep the peace ordered to be executed under Chapter VIII of the said Code.][1]

(3) If the conviction is set aside on appeal or in revision, the bond, so executed shall become void.

(4) An order under this section may also be made by an appellate court, or by the High Court, when exercising its powers of revision.

70. Penalty for excise officer making vexatious, search, etc.—If an excise officer—

(a) vexatiously and unnecessarily enters or searches, or causes to be entered or searched, any place under colour of exercising any power conferred by this Act; or

(b) vexatiously and unnecessarily seizes the moveable property of any person on the presence of seizing or searching for any article liable to confiscation under this Act; or

(c) vexatiously and unnecessarily searches, arrests, or detains any person; or

(d) without lawful excuse ceases or refuses to perform or withdraws himself from the duties of his office unless expressly allowed to do so in writing by the Collector or unless he shall have given to his immediate superior officer two months notice in writing of his intention to do so;

he shall be liable to imprisonment for a term which may extend to three months, or with fine which may extend to five hundred rupees or with both.

71. Report by investigation officer for institution of proceedings.—If on an investigation by an excise officer, empowered under section 46 sub-section (1), it appears that there is sufficient evidence to justify the prosecution of the accused, the investigating officer unless he submits the case for the orders of the Collector under section 80, shall submit a report [(which shall deem to be a Police report under Code of Criminal Procedure, 1973)][1] to a Magistrate having jurisdiction to enquiry into or try the case and empowered to take cognizance of offences on police reports.

72. Offences to be bailable.—All offences, punishable under this Act shall be bailable within the meaning of the Code of Criminal Procedure, 1973[1].

[2][Provided that the offences punishable under clauses (i), (ii), (iv) and (v)][1] and of possession of country of liquor in a quantity exceeding ten bottles of 750 millilitres

---

1. Subs. *vide* Punjab Act No. 20 of 1998.
2. Amended by Punjab Act No. 14 of 1983.

capacity each, punishable under clause (iii) of the proviso to sub-section (1) of section 61 shall be non-bailable.]

73. Security for appearance in case of arrest without warrant.—The State Government may empower any excise officer to grant bail notwithstanding that such officer is not empowered under section 46.

(2) When a person is arrested under this Act, otherwise than on warrant, by a person or officer who is not empowered to grant bail, he shall be produced before or forwarded to:—

(a) the nearest Excise Officer empowered to grant bail; or

(b) the nearest officer-in-charge of a police station whoever is nearer.

(3) Whenever any person arrested under this Act, otherwise than on a warrant, is prepared to give bail, and is arrested by or produced in accordance with sub-section (2) before an officer empowered to grant bail, he shall be released upon bail, or, at the discretion of the officer, releasing him on his own bond.

(4) The provisions of [sections 441 to 446 and 449 of the Code of Criminal Procedure, 1973][1], shall apply so far as may be, in every case in which bail is accepted or a bond taken under this section.

74. Repealed.

75. Cognizance of offences.—(1) No [2][judicial Magistrate] shall take cognizance of an offence punishable.

(a) under section 61 or section 66 except on his own knowledge or suspicion or on the complaint or report of an excise officer; or

(b) under section 62, section 63, section 64, section 65, section 68, or section 70, except on the complaint or report of the Collector or a excise officer authorized by him in that behalf.

(2) Except with the special sanction of the State Government no [Judicial Magistrate] shall take cognizance of any offence punishable under this Act unless the prosecution is instituted within a year after the date on which the offence is alleged to have been committed.

76. Presumption as to commission of offence in certain cases.—Whenever any person is found in possession of:—

(a) any still utensil, implement or apparatus whatsoever or any part or thereof such as are ordinarily used for the manufacture of any intoxicant other than tari.

(b) any materials which have undergone any process towards the manufacture of an intoxicant or from which an intoxicant has been manufactured;

it shall be presumed until the contrary is proved, that his possession was in contravention of the provisions of this Act.

76A. Presumption as to commission of offence in prosecution under section 63 of the Act.—In prosecution under section 63, it shall be presumed without further evidence, until the contrary is proved, that the accused person has committed an offence under that section in respect of any denatured spirit which has been or attempted to be rendered fit for human consumption.

77. Liability of employer for offence committed by employee or Agent.—The holder of a license, permit or pass under this Act as well as the actual offender, shall be

1. Subs. *vide* Punjab Act No. 20 of 1998.
2. Subs. for the word "Magistrate" by Punjab Separation of Judicial and Executive Functions Act, 1964 (25 of 1964).

liable to punishment, of any offence punishable under section 61, section 62, section 63, section 64 or section 65, committed by any person in his employ or acting on his behalf as if he had himself committed the same, unless he shall establish that all due and reasonable precautions were exercised by him to prevent the commission of such offence.

78. Confiscation of article in respect of which offence committed.—(1) Whenever an offence punishable under this Act has been committed;

(a) every intoxicant or excise bottle in respect of which such offence has been committed together with the contents of such bottle, if any;

(b) every still, utensil, implement or apparatus and all material in respect of or by means of which such, offence has been committed;

(c) every intoxicant or excise bottle lawfully imported, transported, manufactured, had in possession or sold along with, or in addition to, any intoxicant or excise bottle liable to confiscation under clause (a);

(d) every receptacle, package and covering in which any intoxicant for excise bottle, materials, still, utensil, implement or apparatus as aforesaid is or are found together with the other contents (if any) of such receptacle or package; and

(e) every animal, cart, vessel, raft or other conveyance used in carrying such, receptacle, or package, covering or articles as aforesaid;

shall be liable to confiscation:

Provided that when it is proved that the receptacles, animals or other articles specified in clauses (d) and (e) are not the property of offenders, they shall not be liable to confiscation if the owner thereof established that he had no reason to believe that such offence was being or was likely to be committed.

(2) When confiscation may be ordered.—When in the trial of any offence punishable under this Act the Magistrate decides that any thing is liable to confiscation under sub-section (1), he may order confiscation;

Provided that in lieu of ordering confiscation he may give the owner of the thing liable to be confiscated an option to pay such fine as the Magistrate thinks fit.

79. Further provisions for confiscation.—When there is reason to believe that an offence under this Act has been committed, but the offenders is not known or cannot be found and when any thing or animal liable to confiscation under this Act and not in the possession of any person cannot be satisfactorily accounted for the case shall be enquired into and determined by the collector, who may order confiscation:

Provided that no such order shall be made until the expiration of one month from the date of seizing the thing or animal in question or without hearing the person (if any) claiming any right thereto, and the evidence (if any) which he produces in support of the claim:

Provided further, that if the thing in question is liable to speedy and natural decay, or if the collector is of opinion that the sale of the thing or animal in question would be for the benefit of its owner, the collector may at any time direct it to be sold; and provisions of this section shall, so far as may be, apply to the net proceeds of such sale.

80. Power of excise officers to compound offences.—(1) The collector may accept from any person who is reasonably suspected of having committed an offence punishable under section 62, section 65 or section 68 of this Act a sum of money by way of composition for such offence; and on the payment of such sum of money to the collector the accused person if in custody shall be discharged and no further proceedings shall be taken against him in respect of such offence.

(2) The cancellation or suspension of any license, permit or pass under section 36(a), (b) or (c) of this Act may be foregone or revoked by and at the sole discretion of the authority having power to cancel or suspend it on payment by the holder of such license, permit or pass of such penalty as such authority may fix.

(3) Where any intoxicant has been seized under the provisions of this Act, the Collector, may in his discretion, at any time before a Magistrate has passed an order under section 78, sub-section (2), release it on receiving payment of the value thereof.

[1][**80A. Imposition of penalty.**—If any violation of any of the provisions of this Act, except sections 61, 61A, 62, 65 and 68 of this Act or the rules made thereunder, is brought to the notice of the [Assistant Excise and Taxation Commissioner in-charge of the district][2], he may, in lieu of criminal proceedings against the offender, pass an order, imposing a penalty, not exceeding the maximum amount of fine as provided for such an offence in the relevant provisions of this Act and also confiscate the liquor and other connected or related goods after giving him a reasonable opportunity of being heard. On payment of such penalty, the offender, if in custody or on bail, shall be discharged and no further criminal proceedings shall be taken against him in respect of such offence.]

[**80AA. Penalty for sale of liquor on prohibited days.**—Whosoever opens a liquor vend on any day on which the sale of liquor is prohibited under this Act, or any rules framed, notification issued or order made thereunder, shall be liable to be imposed a minimum penalty of fifty thousand rupees.][3]

[**80B. Appeal.**—Any person aggrieved by the order of the Assistant Excise and Taxation Commissioner in-charge of the district, under sections 80A and 80AA, may file an appeal to the Excise and Taxation Commissioner, Punjab, within a period of one month from the date of passing of the order.][4]

---

1. Added *vide* Punjab Act 10 of 2003.
2. Subs. for the words "Deputy Excise and Taxation Commissioner in-charge of the Division" by Punjab Act No. 10 of 2004.
3. Ins. by Punjab Act No. 10 of 2004.
4. Subs. by Punjab Act No. 10 of 2004.

SUBJECT INDEX

F

•••